28th International Conference on Computational Linguistics (COLING 2020)

Industry Track

Held online due to COVID-19

Barcelona, Spain
12 December 2020

ISBN: 978-1-7138-2522-7

COLING 2020

**The 28th International Conference
on Computational Linguistics**

Proceedings of the Industry Track

December 12, 2020
Barcelona, Spain (Online)

Preface

We welcome you to the 28th International Conference on Computational Linguistics (COLING 2020) Industry Track. This year marks the first in which COLING has a dedicated track for research related to computational linguistics deployed in real-world settings. In recent years, industrial research has been increasingly influential in the field of computational linguistics—both in the form of research departments that contribute to the advancement of computational linguistics, and also by way of the knowledgeable inventors and developers of innovative language and speech products.

The goals of this session are to foster connections between industry practitioners, share insights from industry research to the broader community, and increase engagement with academia on research questions of high priority in industry. This session will showcase commercially-driven research from diverse angles, including the challenges of doing applied research at scale, production scalability, and a shifting data landscape.

We received 124 submissions (79 long and 45 short) and had an acceptance rate of 23%.[1] Based on the first author's affiliation, an estimated 76% of submissions came from industry and 24% from academia. Geographically, most submissions were from North America (44%), 27–28% from Europe and Asia (respectively), and 1% from Africa.

We thank the many people who have made this track a success. We are grateful to Donia Scott, general chair, for her support and for providing us with this opportunity. Thank you to program chairs Núria Bel and Chengqing Zong; local chairs Leo Wanner, Horacio Saggion, and Mónica Domínguez; publication chairs Derek Wong, Liang Huang, and Yang Zhao; web chairs Laura Pérez-Mayos and Amita Misra; virtual infrastructure chairs Paul Piwek, Lluís Padró Cirera, and Luis Espinosa Anke; publicity chairs Ghazaleh Kazeminejad, Tiejun Zhao, Ted Pedersen, and Anna Rogers; and all other members of the organizing committee. We were inspired by the success of the NAACL 2018 and 2019 industry tracks, and we thank Anastassia Loukin and the organizers of the NAACL 2019 Industry Track for their guidance. We are grateful to area chairs Juri Ganitkevitch and Greg Hanneman, and the program committee, whose dedication and hard work made this program possible.

Organizers
COLING 2020 Industry Track

---

[1] Not including 17 desk rejects and 13 withdrawals.

Industry Track Chairs

Ann Clifton, Spotify, USA
Courtney Napoles, Grammarly, USA

Area Chairs

Juri Ganitkevitch, Apple, USA
Greg Hanneman, Amazon, USA

Program Committee

Shazia Afzal, IBM Research, India
Sachin Agarwal, Apple, USA
Khaled Ammar, Thomson Reuters Labs, Canada
Arturo Argueta, Apple, USA
Mehdi Bahrami, Fujitsu Laboratories of America, USA
Tamali Banerjee, IIT Bombay, India
Oren Barkan, Microsoft, Israel
Frederic Bechet, Aix Marseille Universite - LIS/CNRS, France
Akash Bharadwaj, Facebook AI Research, USA
Sravan Bodapati, Amazon, USA
Daniele Bonadiman, Amazon AI, USA
Trung Bui, Adobe Research, USA
Vitor Carvalho, Carnegie Mellon University, USA
Alessandra Cervone, Amazon Alexa AI, Italy
Ashwini Challa, Facebook, USA
Nicholas Chamansingh, TTLab, Trinidad and Tobago
Praveen Chandar, University of Delaware, USA
Sourish Chaudhuri, Google Inc, USA
John Chen, Interactions LLC, USA
Li Chen, JD.COM, USA
Yue Chen, Indiana University, USA
Laura Chiticariu, IBM Data & AI, USA
Eunah Cho, Amazon Alexa AI, USA
Ido Cohn, Google, Israel
Deborah Dahl, Conversational Technologies, USA
Tirthankar Dasgupta, Tata Consultancy Services Ltd., India
Heidar Davoudi, Ontario Tech University, Canada
Budhaditya Deb, Microsoft Corporation, USA
Lingjia Deng, Bloomberg L.P., USA
Giuseppe Di Fabbrizio, VUI, Inc., USA
Erika Doggett, Walt Disney Studios, USA
Xin Dong, Rutgers University, USA
Matthew Dunn, LivePerson, USA
Jonathan Engel, Megagon Labs, USA

Keelan Evanini, Educational Testing Service, USA
Adam Faulkner, Capital One, USA
Michael Flor, Educational Testing Service, USA
Kavita Ganesan, GitHub, USA
Rashmi Gangadharaiah, Amazon AWS AI, USA
Anna Lisa Gentile, IBM Research Almaden, USA
Fréderic Godin, Chatlayer.ai, Belgium
Anuj Goyal, Amazon Alexa, USA
Abhirut Gupta, Google Research, India
Le An Ha, RGCL, RIILP, University of Wolverhampton, UK
Kristian Hammond, Northwestern University, USA
Bo Han, Accenture, Australia
Sanjika Hewavitharana, eBay, USA
Derrick Higgins, Illinois Institute of Technology, USA
Silja Hildebrand, Amazon, USA
Lynette Hirschman, MITRE, USA
Yuta Hitomi, Media Lab, The Asahi Shimbun Company, Japan
Yufang Hou, IBM Research, Ireland
Jinxin Hu, Alibaba, China
David Huggins Daines, Nuance Communications, Canada
Javid Huseynov, IBM, USA
Tomoki Ito, The University of Tokyo, Japan
Michael Johnston, Interactions Corporation, USA
Mahesh Joshi, LinkedIn, USA
Anup Kalia, IBM T. J. Watson Research Center, USA
Saurabh Khanwalkar, Bose Corporation, USA
Doo Soon Kim, Adobe Research, USA
Kunho Kim, Microsoft Corporation, USA
Young-Bum Kim, Amazon Alexa Brain, USA
Sun Kim, Amazon Alexa AI; NCBI/NIH, USA
Jared Kramer, Amazon, USA
Rohit Kumar, VoiceThesis LLC, USA
Sanjeev Kumar, Quark.ai, USA
Varun Kumar, Amazon Alexa, USA
Gakuto Kurata, IBM Research, Japan
Claudia Leacock, Consultant, USA
Jennifer J Liang, IBM Research, USA
Zhengyuan Liu, Institute for Infocomm Research, A*STAR, Singapore
Phoebe Liu, Figure Eight, USA
Honglei Liu, Facebook Conversational AI, USA
Alexander Loeser, Beuth-University of Applied Sciences Berlin, Germany
Anastassia Loukina, Educational Testing Service, USA
Xiaoqiang Luo, Google, USA
Nitin Madnani, Educational Testing Service, USA
Ashraf Mahgoub, Purdue University, USA
Courtney Mansfield, University of Washington, USA
Gabriel Marzinotto, Orange Labs, Aix Marseille Univ, CNRS, LIS, France
Yuji Matsumoto, Riken Center for Advanced Intelligence Project, Japan
Tomoki Matsuno, LAPRAS Inc., Japan
David McClosky, Google, USA
Mahnoosh Mehrabani, Interactions LLC, USA

Marie Meteer, Pryon, USA
Chad Mills, University of Washington, USA
Prateeti Mohapatra, IBM Research Lab, India
Michelle Morales, CUNY Graduate Center, USA
Isabelle Moulinier, Capital One, USA
Matthew Mulholland, Educational Testing Service, USA
Maria Nadejde, Amazon AWS AI, USA
Nobal B. Niraula, Boeing Research & Technology, USA
Mari Olsen, Lionbridge AI, USA
Girish Palshikar, Tata Consultancy Services Limited, India
Shimei Pan, UMBC, USA
Youngja Park, IBM T. J. Watson Research Center, USA
Ioannis Partalas, Expedia Group, Switzerland
Siddharth Patwardhan, Apple, USA
Stanislav Peshterliev, Facebook, USA
Lahari Poddar, Amazon, Germany
Rashmi Prasad, Interactions Corporation, USA
Nishant Prateek, Amazon Research Cambridge, UK
Long Qin, Singsound Inc, China
Ying Qin, Beijing Foreign Studies University, China
Preethi Raghavan, IBM Research, USA
Vipul Raheja, Grammarly, USA
Anil Ramakrishna, Amazon, USA
Meghana Ravikumar, SigOpt, USA
Anupama Ray, IBM Research, India
Sravana Reddy, Spotify, USA
Ehud Reiter, University of Aberdeen, UK
Brian Riordan, ETS, USA
Salim Roukos, IBM Research AI, USA
Nicholas Ruiz, Interactions, LLC, USA
Alicia Sagae, Consulting Scientist, USA
Avneesh Saluja, Netflix, USA
Rajhans Samdani, Spoke, USA
Stefan Scherer, Embodied, Inc., USA
Frank Schilder, Thomson Reuters, USA
Ethan Selfridge, Interactions LLC, USA
Sapan Shah, Tata Consultancy Services Ltd, India
Arpit Sharma, WalmartLabs, USA
Michal Shmueli-Scheuer, IBM Research, Israel
Sunayana Sitaram, Microsoft Research India, India
Kazoo Sone, Google, USA
Biplav Srivastava, IBM, USA
Fabian Suchanek, Telecom ParisTech University, France
Lichao Sun, University of Illinois at Chicago, USA
Lin Sun, Zhejiang University City College, China
Kyle Swanson, ASAPP, Inc., USA
György Szarvas, Amazon Development Center Germany GmbH, Germany
Aniruddha Tammewar, University Of Trento, Italy
Isabel Trancoso, INESC-ID / IST Univ. Lisbon, Portugal
Keith Trnka, 98point6, Inc., USA
Ling Tsou, SDL, USA

Elena Tutubalina, Insilico Medicine, Russian Federation
Ngoc Phuoc An Vo, IBM Research, USA
Stephen Wan, CSIRO, Australia
Yao Wan, Huazhong University of Science and Technology, China
Varden Wang, Google Inc, USA
Xinhao Wang, Educational Testing Service, USA
Yi-Chia Wang, Facebook AI, USA
Jason D Williams, Apple, USA
Kyle Williams, Microsoft, USA
Joan Xiao, Figure Eight, USA
Wei Yang, Borealis AI, Canada
Jianguo Zhang, University of Illinois at Chicago, USA
Wen Zhang, Zhejiang University, China

Table of Contents

Conference Program

Tuesday, December 8, 2020 (UTC+1)

16:00–16:30   **Session Industry 1: Dialogue**

16:00–16:06   *Evaluating Cross-Lingual Transfer Learning Approaches in Multilingual Conversational Agent Models*
Lizhen Tan and Olga Golovneva

16:06–16:12   *Data-Efficient Paraphrase Generation to Bootstrap Intent Classification and Slot Labeling for New Features in Task-Oriented Dialog Systems*
Shailza Jolly, Tobias Falke, Caglar Tirkaz and Daniil Sorokin

16:12–16:18   *Leveraging User Paraphrasing Behavior In Dialog Systems To Automatically Collect Annotations For Long-Tail Utterances*
Tobias Falke, Markus Boese, Daniil Sorokin, Caglar Tirkaz and Patrick Lehnen

16:18–16:24   *Query Distillation: BERT-based Distillation for Ensemble Ranking*
Wangshu Zhang, Junhong Liu, Zujie Wen, Yafang Wang and Gerard de Melo

16:24–16:30   *Semantic Diversity for Natural Language Understanding Evaluation in Dialog Systems*
Enrico Palumbo, Andrea Mezzalira, Cristina Marco, Alessandro Manzotti and Daniele Amberti

Wednesday, December 9, 2020 (UTC+1)

16:00–16:30   **Session Industry 2: Generation and Question Answering**

16:00–16:06   *An Empirical Study on Multi-Task Learning for Text Style Transfer and Paraphrase Generation*
Pawel Bujnowski, Kseniia Ryzhova, Hyungtak Choi, Katarzyna Witkowska, Jaroslaw Piersa, Tymoteusz Krumholc and Katarzyna Beksa

16:06–16:12   *Best Practices for Data-Efficient Modeling in NLG:How to Train Production-Ready Neural Models with Less Data*
Ankit Arun, Soumya Batra, Vikas Bhardwaj, Ashwini Challa, Pinar Donmez, Peyman Heidari, Hakan Inan, Shashank Jain, Anuj Kumar, Shawn Mei, Karthik Mohan and Michael White

16:12–16:18   *Interactive Question Clarification in Dialogue via Reinforcement Learning*
Xiang Hu, Zujie Wen, Yafang Wang, Xiaolong Li and Gerard de Melo

16:18–16:24   *Towards building a Robust Industry-scale Question Answering System*
Rishav Chakravarti, Anthony Ferritto, Bhavani Iyer, Lin Pan, Radu Florian, Salim Roukos and Avi Sil

Friday, December 11, 2020 (UTC+1)

16:00–16:30   Session Industry 4: Machine Learning Applications

16:00–16:06   *An Industry Evaluation of Embedding-based Entity Alignment*
Ziheng Zhang, Hualuo Liu, Jiaoyan Chen, Xi Chen, Bo Liu, YueJia Xiang and Yefeng Zheng

16:06–16:12   *Learning Domain Terms - Empirical Methods to Enhance Enterprise Text Analytics Performance*
Gargi Roy, Lipika Dey, Mohammad Shakir and Tirthankar Dasgupta

16:12–16:18   *Model-agnostic Methods for Text Classification with Inherent Noise*
Kshitij Tayal, Rahul Ghosh and Vipin Kumar

16:18–16:24   *ScopeIt: Scoping Task Relevant Sentences in Documents*
Barun Patra, Vishwas Suryanarayanan, Chala Fufa, Pamela Bhattacharya and Charles Lee

16:24–16:27   *Uncertainty Modeling for Machine Comprehension Systems using Efficient Bayesian Neural Networks*
Zhengyuan Liu, Pavitra Krishnaswamy, Ai Ti Aw and Nancy Chen

16:27–16:30   *Regularized Graph Convolutional Networks for Short Text Classification*
Kshitij Tayal, Nikhil Rao, Saurabh Agarwal, Xiaowei Jia, Karthik Subbian and Vipin Kumar

Evaluating Cross-Lingual Transfer Learning Approaches in Multilingual Conversational Agent Models

Lizhen Tan
Amazon
ltn@amazon.com

Olga Golovneva
Amazon
olggol@amazon.com

Abstract

With the recent explosion in popularity of voice assistant devices, there is a growing interest in making them available to user populations in additional countries and languages. However, to provide the highest accuracy and best performance for specific user populations, most existing voice assistant models are developed individually for each region or language, which requires linear investment of effort. In this paper, we propose a general multilingual model framework for Natural Language Understanding (NLU) models, which can help bootstrap new language models faster and reduce the amount of effort required to develop each language separately. We explore how different deep learning architectures affect multilingual NLU model performance. Our experimental results show that these multilingual models can reach same or better performance compared to monolingual models across language-specific test data while require less effort in creating features and model maintenance.

1 Introduction

The recent surge in popularity of voice assistants, such as Google Home, Apple's Siri, or Amazon's Alexa resulted in interest in scaling these products to more regions and languages. This means that all the components supporting Spoken Language Understanding (SLU) in these devices, such as Automatic Speech Recognition (ASR), Natural Language Understanding (NLU), and Entity Resolution (ER) are facing the challenges of scaling the development and maintenance processes for multiple languages and dialects.

When a voice assistant is launched in a new locale, its underlying speech processing components are often developed specifically for the targeted country, marketplace, and the main language variant of that country. Many people assume that if a device "understands" and "speaks" in a specific language, for example English, it should be able to work equally well for any English speaking country, but this is a misunderstanding. For instance, if a speaker of UK English asks a device trained on data collected in the United States *"tell me a famous football player"*, it is highly unlikely that this device will provide the user's desired answer, since *football* means different things in the US and UK cultures. As a result, developers need to take into account not only the language or dialectal differences, but also local culture, to provide the right information in the right language setup. An increase in the number of target marketplaces often means a linear increase in effort needed to develop and maintain such locale-specific models.

NLU models, which classify the user's intent and extract any significant entities from the user's utterance, face the same challenge of maintaining high accuracy while being able to accommodate multiple dialects or language content. The major tasks in NLU are intent classification and slot filling. Intent classification is a task to predict what action the user intends the voice assistant to take. Slot filling is a task to identify the specific semantic arguments for the intention. For example, if the user's request is to *"play Poker Face by Lady Gaga"*, the user's intention will be *"play music"*, while in order to fulfill this command with specified details, the system needs to capture the slots for {*song name = Poker*

Proceedings of the 28th International Conference on Computational Linguistics: Industry Track, pages 1–9
Barcelona, Spain (Online), December 12, 2020

Face}, and {*artist name = Lady Gaga*}. These tasks are called intent classification (IC) and named entity recognition (NER), respectively.

One common approach is to use a max-entropy (MaxEnt) classification model for the IC task and a conditional random fields (CRF) model for the NER task. Following the advent of deep learning techniques in related fields, such as computer vision and natural language processing, deep learning is becoming more popular in NLU as well. Some of the recent multilingual approaches to NLU include, for example, the Convolutional Neural Network (CNN) model for sentence classification (Kim, 2014), or the Long Short-Term Memory (LSTM) model for NER prediction (Lample et al., 2016; Kurata et al., 2016). In the deep neural network architecture, the aforementioned NLU tasks can be combined into a single multi-task classification model. An increasing number of experiments also focus on multilingual setups, especially in the field of machine translation, where the task is to translate input from one language to another (Johnson et al., 2016).

One recent thread of multilingual research centers around learning multilingual word representation. Multilingual word embeddings in the shared cross-lingual vector space have one main property: words from different languages but with similar meaning must be geometrically close. This property allows for transfer learning from one language to another in various multilingual tasks, such as dependency parsing (Kondratyuk, 2019; Wang et al., 2019) or classification and NER (Lample and Conneau, 2019; Pires et al., 2019). A number of model architectures have been proposed to pre-train multilingual word representations, such as leveraging large-scaled LSTM networks trained on monolingual corpora and adversarial setup for space alignment (Conneau et al., 2017; Lample et al., 2017), or transformers trained on multilingual corpora as a single language model (Lample and Conneau, 2019).

Although some of these models can be used to solve IC and NER tasks by appending corresponding decoders to generate final predictions, it is not straightforward to use them in production environments due to latency and memory constrains. A different way of benefitting from larger models could be to use them for transfer learning to smaller-size models to improve their performance by initializing some parts of the model with close-to-optimal rather than random weights. In this paper, we extend the multi-task approach studied in (Do and Gaspers, 2019) to a general multilingual model for IC and NER tasks, based on deep learning techniques, such as a bidirectional Long Short-Term Memory (biLSTM) CRF sequence labeling model for NER along with a multilayer perceptron (MLP) for IC.

We also explore multilingual transfer learning and its benefits to our setup. Transfer learning is widely adapted for zero-shot or few-shot setups, and was explored in some multilingual NLP studies (McDonald et al., 2011; Naseem et al., 2012; Chen et al., 2018), and also has been used in multi-task IC-NER models (Do and Gaspers, 2019), yet to the best of our knowledge, there is no study applying transfer learning for data-rich target languages in a multilingual setup. In our experiment, we apply few-shot transfer learning from data-rich languages to a language with a smaller amout of training data. In additon, we also apply transfer learning to mimic the situation of expanding the model ability to same-level-resource language with known context from another high-resource language(s), such that the new multilingual model will "inherit" context information from its ancestors. We investigate these approaches to transfer learning and their effects on model performance. We show that transfer learning can improve NLU model performance even in data-rich conditions.

2 Multilingual model architecture for DC, IC, and NER tasks

Single-language models are usually trained with data in a specific language, yet the model architecture is shared among different model instances (one per language). It follows that using the same model architecture, we should be able to train a generalized multilingual model which is fed by data from multiple languages.

NLU model is first trained to recognize the utterance domain, such as Music, Weather, Notifications, and then it is trained to perform domain-specific IC and NER tasks. In our experiments, the domain classification (DC) model is a MaxEnt logistic regression model. Despite the relatively simple architecture, this model shows good performance on DC task in data-rich conditions. For IC and NER tasks, we build a multi-task deep neural network (DNN) model. We first map input tokens into a share-space word embedding, and then feed them into a biLSTM encoder to obtain context information; this content then propagates to the downstream tasks, with CRF used for NER prediction, and an MLP classifier used for IC prediction. We call this a self-trained multilingual (STM) model. Figure 1 shows the model architecture.

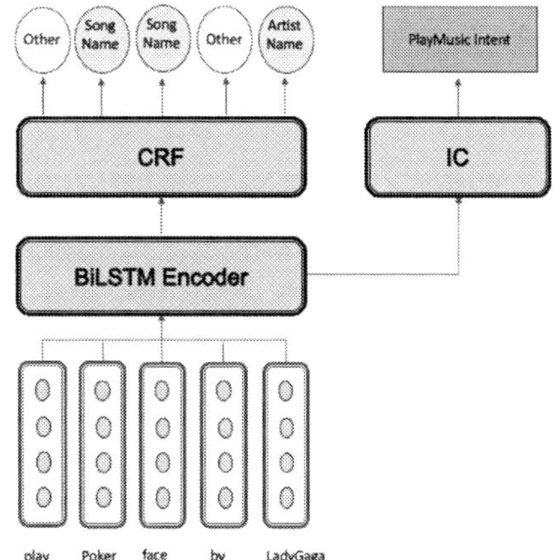

Figure 1: Multi-task model for IC and NER prediction. Tokens are first embedded into word vectors, then fed in to a biLSTM encoder, whose output is used in both CRF and MLP for NER and IC, respectively.

In the transfer learning experiments, we examined the following approaches:

1. Trained model on high-resource language(s), then transferred both encoder and decoder to the new multi-lingual model with fine-tuning (EncDecTL models).

2. Trained model on high-resource language(s), then transferred only encoder with fixed parameters to the new multi-lingual model (EncTL models).

3. Trained model on high-resource language(s), then transferred only encoder with variable learning rate, that we gradually unfreeze embeddings with training steps during fine-tuning (EncVLRTL models).

Figure 2(a) shows the architecture for approach 1, and Figure 2(b) shows the architecture for approaches 2 and 3.

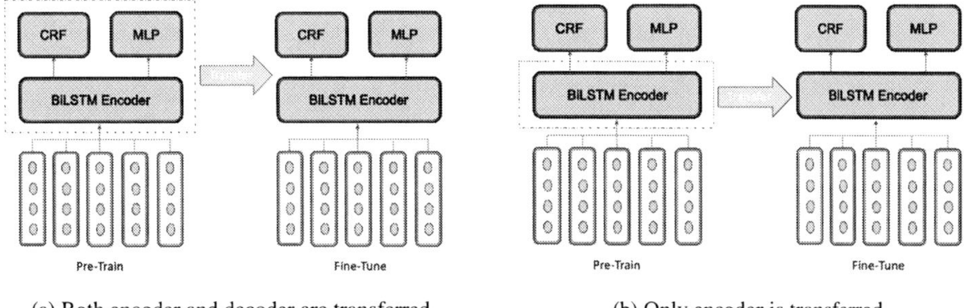

(a) Both encoder and decoder are transferred   (b) Only encoder is transferred

Figure 2: Transfer learning model architectures

We limit our architecture to a small-sized DNN model to avoid memory and latency issues in production environment:

- **Embedding**: Concatenation of share-spaced word embedding and character embedding trained on a 3-filter convolutional neural network (CNN). All embeddings for DNN models are initialized with fastText supervised multilingual word embeddings, aligned in a single vector space (Conneau et al., 2017). Aligned multilingual word embeddings kept fixed in pre-training model, and trained during fine-tuning.

- **Encoder**: 2-layer biLSTM with 512 dimensions in each hidden layer.

- **Decoders**: Both the MLP classifier used for IC task and the CRF sequence labeler used for the NER task have 512 dimensions in each block's hidden layer, and GELU activation function. We also used dropout to prevent overfitting. All models were trained for 160 epochs with early stopping (experiments were attempted to increase the number of epochs, yet this did not show much change in model performance).

- **Loss function**: A combination of loss from both tasks of IC and NER: $L_{total} = \alpha L_{ic} + \beta L_{ner}$, where α and β are the associated weight of each loss contribution. In our experiments, we have fixed both α and β to 1.

3 Experiments and discussion

3.1 Data

We train our models using data collected for four languages, including three relatively closely related language: UK English, Spanish, and Italian. In additon to these three similar languages, we also collected a dataset of Hindi, a language which is lexically and grammatically different from the other three. All utterances represent users' requests and are annotated with corresponding DC, IC, and NER tags. Summary statistics of the data set is shown in Table 1. We limit our experiments to the seven NLU domains: Communication, General Media, Home Automation, Music, Notifications, Shopping, and Video. Each training set is further divided into training and validation split in ratio 9:1.

Language	Number of utterances in train/test split	Intent types	Slot types
English	2,121,583 / 117,546	316	282
Spanish	2,927,850 / 144,156	365	311
Italian	2,435,459 / 107,298	379	324
Hindi	370,465 / 69,024	302	267

Table 1: Summary statistics of the data set

3.2 Results and discussion

Following (Schuster et al., 2019), we evaluate our models according to four metrics: domain accuracy for the DC task, intent accuracy for the IC task, micro-averaged slot F1 for NER prediction, and frame accuracy which is the relative number of utterances for which the domain, intent, and all slots are correctly identified. Relative performance for all model architectures evaluated on each language-specific test set is shown in Figure 3. Metrics are averaged across three model runs for English, Spanish and Italian test results, whereas two model runs were performed for Hindi; detailed numbers are provided in Appendix A. The baseline models used for the relative metric performance are monolingual models with a MaxEnt classifier for IC and a CRF model for NER (*Mono MaxEnt*) trained on data set which consists of utterances in the target language only. For example, in the case of Spanish, the relative performance for all models is calculated against the Mono MaxEnt model trained on Spanish data only.

All performance metrics show similar pattern: multilingual DNN models usually perform better than monolingual models, benefitting from biLSTM setup and encoder transfer learning. The only exception is domain accuracy score, where we observe only slight variations for mono- and multilingual models. The reason is because the DC model in all experiments is governed by MaxEnt model and is not affected by the changing DNN setup, but only training data mixing. Non-English models benefit from encoder transferred from pre-trained mono- and multilingual models, whereas additional decoder transfer slightly

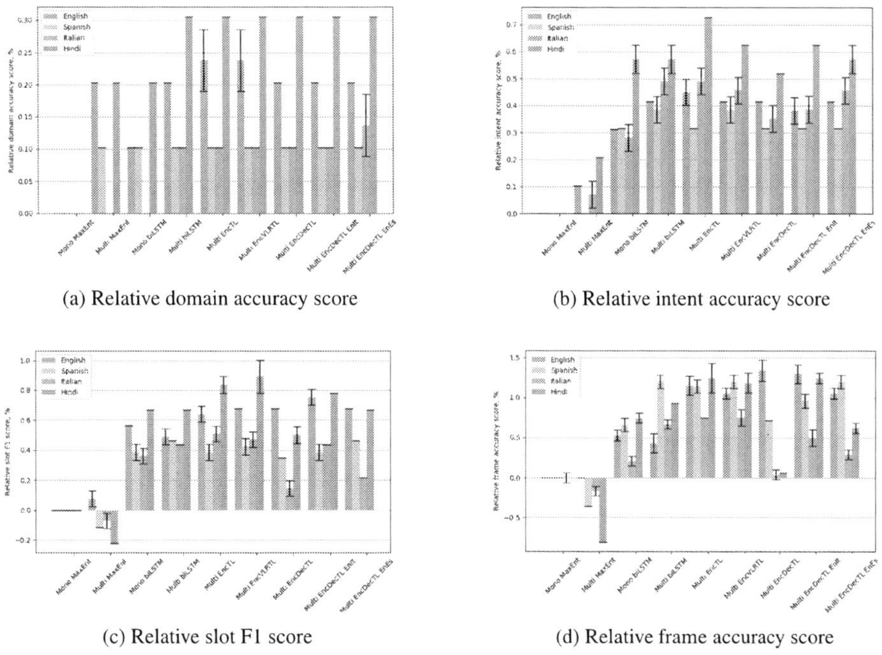

(a) Relative domain accuracy score   (b) Relative intent accuracy score

(c) Relative slot F1 score   (d) Relative frame accuracy score

Figure 3: Percentage change in model performance for mono- and multilingual models with respect to the monolingual MaxEnt model. All models for transfer learning were pre-trained on English data. In addition, two encoder-decoder transfer learning models were built on the mix of English and Italian (EnIt) and English and Spanish (EnEs) models

degrades model performance, but still beats the baseline. Mixing languages in pre-training phase (Table 2 only slightly improves target model performance). For English, EncDecTL model with transfer learning performs the best across all metrics, with EncTL model showing similar performance; while for Spanish and Italian, EncVLRTL pretrained on English is the best model among the pool (see Appendix A for detailed pairwise model comparison). Overall the best average performance across the languages is observed in DNN models with encoder transfer learning, which has about 1% improvement in frame accuracy. Interestingly, more improvement ($> 1\%$) in frame accuracy is observed in applying transfer learning on Hindi; a lexically and grammatically different language than the family of the pretrained languages. This improvement may be due to the fact that the baseline model for Hindi language was trained on a low-resource dataset, thus the encoder and decoders can learn more information from the added data, whereas encoder and decoder learning from a similar language have already been near-to-optimal, and the added data do not contribute more information gain in training. Default DNN models without transfer learning are the next best performing models (Table 3). These model results demonstrate that it is possible not only to create a single model that will serve multiple languages simultaneously, but also to expect some performance improvements.

Deep diving into EncDecTL errors for non-English languages, we found that the failures occur due to the differences in intent and slot label distributions in training data across different languages. When intents or slot labels from target language are missing in the pre-trained model, these entities are not represented in decoder's vocabulary. In our setup, the decoder's vocabulary is being transferred along with weights matrices, so the decoder fails to learn and predict new labels simply because they are missing from the list of the possible outputs. Since differences in slot labeling are more common than in intent labelling, we observe higher degradations for slot F1 and frame accuracy scores than for intent accuracy. Encoder, on the other hand, operates with aligned multilingual word embeddings only, and is not affected by the differences in annotations. This label/intent missing issue could be mitigated by the

5

Target language	Pre-training language	SEMER	Domain accuracy	Intent accuracy	Slot F1	Frame accuracy
Italian	English	1.004	1.000	0.999	0.997	0.994
	English & Spanish	1.002	1.000	1.000	0.998	0.996
Spanish	English	1.000	1.000	0.999	0.996	0.996
	English & Italian	1.000	1.000	0.999	0.999	0.998

Table 2: *Multi-lingual biLSTM* model performance for the targeted languages with monolingual and multilingual encoder-decoder transfer learning on both Italian and Spanish test data. (Values are normalized based on *Multi-lingual biLSTM*. See Appendix A for more details.)

Model	Average intent accuracy improvement(%)	Average slot F1 improvement(%)	Average frame accuracy improvement(%)
DNN without transfer learning	0.45	0.45	0.71
DNN with encoder transfer learning	0.42	0.53	0.99
DNN with encoder transfer learning and variable learning rate	0.42	0.53	1.00

Table 3: Average multilingual model performance change across English, Spanish and Italian test sets for different DNN setups.

expanding decoder's vocabulary in the fine-tuning model with intent and slot labels specific to the target language.

Finally, to understand how the DNN models affect latency, we measure average time taken by the statistical model to evaluate performance on the full multilingual test set over three runs. We found that the latency between the models is comparable, the DDN models even have a slightly lower relative average runtime of 0.95 versus 1.05 for MaxEnt models (detailed can be found in Appendix B for each model architecture).

4   Conclusions

In this paper, we propose a framework for building general multilingual NLU models, which can be used across different marketplaces and languages.

To choose the model with the best performance, we use language-specific test sets to evaluate the candidate models and their corresponding baseline models (e.g. English biLSTM-CRF model vs. monolingual English MaxEnt-CRF model) along four metrics, domain accuracy, intent accuracy, slot F1, and frame accuracy. The models which win in most of the evaluation metrics are the final picks. We find that models built from a simple multi-task biLSTM-CRF model setup are comparable to standard production models in terms of latency constraints required for on-the-fly voice assistant conversational models.

We observe performance improvements in all models with the introduction of transfer learning. Encoder transfer produced the greatest improvements whereas the transfer of the decoder did not bring much change when compared to the baseline model performance, except when tested on an English test set, when the transfer learning is performed from the model trained on English data. This is due to the fact that the target non-English language contains slots or intents which are not included in the pre-trained model, thus the decoder fails to predict correct classes simply because they are missing in the vocabulary. To mitigate this effect, a decoder with default initialization gives better performance because it now can embrace all available slots and intents in the target language realm.

Furthermore, we find that a model pre-trained in a multilingual setup performs better than the one trained on a monolingual data set. This confirms that a multilingual model built based on lexically and orthographically similar languages may provide more beneficial context information to any similar target language. Experimental result on Hindi show that such a multilingual model can work even for non-alike languages with the same or better performance improvement. This confirms that a common multilingual model can be used to support multiple language with better results than a set of monolingual models.

With a single general multilingual NLU model, bootstrapping new languages can be faster as we can use cross-lingual contextual information from all existing high-resource languages. At the same time, maintaining only one model requires much less effort in terms of regular model updates.

References

Xilun Chen, Ahmed Hassan Awadallah, Hany Hassan, Wei Wang, and Claire Cardie. 2018. Zero-resource multilingual model transfer: Learning what to share. *CoRR*, abs/1810.03552.

Alexis Conneau, Guillaume Lample, Marc'Aurelio Ranzato, Ludovic Denoyer, and Hervé Jégou. 2017. Word translation without parallel data. *CoRR*, abs/1710.04087.

Jacob Devlin, Ming-Wei Chang, Kenton Lee, and Kristina Toutanova. 2018. BERT: pre-training of deep bidirectional transformers for language understanding. *CoRR*, abs/1810.04805.

Quynh Ngoc Thi Do and Judith Gaspers. 2019. Cross-lingual transfer learning for spoken language understanding. *CoRR*, abs/1904.01825.

Melvin Johnson, Mike Schuster, Quoc V. Le, Maxim Krikun, Yonghui Wu, Zhifeng Chen, Nikhil Thorat, Fernanda B. Viégas, Martin Wattenberg, Greg Corrado, Macduff Hughes, and Jeffrey Dean. 2016. Google's multilingual neural machine translation system: Enabling zero-shot translation. *CoRR*, abs/1611.04558.

Yoon Kim. 2014. Convolutional neural networks for sentence classification. In *Proceedings of the 2014 Conference on Empirical Methods in Natural Language Processing (EMNLP)*, pages 1746–1751, Doha, Qatar, October. Association for Computational Linguistics.

Daniel Kondratyuk. 2019. 75 languages, 1 model: Parsing universal dependencies universally. *CoRR*, abs/1904.02099.

Gakuto Kurata, Bing Xiang, Bowen Zhou, and Mo Yu. 2016. Leveraging sentence-level information with encoder LSTM for natural language understanding. *CoRR*, abs/1601.01530.

Guillaume Lample and Alexis Conneau. 2019. Cross-lingual language model pretraining. *CoRR*, abs/1901.07291.

Guillaume Lample, Miguel Ballesteros, Sandeep Subramanian, Kazuya Kawakami, and Chris Dyer. 2016. Neural architectures for named entity recognition. In *Proceedings of the 2016 Conference of the North American Chapter of the Association for Computational Linguistics: Human Language Technologies*, pages 260–270, San Diego, California, June. Association for Computational Linguistics.

Guillaume Lample, Ludovic Denoyer, and Marc'Aurelio Ranzato. 2017. Unsupervised machine translation using monolingual corpora only. *CoRR*, abs/1711.00043.

Ryan McDonald, Slav Petrov, and Keith Hall. 2011. Multi-source transfer of delexicalized dependency parsers In *Proceedings of the 2011 Conference on Empirical Methods in Natural Language Processing*, pages 62–72, Edinburgh, Scotland, UK., July. Association for Computational Linguistics.

Tahira Naseem, Regina Barzilay, and Amir Globerson. 2012. Selective sharing for multilingual dependency parsing. In *Proceedings of the 50th Annual Meeting of the Association for Computational Linguistics (Volume 1: Long Papers)*, pages 629–637, Jeju Island, Korea, July. Association for Computational Linguistics.

Telmo Pires, Eva Schlinger, and Dan Garrette. 2019. How multilingual is multilingual BERT? In *Proceedings of the 57th Annual Meeting of the Association for Computational Linguistics*, pages 4996–5001, Florence, Italy, July. Association for Computational Linguistics.

Sebastian Schuster, Sonal Gupta, Rushin Shah, and Mike Lewis. 2019. Cross-lingual transfer learning for multilingual task oriented dialog. In *Proceedings of the 2019 Conference of the North American Chapter of the Association for Computational Linguistics: Human Language Technologies, Volume 1 (Long and Short Papers)*, pages 3795–3805, Minneapolis, Minnesota, June. Association for Computational Linguistics.

Yuxuan Wang, Wanxiang Che, Jiang Guo, Yijia Liu, and Ting Liu. 2019. Cross-lingual BERT transformation for zero-shot dependency parsing. In *Proceedings of the 2019 Conference on Empirical Methods in Natural Language Processing and the 9th International Joint Conference on Natural Language Processing (EMNLP-IJCNLP)*, pages 5721–5727, Hong Kong, China, November. Association for Computational Linguistics.

Appendices

A   Multilingual test results on language-specific datasets

Three model runs are performed on English, Spanish and Italian, while two model runs are performed on Hindi. All values are normalized based on *Multi-lingual biLSTM*, the 2-layer biLSTM CRF cross-lingual model.

Model #		Model type	Embedding transfer	Model blocks transfer	English					Spanish				
					SEMER	Domain accuracy	Intent accuracy	Slot F1	Frame accuracy	SEMER	Domain accuracy	Intent accuracy	Slot F1	Frame accuracy
1	Target only	CRF Max Ent	N/A	N/A	1.044	1.000	0.996	0.995	0.995	1.011	0.999	0.996	0.995	0.989
2	Cross-lingual	CRF Max Ent	N/A	N/A	1.031	1.000	0.997	0.996	0.995	1.014	0.999	0.996	0.994	0.985
3	Target only	2-layer biLSTM CRF +	Target only	-	1.014	1.000	0.999	1.001	1.001	1.006	0.999	0.999	0.999	0.995
4	Cross-lingual	2-layer biLSTM CRF +	Cross-lingual	-	1.000	1.000	1.000	1.000	1.000	1.000	1.000	1.000	1.000	1.000
5	Cross-lingual	2-layer biLSTM CRF +	Cross-lingual	English: encoder	0.996	1.000	1.000	1.002	1.007	1.000	1.000	1.000	1.000	1.000
6	Cross-lingual	2-layer biLSTM CRF +	Cross-lingual	English: encoder + steps lr scheduler	0.995	1.000	1.000	1.001	1.006	0.999	1.000	1.000	1.000	1.000
7	Cross-lingual	2-layer biLSTM CRF +	Cross-lingual	English: encoder + decoder	0.995	1.000	1.000	1.002	1.008	1.000	1.000	0.999	0.999	0.996
8	Cross-lingual	2-layer biLSTM CRF +	Cross-lingual	English + Italian: encoder + decoder	0.996	1.000	1.000	1.003	1.009	1.000	1.000	0.999	0.999	0.998
9	Cross-lingual	2-layer biLSTM CRF +	Cross-lingual	English + Spanish: encoder decoder	0.994	1.000	1.000	1.002	1.006	0.998	1.000	1.000	1.000	1.001
Model Comparison	Relative model performance across metrics (notation: model 1 vs. model 2 means how model 1 performs relatviely to model 2)													
2 vs. 1					-1.200	0.000	0.082	0.068	0.008	0.301	0.036	0.016	-0.058	-0.355
4 vs. 3					-1.416	0.000	0.120	-0.061	-0.074	-0.615	0.064	0.088	0.074	0.526
8 vs. 7					0.185	0.000	-0.007	0.062	0.011	-0.056	-0.011	0.029	0.025	0.227
9 vs. 7					-0.034	0.000	0.024	-0.017	-0.226	-0.259	-0.007	0.048	0.102	0.462
6 vs. 7					0.034	0.000	0.017	-0.054	-0.251	-0.101	-0.015	0.070	0.060	0.448
6 vs. 3					-1.910	0.000	0.123	0.088	0.521	-0.671	0.055	0.076	0.037	0.564

Italian					Hindi (only 2 model runs)				
SEMER	Domain accuracy	Intent accuracy	Slot F1	Frame accuracy	SEMER	Domain accuracy	Intent accuracy	Slot F1	Frame accuracy
1.011	0.998	0.995	0.996	0.993	1.024	0.997	0.995	0.993	0.991
1.010	0.999	0.996	0.995	0.992	1.029	0.999	0.996	0.991	0.983
1.012	0.999	0.998	0.999	0.995	1.015	0.999	1.000	1.000	0.998
1.000	1.000	1.000	1.000	1.000	1.000	1.000	1.000	1.000	1.000
1.000	1.000	1.000	1.000	1.001	0.995	1.000	1.001	1.001	1.003
1.001	1.000	1.000	1.000	1.001	0.995	1.000	1.001	1.002	1.003
1.004	1.000	0.999	0.997	0.994	1.010	1.000	1.000	0.998	0.991
1.005	1.000	0.999	1.000	0.998	0.995	1.000	1.001	1.001	1.003
1.002	1.000	1.000	0.998	0.996	1.001	1.000	1.000	1.000	0.997
-0.010	0.089	0.082	-0.055	-0.140	0.497	0.160	0.150	-0.273	-0.791
-1.171	0.124	0.183	0.068	0.467	-1.505	0.060	0.014	0.002	0.171
0.126	-0.013	0.009	0.241	0.463	-1.450	-0.003	0.070	0.253	1.166
-0.179	0.013	0.091	0.052	0.243	-0.882	-0.017	0.026	0.146	0.536
-0.337	-0.002	0.054	0.298	0.682	-1.492	-0.020	0.075	0.349	1.135
-1.098	0.109	0.148	0.105	-0.461	1.471	0.003	-0.070	-0.253	-1.153

B   Average relative evaluation runtime for each model on the full test set

All values are normalized based on *Multi-lingual biLSTM*, the 2-layer biLSTM CRF cross-lingual model.

Model #	Training set	Model type	Embedding transfer	Model blocks transfer	Runtime (rel)
1	Target only	CRF Max Ent	N/A	N/A	1.00
2	Cross-lingual	CRF Max Ent	N/A	N/A	1.05
3	Target only	2-layer biLSRTM + CRF	Target only	-	0.97
4	Cross-lingual	2-layer biLSRTM + CRF	Cross-lingual	-	1.00
5	Cross-lingual	2-layer biLSRTM + CRF	Cross-lingual	English: encoder	0.97
6	Cross-lingual	2-layer biLSRTM + CRF	Cross-lingual	English: encoder + steps lr scheduler	0.95
7	Cross-lingual	2-layer biLSRTM + CRF	Cross-lingual	English: encoder + decoder	0.98
8	Cross-lingual	2-layer biLSRTM + CRF	Cross-lingual	English + Italian: encoder + decoder	1.02
9	Cross-lingual	2-layer biLSRTM + CRF	Cross-lingual	English + Spanish: encoder + decoder	1.02

Data-Efficient Paraphrase Generation to Bootstrap Intent Classification and Slot Labeling for New Features in Task-Oriented Dialog Systems

Shailza Jolly[1,2,*], **Tobias Falke**[3], **Caglar Tirkaz**[3] and **Daniil Sorokin**[3]

[1]Technische Universität Kaiserslautern, Germany
[2]German Research Center for Artificial Intelligence (DFKI GmbH)
[3]Amazon Alexa AI, Aachen, Germany

`shailza.jolly@dfki.de, {falket,caglart,dsorokin}@amazon.com`

Abstract

Recent progress through advanced neural models pushed the performance of task-oriented dialog systems to almost perfect accuracy on existing benchmark datasets for intent classification and slot labeling. However, in evolving real-world dialog systems, where new functionality is regularly added, a major additional challenge is the lack of annotated training data for such new functionality, as the necessary data collection efforts are laborious and time-consuming. A potential solution to reduce the effort is to augment initial seed data by paraphrasing existing utterances automatically. In this paper, we propose a new, data-efficient approach following this idea. Using an interpretation-to-text model for paraphrase generation, we are able to rely on existing dialog system training data, and, in combination with shuffling-based sampling techniques, we can obtain diverse and novel paraphrases from small amounts of seed data. In experiments on a public dataset and with a real-world dialog system, we observe improvements for both intent classification and slot labeling, demonstrating the usefulness of our approach.

1 Introduction

Intent classification and slot labeling are two fundamental components in task-oriented dialog systems, producing a formal meaning representation for an utterance that the system can act upon to fulfill the user's request. As shown in Figure 1, it is typically modeled by classifying the utterance into a set of supported intents and labeling its sequence of tokens with expressed slots. We refer to the combined output of these two steps as the *interpretation* of the utterance. While the performance on these tasks has by now reached high accuracies on benchmarks like SNIPS (Coucke et al., 2018), the widespread use of real-world systems like Apple's Siri, Amazon's Alexa and Google's Assistant leads to new research challenges. As such systems are constantly expanding their functionality, bootstrapping new features is a common task that we focus on in this work.

In this paper, we define a *new feature* as a set of one or more intents and related slots that were not known to the system before. The main challenge when introducing a new feature is that typically, only very little seed training data is available, which makes it difficult to train good intent and slot models for the feature. However, manually collecting annotated data is expensive and time-consuming, slowing down the expansion of the system's functionality. We therefore aim to reduce that time and effort by automatically augmenting the seed training data and follow the idea of recent work to leverage paraphrase generation (Malandrakis et al., 2019; Cho et al., 2019). Through paraphrasing, we can automatically increase the amount of training data, but for the data to be useful, we have to ensure that the new utterances are diverse and different from what we already have. If not, the data augmentation would degenerate to simply upsampling the seed data. That can on its own already be helpful, but it does not expose any new input examples to the model during training which can help the model learn and generalize even better. On the other hand, we also have to ensure that paraphrases remain realistic and natural utterances that are representative of the real-world data distribution.

Proceedings of the 28th International Conference on Computational Linguistics: Industry Track, pages 10–20
Barcelona, Spain (Online), December 12, 2020

U: find movies playing at the closest movie theatre

I:	SearchScreeningEvent						
S:	O	B-Movie-Type	O	O	O	B-Spatial-Rel	B-Loc-Type	I-Loc-Type

Figure 1: Example utterance with intent and slot labels from SNIPS.

In contrast to previous work, we propose a data-efficient augmentation approach that can work with very small amounts of seed examples. First, we propose using an *interpretation-to-text* model that can leverage similarities to existing intents and shared slots when generating paraphrases for new features. In addition, instead of requiring pairs of paraphrases, it can be trained on single utterances annotated with intents and slots as they already exist for the downstream tasks. Second, we further propose new *paraphrase sampling strategies* that increase the amount and diversity of obtained paraphrases by using random sampling and shuffling the input representation. And third, we obtain token-level slot labels for the paraphrases via *alignment-based label projection*, instead of relying on self-labeling with a baseline model as in prior work. These differences make our approach very data-efficient, such that it can produce diverse and novel training examples for a new feature from just 100 seed utterances.

We evaluate our technique by simulating the introduction of new features on SNIPS, a common benchmark for intent classification and slot labeling in English, and on German data from a real-world dialog system. In both settings, we see substantial improvements for new features without negative effects on existing features, demonstrating the usefulness of our approach despite little seed data being available.

2 Related Work

Intent classification and slot labeling have been studied for several decades as fundamental building blocks of task-oriented dialog systems, dating back at least to the introduction of the ATIS corpus (Price, 1990) and subsequent work, e.g. (Pieraccini et al., 1992). In recent years, much progress has been made by applying deep learning techniques, such as recurrent networks (Mesnil et al., 2013), and modeling both tasks jointly with a single model (Zhang and Wang, 2016; Hakkani-Tür et al., 2016). Approaches that further improve knowledge sharing between the tasks, such as slot-gates (Goo et al., 2018) or bi-directional task connections (E et al., 2019), continued this line of work. Yet, sufficiently large training datasets are required for such advanced machine learning approaches to be effective.

To overcome the lack of training data for new features and avoid costly data collections, several proposals have been made in the recent past. Machine translation can be used to obtain training examples if the feature already exists for other languages (Gaspers et al., 2018). Cross-lingual transfer learning is another technique to effectively use such existing data (Do and Gaspers, 2019). If a feature is already being actively used, feedback signals from users, such as paraphrases or interruptions, can be identified in user interactions to obtain additional training data (Muralidharan et al., 2019). If unlabeled utterances exist for the feature, pairs of paraphrases between labeled and unlabeled data might be found, which allows deducing labels for the unlabeled utterance from the paraphrase relationship (Qiu et al., 2019).

In our work, we make no assumption about the availability of labeled data in other languages, user feedback or unlabeled data, as none of them is necessarily available when bootstrapping a new feature. Therefore, the closest existing work to ours is (Cho et al., 2019) and (Malandrakis et al., 2019), who both deal with the setup where only seed examples are available. Malandrakis et al. (2019) propose using conditional variational auto-encoders to generate paraphrases for the seed data and show that the paraphrases increase intent classification performance in their experiment. In contrast to our work, they do not evaluate on slot labeling and do not suggest a technique to add slot labels to the paraphrases.

Cho et al. (2019) generate paraphrases for seed examples with a transformer network and self-label them with a baseline intent and slot model. When added as training data, this combination of paraphrasing with self-supervised learning improves both tasks in their experiment. Our approach differs mainly in terms of data efficiency, as we do not rely on a baseline model for self-labeling – which in turn requires sufficient seed data for training – and in addition, we leverage data from existing features and use more advanced sampling strategies to obtain sufficient amounts of high-quality paraphrases from little seed data. We therefore demonstrate that our approach is applicable to earlier stages of bootstrapping by running our experiments on orders of magnitude less seed data than Cho et al. (2019). Furthermore, our paraphrase generation approach differs by training an interpretation-to-text model instead of a text-to-text model, such that no corpus of paraphrase pairs is needed. We rely exclusively on the already existing data for the downstream tasks of intent classification and slot labeling.

Beyond our specific use case, the task of paraphrase generation in general has gained much attention in recent years, driven partly by large-scale datasets such as Quora Questions Pairs[1] and the WikiAnswers[2] corpus, which enabled training complex models. Prakash et al. (2016) proposed one of the first neural models, relying on residual LSTMs. Further work explored auto-encoders (Gupta et al., 2018), generator-discriminator models trained with reinforcement learning (Li et al., 2018) or decompositions into multiple recurrent and transformer models that paraphrase at different levels (Li et al., 2019). All approaches in this line of work follow the text-to-text approach and assume training data in the form of paraphrase pairs. Because existing large datasets of this type focus on questions, we found direct application of models trained on them to the dialog domain to yield very unnatural paraphrases.

More closely related to the interpretation-to-text approach we use in this paper is work on generating natural language from structured data. Various versions of this task, differing mainly by the type of input, have been studied, e.g. generation from abstract meaning representations (Konstas et al., 2017) or from tabular data (Chen et al., 2019), as well as generation in unsupervised settings with denoising auto-encoders (Freitag and Roy, 2018). The E2E NLG challenge (Dušek et al., 2020), a recent competition carried out on a dataset from the restaurant domain with slot-based input representations, resembles our paraphrase generation scenario very closely. Among 62 competition entries, the organizers found that sequence-to-sequence models, as also used in our work, were most popular and also very competitive. However, a difference of that line of work is that paraphrases are evaluated only intrinsically, which does not necessarily reflect their usefulness for intent classification and slot labeling.

3 Data Augmentation Approach

We formalize the introduction of a new feature as having two sets of training data $\mathcal{D}_N$ and $\mathcal{D}_O$, where the former contains the seed examples for the new feature and the latter has all available examples for existing features. An example $(u, i, s) \in \mathcal{D}_O \cup \mathcal{D}_N$ consists of a tokenized utterance u, the true intent label i and true slot labels s in BIO-format. We refer to the label of a slot as the *slot name* and the covered tokens as its *slot value*. Let $\hat{s}$ be the mapping of slot names to their values, e.g. $\hat{s} = \{$*Movie-Type* : *movies, Spatial-Rel* : *closest, Loc-Type* : *movie theatre*$\}$ for the example in Figure 1.

In our scenario, $\mathcal{D}_N$ contains one or a few new intents not yet in $\mathcal{D}_O$[3] and is very small. We propose a paraphrase generation model $\mathcal{PG}$ that produces new examples $\mathcal{D}_P = \mathcal{PG}(\mathcal{D}_N)$ with the goal of improving intent classification and slot labeling performance when those models are trained on $\mathcal{D}_O \cup \mathcal{D}_N \cup \mathcal{D}_P$ instead of just $\mathcal{D}_O \cup \mathcal{D}_N$. In this section, we will describe how $\mathcal{PG}$ learns to paraphrase utterances, how we sample diverse paraphrases from it and how we project labels onto them to obtain examples $\mathcal{D}_P$.

3.1 Interpretation-to-Text Paraphrase Generation

In our interpretation-to-text approach, rather than learning to map utterances to paraphrases, we instead use examples (u, i, s) to model utterance sequences token by token conditioned on their interpretation:

$$p(u \mid i, \hat{s}) = \prod_{j=1}^{n} p(u_j \mid u_{1:j-1}, enc_j(i, \hat{s})) \tag{1}$$

where $enc_j(i, \hat{s})$ is an attention-based encoding of the interpretation $(i, \hat{s})$ at decoding step j. The idea behind this approach is that the notion of two utterances being paraphrases is, for our purposes, equivalent

---

[1] https://www.kaggle.com/c/quora-question-pairs
[2] http://knowitall.cs.washington.edu/paralex/
[3] Note that while all intents in $\mathcal{D}_N$ are new, slots might overlap with $\mathcal{D}_O$ since generic slots are used across many intents.

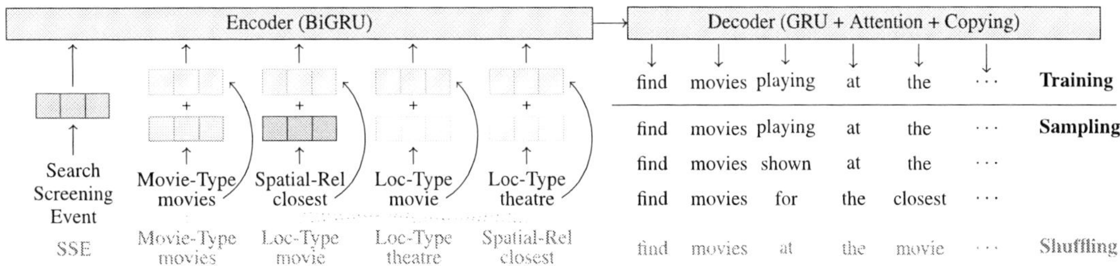

Figure 2: The interpretation-to-text model encodes an interpretation as a sequence of intent, slot name and slot value embeddings and is trained to predict the utterance. At inference time, we sample token by token and shuffle the input slot order (bottom) to obtain diverse paraphrases.

with them having the same interpretation. Thus, we model a mapping from that unique representation of a set of paraphrases – the shared interpretation – to all its realizations. At inference time, the conditional language model $p(u \mid i, \hat{s})$ can then, once conditioned on a specific interpretation, provide a distribution over all possible realizations from which paraphrases can be sampled.

In terms of data-efficiency, an obvious advantage is that downstream training data $\mathcal{D}$ can be used to directly train the model. We can also include the large set $\mathcal{D}_O$ in addition to the seed data $\mathcal{D}_N$ to train a much more powerful paraphrase model than with $\mathcal{D}_N$ alone or with out-of-domain paraphrase data. Thereby, the model can learn more general properties of the language used with dialog systems and similarities of utterances across intents and slots. At inference time, when sampling paraphrases for interpretations from $\mathcal{D}_N$ token by token, the model can interpolate between utterances seen in $\mathcal{D}_N$ or $\mathcal{D}_O$ and thus is able to create novel utterances not seen during training but that reflect the interpretation.

We implement $p(u \mid i, \hat{s})$ following the sequence-to-sequence paradigm using a bi-directional GRU for encoding and a GRU equipped with attention and a pointer mechanism for decoding (See et al., 2017). Embeddings for utterance tokens, slot names and intents are learned. An interpretation is fed into the model as a sequence starting with the embedded intent, followed by vectors that are the sum of a slot name and slot value token embedding. See Figure 2 for an illustration. The same vocabulary and embeddings are used in encoder and decoder, but only tokens can be generated on the output side. We train minimizing cross-entropy for the utterances in $\mathcal{D}_O \cup \mathcal{D}_N$.

3.2 Paraphrase Sampling Strategies

At inference time, sequence-to-sequence models typically use greedy decoding or beam search to find the (approximately) best sequence given an input. In our use case of obtaining additional training data, however, we are not only interested in the most likely realization of an interpretation, but rather want multiple diverse and novel utterances. We therefore rely on *input shuffling* and *random sampling*.

3.2.1 Input Representation Shuffling

The fact that feeding a sequence to the model requires us to order the slots in a certain way provides a simple way for obtaining multiple paraphrases: shuffling the order. We observed that although we train the model using one order (corresponding to the utterance), decoding with alternative ones provides paraphrases that also mention the values in that alternative order. A problem is that decoded utterances sometimes miss a slot, which motivates our quality metric *partial slot carry-over (PSCO)*, measuring the fraction of slots $\hat{s}$ for which at least one token of the slot value $\hat{s}_j^v$ occurs in the decoded utterance u'.

$$PSCO(u', \hat{s}) = \frac{1}{|\hat{s}|} \sum_{j=1}^{|\hat{s}|} \min(1, |\{t \mid t \in u' \wedge t \in \hat{s}_j^v\}|) \tag{2}$$

Using that metric, we collect k paraphrases given a seed utterance u as follows: First, we create input sequences corresponding to all permutations of the slot values. Next, we decode the best utterance for each input with beam search, compute its PSCO and keep only candidates with a rate of 1. From the remaining candidates, we sample k (if they are more) or upsample to k (if they are less). The last step is to ensure that each seed leads to exactly k paraphrases and the initial distribution is thereby preserved.

3.2.2   Random Sampling

As a second strategy, we replace beam search with random sampling, which samples an utterance token by token according to the probability distribution over the vocabulary rather than trying to find the most likely sequence. Since this decoding process is not deterministic, multiple rounds of sampling yield different utterances, which allows us to obtain multiple paraphrases per seed. When decoding token u_j, we scale the logits z_t over the vocabulary with a temperature α before applying softmax

$$p(u_j = t \mid u_{1:j-1}, h_j) = \frac{\exp(z_t/\alpha)}{\sum_{t' \in V} \exp(z_{t'}/\alpha)} \tag{3}$$

and then sample from the top-β tokens according to their probabilities. $\alpha < 1$ makes the distribution spikier, such that the most likely tokens are sampled more often, while $\alpha > 1$ promotes less likely ones, as does a larger β which defines the size of the distribution's head to consider. With higher values, a larger part of the distribution will be explored, leading to higher novelty and diversity of the utterances, but potentially also to more unnatural sequences.

3.3   Label Projection

Given a paraphrase u' for a seed example (u, i, s), we finally need to project labels i and s to turn u' into a useful example for the downstream tasks. While this is trivial for intent labels – we can simply use i – it is more intricate for per-token slot labels as u and u' differ. Nevertheless, many tokens typically overlap, which motivates using a token alignment-based approach inspired by Fürstenau and Lapata (2009).

For each source-target token pair (u_j, u'_k), we first compute a similarity $sim(u_j, u'_k) \in [0, 1]$. We use the inverse of character-level Levenshtein edit distance normalized by length, which works well to identify identical tokens or slight morphological variations. Experiments with word embeddings to capture more semantic similarities made only small differences on our data. Based on the pairwise similarities, we then consider all alignments of source tokens in u to targets in u' and score them by their average similarity of the chosen alignments, allowing that a source is aligned to a virtual empty target token if no better target is found. Rather than exactly solving this optimization problem as done in (Fürstenau and Lapata, 2009), we find the best alignment greedily, choosing the most similar target for each source from left to right. Finally, we project slot labels s along that alignment, restore BIO prefixes, and use the result s' to form the new training example (u', i, s') for $\mathcal{D}_P$.

4   Experimental Setup

We experiment with our data augmentation approach by simulating the introduction of a new feature on a public dataset with English utterances and on internal data from a real-world dialog system in German.

4.1   Data

SNIPS   The Snips NLU dataset (Coucke et al., 2018) is a commonly used benchmark for intent classification and slot labeling covering 7 intents and 39 slots. It is typically split into 13,084 train, 700 validation, and 700 test examples. We run 7 experiments, each time picking one of the intents to be the new feature. For each, we use the full training and validation data of the remaining 6 intents as $\mathcal{D}_O^{train}$ and $\mathcal{D}_O^{val}$ (together about 11,815 instances), while we sample 5% of the data for the new feature to be the seed data $\mathcal{D}_N^{train}$ and $\mathcal{D}_N^{val}$ (together 100 instances). We use the regular test split of SNIPS for evaluation. Since SNIPS is moderate in size and our experimental setup involves several randomized parts, we repeat the experiments multiple times and report averaged results. We use each of the 7 intents as the simulated new feature, sample three different 5% seed subsets for it and train models with 10 different seeds, resulting in 210 different experiment runs per approach.

Internal Data In addition to SNIPS, we use randomly sampled data from logs of a commercial dialog system in German to simulate the introduction of 5 different features that have been introduced in the past. For each, we use $|\mathcal{D}_N^{train}| = 450$ and $|\mathcal{D}_N^{val}| = 50$ seed utterances. The datasets $\mathcal{D}_O^{train}$ and $\mathcal{D}_O^{val}$ are significantly larger and cover several hundred other intents, not including examples for any of the 5 features we simulate to be new. For evaluation, we test against two disjoint test sets, one from the same distribution as $\mathcal{D}_O^{train}$ and one having examples for the new feature.

4.2 Intent and Slot Model

For intent classification and slot labeling, we use a neural model inspired by existing work. Tokens are embedded as 300-dimensional vectors and encoded with a bi-directional GRU with hidden size 512. For intent classification, the concatenated final representations of the GRUs are fed through a 300-d ReLU layer, followed by dropout and a final softmax layer over intent labels. For slot labeling, we use a similar two-layer network, but apply it to the GRU states from each timestep to predict slot labels per token. The model is trained with Adam, a batch size of 64 and dropout of 0.2 until the performance stops improving on the validation data. We train the model separately for intent classification and slot labeling, which departs from recent work that observed improvements through joint training (see Section 2). However, we choose this setup to be able to study the effect of our data augmentation on both tasks in isolation.

4.3 Compared Approaches

In our experiments, we compare the following variations of the techniques presented in Section 3:

- **Baseline** A model trained using just the seed data $\mathcal{D}_N$ and existing data $\mathcal{D}_O$. The goal for all data augmentation approaches is to improve upon this baseline.

- **Upsampling5** A variation of the baseline that repeats each seed example 5 times to match the amount of training data for the new feature obtained with the augmentation techniques below.

- **Beam1** A model trained on $\mathcal{D}_O$, $\mathcal{D}_N$ and $\mathcal{D}_P$, where the latter comes from decoding one paraphrase for each seed in $\mathcal{D}_N$ with beam search. We use a beam size of 5 and normalize scores by length.

- **Beam5** Same as Beam1, but using the top-5 hypotheses from the beam for each seed.

- **Shuffle+Beam5** Same as Beam5, but also using input shuffling. We select 5 paraphrases per seed based on PSCO from the beams across all shuffles as described in Section 3.2.1.

- **Rand1** Same as Beam1, but decoding with random sampling. We sample with $\alpha = 2$ and $\beta - 3$.[4]

- **Rand5** Same as Rand1, but sampling 5 paraphrases per seed.

- **Shuffle+Rand5** Same as Shuffle+Beam5, but using random sampling as in Rand1. We sample 3 paraphrases per shuffle and then select 5 across all shuffles by PSCO as in Section 3.2.1.

Given the number of seed examples available for the new feature – 100 on SNIPS and 500 on our internal dataset – the absolute number of examples added by the augmentation methods and baselines are 100 or 500 on SNIPS and 500 or 2,500 on the internal dataset. Beyond these two settings, it would be interesting to explore more seed-paraphrase-ratios and to determine an optimal one, but we leave this for future work to instead focus on the comparison of different sampling techniques in this work.

The paraphrasing model is trained on $\mathcal{D}_N \cup \mathcal{D}_O$ with a vocabulary of 30,000 tokens. Embeddings for tokens, intents and slot names are initialized with 300-dimensional GloVe vectors (Pennington et al., 2014) (or randomly if not found) and updated during training. The encoder and decoder GRUs have a size of 300 and two layers each. We train with a batch size of 64 and dropout of 0.3 with early stopping.

---

[4]We selected these parameters after manually inspecting paraphrases for a range of parameter settings and found them to represent a good trade-off between novelty and quality.

A i'm looking for a table at a pasta restaurant in serbia	1 *BookRestaurant, Dish=pasta, Type=restaurant, Country=serbia* i'm looking to find a table at a pasta restaurant in serbia 2 *BookRestaurant, Dish=pasta, Country=serbia, Type=restaurant* book a pasta in serbia restaurant 3 *BookRestaurant, Type=restaurant, Dish=pasta, Country=serbia* i'm looking for a restaurant that serves pasta in serbia
B please play the newest music by evil jared hasselhoff	1 *PlayMusic, Sort=newest, Artist=evil jared hasselhoff* play the newest music by evil jared 2 *PlayMusic, Artist=evil jared hasselhoff, Sort=newest* play music by evil jared hasselhoff on the newest
C closest movie theatre with no time for sergeants	1 *SearchScreeningEvent, Sp.-Rel=closest, Movie=no time for ...* is the closest no time for sergeants at the movie theatre

Figure 3: Paraphrases of varying quality sampled for seeds from SNIPS using beam search and input shuffling (Shuffle+Beam5). Left side shows the seed, right the input and output of the paraphrase model. Note that the examples were manually chosen to demonstrate both good and bad examples.

4.4 Evaluation Metrics

Our main evaluation metric is the performance of the downstream tasks, measured by accuracy for intent classification and slot F1-score for slot labeling. We focus on the change in performance when using data augmentation compared to the baseline, as it shows whether the augmentation is helpful to bootstrap a new feature. Because bootstrapping a new feature can be detrimental to existing ones, we separately look at changes for the new feature (should be positive) and for existing features (should not be negative).

To be able to get additional insights into relative strengths of different paraphrase generation approaches, we also adopt the following metrics to compare paraphrases:

- **ESCO** Similar to PSCO defined in Eq. 2, we compute the *exact slot carry over (ESCO)*, which differs in counting only slots whose complete slot value has been carried over. Where we use PSCO=1 for candidate selection, this stricter version can still differentiate among the selections.

- **Novelty** In our use case, new examples need to be different from the seeds, otherwise, the augmentation degenerates to simply upsampling the data. We therefore use BLEU (Papineni et al., 2002) as a measure of similarity and compute for each paraphrase u' of seed u the score $1 - \text{BLEU4}(u, u')$. Higher scores indicate higher novelty. We report averages over all sampled paraphrases.

- **Diversity** In addition, we want paraphrases to be diverse instead of sampling the same paraphrase repeatedly. To measure diversity, we also compute $1 - \text{BLEU4}(u', u'')$, but among pairs of paraphrases u', u'' of the same seed. We report the average over all pairs, higher means more diversity.

Note that we report the three metrics introduced above primarily to better understand how paraphrases sampled with different methods differ. Whether such differences, e.g. higher novelty or diversity, are in fact beneficial is reflected by the downstream performance measured as intent accuracy and slot F1.

5 Results

5.1 Generated Paraphrases

Figure 3 shows several examples for paraphrases obtained with our approach. As the examples show, utterances range from slight variations of the original utterance, dropping only some tokens (B1, A1) or changing the order as encouraged by input shuffling (A2, A3), to more strongly deviating ones that can in the extreme become unnatural and ungrammatical (B2, C1).

Table 1 compares the generated paraphrases with our quality metrics. As expected, paraphrases from random sampling are more novel and more diverse than from beam search, but at the expense of carrying

	Upsampling5	Beam1	Beam5	Shuffle +Beam5	Rand1	Rand5	Shuffle +Rand5
PSCO	1.000	0.988	0.984	**1.000**	0.911	0.910	**1.000**
ESCO	1.000	0.969	0.956	**0.972**	0.773	0.772	0.878
Novelty	0.000	0.486	0.574	0.742	0.767	0.766	**0.864**
Diversity	0.000	–	0.522	0.594	–	0.837	**0.881**

Table 1: Quality comparison of paraphrases generated on SNIPS with different approaches along our four metrics. Bold marks best technique per metric (excluding the edge case Upsampling5).

SNIPS		New Feature				Existing Features			
Method	#Train	IC	Δ	SL	Δ	IC	Δ	SL	Δ
Baseline	100	88.1		52.1		98.9		88.8	
Upsampling5	600	90.5	+2.46	63.6	+11.47	98.8	-0.10	88.4	-0.40
Beam1	200	89.7	+1.67	57.7	+5.58	98.8	-0.06	88.7	**-0.08**
Beam5	600	90.6	+2.50	62.9	+10.78	98.8	-0.10	88.5	-0.23
Shuffle+Beam5	600	88.7	+0.67	63.1	+11.02	98.7	-0.15	88.5	-0.23
Rand1	200	91.0	+2.97	57.5	+5.36	98.9	**-0.02**	88.6	-0.11
Rand5	600	92.0	**+3.95**	63.4	+11.32	98.8	-0.14	88.5	-0.27
Shuffle+Rand5	600	91.3	+3.26	64.7	**+12.66**	98.8	-0.14	88.4	-0.31

Table 2: Intent classification (IC) accuracy and slot labeling (SL) F1-scores on the SNIPS test set (English) after adding generated paraphrases as additional training data. Δ denotes the absolute change with regard to the baseline. Each result is an average over 210 runs of the experiments (see Section 4).

over less slots, indicating that too novel paraphrases might no longer fully represent the intended interpretation. Note that by design (see Section 3.2.1), PSCO is 1 for both input shuffling–based methods, but ESCO reveals that the slot carry over rate is in fact lower for random sampling. While we observe a trade-off between slot carry over and novelty/diversity in general, it is notable that input shuffling increases novelty and diversity while at the same time also achieving the highest slot carry over, for both beam search and random sampling. Hence, our proposed combination of shuffling and selection by PSCO appears to be an effective way to improve paraphrases among all dimensions.

5.2 Effect on Downstream Tasks

Table 2 shows the effect of adding the paraphrases as training data on SNIPS. Comparing the variations of our method, we make the following observations: Across both tasks and both sampling methods, generating more paraphrases per seed utterance (500 vs. 100) improves performance more. With regard to sampling methods, the results show that random sampling helps more than beam search, which is in line with the increased novelty and diversity observed in Table 1. However, that effect is less pronounced for slot labeling, as the lower slot carry over coming with higher novelty and diversity is more problematic for learning slot labeling, but almost irrelevant for intent classification. Input shuffling, on the other hand, seems beneficial for slot labeling but not for intent classification, which could be because word order is less relevant for intent classification in general. When evaluating on existing features, there is a small performance drop, but it is negligibly small, in particular when compared to the gain on the new feature. Finally, we note that the Upsampling baseline is strong, but, while it beats several of our ablations, its performance is not as good as our full method, indicating that the higher novelty and diversity of the sampled paraphrases (see Table 1) are beneficial for the downstream task.

On the internal data, we compared only our full method including input shuffling across the two sampling methods. The average improvement over all simulated new features is even bigger for intent

Internal Data	New Feature				Existing Features			
	ICΔ		SLΔ		ICΔ		SLΔ	
New Feature	S+B5	S+R5	S+B5	S+R5	S+B5	S+R5	S+B5	S+R5
WeatherForecast	+1.48	+4.81	+3.91	+4.98	-0.02	-0.04	-0.02	-0.01
SendMessage	+4.84	+7.73	+0.65	+0.47	-0.13	-0.11	-0.01	-0.02
PlayMusic	+8.79	+10.12	+1.35	-0.12	+0.11	+0.10	-0.05	-0.13
MovieListing	+9.50	+10.32	+1.28	+0.92	+0.05	+0.05	-0.09	-0.06
ApplianceOnOff	+0.91	+12.53	+1.25	+0.79	-0.02	-0.18	+0.04	-0.07
Average	+5.10	+9.10	+1.69	+1.41	0.00	-0.04	-0.03	-0.06

Table 3: Intent classification (IC) and slot labeling (SL) performance change on internal data (German) across 5 (simulated) new features when adding paraphrases generated with Shuffle+Beam5 (S+B5) or Shuffle+Rand5 (S+R5). Numbers are absolute changes with regard to the baseline.

classification, as Table 3 shows, again with random sampling providing bigger improvements than beam search. Also, none of the improvements for the new feature changes the performance on existing features substantially, as desired. Compared to SNIPS, however, improvements are smaller for slots, and beam search outperforms random sampling. We attribute the smaller improvement to the fact that more (shared) slots are already known to the model since the set of existing features is larger. Thus, the baseline can already perform better, which makes it harder to improve. The breakdown by new feature in Table 3 illustrates that changes are different across features, which we attribute to the degree of variety within utterances for specific features and their similarity to already existing features.

5.3 Discussion and Future Work

Our results are promising and show that improvements are possible even with small seed datasets. That being said, we want to emphasize that finding the paraphrases that provide the combination of novelty, diversity and meaning-preservation that benefit the downstream task the most is challenging, as two different models with hyper-parameters and the sampling parameters are involved. Tuning them carefully is therefore very costly, and we leave exploring methods for that to future work. In addition, future work should study the optimal number of paraphrases for a new feature, whether sampling methods, in particular slot shuffling, work equally well across domains and how the paraphrase generation model could benefit from language model pretraining. Finally, we would like to point out that in practice, our approach can be combined with any other data augmentation technique discussed in Section 2, such as using machine translation or user feedback, to bootstrap new features even further.

6 Conclusion

We proposed a data augmentation approach for seed data of new features in dialog systems that relies on interpretation-to-text paraphrase models, shuffling and random sampling to generate paraphrases and alignment-based label projection. We demonstrated that using the resulting new training examples improves performance for intents and slots on an English benchmark and German dialog system data.

Acknowledgements

We would like to thank Markus Boese, Judith Gaspers, Patrick Lehnen, Fabian Triefenbach and our anonymous reviewers for their thoughtful comments and suggestions that improved this paper.

References

Zhiyu Chen, Harini Eavani, Yinyin Liu, and William Yang Wang. 2019. Few-shot NLG with Pre-trained Language Model. *arXiv*, 1904.09521.

Eunah Cho, He Xie, and William M. Campbell. 2019. Paraphrase Generation for Semi-Supervised Learning in NLU. In *Proceedings of the Workshop on Methods for Optimizing and Evaluating NLG*, pages 45–54, Minneapolis, MN, USA.

Alice Coucke, Alaa Saade, Adrien Ball, Théodore Bluche, Alexandre Caulier, David Leroy, Clément Doumouro, Thibault Gisselbrecht, Francesco Caltagirone, Thibaut Lavril, et al. 2018. Snips Voice Platform: An Embedded Spoken Language Understanding System for Private-By-Design Voice Interfaces. *arXiv*, 1805.10190.

Quynh Do and Judith Gaspers. 2019. Cross-lingual Transfer Learning with Data Selection for Large-Scale Spoken Language Understanding. In *Proceedings of the 2019 Conference on EMNLP and the 9th IJCNLP*, pages 1455–1460, Hong Kong, China.

Ondřej Dušek, Jekaterina Novikova, and Verena Rieser. 2020. Evaluating the state-of-the-art of End-to-End Natural Language Generation: The E2E NLG challenge. *Computer Speech & Language*, 59:123–156.

Haihong E, Peiqing Niu, Zhongfu Chen, and Meina Song. 2019. A Novel Bi-directional Interrelated Model for Joint Intent Detection and Slot Filling. In *Proceedings of the 57th Annual Meeting of the ACL*, pages 5467–5471, Florence, Italy.

Markus Freitag and Scott Roy. 2018. Unsupervised Natural Language Generation with Denoising Autoencoders. In *Proceedings of the 2018 Conference on EMNLP*, pages 3922–3929, Brussels, Belgium.

Hagen Fürstenau and Mirella Lapata. 2009. Semi-Supervised Semantic Role Labeling. In *Proceedings of the 12th Conference of the EACL*, pages 220–228, Athens, Greece.

Judith Gaspers, Penny Karanasou, and Rajen Chatterjee. 2018. Selecting Machine-Translated Data for Quick Bootstrapping of a Natural Language Understanding System. In *Proceedings of the 2018 Conference of the NAACL-HLT*, pages 137–144, New Orleans, LA, USA.

Chih-Wen Goo, Guang Gao, Yun-Kai Hsu, Chih-Li Huo, Tsung-Chieh Chen, Keng-Wei Hsu, and Yun-Nung Chen. 2018. Slot-Gated Modeling for Joint Slot Filling and Intent Prediction. In *Proceedings of the 2018 Conference of the NAACL-HLT*, pages 753–757, New Orleans, LA, USA.

Ankush Gupta, Arvind Agarwal, Prawaan Singh, and Piyush Rai. 2018. A Deep Generative Framework for Paraphrase Generation. In *Proceedings of the Thirty-Second AAAI Conference on Artificial Intelligence*, pages 5149–5156, New Orleans, LA, USA.

Dilek Hakkani-Tür, Gökhan Tür, Asli Celikyilmaz, Yun-Nung Chen, Jianfeng Gao, Li Deng, and Ye-Yi Wang. 2016. Multi-Domain Joint Semantic Frame Parsing Using Bi-Directional RNN-LSTM. In *Interspeech*, pages 715–719, San Francisco, CA, USA.

Ioannis Konstas, Srinivasan Iyer, Mark Yatskar, Yejin Choi, and Luke Zettlemoyer. 2017. Neural AMR: Sequence-to-Sequence Models for Parsing and Generation. In *Proceedings of the 55th Annual Meeting of the ACL*, pages 146–157, Vancouver, Canada.

Zichao Li, Xin Jiang, Lifeng Shang, and Hang Li. 2018. Paraphrase Generation with Deep Reinforcement Learning. In *Proceedings of the 2018 Conference on EMNLP*, pages 3865–3878, Brussels, Belgium.

Zichao Li, Xin Jiang, Lifeng Shang, and Qun Liu. 2019. Decomposable Neural Paraphrase Generation. In *Proceedings of the 57th Annual Meeting of the ACL*, pages 3403–3414, Florence, Italy.

Nikolaos Malandrakis, Minmin Shen, Anuj Goyal, Shuyang Gao, Abhishek Sethi, and Angeliki Metallinou. 2019. Controlled Text Generation for Data Augmentation in Intelligent Artificial Agents. In *Proceedings of the 3rd Workshop on Neural Generation and Translation*, pages 90–98, Hong Kong, China.

Grégoire Mesnil, Xiaodong He, Li Deng, and Yoshua Bengio. 2013. Investigation of Recurrent-Neural-Network Architectures and Learning Methods for Spoken Language Understanding. In *Interspeech*, pages 3771–3775, Lyon, France.

Deepak Muralidharan, Justine Kao, Xiao Yang, Lin Li, Lavanya Viswanathan, Mubarak Seyed Ibrahim, Kevin Luikens, Stephen Pulman, Ashish Garg, Atish Kothari, and Jason Williams. 2019. Leveraging User Engagement Signals For Entity Labeling in a Virtual Assistant. *arXiv*, 1909.09143.

Kishore Papineni, Salim Roukos, Todd Ward, and Wei-Jing Zhu. 2002. Bleu: a Method for Automatic Evaluation of Machine Translation. In *Proceedings of the Annual Meeting of the ACL*, pages 311–318, Philadelphia, PA, USA.

Jeffrey Pennington, Richard Socher, and Christopher Manning. 2014. Glove: Global Vectors for Word Representation. In *Proceedings of the 2014 Conference on EMNLP*, pages 1532–1543, Doha, Qatar.

Roberto Pieraccini, Evelyne Tzoukermann, Zakhar Gorelov, Jean-Luc Gauvain, Esther Levin, Chin-Hui Lee, and Jay G. Wilpon. 1992. A Speech Understanding System Based on Statistical Representation of Semantics. In *Proceedings of the 1992 IEEE ICASSP*, page 193–196, San Francisco, CA, USA.

Aaditya Prakash, Sadid A. Hasan, Kathy Lee, Vivek Datla, Ashequl Qadir, Joey Liu, and Oladimeji Farri. 2016. Neural Paraphrase Generation with Stacked Residual LSTM Networks. In *Proceedings of the 26th International Conference on Computational Linguistics*, pages 2923–2934, Osaka, Japan.

P. J. Price. 1990. Evaluation of Spoken Language Systems: the ATIS Domain. In *Speech and Natural Language: Proceedings of a Workshop*, Hidden Valley, PA, USA.

Zimeng Qiu, Eunah Cho, Xiaochun Ma, and William Campbell. 2019. Graph-Based Semi-Supervised Learning for Natural Language Understanding. In *Proceedings of the Thirteenth Workshop on Graph-Based Methods for NLP*, pages 151–158, Hong Kong, China.

Abigail See, Peter J. Liu, and Christopher D. Manning. 2017. Get To The Point: Summarization with Pointer-Generator Networks. In *Proceedings of the 55th Annual Meeting of the ACL*, pages 1073–1083, Vancouver, Canada.

Xiaodong Zhang and Houfeng Wang. 2016. A Joint Model of Intent Determination and Slot Filling for Spoken Language Understanding. In *Proceedings of the Twenty-Fifth IJCAI*, page 2993–2999, New York, NY, USA.

Leveraging User Paraphrasing Behavior In Dialog Systems To Automatically Collect Annotations For Long-Tail Utterances

Tobias Falke, Markus Boese, Daniil Sorokin, Caglar Tirkaz and **Patrick Lehnen**
Amazon Alexa AI, Aachen, Germany
`{falket,boesem,dsorokin,caglart,plehnen}@amazon.com`

Abstract

In large-scale commercial dialog systems, users express the same request in a wide variety of alternative ways with a long tail of less frequent alternatives. Handling the full range of this distribution is challenging, in particular when relying on manual annotations. However, the same users also provide useful implicit feedback as they often paraphrase an utterance if the dialog system failed to understand it. We propose MARUPA, a method to leverage this type of feedback by creating annotated training examples from it. MARUPA creates new data in a fully automatic way, without manual intervention or effort from annotators, and specifically for currently failing utterances. By re-training the dialog system on this new data, accuracy and coverage for long-tail utterances can be improved. In experiments, we study the effectiveness of this approach in a commercial dialog system across various domains and three languages.

1 Introduction

A core component of voice- and text-based dialog systems is a language understanding component, responsible for producing a formal meaning representation of an utterance that the system can act upon to fulfill a user's request (Tur and De Mori, 2011). This component is often modeled as the combination of two tasks: intent classification (IC) – determining which intent from a set of known intents is expressed – and slot labeling (SL) – finding sequences of tokens that express slots relevant for the intent. As an example, consider the utterance *Play Blinding Lights*, which expresses the *PlayMusic* intent and the tokens *Blinding Lights* refer to the *Song* slot whereas *Play* expresses no slot.

As in many other language processing tasks, an important challenge arises from the fact that natural language allows one to express the same meaning in many different ways. In commercial systems at the scale of Apple's Siri, Amazon's Alexa or Google's Assistant, the variety of alternative utterances used to express the same request is immense, stemming from the scale of the system, the heterogenous language use among users and noise such as speech recognition errors (Muralidharan et al., 2019). In addition, the frequency distribution of alternative utterances follows a power law distribution, such that a system can handle a substantial part of the distribution by understanding just a few utterances, but needs to understand orders of magnitude more to also cover the long tail of the distribution. Although utterances from the tail occur rarely, humans have little difficulties understanding them, imposing the same expectation on a dialog system with true language understanding. However, the traditional way of building a language understanding component – supervised learning with manually annotated examples – is impractical to scale to that challenge as the necessary annotation effort becomes prohibitively expensive.

We propose to leverage implicit user feedback to reduce the need for manual annotation and thereby scale language understanding in dialog systems to more long-tail utterances. In this paper, we focus on cases where a user's utterance has not been correctly interpreted by the system, causing *friction* for the user, and the user gives implicit feedback by *paraphrasing* the utterance (see Figure 1). Such behavior is common in commercial systems, where many users make repeated attempts to receive a response. Predicted intents and slots of the eventually successful utterance can in these cases be used to infer labels

Proceedings of the 28th International Conference on Computational Linguistics: Industry Track, pages 21–32
Barcelona, Spain (Online), December 12, 2020

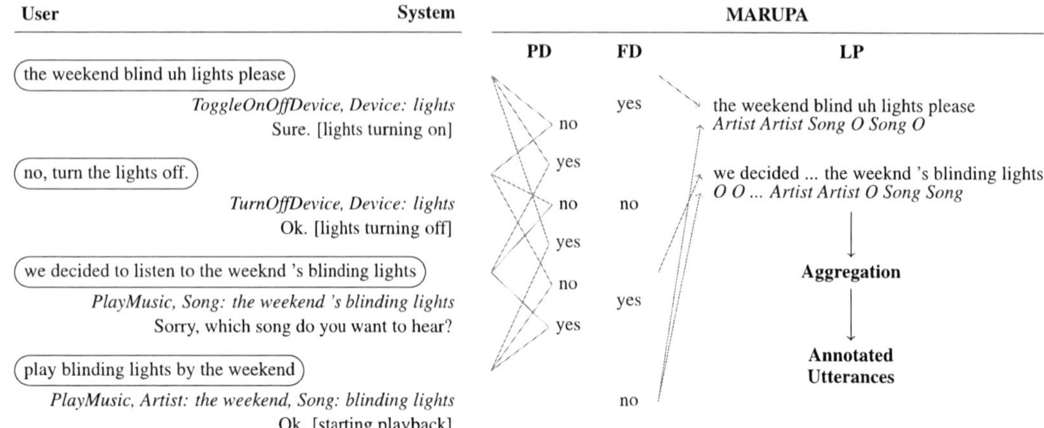

Figure 1: During the interaction (left), the first and third user utterances, exemplary for noisy and long-tail utterances, are mis-interpreted by the system. The final, more common paraphrase succeeds. MARUPA (right) uses PD and FD to detect two paraphrase pairs with a friction-causing and a successful utterance (1+4 and 3+4). For both, the successful interpretation is projected onto the failed utterance (LP). Utterance 2 is not used. After aggregation across interactions, the new data is used to re-train the model.

for the friction-causing utterances. Our proposed method, **MARUPA** (**M**ining **A**nnotations f**r**om **U**ser **Pa**raphrasing), combines *paraphrase detection (PD), friction detection (FD)* and *label projection (LP)* models to automatically detect relevant paraphrasing behavior in interactions with a dialog system and to turn it into new, annotated utterances.

The proposed data collection approach has several advantages: First, it is fully automatic, thus reducing effort and cost for annotation and making data collection scalable. Second, the friction-causing utterances that are followed by paraphrases tend to be the less frequent ones from the long tail, such that the collected data helps in particular to increase coverage and improve accuracy on that part of the distribution. And third, using user feedback to annotate data integrates seamlessly with supervised learning and is agnostic to the type of model being used for IC and SL. It requires only user feedback and predictions of the underlying model. It can also be applied repeatedly with improving underlying models and is essentially an extension of self-learning, as we discuss in Section 2.

We present experiments with MARUPA on anonymized data from a commercial dialog system across many domains and three different languages. In addition, we also report component-wise evaluations and experiments on public datasets where possible. We observe improvements of IC and SL performance when using the collected data for training, demonstrating that the approach can effectively collect useful annotated utterances automatically from user paraphrasing behavior.

2   Related Work

Intent classification (IC) and slot labeling (SL) have been studied for several decades as fundamental building blocks of task-oriented dialog systems, dating back at least to the creation of the ATIS corpus (Price, 1990). In recent years, progress has been been made by applying deep learning, such as using recurrent networks (Mesnil et al., 2013), jointly learning both tasks (Zhang and Wang, 2016; Hakkani-Tür et al., 2016) and improving knowledge-sharing between them (Goo et al., 2018; E et al., 2019).

Methods to leverage user feedback for IC and SL have received less attention in the past, presumably because such work is difficult to perform without access to a deployed dialog system. Most similar to ours is the work of Muralidharan et al. (2019), which proposes to use positive and negative user feedback to automatically turn cheap-to-obtain coarse-grained annotations for SL into more fine-grained ones. Coarse and fine-grained annotations are used together in a multi-task learning setup. They apply that idea to playback requests for music, and rely on whether a user kept a song playing for more than 30 seconds as the feedback. The main differences to this work are that MARUPA is not music-specific but domain-agnostic, that it does not require a coarse-grained annotation to start with and that it integrates with existing IC/SL models more seamlessly, as it works in the same label space and requires no multi-task learning. We also report experiments across many domains and different languages.

Other related work is presented by Ponnusamy et al. (2020), who describe an online method to make use of paraphrasing behavior: They use absorbing Markov chains to distill common successful paraphrase pairs from paraphrasing behavior across many users and use them to re-write utterances at runtime; similar to query-rewriting in search engines. While focusing on the same user behavior, our methods are mostly orthogonal to that work, as it focuses on simplifying the utterance given a fixed IC/SL model while we aim to improve the IC/SL model. In less similar work, Qiu et al. (2019) propose a method to leverage paraphrase relationships between utterances to improve IC. Different to ours and the aforementioned methods, they try to find pairs of paraphrases among large, unstructured collections of unlabeled utterances rather than relying on the dialog flow and feedback given by users. More over, Yaghoub-Zadeh-Fard et al. (2019) study utterance paraphrases collected via crowdsourcing and develop methods to address common paraphrasing errors that occur in such crowdsourced data. Since our method relies on naturally occurring paraphrases, it does not face these challenges.

Beyond the IC and SL tasks of task-oriented dialog, incorporating user feedback is much more common for chit-chat dialog systems and for learning dialog management policies. For the latter, reinforcement learning based on simulated or real user feedback has been studied for a long time (Levin et al., 2000; Schatzmann et al., 2006; Liu et al., 2018). Similarly, chit-chat dialog systems are usually trained end-to-end with reinforcement learning and estimated user satisfaction has been part of proposed reward functions (Serban et al., 2018; Zhang et al., 2018). Hancock et al. (2019) propose a dialog agent that incorporates feedback via supervised multi-task learning and gathers the feedback by learning to explicitly ask a user for it. Through online learning, the feedback is incorporated while the system is actively used. Another line of work focuses on the detection of user feedback itself, rather than also trying to use it. Several models have been proposed to find positive and negative feedback utterances or predict a user's emotion (Wang et al., 2017; Hashimoto and Sassano, 2018; Eskenazi et al., 2019; Ghosal et al., 2019).

Our work is also related to the semi-supervised learning approach known as self-learning or pseudo-labeling, in which models are trained on predictions that a previous version of the model made on unlabeled data. This idea has been successfully applied to a wide range of language tasks, e.g. named entity recognition (Collins and Singer, 1999), word sense disambiguation (Mihalcea, 2004) and parsing (McClosky et al., 2006). Successful applications are also known from computer vision, of which Xie et al. (2019) gives an overview. For task-oriented dialog systems, Cho et al. (2019) report substantial error reductions using self-learning to bootstrap new features. While the use of MARUPA-labeled data for training is at its core self-learning, our approach goes further by leveraging user feedback in the form of paraphrasing and friction as additional signals to guide the self-learning process.

3 MARUPA

Before describing our approach, we start defining important terminology. An *utterance* u is a sequence of tokens, directed from a user to a dialog system. Annotated utterances are triples (u, i, s) with an *intent* label i and *slots* s. Each slot s_i has a *slot name* and a *slot value*, the latter being a subset of tokens from the utterance. As an example, consider $u = $ *"play blinding lights by the weekend"* with intent $i = $ *PlayMusic*. Slots can be written as a mapping $s = \{Artist : $ *"the weekend"*$, Song : $ *"blinding lights"*$\}$ or as token-level labels *"O B-Song I-Song O B-Artist I-Artist"* using BIO-encoding.

MARUPA relies on paraphrase detection (PD), friction detection (FD) and label projection (LP) components as illustrated in Figure 1. Given an interaction between a user and the dialog system, consisting of a sequence of user utterances u along with intent and slots $(\hat{i}, \hat{s})$ predicted by the dialog system, we find all pairs (u_j, u_k), where u_j occurs before u_k, that satisfy the following condition:

$$time(u_k) - time(u_j) \leq \delta \;\; \wedge \;\; u_j \neq u_k \;\; \wedge \;\; PD(u_j, u_k) = 1 \;\; \wedge$$
$$FD(u_j, \hat{i}_j, \hat{s}_j) = 1 \;\; \wedge \;\; FD(u_k, \hat{i}_k, \hat{s}_k) = 0 \;\; \wedge \;\; LP(u_j, u_k) \geq \theta \tag{1}$$

It captures pairs that occur within a maximum time distance δ, that are paraphrases according to a classifier $PD(u_j, u_k) \in \{0, 1\}$ and have the desired friction classifications $FD(\cdot) \in \{0, 1\}$, i.e. u_j causing friction but not u_k. The threshold θ is imposed on the label projection score $LP(u_j, u_k) \in [0, 1]$ defined later in Equation 5 to ensure that unsuccessful projections are discarded. Each pair that satisfies Equation 1 yields a new training example for IC and SL, which are finally aggregated.

In the following, we describe each of the involved components in detail, starting with PD (Section 3.1), then FD (Section 3.2), LP (Section 3.3) and aggregation (Section 3.4).

3.1 Paraphrase Detection

Sentential paraphrases are commonly defined as different sentences with the same, or very similar, meaning (Dolan and Brockett, 2005; Ganitkevitch et al., 2013). Paraphrase detection is the corresponding binary classification task on sentence pairs. In this work, we apply it to pairs of dialog system utterances.

Compared to paraphrase detection in general, our context has one advantage: The notion of meaning, on which the definition of paraphrase relies, can be formalized precisely with regard to the downstream task, i.e. by relying on intents and slots. If two utterances are annotated with the same intent and the same set of slots, we consider them to be paraphrases. On the other hand, the context also brings several challenges. While paraphrases can be very different in its surface form, non-paraphrases can be extremely similar, such as *set volume to 3* and *set volume to 6*. In addition, speech recognition and end-pointing errors make the utterances noisy and the intended meaning often hard to recover. Crucially, in-domain paraphrase detection data is needed to address those challenges, but to the best of our knowledge, no such dataset exists. To overcome this issue, we propose an automatic corpus creation method.

Corpus Creation   To overcome the lack of in-domain paraphrase datasets, we propose a corpus creation approach that automatically derives paraphrase pairs from annotated utterances as used for IC and SL. Such data is necessarily available in our context and using it ensures that the paraphrase pairs resemble the domain of interest. The core idea is that two utterances with the same signature and same slot values but different carrier phrases must be paraphrases. We define the *signature* of an annotated utterance to be the set of its intent and slot names, e.g. {*PlayMusic, Artist, Song*}. The *carrier phrase* of an utterance is the utterance without slot values, e.g. *"play $Song by $Artist"*.

Algorithm 1 shows the corpus creation procedure. Given annotated utterances and a target size, it repeatedly samples signatures occurring in the utterances. To create a positive paraphrase example, we sample two different carrier phrases for that signature and inject the same sampled slot values into them. As an example, consider the signature {*PlayMusic, Artist, Song*}. We obtain a positive pair by sampling slot values {*Artist: "the weekend", Song: "blinding lights"*} and the following two carrier phrases:

$$
\begin{array}{llll}
\textit{play \$Song by \$Artist} & \rightarrow & \textit{play blinding lights by the weekend} & \text{(2a)} \\
\textit{\$Artist \$Song please} & \rightarrow & \textit{the weekend blinding lights please} & \text{(2b)}
\end{array}
$$

The more interesting part is how negative pairs are sampled, which are crucial to make the task non-trivial for paraphrase models. We sample a second, very similar signature from the k nearest signatures in lines 10 and 11 using Jaccard distance between signatures σ_a and σ_b:

$$
d_{sig}(\sigma_a, \sigma_b) = 1 - \frac{|\sigma_a \cap \sigma_b|}{|\sigma_a \cup \sigma_b|} \tag{3}
$$

To continue with the previous example, consider the second signature {*PlayMusic, Song, Room*} with a Jaccard distance of 0.33 that leads, when sampling carrier phrases, to a negative utterance pair:

$$
\begin{array}{lllll}
\{\textit{PlayMusic, Artist, Song}\} \rightarrow & \textit{play \$S by \$A} & \rightarrow & \textit{play blinding lights by the weekend} & \text{(4a)} \\
\{\textit{PlayMusic, Song, Room}\} \rightarrow & \textit{play \$S in the \$R} & \rightarrow & \textit{play blinding lights in the kitchen} & \text{(4b)}
\end{array}
$$

Note that slots shared by both signatures will be filled with the same values, making the utterances of negative examples very similar. Another important detail is that line 3 samples according to the frequency distribution in $\mathcal{D}$, to ensure intents and slots have a similar distribution in $\mathcal{P}$, but all other sampling steps choose uniformly from the possible unique values (carrier phrases, slot values, nearest signatures) to ensure diversity. Slot values are sampled from all values seen for the slot name and intent.

Algorithm 1 Paraphrase Corpus Creation

Input: Set $\mathcal{D}$ of triples (u, i, s), size n, nearest k
Output: Set $\mathcal{P}$ of triples (u, u', l) with $l \in \{0, 1\}$
1: $\mathcal{P} = \emptyset$
2: **for** $n/2$ **do**
3:     Sample a signature σ from all in $\mathcal{D}$.
4:     Sample a carrier phrase c for σ.
5:     // *Create positive example*
6:     Sample another $c_{pos} \neq c$ for σ.
7:     Sample slot values for slot names in σ and inject into c, c_{pos} to obtain u, u_{pos}.
8:     Add $(u, u_{pos}, 1)$ to $\mathcal{P}$.
9:     // *Create negative example*
10:    Compute $d_{sig}(\sigma, \sigma')$ for all $\sigma' \neq \sigma$.
11:    Sample σ_{neg} from k nearest signatures.
12:    Sample a carrier phrase c_{neg} for σ_{neg}.
13:    Inject values from 7, plus samples for new slots in c_{neg}, into c, c_{neg} to obtain u, u_{neg}.
14:    Add $(u, u_{neg}, 0)$ to $\mathcal{P}$.
15: **end for**
16: Return $\mathcal{P}$.

Model For paraphrase detection, we rely on BERT (Devlin et al., 2019), a pre-trained neural model that reached state-of-the-art performance on the common paraphrase detection benchmarks QQP and MRPC. We combine paraphrase pairs into sequences as in the BERT paper, e.g. *"[CLS] play blinding lights [SEP] blinding lights please [SEP]"*. The model encodes the sequence and feeds the output through a 256-d ReLU layer followed by a binary classification. The whole model is fine-tuned on our paraphrase corpus to ensure it addresses the unique challenges of dialog. To support different languages, we use a multilingually pre-trained BERT model (Devlin et al., 2019) and fine-tune it in the target language.

3.2 Friction Detection

Friction occurs for a user of a dialog system if their utterance is not correctly interpreted and the system does not show the desired reaction. It is thus closely related to work on user satisfaction and user feedback detection discussed in Section 2. While friction can in general be caused by many parts of a dialog system – speech recognition, entity resolution, request fulfillment – we are particularly interested in friction caused by IC and SL for our data collection. Therefore, given a small amount of hand-labeled friction examples, we train a model that can automatically detect such friction cases.

Given an utterance u and predictions $\hat{i}$ and $\hat{s}$, we model friction detection as a binary classification task. We use a linear SVM for classification. Our set of binary features (see Table 1) captures the utterance itself, the intent and slots predicted for it, utterance-level confidence scores as well as status codes received from downstream components that try to act upon the provided interpretation. Since these features capture only the utterance and how the dialog system reacts to it, but no additional feedback a user might give afterwards, this modeling approach relies on the friction detector to become aware of current limitations of the underlying model and where they are, rather than relying on explicit feedback. In fact, we found that confidences and status codes from fulfillment components are strong predictors for that. Although other work found it beneficial to include the user's next utterance in similar tasks (Eskenazi et al., 2019), we observed no improvements in classification performance when doing so.

3.3 Label Projection

Once we found a paraphrase pair (u, u') with predictions $\hat{i}, \hat{s}$ and $\hat{i}', \hat{s}'$, of which the first caused friction but not the second, we want to use the successful interpretation $\hat{i}', \hat{s}'$ with the utterance u as a new training example. While this is trivial for intents, it is more intricate for slot labels as they are per token, which differ between u and its paraphrase u'. See Figure 2 for an example. Nevertheless, many tokens typically overlap, which motivates our token alignment-based approach inspired by Fürstenau and Lapata (2009).

For each source-target token pair (u_j, u'_k), we first compute a similarity $sim(u_j, u'_k) \in [0, 1]$. Based on these pairwise similarities, we then consider all alignments of the n source tokens in u to the m targets

Group	Features
N-Grams	uni- and bi-grams of u
Predictions	intent $\hat{\imath}$, slot names in $\hat{s}$
Confidences	IC, SL, speech recognition
Fulfillment	status code

Table 1: Friction detection feature groups.

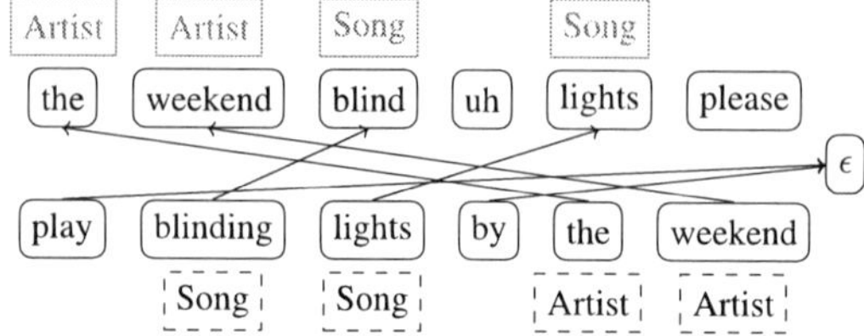

Figure 2: Alignment-based slot label projection.

in u' and score them by the average similarity of the chosen alignments

$$LP(u, u') = \frac{1}{n} \sum_{j=1}^{n} \sum_{k=1}^{m+1} sim(u_j, u'_k)\, x_{jk} \tag{5}$$

where x_{jk} is a binary decision variable representing the alignment. We enforce that all source tokens must have an alignment, only one source can align to one target, but allow alignment to a virtual empty target as a fallback. We experimented with different similarities and optimization methods. For MARUPA, we settled to using as similarity the inverse of character-level Levenshtein edit distance normalized by length, which works well to identify identical tokens or slight morphological variations. The optimization is done greedily, choosing the most similar target for each source from left to right. As we show in experiments in Section 5, this choice offers a good trade-off of alignment accuracy and runtime. Finally, given the alignment, we project slot labels $\hat{s}'$ to the target tokens accordingly (see Figure 2).

3.4 Aggregation

Once PD and FD identified relevant utterance pairs and LP projected slot labels, we obtain new annotated training examples. However, due to noise in the source data and noise introduced by the components of our method, they can be of varying quality. We therefore introduce a final aggregation step that takes examples collected from many user interactions and filters them by consistency. Only if we create an annotation for a specific utterance repeatedly and consistently, we keep the examples. In addition, we also test the effect of adding the training examples to the IC/SL model in terms of accuracy changes on a development set and filter out examples for intent/slot-combinations with accuracy degradations.

Note also that the conditions in Equation 1 are conjunctive, allowing us to enforce them in an arbitrary order on potential utterance pairs. In practice, this enables enforcing the least resource intense checks first, which will reduce the amount of pairs that have to be processed by more time-consuming methods such as paraphrase classification with the fine-tuned BERT model.

4 Experimental Results

In this section, we present experiments with MARUPA in the context of a commercial dialog system across multiple languages. They demonstrate that the newly collected training examples can help to improve the IC and SL performance, in particular on long-tail utterances.

4.1 Setup

We experiment with German, Italian and Hindi utterances. In each case, we use the production IC/SL model of the dialog system as the baseline and compare it against a model re-trained after adding our additional training examples. We report relative changes of a combined IC/SL error rate. In each language, the train and test data contains several hundred different intents and slots.

To collect new training examples, we apply MARUPA to a sample of anonymized user interactions with the dialog system. We set $\delta = 30s$ and $\theta = 0.4$ in Equation 1. For paraphrase detection, we use Algorithm 1 to derive a corpus of 300k paraphrase pairs with $k = 30$ from the training data of the baseline model, and split it into a train, validation and test split (70/10/20). As discussed in Section 3.1,

Language	Used Since	Added Data	Test Set (by utterance frequency)							Held-Out Data
			Total	[0,1)	[1,2)	[2,4)	[4,7)	[7,10)	$\geq$10	
German	3.0 y	70k	-0.01	+0.47	-2.91	-1.34	0.00	0.00	0.00	-79.51
Italian	1.0 y	71k	+0.08	+0.11	+0.42	-0.05	-0.96	0.00	0.00	-91.27
Hindi	0.5 y	2k	+0.53	+0.40	+1.39	+0.74	+0.85	0.00	0.00	-72.55

Table 2: Relative changes in error rates when adding MARUPA-collected data, evaluated on the main IC/SL test set and held-out collected instances. Frequency bin thresholds in $\log_2$ scale.

we fine-tune *BERT-Base Multilingual Cased*[1]. We use a batch size of 64 and dropout of 0.2. The model is trained using Adam with a learning rate of $5 \cdot 10^{-5}$ and with early stopping. For friction detection, we use the model described in Section 3.2 and tune the SVM's regularization constant via grid search. Labels are projected as described in Section 3.3. Finally, we aggregate the collected examples by keeping only utterances that occur at least 10 times and for which the same annotation was created in at least 80% of the cases. In addition, we filter out collected examples belonging to intent/slot-combinations for which the error rate on the IC/SL development set increases after retraining the model.

4.2 Results

Table 2 shows the results of our experiment for German, Italian and Hindi. We evaluate the model's error rate on its main test set, obtained via manual annotation, and on a set of held-out MARUPA-collected examples (20%). For the former, we break down results by utterance frequency.[2] While the overall change on the main test set (*Total*) is negligible, the break down reveals that for low-frequency utterances the new data leads to error rate reductions of up to 3%. As desired, this comes with no negative effects for high-frequency utterances. Even stronger error reductions can be seen for the held-out MARUPA examples, on which the baseline's error rate is by design high. We observed that many collected utterances are so rare that they are not captured even by the lowest-frequency bin of the main test set, making it difficult to assess the full impact of MARUPA. Across languages, we observe that for newer languages like Hindi, less useful examples can be collected and their quality is lower, which is because fewer user interactions are available and the underlying IC/SL is less mature. Overall, the results demonstrate that MARUPA can improve accuracy on long-tail utterances.

5 Analysis

In addition to the previous section, which presented our main experimental results, the following sections show further experiments to provide additional insights into our proposed method.

5.1 Application to Public Datasets

Since the core of our approach is to leverage user paraphrasing behavior, it is difficult to conduct experiments on academic datasets for IC and SL, which to the best of our knowledge contain neither examples for friction nor paraphrasing. However, we try to replicate our application scenario as closely as possible.

Setup We use SNIPS (Coucke et al., 2018), a common benchmark with 14,484 English utterances annotated for IC and SL. We sample a subset of 10% of the training set as labeled data and treat the remaining part as unlabeled. On the unlabeled part, we create paraphrase pairs re-using ideas from Section 3.1: We group all utterances by signature and compute the frequency of unique carrier phrases. Per signature, we use all utterances from the 70%-head of the carrier phrase distribution, and for each, create a paraphrase by sampling another carrier phrase from the remaining 30%-tail and inject the same slot values. This process turns the unlabeled data into pairs of paraphrases, each pair consisting of a

---

[1] https://github.com/google-research/bert/blob/master/multilingual.md

[2] Bins are chosen to contain roughly equal amounts of examples, except for [0,1) with unique utterances (40% of examples).

Setting		Training Data				Evaluation Metrics		
		Labeled	Unl.-Head	Unl.-Tail	Count	IC	SL	IC+SL
Baseline	1	All	—	—	1,309	97.54	76.11	56.27
No Selection	2.1	All	All	—	9,253	-0.13	+1.47	+1.90
	2.2	All	All	All, Self	17,197	+0.17	+1.37	+1.86
	2.3	All	All	All, LP	17,197	+0.51	+2.09	+3.21
Self-Labeled vs.	3.1	All	—	FD, Self	2,807	-0.16	-0.77	-1.23
Projection on Tail	3.2	All	—	FD, LP	2,807	**+0.99**	+2.63	+3.07
Confidence vs.	4.1	All	Conf	—	4,293	+0.23	+2.72	+4.74
Friction Detection	4.2	All	FD	—	6,208	+0.01	+3.42	+5.41
	4.3	All	Conf	Conf, LP	7,277	+0.74	+3.47	+5.01
MARUPA (FD+LP)	5	All	FD	FD, LP	7,706	+0.87	**+4.42**	**+6.57**

Table 3: Experiments with unlabeled head/tail–paraphrase pairs created for SNIPS (English), comparing label projection to self-labeling and selection by friction to selection by confidence. Metrics are accuracy (IC), slot-based F1 (SL) and full frame accuracy (IC+SL). All results are averages of 10 re-runs.

less common (tail) and a more common (head) utterance, similar to our real-world friction scenario. For SNIPS, the process yields 1,309 labeled utterances and 7,944 unlabeled paraphrase pairs.

Note that we can only apply FD and LP of MARUPA, but not PD, as paraphrase pairs are already given in this setup. For IC and SL, we train a joint neural model that encodes utterances with ELMO embeddings (Peters et al., 2018) and then feeds them through a BiLSTM. Slot labels are predicted from each hidden state and intent labels from the mean of them. We use 1024-d ELMO embeddings, a single-layer 200-d BiLSTM and dropout of 0.2 after both. The model is trained with Adam, batch size 16 and early stopping. For evaluation (and stopping) we use the original test (and validation) set of SNIPS.

Results Table 3 shows results for various ways to leverage the unlabeled paraphrase pairs, including using FD and LP of MARUPA (see row 5). The baseline (1) uses only labeled data, and all other methods make use of this model's predictions on the unlabeled pairs. The most simple approach of ingesting all self-labeled data back into training, for just head utterances (2.1) or head and tail (2.2), already boosts performance on both tasks. However, when using label projection from self-labeled head utterances to tail utterances (2.3), the performance is even better, demonstrating the effectiveness of label projection.

To apply FD in this setup, we train the IC/SL model with cross-validation on the labeled data and then train the detector on the out-of-fold predictions.[3] If we apply label projection only to paraphrase pairs selected by FD (3.2), i.e. pairs with friction for the tail but not for the head, we see that projection outperforms self-labeling (3.1) on these cases even more, as the tail's self-label is expected to cause friction. Finally, we compare selecting paraphrase pairs by FD to selecting based on the baseline model's confidence, a common approach for self-supervised learning (see Section 2). We tune a confidence threshold on the validation set.[4] Selecting with FD is superior both when using only head utterances (4.1 vs. 4.2) and when including tail utterances with label projection (4.3 vs. 5). Thus, we conclude that our self-learning approach based on friction detection is effective also beyond our exact application scenario.

5.2 Quality of Derived Paraphrase Corpora

Next, we give more insight into the effectiveness of the proposed paraphrase corpus creation. We include public datasets, as paraphrase detection was not included in the previous experiment.

---

[3] We omit the fulfillment and speech recognition features described in Table 6, as they are not available in this setup.

[4] We tried thresholds 0.8, 0.85, 0.9, 0.95, 0.97, 0.99, 0.999 based on plotting the distribution, finding 0.95 to perform best.

Method	German Internal	Italian Internal	Hindi Internal	English SNIPS	English ATIS
Edit-Distance	59.75	65.29	64.65	65.95	61.00
Jaccard Similarity	61.02	66.04	67.82	68.80	63.10
N-Gram SVM	80.36	83.22	83.79	86.85	93.40
Fine-tuned mBERT	**92.33**	**92.99**	**94.61**	**97.75**	**97.55**

Table 4: Paraphrase detection accuracy of fine-tuned mBERT and baselines across paraphrase corpora.

Language	Maturity	Prec.	Rec.	F1
English	5.0	76.9	55.2	64.3
German	3.0	76.3	60.0	67.2
French	1.5	82.6	69.7	75.6
Italian	1.0	85.5	72.5	78.4
Hindi	0.5	**92.0**	**81.6**	**86.5**

Table 5: Friction detection performance across languages with IC/SL model maturity in years.

Features	F1	Delta
All	67.2	
- N-Grams	65.2	-2.0
- Predictions	65.3	-1.9
- Confidences	62.4	-4.8
- Fulfillment	56.2	-11.0

Table 6: Feature ablation for friction detection on German utterances.

Setup   We use our internal IC/SL training data for German, Italian and Hindi as well as the commonly used SNIPS and ATIS (Price, 1990) corpora (both English) to derive paraphrase pairs and fine-tune mBERT models as outlined in Section 4.1 on them. For each, we report accuracy for paraphrase detection evaluated on the 20% test split of the paraphrase pairs. For ATIS and SNIPS, due to their small size, we derive corpora with 10k pairs and $k = 10$. As baselines, we include simple threshold-based classifiers using character-level edit-distance or token-level Jaccard similarity and a linear SVM using binary uni- and bigram features, and- and xor-combined between the two utterances.

Results   Table 4 shows paraphrase detection results. We observe that the simple baselines relying on surface-level similarities perform much worse than BERT, which demonstrates that our approach of selecting negative examples with high similarity (see Section 3.1) is effective for creating a challenging corpus. We saw in preliminary experiments that sampling negative pairs fully randomly makes the baselines perform much better. Furthermore, we observe that the trained SVM performs much better than the simple baselines, but using a fine-tuned BERT model substantially improves upon it. Finally, this experiment also shows that our approach can be applied across different languages and domains.

5.3   Analysis of Friction Detection

For friction detection, we report classification performance for the task in Table 5, evaluated on a held-out set of the same data the models are trained on for MARUPA. Performance, and in particular precision, is generally high across languages, showing that the model can reliable find many friction cases. That also confirms that the approach is largely language independent and works for any of the tested ones. An interesting trend is that friction detection, using the set of features proposed in this work, tends to become more difficult the more mature the underlying IC/SL model for the language is, indicating that the causes of friction most easy to detect are also being resolved the earliest.

In Table 6, we show ablation results for the friction detector trained on German utterances. Removing any of the features decreases F1-scores by at least 2 points, showing that they all contribute to the task. Among them, the status codes received from the fulfillment component are by far the most useful features. This underlines the point made earlier that the dialog system is already aware of many friction cases and does not necessarily require explicit or implicit feedback from the user to detect friction – but, we do require feedback in terms of paraphrasing to go further and avoid the friction in the future.

Optimization	Similarity	Exact Match	Token F1	Runtime
	Word Identity	82.65	92.89	**3.8s**
Greedy	Norm. Character Edit-Distance	85.46	94.17	8.8s
	Word2Vec Cosine Similarity	81.47	92.64	51.8s
	Word Identity	84.87	94.26	61.8s
Exact	Norm. Character Edit-Distance	**87.03**	**95.52**	75.1s
	Word2Vec Cosine Similarity	86.41	95.23	120.5s

Table 7: Label projection accuracy and runtime across similarity measures and optimization strategies.

5.4 Quality vs. Runtime Trade-Offs in Label Projection

Finally, Table 7 shows different instantiations of our label projection approach, tested on a dataset of 11k German utterance pairs for which reference projections have been derived from gold IC/SL annotations. We report whether the projection matches the reference completely (Exact Match) and F1-scores over token-level matches (Token F1). We observed that using word embeddings to compute similarities provided no improvements, as cases where that would be needed, i.e. aligning synonyms, are rare in the data. Exact optimization using linear programming, on the other hand, does improve the projection regardless of similarity being used, but comes at a large increase in runtime. Trading off quality and runtime, we therefore rely on greedy optimization with character-level edit-distance in MARUPA.

6 Conclusion

We proposed MARUPA, an approach to collect annotations for friction-causing long-tail utterances automatically from user feedback by using paraphrase detection, friction detection and label projection. We demonstrated that this form of user feedback-driven self-learning can effectively improve intent classification and slot labeling in dialog systems across several languages and on SNIPS. In the future, we plan to integrate more advanced aggregation methods to reduce noise and to more closely study the effect of the feedback loops that emerge when our data collection and re-training are applied repeatedly.

Acknowledgements

We would like to thank Judith Gaspers, Fabian Triefenbach and our anonymous reviewers for their thoughtful comments and suggestions that improved this paper.

References

Eunah Cho, He Xie, and William M. Campbell. 2019. Paraphrase Generation for Semi-Supervised Learning in NLU. In *Proceedings of the Workshop on Methods for Optimizing and Evaluating NLG*, pages 45–54, Minneapolis, MN, USA.

Michael Collins and Yoram Singer. 1999. Unsupervised models for named entity classification. In *1999 Joint SIGDAT Conference on Empirical Methods in Natural Language Processing and Very Large Corpora*, pages 100–110, College Park, MD, USA.

Alice Coucke, Alaa Saade, Adrien Ball, Théodore Bluche, Alexandre Caulier, David Leroy, Clément Doumouro, Thibault Gisselbrecht, Francesco Caltagirone, Thibaut Lavril, et al. 2018. Snips Voice Platform: An Embedded Spoken Language Understanding System for Private-By-Design Voice Interfaces. *arXiv*, 1805.10190.

Jacob Devlin, Ming-Wei Chang, Kenton Lee, and Kristina Toutanova. 2019. BERT: Pre-training of deep bidirectional transformers for language understanding. In *Proceedings of the 2019 Conference of the North American Chapter of the Association for Computational Linguistics: Human Language Technologies, Volume 1 (Long and Short Papers)*, pages 4171–4186, Minneapolis, MN, USA.

William B. Dolan and Chris Brockett. 2005. Automatically constructing a corpus of sentential paraphrases. In *Proceedings of the Third International Workshop on Paraphrasing (IWP2005)*, pages 9–16, Jeju Island, Korea.

Haihong E, Peiqing Niu, Zhongfu Chen, and Meina Song. 2019. A Novel Bi-directional Interrelated Model for Joint Intent Detection and Slot Filling. In *Proceedings of the 57th Annual Meeting of the ACL*, pages 5467–5471, Florence, Italy.

Maxine Eskenazi, Shikib Mehri, Evgeniia Razumovskaia, and Tiancheng Zhao. 2019. Beyond turing: Intelligent agents centered on the user. *arXiv*, 1901.06613.

Hagen Fürstenau and Mirella Lapata. 2009. Semi-Supervised Semantic Role Labeling. In *Proceedings of the 12th Conference of the EACL*, pages 220–228, Athens, Greece.

Juri Ganitkevitch, Benjamin Van Durme, and Chris Callison-Burch. 2013. PPDB: The paraphrase database. In *Proceedings of the 2013 Conference of the North American Chapter of the Association for Computational Linguistics: Human Language Technologies*, pages 758–764, Atlanta, GA, USA.

Deepanway Ghosal, Navonil Majumder, Soujanya Poria, Niyati Chhaya, and Alexander Gelbukh. 2019. DialogueGCN: A graph convolutional neural network for emotion recognition in conversation. In *Proceedings of the 2019 Conference on Empirical Methods in Natural Language Processing and the 9th International Joint Conference on Natural Language Processing (EMNLP-IJCNLP)*, pages 154–164, Hong Kong, China.

Chih-Wen Goo, Guang Gao, Yun-Kai Hsu, Chih-Li Huo, Tsung-Chieh Chen, Keng-Wei Hsu, and Yun-Nung Chen. 2018. Slot-Gated Modeling for Joint Slot Filling and Intent Prediction. In *Proceedings of the 2018 Conference of the NAACL-HLT*, pages 753–757, New Orleans, LA, USA.

Dilek Hakkani-Tür, Gökhan Tür, Asli Celikyilmaz, Yun-Nung Chen, Jianfeng Gao, Li Deng, and Ye-Yi Wang. 2016. Multi-Domain Joint Semantic Frame Parsing Using Bi-Directional RNN-LSTM. In *Interspeech*, pages 715–719, San Francisco, CA, USA.

Braden Hancock, Antoine Bordes, Pierre-Emmanuel Mazare, and Jason Weston. 2019. Learning from dialogue after deployment: Feed yourself, chatbot! In *Proceedings of the 57th Annual Meeting of the Association for Computational Linguistics*, pages 3667–3684, Florence, Italy.

Chikara Hashimoto and Manabu Sassano. 2018. Detecting absurd conversations from intelligent assistant logs by exploiting user feedback utterances. In *Proceedings of the 2018 World Wide Web Conference*, WWW '18, page 147–156, Lyon, France.

Esther Levin, Roberto Pieraccini, and Wieland Eckert. 2000. A stochastic model of human-machine interaction for learning dialog strategies. *IEEE Transactions on Speech and Audio Processing*, 8(1):11–23.

Bing Liu, Gokhan Tür, Dilek Hakkani-Tür, Pararth Shah, and Larry Heck. 2018. Dialogue learning with human teaching and feedback in end-to-end trainable task-oriented dialogue systems. In *Proceedings of the 2018 Conference of the North American Chapter of the Association for Computational Linguistics: Human Language Technologies*, pages 2060–2069, New Orleans, LA, USA.

David McClosky, Eugene Charniak, and Mark Johnson. 2006. Effective self-training for parsing. In *Proceedings of the Human Language Technology Conference of the NAACL*, pages 152–159, New York, NY, USA.

Grégoire Mesnil, Xiaodong He, Li Deng, and Yoshua Bengio. 2013. Investigation of Recurrent-Neural-Network Architectures and Learning Methods for Spoken Language Understanding. In *Interspeech*, pages 3771–3775, Lyon, France.

Rada Mihalcea. 2004. Co-training and self-training for word sense disambiguation. In *Proceedings of the Eighth Conference on Computational Natural Language Learning (CoNLL-2004) at HLT-NAACL 2004*, pages 33–40, Boston, MA, USA.

Deepak Muralidharan, Justine Kao, Xiao Yang, Lin Li, Lavanya Viswanathan, Mubarak Seyed Ibrahim, Kevin Luikens, Stephen Pulman, Ashish Garg, Atish Kothari, and Jason Williams. 2019. Leveraging User Engagement Signals For Entity Labeling in a Virtual Assistant. *arXiv*, 1909.09143.

Matthew Peters, Mark Neumann, Mohit Iyyer, Matt Gardner, Christopher Clark, Kenton Lee, and Luke Zettlemoyer. 2018. Deep contextualized word representations. In *Proceedings of the 2018 Conference of the North American Chapter of the Association for Computational Linguistics: Human Language Technologies*, pages 2227–2237, New Orleans, LA, USA.

Pragaash Ponnusamy, Alireza Roshan-Ghias, Chenlei Guo, and Ruhi Sarikaya. 2020. Feedback-based self-learning in large-scale conversational ai agents. In *Proceedings of the Thirty-Fourth AAAI Conference on Artificial Intelligence*, New York, NY, USA.

P. J. Price. 1990. Evaluation of Spoken Language Systems: the ATIS Domain. In *Speech and Natural Language: Proceedings of a Workshop*, Hidden Valley, PA, USA.

Zimeng Qiu, Eunah Cho, Xiaochun Ma, and William Campbell. 2019. Graph-Based Semi-Supervised Learning for Natural Language Understanding. In *Proceedings of the Thirteenth Workshop on Graph-Based Methods for NLP*, pages 151–158, Hong Kong, China.

Jost Schatzmann, Karl Weilhammer, Matt Stuttle, and Steve Young. 2006. A survey of statistical user simulation techniques for reinforcement-learning of dialogue management strategies. *The Knowledge Engineering Review*, 21(2):97–126.

Iulian V. Serban, Chinnadhurai Sankar, Mathieu Germain, Saizheng Zhang, Zhouhan Lin, Sandeep Subramanian, Taesup Kim, Michael Pieper, Sarath Chandar, Nan Rosemary Ke, Sai Rajeswar, Alexandre de Brebisson, Jose M. R. Sotelo, Dendi Suhubdy, Vincent Michalski, Alexandre Nguyen, Joelle Pineau, and Yoshua Bengio. 2018. A Deep Reinforcement Learning Chatbot (Short Version). *arXiv*, 1801.06700.

Gokhan Tur and Renato De Mori. 2011. *Spoken Language Understanding: Systems for Extracting Semantic Information from Speech*. John Wiley and Sons.

Xin Wang, Jianan Wang, Yuanchao Liu, Xiaolong Wang, Zhuoran Wang, and Baoxun Wang. 2017. Predicting users' negative feedbacks in multi-turn human-computer dialogues. In *Proceedings of the Eighth International Joint Conference on Natural Language Processing*, pages 713–722, Taipei, Taiwan.

Qizhe Xie, Minh-Thang Luong, Eduard Hovy, and Quoc V. Le. 2019. Self-training with noisy student improves imagenet classification. *arXiv*, 1911.04252.

Mohammad-Ali Yaghoub-Zadeh-Fard, Boualem Benatallah, Moshe Chai Barukh, and Shayan Zamanirad. 2019. A study of incorrect paraphrases in crowdsourced user utterances. In *Proceedings of the 2019 Conference of the North American Chapter of the Association for Computational Linguistics*, pages 295–306, Minneapolis, MN, USA.

Xiaodong Zhang and Houfeng Wang. 2016. A Joint Model of Intent Determination and Slot Filling for Spoken Language Understanding. In *Proceedings of the Twenty-Fifth IJCAI*, page 2993–2999, New York, NY, USA.

Wei-Nan Zhang, Lingzhi Li, Dongyan Cao, and Ting Liu. 2018. Exploring implicit feedback for open domain conversation generation. In *Proceedings of the Thirty-Second AAAI Conference on Artificial Intelligence*, New Orleans, LA, USA.

Query Distillation: BERT-based Distillation for Ensemble Ranking

Wangshu Zhang[†]   **Junhong Liu**[†]   **Zujie Wen**[†]   **Yafang Wang** [†*]   **Gerard de Melo**[‡]

Ant Financial Services Group[†]
Hasso Plattner Institute, University of Potsdam[‡]

Abstract

Recent years have witnessed substantial progress in the development of neural ranking networks, but also an increasingly heavy computational burden due to growing numbers of parameters and the adoption of model ensembles. Knowledge Distillation (KD) is a common solution to balance the effectiveness and efficiency. However, it is not straightforward to apply KD to ranking problems. Ranking Distillation (RD) has been proposed to address this issue, but only shows effectiveness on recommendation tasks. We present a novel two-stage distillation method for ranking problems that allows a smaller student model to be trained while benefitting from the better performance of the teacher model, providing better control of the inference latency and computational burden. We design a novel BERT-based ranking model structure for list-wise ranking to serve as our student model. All ranking candidates are fed to the BERT model simultaneously, such that the self-attention mechanism can enable joint inference to rank the document list. Our experiments confirm the advantages of our method, not just with regard to the inference latency but also in terms of higher-quality rankings compared to the original teacher model.

1   Introduction

The information retrieval (IR) community has witnessed the flourishing development of neural ranking models in the past several years, examples including DRMM (Guo et al., 2016), DUET (Mitra et al., 2017), PACRR (Hui et al., 2017), and Co-PACRR (Hui et al., 2018). Recently, BERT (Devlin et al., 2018), the pre-trained deep bidirectional Transformer, has shown strong performance on a broad range of language processing tasks and has wide application in ranking tasks as well (MacAvaney et al., 2019; Nogueira and Cho, 2019; Nogueira et al., 2019; Qiao et al., 2019). To further boost the results, it is common to adopt model ensembles, as modern neural ranking models provide a wealth of options for sub-models. The scores of all such sub-models with regard to the relevance of a candidate document to a query are collected and fed into a LambdaMART (Burges, 2010) or XGBoost (Chen and Guestrin, 2016) model to obtain the final ensemble relevance score. However, the computational burden is extremely heavy when drawing on such ensembles, and the prominence of increasingly deep and large neural networks such as BERT exacerbates this problem even more. Furthermore, it is rather inconvenient to update and maintain an ensemble of large models, which is concerning in real-world online deployments.

Knowledge Distillation (KD) is a common approach to balance effectiveness and efficiency (Ba and Caruana, 2014; Hinton et al., 2015). A well-trained large model serves as a teacher for a smaller student model that is trained not only based on the ground truth labeled data, but also using the label distribution emitted by the teacher, such that the student is ultimately able to replace the teacher. However, it is not straightforward to apply KD to ranking problems. First of all, in ranking, we focus on the relative order of documents rather than the label distribution in classification problems, which KD is designed for. On top of this, the total number of documents is often so large that we retrieve only a subset of relevant documents to reduce the size of the ranking list, and computing the overall distribution over all documents is impractical.

Proceedings of the 28th International Conference on Computational Linguistics: Industry Track, pages 33–43
Barcelona, Spain (Online), December 12, 2020

Recently, Tang and Wang (2018) proposed Ranking Distillation (RD) to address these issues in the context of recommender systems. Based on the ground truth training data set, the teacher model makes predictions for additional unlabeled documents to obtain a top-k unlabeled document ranking. The student model is then trained to minimize not just the ranking loss on the training data set but also a distillation loss with the example top-k ranking of unlabeled documents generated by its teacher. This method is reminiscent of that of Urner et al. (2011) and has shown its effectiveness in recommender systems.

However, this approach is beset by several problems when considering standard query document ranking tasks. Unlike recommender systems, in the case of search engines, it is rare for the teacher to predict an unlabeled document as being a positive sample, since the set of unlabeled documents consists of all documents that are not in the recall set, and the vast majority of these documents bear little connection with the query. Also, the weight of unlabeled samples needs to be set empirically, making it unclear whether this method can be effective for query document ranking.

In this paper, we propose a substantially different distillation method for ranking tasks. Instead of adding additional unlabeled documents for all the queries in the training data, our *Query Distillation* approach incorporates additional queries. It uses the teacher to predict top-ranked documents for these queries, enabling the teacher to guide the student's training. Furthermore, we divide the student training into two phases: The student model is first trained using teacher-labeled ranking data as teacher guidance and subsequently is fine-tuned using the ground truth labeled training data so as to obtain higher-quality rankings. Through this two-stage fine-tuned training regimen, we hope to obtain a student model that benefits from the strong retrieval effectiveness of the richer model but reduces the inference latency and computational burden.

We adopt a BERT-based model as the student in light of its outstanding performance in ranking tasks (Nogueira and Cho, 2019; Nogueira et al., 2019; Qiao et al., 2019). We also propose a novel BERT QD-list model structure for ranking, which, contrary to the common practice of treating a query document pair (BERT QD-pair) as the input to BERT, jointly considers a query and the entire candidate document list. The self-attention mechanism in BERT allows the query to be evaluated with regard to all documents simultaneously. In addition, a custom attention mask is applied to the KQV self-attention layers to help boost the results. Our experiments show that a single student model outperforms the original large ensemble model through the two-stage teacher–student training and our QD-list model saves substantial inference time while obtaining better results compared to the BERT QD-pair model.

The contributions of our work are two-fold: (1) We introduce a novel two-stage fine-tuned teacher–student training method and obtain a single student model that benefits from the high quality of the ensemble model while reducing the inference latency and computational burden. (2) We propose a list-wise BERT-based ranking model, which through self-attention, allows the model to observe more information while ranking. The experiments confirm the advantages of our contributions.

2 Related Work

2.1 Neural Ranking

The advent of deep learning has brought invigorating new progress to the information retrieval community. Although ranking models have been studied extensively since the mid-2000s, the traditional learning-to-rank paradigm heavily relies on manual feature engineering (Liu and others, 2009; Li, 2011). Commercial web search engines are known to incorporate thousands of carefully designed features, and the feature engineering process is time-consuming, incomplete, and over-specified. In recent years, neural models have attracted attention in light of their ability to obviate the need for handcrafted features. Well-known neural ranking models include DSSM (Huang et al., 2013), DRMM (Guo et al., 2016), DUET (Mitra et al., 2017), PACRR (Hui et al., 2017), and Co-PACRR (Hui et al., 2018).

2.2 Pre-trained Lanuage Models

Recently, neural models pre-trained on language modeling tasks such as ELMo (Peters et al., 2017), Open-AI GPT (Radford et al., 2019), and BERT (Devlin et al., 2018) have achieved impressive results across wide swaths of the NLP landscape. Among these model variants, BERT, the pre-trained deep bidirectional Transformer, has shown strong performance on search-related tasks, including retrieval-based question answering (Yang et al., 2019a), and numerous experiments confirm that BERT-based methods can outperform state-of-the-art ad-hoc ranking baselines (MacAvaney et al., 2019; Nogueira and Cho, 2019; Nogueira et al., 2019; Qiao et al., 2019).

2.3 Knowledge Distilling

To address the computational overhead of large models, techniques such as the Knowledge Distillation (KD) framework have been proposed (Ba and Caruana, 2014; Hinton et al., 2015). These have shown remarkable potential in accelerating the inference time and improving the performance. Well-trained wide and deep networks are recruited as teachers, and the target student model is supervised not solely by the ground truth, but also by signals from the teacher model. A common approach towards mimicking teacher behaviour is to train the student model to additionally produce a softmax distribution matching that of the teacher model as closely as possible (Hinton et al., 2015). Another way of using teacher guidance for students is to directly mimic the hidden layers of the teacher model (Romero et al., 2014). Learning from multiple neural networks has as well been studied. Distilling an ensemble of neural networks was first introduced by Buciluǎ et al. (2006), where large amounts of pseudo-data are created by a teacher and serve to train a student to approximate the function learned by the teacher model. Learning from multiple teachers also leads to a better student, as shown by You et al. (2017). In their work, multiple teachers are combined via a voting strategy, and the student is required to mimic both the internal layers and the outputs of multiple teachers.

It is not straightforward to apply knowledge distillation to ranking problems, which has only recently been approached in the Ranking Distillation method (Tang and Wang, 2018). By introducing additional teacher-predicted unlabeled documents as teacher guidance, RD shows its effectiveness in recommendation problems, but as mentioned in the introduction, there still remain problems in applying this method to query-based retrieval of documents. Distilled Sentence Embedding (DSE), introduced by Barkan et al. (2020), is a method for sentence embedding distillation that has been shown effective on the GLUE benchmark, but encoding query and documents independently disregards the interaction between query and documents, which is important for ranking problems. In this paper, we will discuss our student training method for ranking problems and propose a novel ranking student model, showing the merit of these ideas.

3 Methodology

3.1 Model Ensemble Ranking

An information retrieval system usually proceeds in two stages. In the first *recall* stage, many potentially relevant documents are collected from a large document index using a simple relevance score such as BM25. These document candidates are then re-ranked according to their predicted relevance to the query in the second stage. Note that, throughout this paper, the term *document* can generally refer to any unit of text being retrieved, such as a passage, sentence, etc.

We focus on the second stage, which has a major contribution to the final result quality. Model ensembling is a common practice to boost the ranking quality and is widely used in state-of-the-art retrieval systems. Specifically, for a given query Q, there are m recalled results $t_0, t_1, \ldots, t_{m-1}, t_i \in T$, $i \in [0, m)$, where T is the set of all available documents. For one such document t_i, n models are separately invoked to score the query–document relevance and all of these scores are combined into a score vector $[s_0^i, s_1^i, \ldots, s_{n-1}^i]$. This feature vector provides the union of all the model scores and is fed into a ranking model such as LambdaMART (Burges, 2010) or XGBoost (Chen and Guestrin, 2016) to obtain the final ensemble score.

The advantages of such model ensembling are straightforward. By drawing on the aggregate ranking abilities of all models, the quality of the ensemble model is normally better than that of any individual model. However, needing multiple models to be deployed online simultaneously may decrease the stability and maintainability of the system.

3.2 Ranking Model Distillation

One method of simplifying a large model while maintaining the result quality is Knowledge Distillation (KD), where a well-trained large model serves as the teacher and a simpler student model is trained to not only predict the ground truth training data, but also mimic the label distribution generated by the teacher. However, it is not straightforward to apply KD to ranking problems. Recently, Tang and Wang (2018) proposed Ranking Distillation (RD) as a means of applying KD to recommendation ranking tasks. The teacher makes predictions on additional unlabeled documents and the top-k ranked list is obtained to train the student based on a distillation loss. However, this method is designed for recommender systems and there remain issues in applying it to query document ranking problems, as discussed in Section 1.

We propose Query Distillation as a novel two-stage distillation method for ranking. First, a large ensemble ranking model is trained on the training data to obtain a high-quality model that can serve as the teacher. Then, instead of adding additional unlabeled documents, we incorporate additional queries and use the recall method as well as the ranking teacher model to produce ranked lists for them. In production systems, additional queries can easily be sampled from query logs. Alternatively, one may also sample keywords and key phrases automatically identified in the document collection.

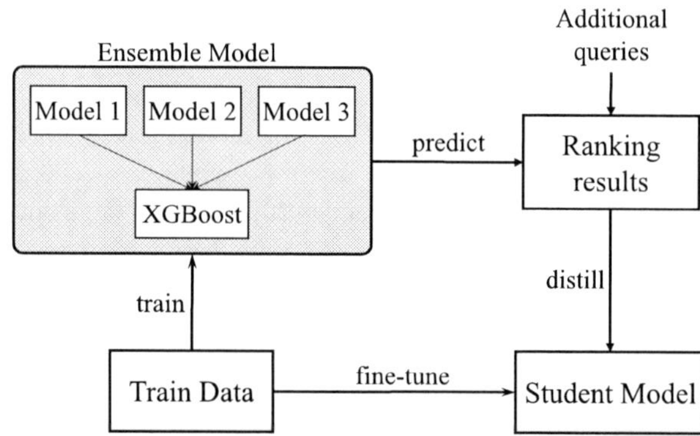

Figure 1: Flowchart of teacher–student training process for an ensemble ranking teacher model

The subsequent student training is guided by the ranking results provisioned by the teacher as well as the ground truth training data. The overall procedure is illustrated in Figure 1. The two stages of student training are as follows:

- *Teacher Guidance.* The student model is first trained based on ranking data generated by the teacher model using supplementary queries.
- *Ground Truth Training.* In the second stage, higher-quality ground truth labeled data is used to fine-tune the student model to attain a better performance.

By applying the two-stage teacher-student training method, we can obtain a student model that benefits from the retrieval quality of the ensemble, while reducing the inference latency and computational cost.

3.3 Student Model

We adopt BERT as our base student model. The standard practice to invoke BERT in ranking tasks is to form pairs of each query and candidate document token sequence. Previous work shows the effectiveness of this structure (Nogueira and Cho, 2019; Nogueira et al., 2019). We refer to this structure as query document pair BERT (BERT QD-pair). In this paper, we advance a new query document list BERT approach (BERT QD-list) that excels both in retrieval quality and inference efficiency. The two model structures are contrasted in Figure 2. We are given a query as a sequence of tokens $Q = (q_0, q_1, \ldots, q_{n-1})$ and top-k document candidates $T_0, T_1, \ldots, T_{k-1}$, where the token sequence of each document is $T_i = (t_0^i, t_1^i, \ldots, t_{l_i}^i)$, and l_i is the sequence length of T_i. Instead of pairing each query and document token sequence, BERT QD-list squeezes the entire document list into a single input sequence. All document tokens are tied together as the second sequence input of the BERT model, and the query tokens as the first sequence input are expected to reveal the most relevant documents among all candidates. We place a marker token [RANK] before each document to represent the document token sequence. Ultimately, all pertinent ranking information between the query and document resides in the marker token.

The advantages of BERT QD-list are two-fold. First of all, it makes the online model prediction more efficient. Furthermore, compared to the input of BERT QD-pair, where the query is only associated with one single document at a time, BERT QD-list enables list-wise joint ranking among all documents.

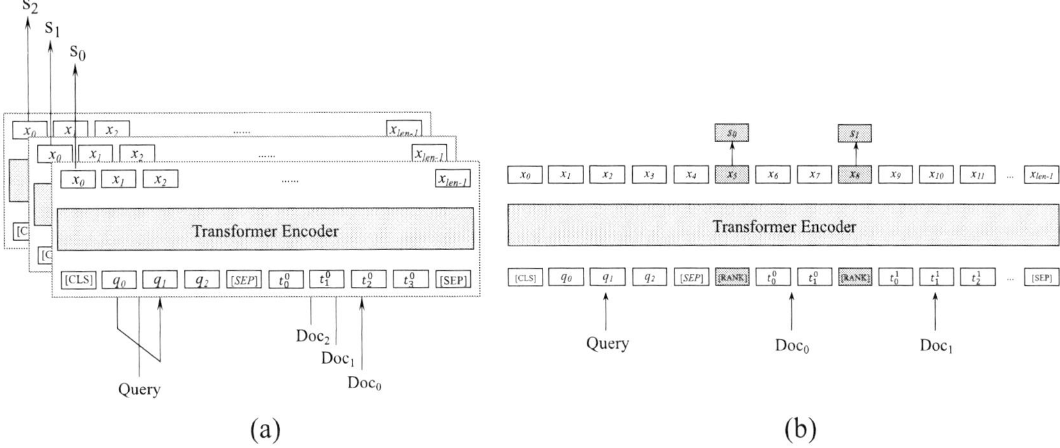

Figure 2: Structure of our student model. Figure (a) shows vanilla query document pair BERT (BERT QD-pair) and Figure (b) illustrates our query document list BERT (BERT QD-list) variant.

3.4 Loss Function

We add an output layer to the final Transformer output to transform every output token to a scalar value, in which the value of the positions of [RANK] tokens are gathered as the output score of every corresponding document. A hinge loss is adopted for our loss function:

$$L = \sum_i \Delta\text{nDCG}_i \, \max(0, \lambda - (\hat{s} - s_i))$$ (1)

Here, $\hat{s}$ is the score of the correct document, and s_i denotes the other document scores. ΔnDCG stands for the absolute difference in nDCG score (Burges, 2010) between the correct document and the current document. λ is a constant set to be 0.1. Note that if there is only one correct document, softmax cross-entropy loss is also an option.

3.5 Multi-Head Self-Attention

Self-attention (Devlin et al., 2018) has proven capable of capturing long-distance dependency information between sentences and attending to evidence information in many tasks such as machine translation, reading comprehension, and text classification. We also adopt self-attention to help capture the relationship between the query and the candidate documents. We represent the L layers of the Transformer as $\mathbf{H}^l = \text{Transformer}_l(\mathbf{H}^{l-1})$, $l \in [1, L]$, where $\mathbf{H}^l = [h_0^l, h_1^l, \ldots, h_{n-1}^l]$, n being the sequence length. For the l-th BERT layer, the output of a self-attention head is

$$\mathbf{Q} = \mathbf{H}^{l-1}\mathbf{W}_l^Q, \quad \mathbf{K} = \mathbf{H}^{l-1}\mathbf{W}_l^K, \quad \mathbf{V} = \mathbf{H}^{l-1}\mathbf{W}_l^V$$ (2)

$$\mathbf{M}_{ij} = \begin{cases} 0, & \text{allow to attend} \\ -\infty, & \text{prevent from attending} \end{cases}$$ (3)

$$\mathbf{A}_l = \text{softmax}\left(\frac{\mathbf{QK}^\mathsf{T} + \mathbf{M}}{\sqrt{d_k}}\right)\mathbf{V}_l$$ (4)

One of the most important challenges of our multiple document ranking problem is how to better make sense of the relationship between the query and the document tokens. The vanilla Transformer works to some extent, but since each pair of tokens has an attention dependency, noise may be introduced between candidate ranking documents. To address this issue, we propose several attention mask patterns applied to the KQV self-attention layer of the BERT model. We wish to grant query tokens access to affect all

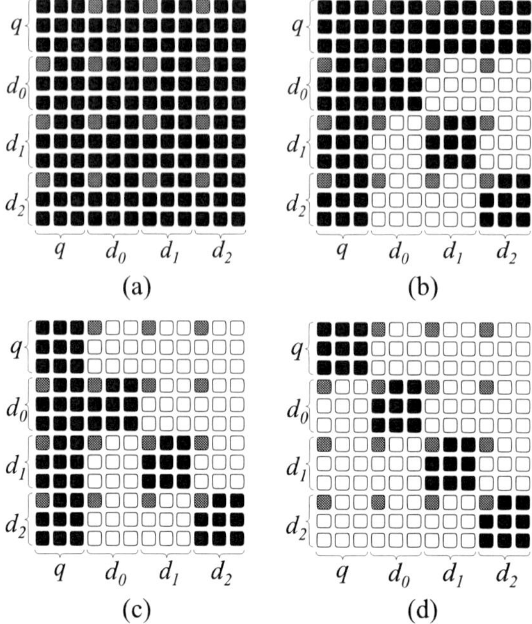

Figure 3: Different patterns of attention masks. q represents the query tokens, while d_k stands for tokens of a document k. For simplicity, only three ranking candidates are illustrated. A dark cell at row i and column j indicates that the i-th token is allowed to attend to the j-th token. A light cell indicates that the self-attention is inhibited between the corresponding pair of i and j. Cells shaded in gray denote the attention between different [RANK] marker tokens.

ranking documents, while the ties between candidate document token are restricted to prevent introducing noise. Only the special [RANK] tokens should attend to each other so as to enable the communication and comparison between candidate documents. We design our own mask matrix to control how tokens can attend to each other, as is shown in Figure 3. We can distinguish four kinds of mask patterns.

1. *No mask (Figure 3(a))*. The numbers in the attention matrix are all 1, and hence all tokens can attend to each other.
2. *Mutual document mask (Figure 3(b))*. Document tokens are inhibited from attending to tokens from other documents, which guarantees that noise from other document tokens cannot creep in, while the [RANK] tokens, which represent the overall document relevance, can have access to each other.
3. *Document–query mask (Figure 3(c))*. Compared to the second pattern, the output document tokens cannot affect any of the query tokens, while the query tokens can have attention bridges to documents, which may make the output document tokens cleaner.
4. *Segment-level self-attention (Figure 3(d))*. The query and each individual document possess only local self-attention, with the exception of the special [RANK] marker token, which can access other [RANK] tokens as well as query tokens.

4 Experiments

4.1 Experimental Settings

4.1.1 Dataset

We conduct experiments on two datasets. The first one is a retrieval based question answer dataset called Alipay Question Answers (Alipay QA), with queries collected from an online customer service with Mandarin Chinese data. For a given query, the system retrieves the most relevant answer from a document database with around $8,000$ documents, which cover the majority of user queries. The collected dataset consists of $38,017$ queries, each with 10 recall document candidates, within which the correct answer is labeled manually. It should be noted that there may be more than one suitable answer for a given query. In addition, another $500,000$ queries and recall document candidates are also collected for distillation usage.

The second dataset is MS MARCO (Microsoft Machine Reading Comprehension) by Nguyen et al. (2016), a large-scale English language dataset focused on machine reading comprehension, question answering, and passage ranking. The passage ranking sub-task consists of a collection of given queries q, each with $1,000$ relevant document passages selected by BM25, among which the most suitable passages that can answer the query have been marked manually. A large number of $532,761$ labeled queries and passages are available as training data. To fit our ranking distilling paradigm, we extract $50,000$ queries for training and test usage respectively, and for each query we keep the correct passage and randomly select 4 other recalled passages as recall candidates, which makes 5 recall documents. In addition, the remainder of around $400,000$ queries and recall documents is used as distillation data.

4.1.2 Baselines and Parameters Setting

An ensemble model is first trained for all datasets. For simplicity, only a BERT-based single model is adopted and we use query document pair BERT and query document list BERT as base single models. We trained two instances for both model types with different parameters so that in total four models are built for the ensemble. For the Alipay QA dataset, the best single model top-1 accuracy is 84.57%, and XGBoost is used for model ensembling, which attains a top-1 accuracy of 86.00%. Similarly, we also build an XGBoost ensemble model for the MS MARCO dataset. We obtain a best single model top-1 accuracy of 91.80%, versus 92.60% for the XGBoost model ensemble. All single and ensemble model baseline results are given in Table 1.

The ensemble model is then invoked as a teacher to label the additional queries and recalled documents. Student models are trained with our two-stage teacher–student training regimen, and we conduct distillation experiments on both the QD-pair and QD-list variants. The results for different model complexities are also collected by gradually reducing the number of hidden layers of the model.

To draw a fair comparison among all experiments, we adopt the same BERT configuration, initialized with the parameters provided by the pre-trained BERT-base model (Devlin et al., 2018). The Chinese BERT base model is used for Alipay QA, while the English version is used for MS MARCO. The maximum sequence length of BERT QD-pair and BERT QD-list on Alipay QA is set to 64 and 228, respectively, and on MS MARCO it is set to 256 and 512, respectively. We apply Adam optimization (Kingma and Ba, 2014) with a learning rate of 4×10^{-5}, and adopt a dropout probability of 0.1. We consider the mutual document masking from Section 3.5 our default masking procedure, except where indicated otherwise.

Model	Alipay QA$_{10\,recall}$		MS MARCO$_{5\,recall}$	
	ACC@1	MRR@5	ACC@1	MRR@5
Best Single	84.57	91.14	91.80	95.59
Ensemble	86.00	91.95	92.60	95.92
BERT RD	83.87	90.61	92.00	95.66
BERT QD-pair	86.27	92.18	92.82	96.11
BERT QD-list	**86.83**	**92.49**	**92.91**	**96.17**

Table 1: ACC@1 and MRR@5 of student models compared to the best single model and the original ensemble model on both Alipay QA and MS MARCO datasets (%).

4.1.3 Evaluation Measure

For both datasets, we consider a) whether the top-1 ranked document can answer the user's query, as well as b) the overall ranking quality. We thus adopt top-1 accuracy (ACC@1) and top-5 Mean Reciprocal Rank (MRR@5) (Burges, 2010) to evaluate the retrieval quality. Additionally, the inference time is also taken into consideration so as to evaluate the model's time efficiency.

4.2 Experimental Results

4.2.1 Ensemble Ranking Model Distillation

The main experimental results are given in Table 1. We first focus on the 12-layer model distilling method. BERT RD stands for the Ranking Distillation method by Tang and Wang (2018) using a base BERT model. BERT QD-pair and BERT QD-list represent our two-stage distillation of the query document pair BERT model and query document list BERT model, respectively.

#Layers	Model	Alipay QA$_{10\,recall}$			MS MARCO$_{5\,recall}$		
		ACC@1	MRR@5	Speed	ACC@1	MRR@5	Speed
12	BERT QD-pair	86.27	92.18	2.6	92.82	96.11	1.5
	BERT QD-list	**86.83**	**92.49**	6.6 ($\times$**2.5**)	**92.91**	**96.17**	2.8 ($\times$**1.9**)
9	BERT QD-pair	86.26	92.21	3.5	92.66	96.01	1.8
	BERT QD-list	**86.56**	**92.38**	8.8 ($\times$**2.5**)	**92.90**	**96.15**	3.7 ($\times$**2.1**)
6	BERT QD-pair	86.24	92.22	5.6	**92.62**	**96.01**	2.6
	BERT QD-list	**86.43**	**92.28**	13.0 ($\times$**2.3**)	92.37	95.87	5.5 ($\times$**2.1**)
3	BERT QD-pair	85.24	91.62	10.5	**91.77**	**95.48**	5.3
	BERT QD-list	**85.27**	**91.63**	25.7 ($\times$**2.4**)	90.91	95.00	11.7 ($\times$**2.2**)

Table 2: ACC@1 and MRR@5 of student model with various numbers of hidden layers (%). The inference time is as well reported in the Speed column, which represents the inference throughput of model (#samples/sec.).

BERT RD shows very limited effectiveness on our query document ranking tasks, since the additional distillation loss is inaccurate for our datasets, as discussed in Section 1. In contrast, both BERT QD-pair and BERT QD-list perform better than the large ensemble teacher model and far better than the original single models, which demonstrates the effectiveness of introducing our two-stage fine-tuned distilling method. While both distilled models outperform the original ensemble model, BERT QD-list obtains better results than the BERT QD pair variant. We conjecture that providing the document list to the model for a single joint prediction helps query tokens exchange information between all documents simultaneously during the KQV attention process. It is more difficult for the BERT QD-pair model to compare between documents and choose the best one because query tokens can only be cross-referenced with tokens from a single document at a time. In addition, the larger the number of candidate documents, the more benefit it appears we can obtain from BERT QD-list, since a larger number of documents can be compared. The experiments show that BERT QD-list outperforms QD-pair by 0.56% (ACC@1) and 0.31% (MRR@5) in absolute percentage points on Alipay QA, which has 10 document candidates, while the respective gains are 0.09% and 0.06% on MS MARCO, which has 5 recall documents.

4.2.2 Model Complexity

To get better inference time efficiency while retaining most of the retrieval quality, we can further shrink our distill model to a smaller size. For simplicity, model complexity is controlled by altering the number of hidden layers of BERT. We conduct experiments reducing the 12 hidden layers to 9, 6, and 3, respectively, as also reported in Table 2. The experiments show that the retrieval quality of both models drops as the number of hidden layers decreases, due to the reduction in model capacity. This reduction is non-linear: Taking BERT QD-list on Alipay QA as an example, ACC@1 decreases by 0.40% when the number of hidden layers drops from 12 to 6, but more drastically falls by 1.19% with a further reduction from 6 to 3. The overall results suggest that 6 hidden layers strikes a good balance between retrieval quality and model complexity. Note that at 3 hidden layers, BERT QD-pair shows little difference with BERT QD-list on Alipay QA and even outperforms the latter on MS MARCO, which suggests that the BERT list model requires a greater model capacity to handle the intricate relationships and comparisons between the query and the various documents. The simpler BERT QD-pair model thus constitutes an alternative in resource-constrained circumstances.

4.2.3 Inference Time Efficiency

In many situations, it is not enough for a model to be highly accurate. It also has to meet stringent time and space requirements. To assess this, we provide one single query document list sample at a time to obtain a prediction and measure how many samples the model can handle per second. All results are collected using PyTorch version 1.0.1 with Python 3.6.8 on a server equipped with Intel Xeon E5-2682 v4 @ 2.50GHz CPU, and the prediction service can access only up to 8 CPU cores. The time efficiency results are shown in the Speed column of Table 2. We collect data of the average number of samples the model can process per second for various numbers of hidden layers and also report the multiplier in time efficiency of the BERT QD-list model compared to the BERT QD-pair model.

We consistently observe an inference time speed-up by using BERT QD-list. On Alipay QA, this amounts to a roughly 2.4 times faster inference of BERT QD-list compared to BERT QD-pair, and it is around 2.1 times faster on MS MARCO. The computational time efficiency of BERT QD-list comes from the fact that all input documents are compressed into a single long token sequence, while the BERT QD-pair model handles a batch of shorter token sequences at a time. The larger the number of candidate documents, the bigger the benefit in time efficiency, as confirmed by the result that the time efficiency advantage is greater on the 10 recall documents for Alipay QA in comparison to the MS MARCO dataset, which has 5 recall documents. In addition, although the throughput of the model increases as the number of hidden layers is reduced, the advantage of BERT QD-list over BERT QD-pair on both datasets remains reasonably consistent.

4.2.4 Mask Patterns

We further assess further variants of self-attention masking, as described in Section 3.5, on both datasets using BERT QD-list with 12 hidden layers. The results are compiled in Table 3. On Alipay QA, we observe that the Mutual-Doc and Doc-Query mask patterns, as illustrated in Figure 3(b) and (c), prevail over models without any mask applied. On MS MARCO, the advantage is weaker, since we have much fewer documents.

	Alipay QA$_{10\,recall}$		MS MARCO$_{5\,recall}$	
Mask Type	ACC@1	MRR@5	ACC@1	MRR@5
No Mask	86.38	92.25	92.90	96.14
Mutual-Doc	**86.83**	**92.50**	**92.91**	**96.15**
Doc-Query	86.54	92.37	92.86	96.14
Segment	86.29	92.16	91.91	95.58

Table 3: ACC@1 and MRR@5 obtained for various mask patterns with the BERT QD-list model on both datasets (%). The different mask patterns are described in Figure 3.

Segment-level masking hampers the model performance dramatically on both datasets, thus establishing the importance of self-attention to bridge query tokens and document tokens.

4.2.5 Sequence Length Limitation

We finally evaluate the influence of the length of input sequence. Taking our 12-layer BERT QD-list model as an example, Table 1 shows that on the Alipay QA dataset the throughput of our model is 6.6 when the sequence length is 228, while on the MS MARCO dataset the throughput is 2.8 with a sequence length of 512, which means that a 2.25 times larger sequence length results in a 2.36 times slower model inference time. Furthermore, the largest position embedded in the pre-trained BERT model is 512, so we would need to train our own BERT position embedding if sequence lengths exceed 512. With larger inference time and sequence length limitation, there appear to be obstacles when applying our model to scenarios involving a large recall set and long input sequence lengths. In practice, a sophisticated ranking system often has multiple ranking processes, which are piped together to gradually obtain fewer but more accurate results. Our list model can be a good choice at the end of the ranking pipeline, since it delivers strong results but is limited by the input sequence length. Another option is to incorporate small changes to the network architecture for much greater scalability to long inputs (Beltagy et al., 2020).

5 Conclusion

In this paper, we introduce Query Distillation as a two-stage fine-tuned distillation training process for large ensemble ranking models. Furthermore, we propose a novel list-wise BERT model structure for ranking tasks (BERT QD-list), which is used as our student model. The experiments confirm the advantages of our query document list model not just with regard to the inference latency but also with regard to the retrieval quality over regular query document pair BERT (BERT QD-pair) as well as the original teacher models. In the future, we will try to apply our ranking distillation method on further tasks, such as answer selection in machine reading. Additionally, BERT variants that can handle larger sequence lengths such as XLNet (Yang et al., 2019b) will be evaluated to process even more documents at a time.

References

Jimmy Ba and Rich Caruana. 2014. Do deep nets really need to be deep? In *NIPS*, pages 2654–2662.

Oren Barkan, Noam Razin, Itzik Malkiel, Ori Katz, Avi Caciularu, and Noam Koenigstein. 2020. Scalable attentive sentence pair modeling via distilled sentence embedding. In *AAAI*, pages 3235–3242.

Iz Beltagy, Matthew E. Peters, and Arman Cohan. 2020. Longformer: The long-document transformer. *arXiv:2004.05150*.

Cristian Buciluǎ, Rich Caruana, and Alexandru Niculescu-Mizil. 2006. Model compression. In *SIGKDD*, pages 535–541. ACM.

Christopher JC Burges. 2010. From ranknet to lambdarank to lambdamart: An overview. *Learning*, 11(23-581):81.

Tianqi Chen and Carlos Guestrin. 2016. Xgboost: A scalable tree boosting system. In *SIGKDD*, pages 785–794. ACM.

Jacob Devlin, Ming-Wei Chang, Kenton Lee, and Kristina Toutanova. 2018. Bert: Pre-training of deep bidirectional transformers for language understanding. *arXiv preprint arXiv:1810.04805*.

Jiafeng Guo, Yixing Fan, Qingyao Ai, and W Bruce Croft. 2016. A deep relevance matching model for ad-hoc retrieval. In *CIKM*, pages 55–64. ACM.

Geoffrey Hinton, Oriol Vinyals, and Jeff Dean. 2015. Distilling the knowledge in a neural network. *arXiv preprint arXiv:1503.02531*.

Po-Sen Huang, Xiaodong He, Jianfeng Gao, Li Deng, Alex Acero, and Larry Heck. 2013. Learning deep structured semantic models for web search using clickthrough data. In *CIKM*, pages 2333–2338. ACM.

Kai Hui, Andrew Yates, Klaus Berberich, and Gerard de Melo. 2017. A position-aware deep model for relevance matching in information retrieval. In *Proceedings of EMNLP 2017*, pages 1049–1058. ACL.

Kai Hui, Andrew Yates, Klaus Berberich, and Gerard De Melo. 2018. Co-pacrr: A context-aware neural ir model for ad-hoc retrieval. In *WSDM*, pages 279–287. ACM.

Diederik P Kingma and Jimmy Ba. 2014. Adam: A method for stochastic optimization. *arXiv preprint arXiv:1412.6980*.

Hang Li. 2011. Learning to rank for information retrieval and natural language processing. *Synthesis Lectures on Human Language Technologies*, 4(1):1–113.

Tie-Yan Liu et al. 2009. Learning to rank for information retrieval. *Foundations and Trends® in Information Retrieval*, 3(3):225–331.

Sean MacAvaney, Andrew Yates, Arman Cohan, and Nazli Goharian. 2019. Cedr: Contextualized embeddings for document ranking. In *SIGIR*, pages 1101–1104. ACM.

Bhaskar Mitra, Fernando Diaz, and Nick Craswell. 2017. Learning to match using local and distributed representations of text for web search. In *WWW*, pages 1291–1299. International World Wide Web Conferences Steering Committee.

Tri Nguyen, Mir Rosenberg, Xia Song, Jianfeng Gao, Saurabh Tiwary, Rangan Majumder, and Li Deng. 2016. Ms marco: A human-generated machine reading comprehension dataset.

Rodrigo Nogueira and Kyunghyun Cho. 2019. Passage re-ranking with bert. *arXiv preprint arXiv:1901.04085*.

Rodrigo Nogueira, Wei Yang, Kyunghyun Cho, and Jimmy Lin. 2019. Multi-stage document ranking with bert. *arXiv preprint arXiv:1910.14424*.

Matthew E Peters, Waleed Ammar, Chandra Bhagavatula, and Russell Power. 2017. Semi-supervised sequence tagging with bidirectional language models. *arXiv preprint arXiv:1705.00108*.

Yifan Qiao, Chenyan Xiong, Zhenghao Liu, and Zhiyuan Liu. 2019. Understanding the behaviors of bert in ranking. *arXiv preprint arXiv:1904.07531*.

Alec Radford, Jeff Wu, Rewon Child, David Luan, Dario Amodei, and Ilya Sutskever. 2019. Language models are unsupervised multitask learners.

Adriana Romero, Nicolas Ballas, Samira Ebrahimi Kahou, Antoine Chassang, Carlo Gatta, and Yoshua Bengio. 2014. Fitnets: Hints for thin deep nets. *arXiv preprint arXiv:1412.6550*.

Jiaxi Tang and Ke Wang. 2018. Ranking distillation: Learning compact ranking models with high performance for recommender system. In *SIGKDD*, pages 2289–2298. ACM.

Ruth Urner, Shai Shalev-Shwartz, and Shai Ben-David. 2011. Access to unlabeled data can speed up prediction time. In *Proceedings of the 28th International Conference on Machine Learning, ICML 2011, Bellevue, Washington, USA, June 28 - July 2, 2011*, pages 641–648.

Wei Yang, Yuqing Xie, Aileen Lin, Xingyu Li, Luchen Tan, Kun Xiong, Ming Li, and Jimmy Lin. 2019a. End-to-end open-domain question answering with bertserini. *arXiv preprint arXiv:1902.01718*.

Zhilin Yang, Zihang Dai, Yiming Yang, Jaime Carbonell, Ruslan Salakhutdinov, and Quoc V Le. 2019b. Xlnet: Generalized autoregressive pretraining for language understanding. *arXiv preprint arXiv:1906.08237*.

Shan You, Chang Xu, Chao Xu, and Dacheng Tao. 2017. Learning from multiple teacher networks. In *SIGKDD*, pages 1285–1294. ACM.

Semantic Diversity for Natural Language Understanding Evaluation in Dialog Systems

Enrico Palumbo
Amazon Alexa
Turin, 10126, Italy
palumboe@amazon.com

Andrea Mezzalira
Amazon Alexa
Turin, 10126, Italy
mezzalir@amazon.com

Cristina Marco
Amazon Alexa
Turin, 10126, Italy
marcocri@amazon.com

Alessandro Manzotti
Amazon Alexa
Turin, 10126, Italy
manzotti@amazon.com

Daniele Amberti
Amazon Alexa
Turin, 10126, Italy
amberti@amazon.com

Abstract

The quality of Natural Language Understanding (NLU) models is typically evaluated using aggregated metrics on a large number of utterances. In a dialog system, though, the manual analysis of failures on specific utterances is a time-consuming and yet critical endeavor to guarantee a high-quality customer experience. A crucial question for this analysis is how to create a test set of utterances that covers a diversity of possible customer requests. In this paper, we introduce the task of generating a test set with high semantic diversity for NLU evaluation in dialog systems and we describe an approach to address it. The approach starts by extracting high-traffic utterance patterns. Then, for each pattern, it achieves high diversity selecting utterances from different regions of the utterance embedding space. We compare three selection strategies based on clustering of utterances in the embedding space, on solving the maximum distance optimization problem and on simple heuristics such as random uniform sampling and popularity. The evaluation shows that the highest semantic and lexicon diversity is obtained by a greedy maximum sum of distance solver in a comparable runtime with the clustering and the heuristics approaches.

1 Background

In the past years, voice-first dialog systems have become ubiquitous in the market, with an ever increasing number of features, languages and customer requests. A crucial component of these systems is the Natural Language Understanding (NLU) model. The NLU model maps customer requests onto specific actions that the device has to perform. In practice, this means classifying an utterance into a domain, intent and slots (Su et al., 2018). For instance, given the customer's utterance "play madonna", an NLU model returns: (*Music, PlayMusicIntent, play ArtistName*) where *Music* is the domain, *PlayMusicIntent* is the intent and the slot is *ArtistName*. When a new algorithm for NLU is proposed in a research environment, the evaluation is typically performed by aggregating metrics such as Slot Error Rate (SER) (Makhoul et al., 1999) and Semantic Error Rate (SemER) (Su et al., 2018) on a large test set of utterances. However, in a production environment, aggregated metrics alone are not sufficient, as they may hide failures on specific business critical utterances. Thus, whenever a change is introduced into an NLU model, failures need to be manually reviewed to determine whether they represent an issue for the customers. The manual review of failures is a crucial, and yet very time-consuming operation. Hence, the question: how to create a test set that makes the analysis more efficient including a diversity of patterns, utterances and possibile failure causes? The problem of maximizing semantic diversity in text is common in tasks such as text summarization (Zhu et al., 2007), text generation (Xu et al., 2018), keyphrase extraction (Bennani-Smires et al., 2018), machine translation (Shu et al., 2019), data augmentation in dialog systems (Hou et al., 2018; Cho et al., 2019). However, to the best our knowledge, semantic diversity has never been used to

Proceedings of the 28th International Conference on Computational Linguistics: Industry Track, pages 44–49
Barcelona, Spain (Online), December 12, 2020

create test sets for the evaluation of natural language understanding models in dialog systems.

In this paper, we introduce an approach to automate the creation of test sets with high semantic diversity for the evaluation of the NLU model in a dialog system. The approach works as follows. First, we filter the dataset extracting a set of high-traffic pattern. Then, for each pattern, we map utterances into an embedding space to represent the semantics of the different slot values. Finally, we create test sets comparing three selection algorithms based on partitioning the space in groups and selecting representatives or on directly solving a maximum sum of distance optimization problem to achieve high diversity.

2   Approach

The approach can be divided in three major steps: pattern extraction, encoding and selection (Fig. 1).

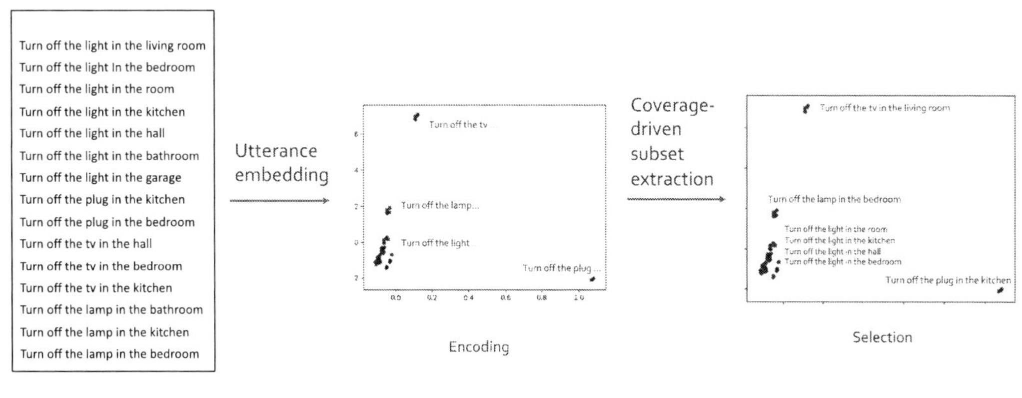

Figure 1: A bird's eye view over the proposed approach. High-traffic patterns are extracted and, for a specific pattern, utterances are embedded into a vector space in the encoding stage. Then, the selection stage selects points that are far apart in the vector space to create a test set with high diversity (red points),

2.1   Pattern Extraction

As of today, pattern-based rules such as Finite State Transducers (FSTs) (Karttunen, 2000) still play a very important role in NLU models. FSTs work by mapping into domain, intent and slots utterances that exactly match structures such as "play SongName", "play SongName please", "please can you play SongName". We call these structures "semantic frames", and, together with domain and intent, they are a suitable definition of "pattern" that can break in an FST. Given a domain $d \in D$, an intent $i \in I$ and a semantic frames $c \in C$, we define a pattern $p \in P$ as:

$$p = (d, i, c) \tag{1}$$

such as "Music, PlayMusicIntent, play SongName" or "Weather, GetWeatherForecastIntent, what is the weather like in CityName". We use a dataset composed by ~5M annotated utterances that contains ~400 high-traffic patterns. Even within a specific pattern, though, the variability can be high and the selection strategy should be diversity-aware. Consider the example of "play SongName": a huge amount of possible songs are present in the dataset. The resulting test set should include a diversity of songs, both in terms of lexicon, that is different wordings, and also in terms of semantics, for instance different musical genres.

2.2   Encoding

A crucial point for measuring diversity is finding an adequate vector representation of words and utterances where similarity metrics can be easily applied. word2vec embeddings (Mikolov et al., 2013) have shown the effectiveness of the Continuous Bag of Words and Skip-gram architectures to learn word representations, gaining tremendous popularity. FastText (Bojanowski et al., 2017) improves the word2vec model including subword information (character n-grams) into the skip-gram architecture. In this work, we use FastText to map utterances into embeddings. This means that the model is trained to predict, given a character n-gram as input, the surrounding character n-grams in a predefined window. Given an utterance $s(p)$ of a pattern p and its K character n-grams $k_i(s(p))$ we obtain the vector representation of the utterance $\hat{s}(p)$:

$$\hat{s}(p) = \frac{1}{K} \sum_{i=1}^{K} fasttext\_pretrained\_vector(k_i(s(p))) \tag{2}$$

Currently, popular models such as ELMo (Peters et al., 2018) or BERT (Devlin et al., 2019) further improve word representations by considering the context or embedding the whole sentence based on neighboring sentences (Kiros et al., 2015). We choose FastText over more sophisticated embedding models because it is frugal (fast at retrieval times on CPU), and it provides pre-trained models for 157 different languages. The major drawback of averaging character n-grams embeddings in this way is that we lose information on how the sentence is structured, e.g. the order of the tokens. However, given that we perform the encoding in pattern-wise manner, the structure of the sentence is fixed as described in Sec.2.1 and the variations mostly come from the values that occur in the slots.

2.3 Selection

Definition 1 *Given a pattern p, $M = |p|$ is the total number of utterances in the pattern*

Definition 2 *Given a pattern p, $m \leq M$ is the total number of utterances to be selected for the pattern*

Definition 3 *Given the vector representation of an utterance $\hat{s}(p)$, $d = |\hat{s}(p)|$ is the number of dimensions of the vector.*

Definition 4 *$X(p) = (\hat{s}_1(p), ..., \hat{s}_M(p))$ is the matrix that contains the vector representations of all the utterances in a pattern p*

We compare the following approaches to select points from the vector space:

PSA The Part and Select Algorithm (PSA) (Salomon et al., 2013) has two steps: first, it partitions the space grouping similar points; then it selects a diverse subset by choosing one member for each of the groups. To partition the space in m subsets, PSA makes $m - 1$ divisions of a single set into two subsets. Given the minimum and maximum values of a feature $a_j = min_i(X_{ij})$ and $b_j = max_i(X_{ij})$, the diameter of a subset is defined as $A = max_j(b_j - a_j)$. The partitioning of the space works iteratively, searching among all the subsets the one that has the maximum diameter A, and splitting in half the subset along the feature j that maximizes the diameter. Then, for each of the m subset, the point that is closest to the center of the hyperretangle is selected. PSA has a runtime complexity that is $O(M * m * d)$.

KMeans KMeans (Hartigan and Wong, 1979) is arguably the most popular clustering algorithm, it works by dividing the data in a predefined number of groups minimizing the within-cluster sum of squares. For each pattern with M utterances, we apply KMeans to obtain m clusters, and then we select the nearest point to the centroid to be part of the subset. KMeans has a runtime complexity of $O(M * m * d)$.

MaxSum MaxSum (Ghosh, 1996) solves the optimization problem of finding a subset of points that have the maximum sum of distances among each other. Given that the problem is NP-hard, we use a greedy approach that iteratively selects points that maximize the objective and has a linear runtime complexity $O(M * m * d)$.

As baselines, we also include the **Random Sampler**, which selects m points per pattern using a uniform distribution, and the **Popularity Sampler**, which selects the most frequently used m utterances for each pattern. For all selection algorithms, we set as the default percentage of utterances to select for each pattern $f = 0.01$. Given the number of utterances in a pattern M and f, we determine the number of points to select and set the number of clusters $m = Mf$ in the clustering algorithms. When using the proposed approach, we recommend to set the value of f depending on the desired size of the test set.

3 Evaluation

We evaluate the inherent diversity of the test sets that the selection algorithms generate measuring how 'distant' two utterances are on average in the subsets that we generate using the following metrics:

- **SelfBLEU** (Zhu et al., 2018) was recently introduced to measure the diversity of artifically generated text, it computes BLEU (Papineni et al., 2002) comparing a set of utterances with themselves rather than with a reference. We use it as follows:

$$SelfBLEU = \frac{1}{N} \sum_{p=1}^{N} avg_{i,j}(1 - BLEU(s(p)_i, s(p)_j)) \qquad (3)$$

- **Jaccard**: average word overlap across test utterances

$$Jaccard = \frac{1}{N} \sum_{p=1}^{N} avg_{i,j}(1 - word\_overlap(s(p)_i, s(p)_j)) \qquad (4)$$

- **Word Embedding Diversity (WED)**: similar to the Word Embedding Similarity (Agirre et al., 2016), it is the average cosine distance between embeddings of vectors in the test set:

$$WED = \frac{1}{N} \sum_{p=1}^{N} avg_{i,j}(1 - cosine\_similarity(\hat{s}(p)_i, \hat{s}(p)_j)) \qquad (5)$$

Note that SelfBLEU and Jaccard only consider word and n-gram level similarities, whereas WED can also take into account word semantics.

4 Results

We compare the selection algorithms computing the relative percentage improvement with respect to random selection on the diversity metrics (Tab. 1). The results show that, in general, all diversity-aware algorithms achieve higher diversity with respect to Random and Popularity generates the lowest diversity. MaxSum solver obtains the best diversity both at the semantic (WED) and at the lexicon level (SelfBLEU, Jaccard). Interestingly, PSA performs better than KMeans for metrics that take into account words and n-grams overlaps, i.e. at a lexicon level, whereas KMeans works better for WED, which measures embedding distance at a semantic level. Random is the fastest algorithm, but the runtime is comparable for all the algorithms.

Algorithm	WED	SelfBLEU-2	SelfBLEU-3	SelfBLEU-4	Jaccard	Runtime (s)
PSA	24.73	2.33	1.97	1.53	1.93	12178
KMeans	26.13	2.20	1.96	1.59	1.87	13679
MaxSum	**38.7**	**6.96**	**6.13**	**4.9**	**5.31**	12219
Random	0.0	0.0	0.0	0.0	0.0	**11959**
Popularity	-12.98	-10.88	-9.66	-7.75	-7.75	12011

Table 1: Diversity comparison of the selectiong algorithms as a relative % change with respect to Random sampling. In SelfBLEU-n, n is the size of the n-gram used. Results are significant for all pairs of algorithms and for all metrics with a paired t-test with p<0.05.

5 Conclusions

In this paper, we have introduced the problem of creating a test set with high semantic diversity to evaluate the NLU model of a dialog system. We have described the problem motivation and we have introduced an approach to address it. The experimental comparison among different diversity-aware selection algorithms shows that the MaxSum sampler obtains the best diversity, both at the semantic (WED) and at the lexicon level (SelfBLEU, Jaccard). For all the diversity-aware approaches (PSA, KMeans, MaxSum), runtime is comparable to simple heuristics such as random and popularity selection. As a future work, we will create a ground truth to see how well our diversity metrics correlate with human judgement. The ground truth will also be key to exploring the effectiveness of hybrid approaches that combine diverisity and coverage, taking into the frequency of customer requests. We also plan to experiment with more encoding algorithms, such as frugal light-weight transformer-based approaches that have been recently proposed (Sanh et al., 2019) and have shown to better represent complex utterances.

References

Eneko Agirre, Carmen Banea, Daniel Cer, Mona Diab, Aitor Gonzalez Agirre, Rada Mihalcea, German Rigau Claramunt, and Janyce Wiebe. 2016. Semeval-2016 task 1: Semantic textual similarity, monolingual and cross-lingual evaluation. In *SemEval-2016. 10th International Workshop on Semantic Evaluation; 2016 Jun 16-17; San Diego, CA. Stroudsburg (PA): ACL; 2016. p. 497-511*. ACL (Association for Computational Linguistics).

Kamil Bennani-Smires, Claudiu Musat, Andreea Hossmann, Michael Baeriswyl, and Martin Jaggi. 2018. Simple unsupervised keyphrase extraction using sentence embeddings. In *Proceedings of the 22nd Conference on Computational Natural Language Learning*, pages 221–229, Brussels, Belgium, October. Association for Computational Linguistics.

Piotr Bojanowski, Edouard Grave, Armand Joulin, and Tomas Mikolov. 2017. Enriching word vectors with subword information. *Transactions of the Association for Computational Linguistics*, 5:135–146.

Eunah Cho, He Xie, John P Lalor, Varun Kumar, and William M Campbell. 2019. Efficient semi-supervised learning for natural language understanding by optimizing diversity. *arXiv preprint arXiv:1910.04196*.

Jacob Devlin, Ming-Wei Chang, Kenton Lee, and Kristina Toutanova. 2019. BERT: Pre-training of deep bidirectional transformers for language understanding. In *Proceedings of the 2019 Conference of the North American Chapter of the Association for Computational Linguistics: Human Language Technologies, Volume 1 (Long and Short Papers)*, pages 4171–4186, Minneapolis, Minnesota, June. Association for Computational Linguistics.

Jay B Ghosh. 1996. Computational aspects of the maximum diversity problem. *Operations research letters*, 19(4):175–181.

John A Hartigan and Manchek A Wong. 1979. Algorithm as 136: A k-means clustering algorithm. *Journal of the Royal Statistical Society. Series C (Applied Statistics)*, 28(1):100–108.

Yutai Hou, Yijia Liu, Wanxiang Che, and Ting Liu. 2018. Sequence-to-sequence data augmentation for dialogue language understanding. *arXiv preprint arXiv:1807.01554*.

Lauri Karttunen. 2000. Applications of finite-state transducers in natural language processing. In *International Conference on Implementation and Application of Automata*, pages 34–46. Springer.

Ryan Kiros, Yukun Zhu, Russ R Salakhutdinov, Richard Zemel, Raquel Urtasun, Antonio Torralba, and Sanja Fidler. 2015. Skip-thought vectors. In *Advances in neural information processing systems*, pages 3294–3302.

John Makhoul, Francis Kubala, Richard Schwartz, Ralph Weischedel, et al. 1999. Performance measures for information extraction. In *Proceedings of DARPA broadcast news workshop*, pages 249–252. Herndon, VA.

Tomas Mikolov, Ilya Sutskever, Kai Chen, Greg S Corrado, and Jeff Dean. 2013. Distributed representations of words and phrases and their compositionality. In *Advances in neural information processing systems*, pages 3111–3119.

Kishore Papineni, Salim Roukos, Todd Ward, and Wei-Jing Zhu. 2002. Bleu: a method for automatic evaluation of machine translation. In *Proceedings of the 40th annual meeting on association for computational linguistics*, pages 311–318. Association for Computational Linguistics.

Matthew E Peters, Mark Neumann, Mohit Iyyer, Matt Gardner, Christopher Clark, Kenton Lee, and Luke Zettlemoyer. 2018. Deep contextualized word representations. *arXiv preprint arXiv:1802.05365*.

Shaul Salomon, Gideon Avigad, Alex Goldvard, and Oliver Schütze. 2013. Psa – a new scalable space partition based selection algorithm for moeas. In Oliver Schütze, Carlos A. Coello Coello, Alexandru-Adrian Tantar, Emilia Tantar, Pascal Bouvry, Pierre Del Moral, and Pierrick Legrand, editors, *EVOLVE - A Bridge between Probability, Set Oriented Numerics, and Evolutionary Computation II*, pages 137–151, Berlin, Heidelberg. Springer Berlin Heidelberg.

Victor Sanh, Lysandre Debut, Julien Chaumond, and Thomas Wolf. 2019. Distilbert, a distilled version of bert: smaller, faster, cheaper and lighter. *arXiv preprint arXiv:1910.01108.*

Raphael Shu, Hideki Nakayama, and Kyunghyun Cho. 2019. Generating diverse translations with sentence codes. In *Proceedings of the 57th Annual Meeting of the Association for Computational Linguistics*, pages 1823–1827.

Chengwei Su, Rahul Gupta, Shankar Ananthakrishnan, and Spyros Matsoukas. 2018. A re-ranker scheme for integrating large scale nlu models. In *2018 IEEE Spoken Language Technology Workshop (SLT)*, pages 670–676. IEEE.

Jingjing Xu, Xuancheng Ren, Junyang Lin, and Xu Sun. 2018. Diversity-promoting gan: A cross-entropy based generative adversarial network for diversified text generation. In *Proceedings of the 2018 Conference on Empirical Methods in Natural Language Processing*, pages 3940–3949.

Xiaojin Zhu, Andrew B Goldberg, Jurgen Van Gael, and David Andrzejewski. 2007. Improving diversity in ranking using absorbing random walks. In *Human Language Technologies 2007: The Conference of the North American Chapter of the Association for Computational Linguistics; Proceedings of the Main Conference*, pages 97–104.

Yaoming Zhu, Sidi Lu, Lei Zheng, Jiaxian Guo, Weinan Zhang, Jun Wang, and Yong Yu. 2018. Texygen: A benchmarking platform for text generation models. In *The 41st International ACM SIGIR Conference on Research & Development in Information Retrieval*, pages 1097–1100.

An Empirical Study on Multi-Task Learning for Text Style Transfer and Paraphrase Generation

Paweł Bujnowski[a], Kseniia Ryzhova[c*], Hyungtak Choi[b], Katarzyna Witkowska[d*],
Jarosław Piersa[a], Tymoteusz Krumholc[a] and Katarzyna Beksa[a]

[a] Samsung R&D Institute, Warsaw, Poland
[b] Samsung Research, Samsung Electronics Co. Ltd., Seoul, Korea
[c] Rankomat, Warsaw, Poland
[d] Polytechnic University of Catalonia, Barcelona, Spain

```
{p.bujnowski, ht777.choi, j.piersa,
   t.krumholc, k.beksa}@samsung.com,
{ksenija.rijova, witek.witkowska}@gmail.com
```


Abstract

The topic of this paper is neural multi-task training for text style transfer. We present an efficient method for neutral-to-style transformation using the transformer framework. We demonstrate how to prepare a robust model utilizing large paraphrases corpora together with a small parallel style transfer corpus. We study how much style transfer data is needed for a model on the example of two transformations: *neutral-to-cute* on internal corpus and *modern-to-antique* on publicly available Bible corpora. Additionally, we propose a synthetic measure for the automatic evaluation of style transfer models. We hope our research is a step towards replacing common but limited rule-based style transfer systems by more flexible machine learning models for both public and commercial usage.

1 Introduction

The goal of text style transfer (ST[1]) is to convert the input sentence into an output, preserving the meaning but modifying the linguistic layer (grammatical or lexical).

Style transfer is extensively studied in academic papers (Li et al., 2018a; Rao and Tetreault, 2018; Carlson et al., 2018; Jhamtani et al., 2017) and also gains popularity in commercialized chatbots. Amazon Alexa introduced styles mimicking celebrities that replace the original Alexa voice (Amazon, 2020). Samsung offers applications personalized in terms of style, e.g. Celebrity Alarm (Samsung, 2019). Both examples offer novel user experience, though the number of available system responses seems to be limited. The two main constraints are voice generation and text content limitations. While voice generation can be implemented with voice synthesis systems, like e.g. by Jia et al. (2018) or Prenger et al. (2018), content limitation might be resolved by flexible machine learning text ST methods: the system could transform neutral answer into one of predefined styles using a machine learning model. The major challenges are the limited amount of style data and the lack of convincing automatic evaluation measures. In our study we try to mitigate these two issues.

The goal of our paper is to present an efficient method to train domain-unlimited ST models using a small style dataset. Inspired by the successful outcomes of multi-task learning (Caruana, 1997; Collobert and Weston, 2008; Johnson et al., 2017), we propose a transformer model (Vaswani et al., 2017) that jointly solves paraphrase generation and style transfer tasks. We hypothesize that training in the multi-task mode on an English large parallel corpus for paraphrasing may help preserve the input content along with successful adjustment of vocabulary and grammar to the target style, even using a small ST corpus.

To verify the hypothesis and add practical value, we perform detailed tests on various sizes of text ST corpora to verify how their volume affects the results. This is a convenient approach, because we have

---

*Work done during an internship at Samsung R&D Institute, Warsaw, Poland.

[1] Abbreviations used throughout the article: ST — Style Transfer, (N)MT — (Neural) Machine Translation, N2C — Neutral to Cute, M2A — Modern to Antique, TS — Text Simplification, DNNs — Deep Neural Networks.

Proceedings of the 28th International Conference on Computational Linguistics: Industry Track, pages 50–63
Barcelona, Spain (Online), December 12, 2020

publicly available large parallel corpora for paraphrasing, but rather small parallel corpora of style transformations we want to achieve. We perform our experiments using openly available paraphrase sources (Rao and Tetreault, 2018; Carlson et al., 2018; Quora, 2017; Wieting and Gimpel, 2018; Williams et al., 2018) and two ST corpora, one for each task: the internal "cute person" style corpus and the processed Bible texts corpus composed of publicly available sources. We examine two style transformations: *neutral-to-cute* and *modern-to-antique* (the latter one on different Bible translations).

Besides studies with various data volumes, we propose a method of creating an automatic measure. We show that simple common measures do not work if separated and instead we propose a fitted compound measure.

2 Related works

2.1 Style transfer: not too far from paraphrasing

Similarly to Xu et al. (2012) we see language ST as a task composed of two linked subtasks: paraphrasing and style adjustment. In our paper we claim that the ST task consists mostly in good paraphrasing and much less in adding the target style. Following this idea, we focus on background methods for the first task – paraphrasing, and then for style transfer.

Traditionally, the paraphrasing task involved rule and dictionary-based approaches (McKeown, 1983; Bolshakov and Gelbukh, 2004; Kauchak and Barzilay, 2006). Another popular method was the statistical paraphrase generation that recombined words probabilistically in order to create new sentences (Quirk et al., 2004; Wan et al., 2005; Zhao et al., 2009). Currently, DNNs are used for automatic paraphrasing, e.g. by sequence-to-sequence (seq2seq) models (Sutskever et al., 2014).

Presumably, the first paper presenting a deep learning model for the paraphrase task is the one by Prakash et al. (2016). The authors successfully compared their residual LSTM to previous LSTM-derived seq2seq models (Hochreiter and Schmidhuber, 1997; Schuster and Paliwal, 1997; Bahdanau et al., 2014; Vaswani et al., 2017). In parallel, upon research on variational autoencoders (VAEs), e.g. Chung et al. (2015), other approaches to paraphrasing emerged (Bowman et al., 2016; Gupta et al., 2018).

More recently Li et al. (2018b) implemented paraphrase generation with deep reinforcement learning that proved better performance than the previous seq2seq results on Twitter (Lan et al., 2017) and Quora (Quora, 2017) datasets. Insufficient corpora for paraphrase generation gave motivation to new practical studies on unsupervised approach (Artetxe et al., 2018; Conneau and Lample, 2019). Recently, Roy and Grangier (2019) proposed a monolingual system for paraphrasing (without translation) and compared it to the unsupervised and translation methods, presenting various linguistic characteristics for each of them.

2.2 Style transfer methods

We name here only some existing solutions. Xu et al. (2012) used a phrase-based MT method on Shakespeare M2A corpus. This research was followed by Jhamtani et al. (2017), who improved the results with the DNN seq2seq approach using a copy mechanism.

Rao and Tetreault (2018) adapted phrased-based and neural MT models for formality transfer using GYAFC corpus. Later Niu et al. (2018) improved results on GYAFC by creating a multi-task system for both formality transfer and English-French MT.

It is worth mentioning Dryjański et al. (2018) who used DNNs both elements: generation of ST phrases and their positions related to the input sentence.

Another distinctive study was conducted for text simplification (TS) task with the matched Wikipedia–Simple Wikipedia parallel data, e.g. Wubben et al. (2012; Wang et al. (2016). What is significant for TS are the results for automatic measures in Xu et al. (2016) followed by Alva-Manchego et al. (2019). We draw our inspiration from the authors, along with the results of Xu et al. (2012) in our measure propositions.

Our solution has common features with Wieting and Gimpel (2018). The authors demonstrated that using pretrained embeddings from a large parallel paraphrase corpus ($\sim$50 millions) and out-of-the-box models, it was possible to reach state-of-the-art results on several SemEval semantic textual similarity competitions. In our work, instead of using pretrained embeddings we follow Johnson et al. (2017) and train the multi-task model on a single language, but with paraphrases and a small *neutral-to-style* dataset. Compared to the previous solutions, our approach can be seen as a universal method to tackle text ST (e.g. formality transfer, simplification and more).

3   Model

3.1   Multilingual model

We used the Multilingual Transformer (Vaswani et al., 2017) model from the Fairseq package (Ott et al., 2019). Using this model we approach the problem similarly to multilingual translation, treating each style as a new language. An overview of the system is presented in Figure 1.

In this architecture all the language pairs share a single Transformer neural network. We fed the model with two paired datasets, {English sentences vs English paraphrase references} and {English sentences vs English sentences with target style}, and trained it on both sets. The parallel training on both datasets following this multilingual (multi-task) approach produces robust results, but requires retraining the model from scratch after any modification of the style corpus. For Multilingual Transformer we preprocessed the sentences with the SentencePiece toolkit (Kudo and Richardson, 2018) without any pretokenization. The vocabulary size was predefined to 16k. We used a shared English dictionary for both the paraphrase pairs and the target style corpus binarization. We also removed lines with more than 250 tokens.

For each training set the target style sample constituted only up to 0.6% of the whole set. It appears that Multilingual Transformer can effectively train the model even with a huge disproportion between paraphrases and style corpora sizes.

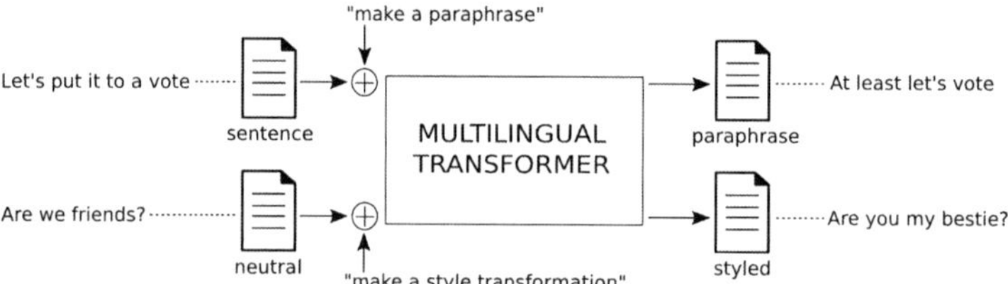

Figure 1: Model overview: Multilingual transformer trained with paraphrases and styled data.

3.2   Training parameters details

For training the models we used multiple GPUs (GeForce GTX 1080 Ti, 11GB), which contributed to more representative updates due to different average sentence length among mini-batches distributed between workers. The training on 8 GPUs lasted about 27 hours. We used Multilingual Transformer models with shared-decoders from the Fairseq package. The architecture consisted of 6 encoder and 6 decoder fully connected layers of dimension 1054 with 4 attention heads. The embeddings were of dimension 512. We set the dropout to 0.3, weight decay to 0.0001 and the optimizer to Adam ($\beta_1 = 0.9, \beta_2 = 0.98$) with the learning rate equal to 0.0005. We used label-smoothed cross entropy loss with label smoothing set to 0.1. For generation we used beam size equal to 5. We stopped the training after 40 epochs.

4   Experiments

Using our ST methods we performed two tasks: N2C and M2A. For each task we prepared a number of target (style) parallel corpora differing only in volumes. For the N2C transformation it was 1k, 3k, 5k, 7k, 10k, 13k, and 17k. For the M2A transformation we prepared the same corpora volumes plus the additional 30k. The proportions for training and validation were equal for all the target datasets with the ratio of 80%:20% respectively. The style corpora are described in subsections 4.1.2 and 4.1.3. As supplementary data, we used much larger parallel paraphrases corpora described in subsection 4.1.1. Firstly, paraphrase data is required for producing high quality sentences. Secondly, the generated utterances must be properly *tuned* to the target style. In our experiments we searched for answers to the following questions.

1. How much style data is needed in multilingual training for style transformations of high quality?

2. How to automatically evaluate the major aspects of ST models? How to create a synthetic measure?

3. What elements are successful and what challenges remain when using transformer models for ST?

4.1 Data

4.1.1 Paraphrases data

For each task we built a large parallel corpus, used as supplementary data in model training. We treat these corpora as domain-unspecific and stylistically neutral. As sources, we used the paraphrases corpus presented in Wieting and Gimpel (2018), MultiNLI corpus (Williams et al., 2018), Quora Kaggle dataset (Quora, 2017) and Bible corpus (Carlson et al., 2018).

Name	Size (lines)	Task
Paraphrases	5,000,000	Netural-to-Cute, Modern-to-Antique
MultiNLI	16,329	Netural-to-Cute, Modern-to-Antique
Quora	145, 000	Neutral-to-Cute, Modern-to-Antique
Bible	1,339,891	Netural-to-Cute

Table 1: Parallel "paraphrases" corpora used in Neutral-to-Cute and Modern-to-Antique tasks.

In the M2A task we removed the Bible subcorpus from the dataset of paraphrases to perform the multi-task training with a small amount of style data (like in the N2C task).

4.1.2 Neutral-to-Cute data

The N2C training corpus contains 17k lines, some longer than one sentence. The efforts of searching for available cute person style corpora turned out to be ineffective. Thus, the set was created with the use of an internal crowdsourcing platform by educated linguists with academic background and experience in style transfer projects. In a series of tasks the linguists rewrote input ("neutral") sentences into "cute person" style unless they were "cute" enough (pairs with no change constituted 15% of the total set). The "cute style" was described as "informal", "positive", "superlative", "excited" and "slangy". The "cute style" was usually created by inserting an adequate "cute style" phrase, paraphrasing a fragment or the whole sentence. The generated corpus covered numerous genres, styles and topics, e.g. self-presentation, jokes, facts, small talk and anecdotes. We also created a 300 lines long test corpus with four "cute style" candidate answers for each input sentence. Linguists were asked to follow the same guidelines as in the training corpus creation task, and additionally to keep a degree of variation between the candidate answers. The same set of neutral sentences is used both for human and automatic evaluation.

4.1.3 Modern-to-Antique Bible data

The idea of using the Bible as a parallel corpus suitable for ST tasks was presented in Carlson et al. (2018). The authors claim that traditionally used sentence and verse demarcation makes for easy sentence alignment. The dataset consists of 8 public domain available Bible versions.[2] For the "antiquification" task's purpose, as the input we chose World English Bible (WEB, released in 2000), being the most stylistically modern version. As the target style, we chose King James Version (KJV, released in 1611), as it is one of the most influential English versions of the Bible, which perfectly shows the "majesty of style".

Using these sources, we built a 30 thousand verse long parallel WEB-KJV Bible corpus. We additionally sampled 300 verses of pairs for human and automatic evaluation. The automatic test set was built in the same way as the one used in the N2C task. Each input (WEB-style) was paired with a target-style (KJV) sentence and three candidate answers from other Bible translations: Darby's, Young's Literal Translation and American Standard Version. For human evaluation we selected 150 Bible verses (half of the automatic sample). Additionally, we test out-of-domain ST capability of the model by adding 150 "neutral style" small talk sentences, previously used in the N2C task, to the M2A test corpus.

---

[2] `https://github.com/keithecarlson/StyleTransferBibleData`

4.1.4 Lexical diversity

Additionally, we tested the lexical diversity of corpora used in both tasks. For this purpose we used MTLD (measure of textual lexical diversity) index (McCarthy, 2005; McCarthy and Jarvis, 2010) for our two tasks (see Table 2). We assume that higher MTLD scores are associated with higher topical and lexical diversity of "neutral" and "cute" corpora. This may indicate the higher difficulty of the N2C task.

We also measured the number of tokens, types (unique tokens), mean and standard deviation of number of sentences and tokens per line. The study revealed the difference between M2A and N2C tasks. In the M2A task, output (KJV style) has two times less sentences than input (WEB style) while maintaining similar (10% lower) number of tokens. In contrast, in the second task, "cute" style outputs tend to have 50% more sentences and 33% more tokens than "neutral" style sentences (inputs).

Corpus	Tokens	Types	MTLD	Mean sentences/line	Mean tokens/line	Median tokens/line
WEB 17k	359871	9461	54.88	2.26 ± 0.80	$32.65 \pm 12{,}36$	31
KJV 17k	346942	9469	54.18	1.12 ± 0.38	$29.52 \pm 12{,}63$	27
Neutral 17k	147190	10876	129.48	1.5 ± 0.87	12.89 ± 10.4	10
Cute 17k	186455	12648	156.11	1.94 ± 1.04	17.17 ± 11.32	15

Table 2: MTLD score for N2C and M2A corpora. The higher score indicates higher lexical diversity.

4.2 Human evaluation method

For human evaluation, a panel of three language experts was employed for each style. Every judge evaluated the same 300 transformations in four criteria, using Likert scale: 1 – very bad, 2 – unacceptable, 3 – flawed, but acceptable, 4 – good, with minor errors, 5 – very good.

The criteria covered four aspects.

- **Language**: the correctness of grammar, spelling, vocabulary usage, lack of unnecessary repetitions or loops, etc.
- **Quality**: semantics, fluency, comprehensibility, logic and the general "feel" of the sentence.
- **Content**: the degree of semantic similarity to the input sentence.
- **Style**: the appropriateness of style in the output sentence.

Our *Content* is similar to *Meaning Preservation* used in Callison-Burch (2008) and Rao and Tetreault (2018), while their *Fluency* is splitted into our *Language* and *Quality*.

The judges were instructed on how to understand the cute person and antique styles. All the sets were evaluated by the same panel of language experts, in order to preserve the common understanding of criteria and keep the results coherent. The judges were attended by the panel of two supervisors who verified their understanding of the criteria. All the evaluators had academic background in linguistics and at least Bachelor's Degree in this or related field.

The evaluated element was the transformation in relation to the input sentence. The examples below show that some transformation elements may produce parallelity of score values (compare Quality and Content). However, the opposite effect occurs as well – raising one score may cause lowering another one (compare Content and Style).

Score	Neutral-to-Cute	Modern-to-Antique
input	Neutral: *I don't want to scare you, but right now there is a skeleton inside you.*	Modern: *Let it be, when these signs have come to you, that you do what is appropriate for the occasion; for God is with you.*
styled output	Cute: *Wow, don't want to scare you, but right now there's a skeleton inside you. So cool, so I'm sure we can try again!*	Antique: *Let it be, when these signs be come unto thee, that thou doest ought for the occasion; for God is with thee.*
Language	5 – The sentence is linguistically correct.	3 – The output contains language mistakes.
Quality	4 – The sentence is logical and semantically correct, but the phrase added at the end is a bit semantically separated from the input meaning.	3 – Small semantic distortion (*ought* used incorrectly as a synonym to *appropriate*).
Content	3 – The score was lowered for the additional sentence introducing a little new meaning.	3 – Small error: incorrect introduction of the word *ought* as a synonym to *appropriate*.
Style	5 – The added phrase *wow* and the contraction *there's* are typical to the excited person style. Although unnecessarily introduced, the sentence which lowers the score for Content raises it for Style.	5 – The changes (*thee, thou, doest*) are compliant with the antique style.

Table 3: Examples of outputs with human evaluation scores.

The two 300-transformation sets (one for *neutral-to-cute* and one for *modern-to-antique*) were evaluated separately for all the trainings with various sizes of corpora (1k, 3k, 5k, 7k, 10k, 13k, 17k for both transformations plus 30k for M2A only) by three language experts and in four criteria (Language, Quality, Content and Style). It gives the total number of 54,000 single assessments.

We also measured the inter-annotator agreement using Krippendorff's alpha (Krippendorff, 2004) for each criterion and each task (see Table 4). The values in Krippendorff's alpha range from $\alpha = 0$ (perfect disagreement) to $\alpha = 1$ (perfect agreement). Customarily, $\alpha \geqslant 0.667$ is considered the minimum threshold for reliable annotation and $\alpha \geqslant 0.8$ is the optimal threshold (Krippendorff, 2004).

For three out of four criteria, inter-annotator agreement was higher in the M2A task. The agreement in Style assessment was significantly higher in the N2C task. We assume that this discrepancy is caused by the limited proficiency of judges in the biblical style.

Task	Language	Quality	Content	Style
Modern-to-Antique	0.715	0.774	0.829	0.683
Neutral-to-Cute	0.641	0.667	0.796	0.858

Table 4: Krippendorff's alpha for Neutral-to-Cute and Modern-to-Antique tasks human evaluation.

4.3 Human evaluation results

In this section we present the outcomes of our generative models for each dataset volume, focusing on the impact of the style data volume on style transformation quality. In order to prove the complexity of the problem, we adopted the proposed human evaluation measures (Language, Quality, Content and Style). As expected, dependencies between the target data volume used in models training and human measures statistics are not strictly linear. We can make an insight into this process. First, we focus on N2C transformations and then we move to Bible ST.

4.3.1 *Neutral-to-Cute* transformation

In Table 5 and in Figure 2 we present the study results for "cute person" data. We counted means and standard deviations of combined datasets of size $N = 900$, putting together the same three datasets of 300 sentences evaluated by independent linguists.

Corpus size	1k	3k	5k	7k	10k	13k	17k
Language (L): $\bar{x} \pm \sigma$	4.33 ± 1.07	**4.69 ± 0.76**	4.57 ± 0.88	4.67 ± 0.76	4.61 ± 0.89	4.58 ± 0.89	4.59 ± 0.91
Quality (Q): $\bar{x} \pm \sigma$	4.38 ± 1.08	**4.64 ± 0.84**	4.54 ± 0.95	4.64 ± 0.84	4.57 ± 0.96	4.50 ± 0.97	4.45 ± 1.04
Content (C): $\bar{x} \pm \sigma$	3.81 ± 1.48	**4.36 ± 1.16**	4.21 ± 1.28	4.27 ± 1.26	4.24 ± 1.25	3.99 ± 1.34	4.09 ± 1.31
Style (S): $\bar{x} \pm \sigma$	3.27 ± 1.72	3.37 ± 1.74	3.21 ± 1.80	3.52 ± 1.73	3.64 ± 1.65	3.92 ± 1.58	**4.04 ± 1.46**
Mean(L,C,S): $\bar{x} \pm \sigma$	3.81 ± 0.80	4.14 ± 0.74	4.00 ± 0.75	4.15 ± 0.71	4.17 ± 0.78	4.16 ± 0.78	**4.24 ± 0.76**
#(output=input): %	19.67%	27.33%	31.00%	26.67%	19.67%	13.67%	13.67%

Table 5: Human measures statistics of Neutral-to-Cute transformation across sizes of target corpora.

First of all, we notice that the scores for all datasets are quite high – above 3 for each human measure – including the smallest 1k style dataset. The lowest score, for Style (3.27) in the 1k style dataset, points that some transformations are stylistically flawed. The 3.81 score for Content shows that most of the generated sentences semantically reflect the input. The highest scores are those for Quality and Language – both over 4.30 – being more than good. The growth of the style dataset volume is also reflected by evaluation scores. The Style factor increases together with the data volume (except for the 5k set). The maximum Style score is 4.04 for the biggest 17k dataset, which demonstrates the high quality of style conversion. As opposed to the Style score, Language, Quality and Content do not improve with larger datasets sizes (between 7k and 17k). It may be due to the negative correlation between Style and the remaining human measures, which we analyze in section 4.4.

In Table 5 and in Figure 2 we added the average of arithmetic mean for Language, Content and Style (i.e. "Average human score"). Quality was omitted because its strong correlation with Language makes it too overlapping. The biggest difference in average human scores is between datasets 1k and 3k. The values for Content and Quality are lower for the largest volumes - 13k and 17k. The reason may be the specific N2C transformation, where more elaborate cute person phrases contrast with context-suitable

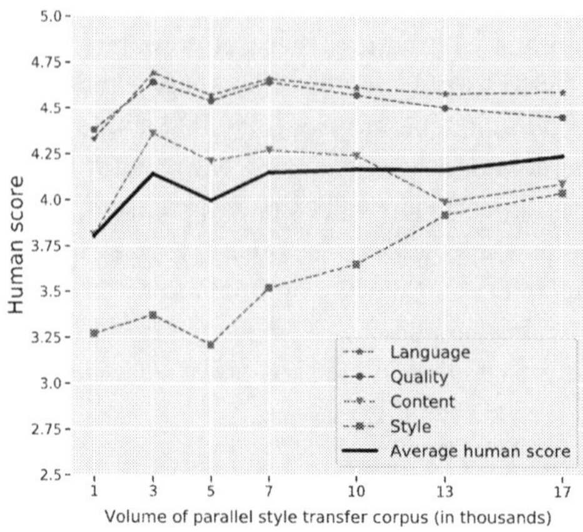

Figure 2: Human evaluation of Neutral-to-Cute transformation (legend: average human score is an arithmetic mean of Language, Content and Style).

ones. Closing the analysis, we also point out the repetition ratio of the input as the model output (the lower the better). The best results are for the largest datasets of 13k and 17k (13.67% in both cases – a bit below the mean of 15% in the training sets).

The following conclusions can be drawn from the N2C data transformation.

1. Style transformation is acceptable even for the 1k style dataset used for the multi-task training model.

2. For the 3k dataset there is the biggest growth in transformation quality, especially for vocabulary, semantics and logic (and smaller for style score).

3. The more style data we use, the better style transformation we obtain. The models trained with the datasets of 13k or larger, provide good quality with a low unchanged sentence ratio.

4.3.2 *Modern-to-Antique* transformation

In this part of the experiment we focus on the "antique" Bible style data as the model's output. We divided our evaluation into two tasks. In the first and main one we examine the evaluation where modern Bible data is used as the input. It is consistent with our model multi-task training, where besides the large corpus of paraphrases we take the style corpus of M2A Bible data. For this evaluation we use 150 sentences. As a supplementary test we employ the neutral dataset of 150 lines, similar to N2C data input. Table 6 and Figure 3 present the two evaluation studies.

Corpus size	1k	3k	5k	7k	10k	13k	17k	30k
Modern Bible input								
Language (L): $\bar{x} \pm \sigma$	3.68 ± 0.95	4.19 ± 0.93	4.29 ± 0.83	4.35 ± 0.86	4.58 ± 0.58	4.60 ± 0.63	4.62 ± 0.57	$\mathbf{4.64 \pm 0.56}$
Quality (Q): $\bar{x} \pm \sigma$	3.36 ± 1.21	4.29 ± 0.98	4.37 ± 0.85	4.38 ± 0.85	4.61 ± 0.62	$\mathbf{4.68 \pm 0.60}$	4.65 ± 0.63	4.66 ± 0.58
Content (C): $\bar{x} \pm \sigma$	3.08 ± 1.29	4.18 ± 1.07	4.27 ± 0.93	4.26 ± 1.02	4.44 ± 0.80	$\mathbf{4.57 \pm 0.74}$	4.45 ± 0.81	4.48 ± 0.77
Style (S): $\bar{x} \pm \sigma$	3.81 ± 1.19	4.38 ± 0.91	4.28 ± 1.04	$\mathbf{4.50 \pm 0.84}$	4.16 ± 0.95	4.17 ± 1.03	4.35 ± 0.88	4.44 ± 0.84
Mean(L,C,S): $\bar{x} \pm \sigma$	3.53 ± 0.86	4.25 ± 0.73	4.28 ± 0.69	4.37 ± 0.67	4.39 ± 0.53	4.45 ± 0.55	4.47 ± 0.52	$\mathbf{4.52 \pm 0.51}$
#(output=input): %	0.00%	0.67%	0.00%	1.33%	0.67%	2.00%	0.67%	0.67%
Neutral input								
Language (L): $\bar{x} \pm \sigma$	3.79 ± 1.11	4.12 ± 1.02	4.31 ± 0.97	4.34 ± 0.92	$\mathbf{4.59 \pm 0.72}$	4.50 ± 0.77	4.45 ± 0.82	4.43 ± 0.81
Quality (Q): $\bar{x} \pm \sigma$	3.52 ± 1.27	4.05 ± 1.14	4.18 ± 1.12	4.34 ± 0.93	$\mathbf{4.49 \pm 0.82}$	4.43 ± 0.84	4.38 ± 0.91	4.34 ± 0.95
Content (C): $\bar{x} \pm \sigma$	3.04 ± 1.44	3.85 ± 1.31	3.96 ± 1.29	$\mathbf{4.16 \pm 1.13}$	4.13 ± 1.12	4.07 ± 1.11	4.05 ± 1.15	4.06 ± 1.17
Style (S): $\bar{x} \pm \sigma$	3.20 ± 1.26	3.48 ± 1.42	3.16 ± 1.37	$\mathbf{3.59 \pm 1.42}$	3.25 ± 1.33	3.32 ± 1.41	3.30 ± 1.37	3.39 ± 1.35
Mean(L,C,S): $\bar{x} \pm \sigma$	3.34 ± 0.92	3.82 ± 0.85	3.81 ± 0.85	$\mathbf{4.03 \pm 0.79}$	3.99 ± 0.74	3.97 ± 0.71	3.93 ± 0.76	3.96 ± 0.79
#(output=input): %	2.67%	7.33%	10.67%	8.67%	7.33%	10.00%	7.33%	7.33%

Table 6: Human measures statistics of Modern-to-Antique transformation across sizes of target corpora.

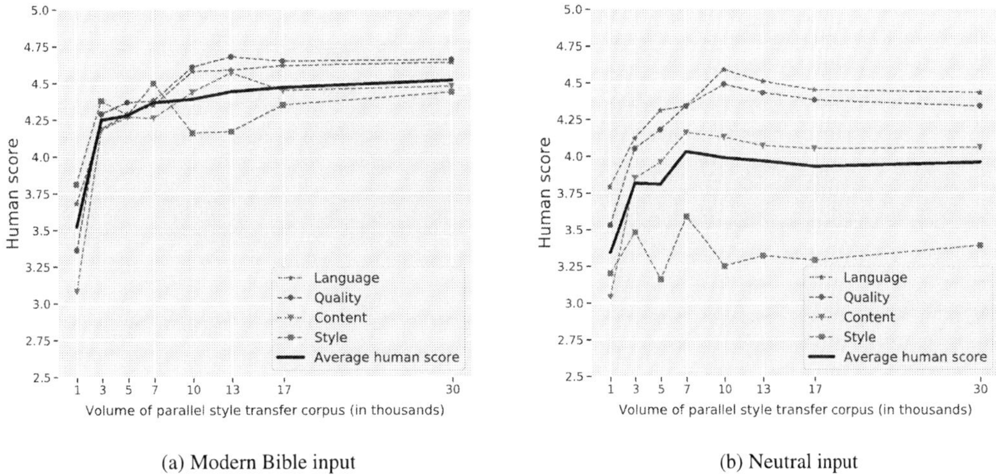

(a) Modern Bible input   (b) Neutral input

Figure 3: Human evaluation of models for Bible Modern-to-Antique transformation (legend: average human score is an arithmetic mean of Language, Content and Style).

Modern Bible input

Comparing curves of Bible and Cute style transformations we see significant differences, but also some similarities. Like for N2C models, in both Bible tests the biggest increase in quality is noticeable between the trainings with 1k and 3k style datasets. The modern Bible input data results are better than good for all human criteria for the model using the 3k style dataset. The Style rank reaches a maximum of 4.50 for the model with 7k Bible data volume. However, the most robust model, referring to the human average score, was trained using the biggest 30k style dataset, with the result of 4.52. The M2A transformation models bring a very low unchanged sentence ratio (0-2%), reflecting the training data proportions. We can notice the nonlinear dependency between the target dataset size and Style scores. However, the average of human scores behaves as expected – it grows with the size of style data used for training.

Neutral input

To some extent, we can treat our test with neutral input for the Bible models as another transfer learning experiment. Surprisingly, the results of this study are quite satisfactory. Although in many examples of the same model, human Style scores are even 1 point lower compared to the dedicated modern Bible input, they are still above 3. Like for modern Bible data, the highest Style mark (3.59) for neutral input was reached with the 7k dataset. Considering the human average score, the largest quality growth is between the models trained with 1k and 3k target datasets – 3.34 and 3.82 respectively. Evaluations for all the test samples show that the ratio of unchanged sentences, although higher than for modern Bible inputs, is still low or medium – between 2.67% and 10.67%.

The comparison of human measure curves on the left side (for modern Bible input) of Figure 3 with similar ones on the right side (for neutral input) shows a very interesting observation: Language and Quality marks have more or less similar values on both plots, while Style means are much lower in neutral input tests (from 0.61 up to 1.12 points). In this study Content for neutral input varies from being the same or slightly lower to being lower up to 0.5 points, compared to modern Bible data.

From this analysis, we draw the following conclusions for Bible data and hypotheses for other styles.

1. Multi-task models built using paraphrases and a small or medium amount of style data can easily generate lexicon and logic that are distinctive for style conversion even for unexpected input data.
2. Moreover, style and semantics are more difficult to generate by multi-task models when new input data differ significantly from training input style data. Though, the results are still acceptable.

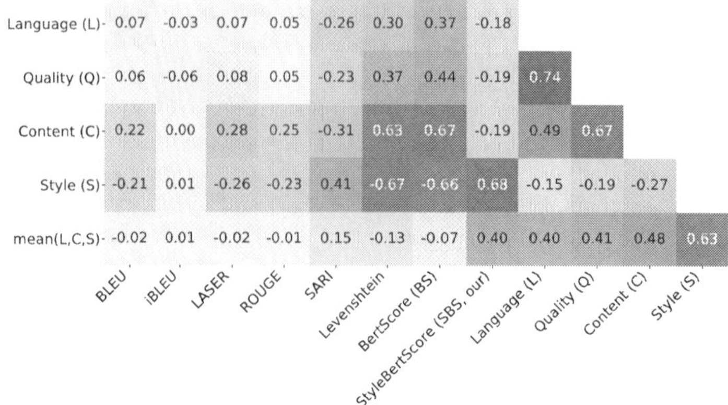

Figure 4: Spearman correlation between various NLP metrics and human judgment for N2C data.

4.4 Automated evaluation

Automated evaluation in text ST is a challenging task. Firstly, the full solution space cannot be clearly predefined (there are many ways of transferring style into a sentence). Secondly, the model should not only add style, but also maintain language correctness and preserve content. Additionally, stylizing text might be manifested in various language components (like syntax or lexis). It is difficult to reflect such multidimensional evaluation in any single synthetic score, especially when those aspects of assessment are poorly correlated or orthogonal.

We examined a few well-known automatic metrics in the NLP field. For computations we used Vizseq toolkit (Wang et al., 2019): BLEU, iBLEU, ROUGE-L, LASER; EASSE package (Alva-Manchego et al., 2019): SARI; python-Levenshtein package: Levenshtein ratio; BERTScore (Zhang et al., 2020). These measures correlate to some extent with human ranks in various tasks: MT (ST might be seen as translation within one language), summarization or text simplification (a special case of ST). In Figure 4 we present Spearman correlations between NLP measures and human scores for N2C transformation.

The analysis reveals a limited correlation of the human Style score with the most of checked measures (the biggest positive value is for SARI: 0.41). In our opinion, the tested ranks are not sufficient to estimate all the factors of style transfer. Thus, in this section, we propose an easy method to compose a synthetic style transfer measure that exhibits better correlation with human judgment than the already known measures, even at the cost of its universality. Due to limited space, we focus on N2C transformation only.

We decided to assemble our score from two factors: one capturing the stylistic aspect and the other covering the paraphrase quality. As the measure of paraphrases quality we chose BertScore (Zhang et al., 2020). It is a metric formed on the BERT model's contextual embeddings (Devlin et al., 2019), adequate for identifying semantic similarity between sentences. Moreover, it handles synonyms and spatial lexical dependencies. For those reasons, it has the strongest correlation with the linguistic Content score.

In order to facilitate the evaluation of the stylistic factor, we built a small classifier tool using BERT. We decided to use out-of-the-box torch-transformers[3], and only apply a fine-tuning step on top. From the validation sets we selected 6k-verse subsets (they were not used for the training in style transfer tasks) and built 12k datasets of balanced positive (target) and negative (neutral) styles. The classifier reached an accuracy of 0.77. We called its softmax StyleBertScore. We assumed that the average human score (the arithmetic mean of Style, Content and Language) can be approximated using BertScore and StyleBertScore. In order to combine scores we built a few regression models, from a simple mean, through linear regression, to ones capable of model complex relations: Random Forest and Support Vector Machine Regression (SVR) (Drucker et al., 1997). Figure 5 depicts the estimation results as a linear chart and a heatmap of correlations with human ranks. In our study, Random Forest has the biggest correlation (0.67) and the smallest mean square error (see Table 7).

---

[3] https://github.com/huggingface/transformers

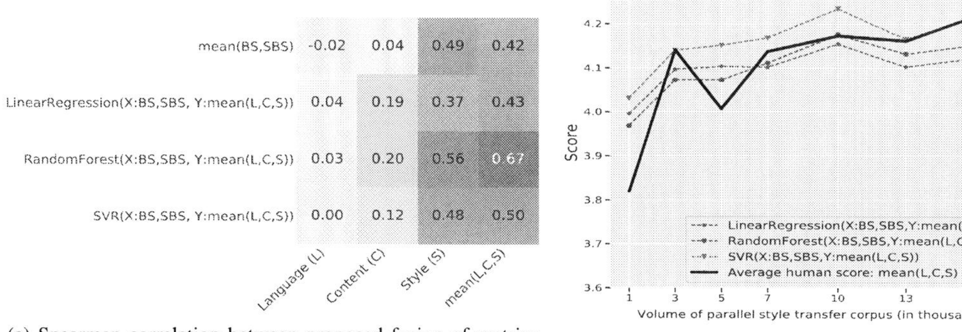

(a) Spearman correlation between proposed fusion of metrics and human scores (for Neutral-to-Cute evaluation data.)

(b) Regression models estimation of average human rank.

Figure 5: Regression methods for approximating the model score.

Our proposal for creation of automatic measure includes application of two machine learning models and some amount of human evaluation engagement. Although annotation is needed to calibrate the synthetic measure well, we need to make it only once for the whole process. Afterwards, created automatic model of the measure can be used to test many style transfer models without multiplication of human evaluation.

	Mean	Linear Regression	Random Forest	SVR
mean square error (MSE)	11.732	0.401	0.278	0.401

Table 7: Average mean square error (MSE) for each regression model.

We showed that a non-linear combination of the selected metrics (BertScore and StyleBertScore) can approximate the arithmetic mean of human scores and be a reliable method for assembling a style specific automatic measure. The novelty of our metric is that it is partly model dependent, though this results from the nature of the ST task.

5 Conclusions

We discussed the method of text style conversion with a multilingual transformer trained for two tasks: paraphrasing and style changing. We showed a successful approach using a large paraphrase parallel corpus with much less data of neutral-target style pairs. In our numerical experiments models trained with varying sizes of style samples were evaluated with four human scores (and their average), revealing nonlinear dependencies. For both studies, Neutral-to-Cute and Modern-to-Antique, we pointed out essential data volumes in models that brought acceptable and good results. In particular, we indicated the meaningful model performance growth between 1k and 3k sizes of target data. Moreover, the transfer learning ability of our multilingual generator was tested with a satisfying outcome for Neutral-to-Bible transformation (not seen during the model training). Finally, we proposed an easy method to automatically measure style transfer results and to approximate average human score with it. A new measure can be used during model training to estimate style transformation quality, besides checking a typical minimum of cross entropy loss function. In our opinion, this opportunity is worth further research.

References

Fernando Alva-Manchego, Louis Martin, Carolina Scarton, and Lucia Specia. 2019. EASSE: Easier automatic sentence simplification evaluation. In *Proceedings of the 2019 Conference on Empirical Methods in Natural Language Processing and the 9th International Joint Conference on Natural Language Processing (EMNLP-IJCNLP): System Demonstrations*, pages 49–54, Hong Kong, China, November. Association for Computational Linguistics.

Amazon. 2020. Samuel L. Jackson - celebrity voice skill for Alexa. *www.amazon.com/gp/product/B07WS3HN5Q*.

Mikel Artetxe, Gorka Labaka, and Eneko Agirre. 2018. Unsupervised statistical machine translation. In *Proceedings of the 2018 Conference on Empirical Methods in Natural Language Processing*, pages 3632–3642, Brussels, Belgium, Oct - Nov. Association for Computational Linguistics.

Dzmitry Bahdanau, Kyunghyun Cho, and Yoshua Bengio. 2014. Neural machine translation by jointly learning to align and translate.

I. A. Bolshakov and Alexander Gelbukh. 2004. Synonymous paraphrasing using wordnet and internet. In *Meziane F., Métais E. (eds) Natural Language Processing and Information Systems. NLDB 2004. Lecture Notes in Computer Science, vol 3136*, pages 312–323, 01.

Samuel R. Bowman, Luke Vilnis, Oriol Vinyals, Andrew Dai, Rafal Jozefowicz, and Samy Bengio. 2016. Generating sentences from a continuous space. In *Proceedings of The 20th SIGNLL Conference on Computational Natural Language Learning*, pages 10–21, Berlin, Germany, August. Association for Computational Linguistics.

Chris Callison-Burch. 2008. Syntactic constraints on paraphrases extracted from parallel corpora. In *Proceedings of the 2008 Conference on Empirical Methods in Natural Language Processing*, pages 196–205, Honolulu, Hawaii, October. Association for Computational Linguistics.

Keith Carlson, Allen Riddell, and Daniel Rockmore. 2018. Evaluating prose style transfer with the Bible. *Royal Society Open Science*, 5:171920, 10.

Rich Caruana. 1997. Multitask learning. *Mach. Learn.*, 28(1):41–75, July.

Junyoung Chung, Kyle Kastner, Laurent Dinh, Kratarth Goel, Aaron C Courville, and Yoshua Bengio. 2015. A recurrent latent variable model for sequential data. In C. Cortes, N. D. Lawrence, D. D. Lee, M. Sugiyama, and R. Garnett, editors, *Advances in Neural Information Processing Systems 28*, pages 2980–2988. Curran Associates, Inc.

Ronan Collobert and Jason Weston. 2008. A unified architecture for natural language processing: Deep neural networks with multitask learning. In *Proceedings of the 25th International Conference on Machine Learning*, ICML '08, page 160–167, New York, NY, USA. Association for Computing Machinery.

Alexis Conneau and Guillaume Lample. 2019. Cross-lingual language model pretraining. In *33rd Conference on Neural Information Processing Systems*.

Jacob Devlin, Ming-Wei Chang, Kenton Lee, and Kristina Toutanova. 2019. BERT: Pre-training of deep bidirectional transformers for language understanding. In *Proceedings of the 2019 Conference of the North American Chapter of the Association for Computational Linguistics: Human Language Technologies, Volume 1 (Long and Short Papers)*, pages 4171–4186, Minneapolis, Minnesota, June. Association for Computational Linguistics.

Harris Drucker, Christopher J. C. Burges, Linda Kaufman, Alex J. Smola, and Vladimir Vapnik. 1997. Support vector regression machines. In M. C. Mozer, M. I. Jordan, and T. Petsche, editors, *Advances in Neural Information Processing Systems 9*, pages 155–161. MIT Press.

T. Dryjański, P. Bujnowski, H. Choi, K. Podlaska, K. Michalski, K. Beksa, and P. Kubik. 2018. Affective natural language generation by phrase insertion. In *2018 IEEE International Conference on Big Data (Big Data)*, pages 4876–4882, Dec.

Ankush Gupta, Arvind Agarwal, Prawaan Singh, and Piyush Rai. 2018. A deep generative framework for paraphrase generation. In *Proceedings of the Thirty-Second AAAI Conference on Artificial Intelligence*, AAAI18. AAAI Publications.

Sepp Hochreiter and Jürgen Schmidhuber. 1997. Long short-term memory. *Neural computation*, 9(8):1735–1780.

Harsh Jhamtani, Varun Gangal, Eduard H. Hovy, and Eric Nyberg. 2017. Shakespearizing modern language using copy-enriched sequence-to-sequence models. *ArXiv*, abs/1707.01161.

Ye Jia, Yu Zhang, Ron J. Weiss, Quan Wang, Jonathan Shen, Fei Ren, Zhifeng Chen, Patrick Nguyen, Ruoming Pang, Ignacio Lopez Moreno, and Yonghui Wu. 2018. Transfer learning from speaker verification to multi-speaker text-to-speech synthesis.

Melvin Johnson, Mike Schuster, Quoc V. Le, Maxim Krikun, Yonghui Wu, Zhifeng Chen, Nikhil Thorat, Fernanda Viégas, Martin Wattenberg, Greg Corrado, Macduff Hughes, and Jeffrey Dean. 2017. Google's multilingual neural machine translation system: Enabling zero-shot translation. *Transactions of the Association for Computational Linguistics*, 5:339–351.

David Kauchak and Regina Barzilay. 2006. Paraphrasing for automatic evaluation. In *Proceedings of the Human Language Technology Conference of the NAACL, Main Conference*, pages 455–462, New York City, USA, June. Association for Computational Linguistics.

Klaus Krippendorff. 2004. Content analysis: An introduction to its methodology thousand oaks. *Calif.: Sage*.

T. Kudo and J. Richardson. 2018. Sentencepiece: A simple and language independent subword tokenizer and detokenizer for neural text processing.

Wuwei Lan, Siyu Qiu, Hua He, and Wei Xu. 2017. A continuously growing dataset of sentential paraphrases. In *Proceedings of the 2017 Conference on Empirical Methods in Natural Language Processing*, pages 1224–1234, Copenhagen, Denmark, September. Association for Computational Linguistics.

Juncen Li, Robin Jia, He He, and Percy Liang. 2018a. Delete, retrieve, generate: a simple approach to sentiment and style transfer. In *Proceedings of the 2018 Conference of the North American Chapter of the Association for Computational Linguistics: Human Language Technologies, Volume 1 (Long Papers)*, pages 1865–1874, New Orleans, Louisiana, June. Association for Computational Linguistics.

Zichao Li, Xin Jiang, Lifeng Shang, and Hang Li. 2018b. Paraphrase generation with deep reinforcement learning. In *Proceedings of the 2018 Conference on Empirical Methods in Natural Language Processing*, pages 3865–3878, Brussels, Belgium, October-November. Association for Computational Linguistics.

Philip M. McCarthy and Scott Jarvis. 2010. Mtld, vocd-d, and hd-d: A validation study of sophisticated approaches to lexical diversity assessment. *Behavior research methods*, 42(2):381–392.

Philip M. McCarthy. 2005. *An assessment of the range and usefulness of lexical diversity measures and the potential of the measure of textual, lexical diversity (MTLD)*. Ph.D. thesis, The University of Memphis.

Kathleen R. McKeown. 1983. Paraphrasing questions using given and new information. *American Journal of Computational Linguistics*, 9(1):1–10.

Xing Niu, Sudha Rao, and Marine Carpuat. 2018. Multi-task neural models for translating between styles within and across languages. In *Proceedings of the 27th International Conference on Computational Linguistics*, pages 1008–1021, Santa Fe, New Mexico, USA, August. Association for Computational Linguistics.

Myle Ott, Sergey Edunov, Alexei Baevski, Angela Fan, Sam Gross, Nathan Ng, David Grangier, and Michael Auli. 2019. fairseq: A fast, extensible toolkit for sequence modeling. In *Proceedings of NAACL-HLT 2019: Demonstrations*.

Aaditya Prakash, Sadid A. Hasan, Kathy Lee, Vivek Datla, Ashequl Qadir, Joey Liu, and Oladimeji Farri. 2016. Neural paraphrase generation with stacked residual LSTM networks. In *Proceedings of COLING 2016, the 26th International Conference on Computational Linguistics: Technical Papers*, pages 2923–2934, Osaka, Japan, December. The COLING 2016 Organizing Committee.

Ryan Prenger, Rafael Valle, and Bryan Catanzaro. 2018. Waveglow: A flow-based generative network for speech synthesis.

Chris Quirk, Chris Brockett, and William Dolan. 2004. Monolingual machine translation for paraphrase generation. In *Proceedings of the 2004 Conference on Empirical Methods in Natural Language Processing*, pages 142–149, Barcelona, Spain, July. Association for Computational Linguistics.

Quora. 2017. Quora question pairs.

Sudha Rao and Joel Tetreault. 2018. Dear sir or madam, may I introduce the GYAFC dataset: Corpus, benchmarks and metrics for formality style transfer. In *Proceedings of the 2018 Conference of the North American Chapter of the Association for Computational Linguistics: Human Language Technologies*, pages 129–140, New Orleans, Louisiana, June. Association for Computational Linguistics.

Aurko Roy and David Grangier. 2019. Unsupervised paraphrasing without translation. *Proceedings of the 57th Annual Meeting of the Association for Computational Linguistics.*

Samsung. 2019. Galaxy's Celebrity Alarm lets you personalize notification alerts with Celebrity Voices. *https://news.samsung.com/global/galaxys-celebrity-alarm-lets-you-personalize-notification-alerts-with-celebrity-voices.*

M. Schuster and K. K. Paliwal. 1997. Bidirectional recurrent neural networks. *Trans. Sig. Proc.*, 45(11):2673–2681, November.

Ilya Sutskever, Oriol Vinyals, and Quoc V. Le. 2014. Sequence to sequence learning with neural networks. In *Proceedings of the 27th International Conference on Neural Information Processing Systems - Volume 2*, NIPS'14, page 3104–3112, Cambridge, MA, USA. MIT Press.

Ashish Vaswani, Noam Shazeer, Niki Parmar, Jakob Uszkoreit, Llion Jones, Aidan N. Gomez, Lukasz Kaiser, and Illia Polosukhin. 2017. Attention is all you need. In *Proceedings of the 31st International Conference on Neural Information Processing Systems*, NIPS'17, page 6000–6010, Red Hook, NY, USA. Curran Associates Inc.

Stephen Wan, Mark Dras, Robert Dale, and Cécile Paris. 2005. Towards statistical paraphrase generation: Preliminary evaluations of grammaticality. In *Proceedings of the Third International Workshop on Paraphrasing (IWP2005).*

Tong Wang, Ping Chen, John Rochford, and Jipeng Qiang. 2016. Text simplification using neural machine translation. In *Proceedings of the Thirtieth AAAI Conference on Artificial Intelligence*, AAAI'16, page 4270–7271. AAAI Press.

Changhan Wang, Anirudh Jain, Danlu Chen, and Jiatao Gu. 2019. Vizseq: A visual analysis toolkit for text generation tasks. In *In Proceedings of the 2019 Conference on Empirical Methods in Natural Language Processing: System Demonstrations.*

John Wieting and Kevin Gimpel. 2018. ParaNMT-50M: Pushing the limits of paraphrastic sentence embeddings with millions of machine translations. In *Proceedings of the 56th Annual Meeting of the Association for Computational Linguistics (Volume 1: Long Papers)*, pages 451–462, Melbourne, Australia, July. Association for Computational Linguistics.

Adina Williams, Nikita Nangia, and Samuel Bowman. 2018. A broad-coverage challenge corpus for sentence understanding through inference. In *Proceedings of the 2018 Conference of the North American Chapter of the Association for Computational Linguistics: Human Language Technologies, Volume 1 (Long Papers)*, pages 1112–1122, New Orleans, Louisiana, June. Association for Computational Linguistics.

Sander Wubben, Antal van den Bosch, and Emiel Krahmer. 2012. Sentence simplification by monolingual machine translation. In *Proceedings of the 50th Annual Meeting of the Association for Computational Linguistics (Volume 1: Long Papers)*, pages 1015–1024, Jeju Island, Korea, July. Association for Computational Linguistics.

Wei Xu, Alan Ritter, Bill Dolan, Ralph Grishman, and Colin Cherry. 2012. Paraphrasing for style. In *Proceedings of COLING 2012*, pages 2899–2914. The COLING 2012 Organizing Committee, December.

Wei Xu, Courtney Napoles, Ellie Pavlick, Quanze Chen, and Chris Callison-Burch. 2016. Optimizing statistical machine translation for text simplification. *Transactions of the Association for Computational Linguistics*, 4:401–415.

Tianyi Zhang, Varsha Kishore, Felix Wu, Kilian Q. Weinberger, and Yoav Artzi. 2020. Bertscore: Evaluating text generation with bert. In *International Conference on Learning Representations.*

Shiqi Zhao, Xiang Lan, Ting Liu, and Sheng Li. 2009. Application-driven statistical paraphrase generation. In *Proceedings of the Joint Conference of the 47th Annual Meeting of the ACL and the 4th International Joint Conference on Natural Language Processing of the AFNLP*, pages 834–842, Suntec, Singapore, August. Association for Computational Linguistics.

Appendix: Style Transfer Results

Every judge evaluated the same 300 transformations in four criteria ("Language" – "L", "Quality" – "Q", "Content" – "C" and "Style" – "S") using Likert scale where 1 – very bad, 2 – unacceptable, 3 – flawed, but acceptable, 4 – good, with minor errors, 5 – very good.

"Bible" stands for Modern-to-Antique dataset. "Cute" refers to the Neutral-to-Cute set. For more information refer to the section 4 of the article.

Training Data	Input sentence	Styled Sentence	L	Q	C	S
Bible 30k	[Neutral] You're cool.	Thou art cool.	5	5	5	5
Bible 1k		Thou art cold!	5	5	2	4
Bible 30k	[Neutral] You should be a superhero and I'm your sidekick.	Thou shouldest be a superhero, and I am thy sidekick.	5	5	5	5
Bible 1k		Thou should be a fool and I am thy sidekhants.	3	3	1	4
Bible 30k	[Modern] My people, what have I done to you? How have I burdened you? Answer me!	My people, what have I done unto thee? how have I straitened thee? hear me.	4	4	3	5
Bible 1k		My people, what have I done unto thee? how hast I buried thee? Aneth me.	3	2	2	5
Bible 30k	[Modern] The fool's talk brings a rod to his back, but the lips of the wise protect them.	The fool's talk bringeth a rod to his back; but the lips of the wise defendeth them.	5	5	5	5
Bible 1k		The fool's speak bringeth a rod to his back, but the lips of the wise man keep them.	4	4	4	3
Bible 30k	[Modern] Where then is the boasting? It is excluded. By what kind of law? Of works? No, but by a law of faith.	Where then is the glorying? it is excluded. By what manner of law? No, but by the law of faith.	4	3	3	3
Bible 1k		Where is the boasting? It is removed from the law of Of works? but by a law of faith.	2	2	3	2
Cute 17k	Take care of yourself and see a doctor if needed.	Don't you worry, darling, take care of yourself and see a doctor if needed.	5	5	5	5
Cute 1k		take care of yourself and see a doctor if necessary.	4	5	5	2
Cute 17k	I don't know much about the president. What's your opinion?	Hey, sweetie! I don't know much about the president. What's your opinion? Cute one, huh?	5	5	5	5
Cute 1k		I don't know much about the president. What's your opinion?	5	5	5	1
Cute 17k	The name's Bond, James Bond. Just kidding, it's me.	haha, the name's Bond, James Bond. Just kidding, its me!	4	5	5	5
Cute 1k		No prob darling, just pick the name is Bond, James Bond, just kidding, it's me.	2	2	2	5
Cute 17k	Am I intelligent?	Seriously, I'm not that intelligent.	5	5	2	3
Cute 1k		Amazing that, sweetie'?	2	2	1	5
Cute 17k	Carpe diem.	Carpe totally diem	4	4	5	5
Cute 1k		Good Morning babe' u have been kinda quite on da' boat!	3	4	2	5

Best Practices for Data-Efficient Modeling in NLG:
How to Train Production-Ready Neural Models with Less Data

Ankit Arun,* Soumya Batra, Vikas Bhardwaj, Ashwini Challa,
Pinar Donmez, Peyman Heidari, Hakan Inan, Shashank Jain,
Anuj Kumar, Shawn Mei, Karthik Mohan, Michael White[†]

Facebook

{ankitarun, sbatra, vikasb, ashwinichalla,
   pinared, peymanheidari, inan, shajain,
anujk, smei, mkarthik, mwhite14850}@fb.com

Abstract

Natural language generation (NLG) is a critical component in conversational systems, owing to its role of formulating a correct and natural text response. Traditionally, NLG components have been deployed using template-based solutions. Although neural network solutions recently developed in the research community have been shown to provide several benefits, deployment of such model-based solutions has been challenging due to high latency, correctness issues, and high data needs. In this paper, we present approaches that have helped us deploy data-efficient neural solutions for NLG in conversational systems to production. We describe a family of sampling and modeling techniques to attain production quality with light-weight neural network models using only a fraction of the data that would be necessary otherwise, and show a thorough comparison between each. Our results show that domain complexity dictates the appropriate approach to achieve high data efficiency. Finally, we distill the lessons from our experimental findings into a list of best practices for production-level NLG model development, and present them in a brief runbook. Importantly, the end products of all of the techniques are small sequence-to-sequence models (~2Mb) that we can reliably deploy in production.

1 Introduction

Task-oriented dialog systems are commonplace in automated systems that interact with end users, including digital assistants, technical support agents, and various website navigation helpers. An essential part in any task-oriented dialog system is *natural language generation* (NLG), which consumes data, typically fed in the form of a *dialog act*, and converts it into natural language output to be served to the end user. The natural language response of the NLG component should 1) contain all essential information, 2) be contextualized around the user request, and 3) be natural sounding. Such a system requires consideration for content planning, correctness, grammaticality, and naturalness.

NLG systems employed in commercial settings are typically based on template-based text generation techniques (Reiter and Dale, 2000; Gatt and Krahmer, 2018; Dale, 2020). In these, humans author a minimal set of responses templates with placeholder slot values. These slots are later filled at runtime, with the dialog input. Although template-based NLG modules are appealing due to their deterministic nature, inherent correctness, and low latency, they have major drawbacks: First, separate templates need to be authored for different response variations; this behavior is unfavorable for scaling. Second, templates authored for a particular domain are commonly not reusable. Lastly, no matter the complexity of the language instilled into templates, they form a strictly discrete set of responses, and therefore are bound to be limited in their response naturalness.

More recently, advances in neural-network-based (conditional) language generation prompted a new direction in NLG research (Novikova et al., 2017; Budzianowski et al., 2018; Chen et al., 2020; Bal-

---

*Author list alphabetical by last name.

[†] Work done while on leave from Ohio State University.

Proceedings of the 28th International Conference on Computational Linguistics: Industry Track, pages 64–77
Barcelona, Spain (Online), December 12, 2020

akrishnan et al., 2019; Peng et al., 2020). The process is typically split into two steps: (1) serialization of input data into a flattened meaning representation (MR), and (2) using the neural generation model to generate a natural language response conditioned on the MR. The models are trained on data that includes ⟨MR, response⟩ pairs, and therefore they are able to not only generate desired responses for MRs in their training data, but they are also expected to form coherent responses for novel MRs, owing to the generalization ability of their machine learning (ML) backbone.

However, deploying neural NLG systems in an industry setting is quite challenging. First, it is not trivial to train a model that reliably presents its input data with the high fidelity required from a user-serving dialog system. Second, the models require much high-quality human-annotated data, which is resource intensive. Consequently, data annotation is a major limiting factor for scaling model-based NLG across domains and languages.

In this work, we detail our approach to production-level neural NLG, with a focus on scalability and data efficiency. Adopting the tree-structured MR framework introduced in Balakrishnan et al. (2019), which allows better control over generated responses, we train sequence-to-sequence RNN models (Sutskever et al., 2014; Bahdanau et al., 2014; Cho et al., 2014) that can produce high-fidelity responses. We then employ a multitude of techniques for reducing the amount of required data, primarily powered by eliminating the "hidden" redundancy by grouping data points with similar semantics into *buckets*. We train models either on the reduced data, or after increasing the size of the dataset using a novel synthetic augmentation technique. We also employ large, pre-trained attention-based language models (Lewis et al., 2019), fine-tuning them on the same datasets, and then using novel methods to distill their knowledge into smaller sequence-to-sequence models. Further, we train models on data from multiple domains, showing gains over models trained on individual domains when the domains are semantically close together. We conclude with a compiled list of best practices for production-level NLG model development based on our analyses, and we present it as a runbook.

2   Related Work

NLG from structured data has been an active research area for decades, facilitated of late by datasets like the E2E Challenge (Novikova et al., 2017), MultiWoz (Budzianowski et al., 2018) and Conversational Weather (Balakrishnan et al., 2019). Recently, Seq2Seq models (Wen et al., 2015; Dušek and Jurcıcek, 2016; Balakrishnan et al., 2019; Rao et al., 2019), have become popular for their superior naturalness and simplicity. These models have achieved high performance on benchmarks like E2E challenge (Novikova et al., 2017) and WebNLG challenge (Gardent et al., 2017). However, they require a lot of data making them resource-intensive to stand up and manage at scale.

Our work introduces an approach for bootstrapping data-efficient NLG models by auto-annotating unlabelled examples using a large pretrained sequence de-noiser model known as BART (Lewis et al., 2019) fine-tuned on a small annotated dataset. Additionally, to increase data collection efficiency, we present several bucketing strategies, which enable a more uniform data collection process over the possible semantic space. We improve upon the BART auto-annotation technique by combining it with an innovative method of dynamic data-augmentation (DDA) and fine-tuning BART auto-annotation on a small subset of data sampled using a medium grained bucketing approach. We also carried out experiments to examine the effects of bucketing granularity combined with domain complexity.

In similar studies, pretrained GPT models (Radford et al., 2019) were used by Chen et al. (2020) and Peng et al. (2020), who fine-tune them on a small set of in-domain data, but they did not distill these models into ones suitable for production.

Interestingly, Wen et al. (2016) demonstrated that the structure of arguments in existing dialogues can be used to guide data collection for low-resource domain adaptation, which is similar to the bucketing strategies explored here. Additionally, Shah et al. (2018) introduce a dialogue self-play method where templates are instantiated with database values to create synthetic utterances, similar to our dynamic data-augmentation method; however, their instantiated templates are then rewritten by crowd-workers, whereas in our DDA method, crowd-sourced utterances are delexicalized and then re-instantiated with random values. Kedzie & McKeown (2019) also make use of a similar technique in their work on

Domain	# of Training	# of CB	# of MB	# of FBQ	# of FB	# of Validation	# of Test
Weather	25390	2240	6406	20343	15456	3078	3121
Reminder	9716	68	562	1907	739	2794	1397
Time	5530	18	288	863	330	1529	790
Alarm	7163	26	126	286	188	2024	1024

Table 1: Number of examples in training, validation, and test sets for all domains in addition to number of different buckets in the training set. CB, MB, FBQ, and FB stand for coarse-grained, medium-grained, fine-grained combined with query, and fine-grained buckets, respectively.

self-training for neural NLG; by comparison, we experiment with DDA in a wider variety of training scenarios.

3 Experimental Approach

3.1 Data

The experiments were conducted using 4 task-oriented datasets: a Conversational Weather dataset introduced in Balakrishnan et al. (2019) and three additional datasets for the Reminder, Time, and Alarm domains. These four datasets were selected due to their varying level of complexity, which will be explained further in the results section.[1] In addition, these domains provide a good representation of various arguments such as tense, date_time, and date_time_range as well as range queries that are typically seen across conversational systems. Descriptive statistics of the datasets are shown in Table 1.

All of the datasets use a tree structure to store the meaning representation (MR) that has been discussed in Balakrishnan et al. (2019). If necessary, they use discourse relations (CONTRAST and JUSTIFY), which encompass a possible list of dialog acts (REQUEST, INFORM, etc.). The dialog acts contain a list of slot key-value pairs to be mentioned. The tree structures are used to present semantic information to the models after flattening. Examples of flattened MRs are shown in Table 2 and Table 3. The synthetic user queries and scenarios were generated by engineers, the annotated responses were created by human annotators following guidelines written by computational linguists. The responses were verified to be grammatical and correct by the linguists to ensure data quality.

Query	How is the weather over the next weekend?
Reference	Next weekend expect a low of 20 and a high of 45. It will be sunny on Saturday but it'll rain on Sunday.

Our MR (Tree-based Scenario)	`INFORM_1[temp_low[20] temp_high[45] date_time[colloquial[ next weekend ]]]`
	`CONTRAST_1[`
	    `INFORM_2[condition[ sun ] date_time[weekday[ Saturday ]]]`
	    `INFORM_3[condition[ rain ] date_time[weekday[ Sunday ]]]`
	`]`

Annotated Reference	`INFORM_1[ date_time[colloquial[next weekend]] expect a low of temp_low[20]`
	    `and a high of  temp_high[45] .]`
	`CONTRAST_1[`
	    `INFORM_2[ it will be condition[sunny] date_time[ on weekday[Saturday]]]`
	    `but`
	    `INFORM_3[ it'll condition[rain] date_time[ on weekday[Sunday]]]`
	`.]`

Table 2: A training example with a discourse relation (bold black node). Blue nodes are the dialog acts, red nodes are the first level arguments under dialog acts and orange nodes are the second level arguments. Argument values at the leaf nodes and terminal tokens are in black.

3.2 Bucketing

All our datasets present tree-structured input. We found the tree structure helpful in grouping the training examples in order to reduce biases in the model-generated responses because of imbalanced distribution and also to improve data efficiency. We investigated several bucketing strategies that assign scenarios into groups based on their tree structures and argument values at different levels of granularity. During data collection, we observed that compared to random, bucket-assisted gradual data collection improved model performance due to more exhaustive MR coverage.

---

[1]The datasets can be found at https://github.com/facebookresearch/DataEfficientNLG

Query	Do I have any reminder to buy milk?
Reference	Yes, there are 3 reminders. The first two are, buy milk at 7 PM and tomorrow. There's 1 other reminder.

Our MR (Scenario)	`INFORM_1[amount[ 3 ]]`
	`INFORM_2[todo[ buy milk ] date_time[time[ 7 pm ]]]`
	`INFORM_3[todo[ buy milk ] date_time[colloquial[ tomorrow ]]]`
	`INFORM_4[amount_remaining[1]]`

Annotated Reference	`INFORM[Yes, there are amount[ 3 ] reminders .]`
	`INFORM[The first two are, todo[ buy milk ]at date_time[time[ 7 pm ]]]`
	and `INFORM[date_time[colloquial[ tomorrow ]].]`
	`INFORM[ There's amount_remaining[ 1 ] other reminder.]`

Delexicalized Query	Do I have any reminder to todo__a ?

Coarse_grained Bucket Hash	`INFORM_1[amount]`
	`INFORM_2[todo date_time]`
	`INFORM_3[todo date_time]`
	`INFORM_4[amount_remaining]`

Medium_grained Bucket Hash	`INFORM_1[amount]`
	`INFORM_2[todo date_time[time]]`
	`INFORM_3[todo date_time[colloquial[ tomorrow ]]]`
	`INFORM_4[amount_remaining]`

Fine_grained Bucket Hash	`INFORM_1[amount[ amount__gr1 ]]`
	`INFORM_2[todo[ todo__a ] date_time[time[ time__a ]]]`
	`INFORM_3[todo[ todo__a ] date_time[colloquial[ tomorrow ]]]`
	`INFORM_4[amount_remaining[ amount_remaining_eq1 ]]`

Table 3: A training example from the reminder domain with its corresponding coarse_grained, medium_grained and fine_grained buckets. There are no discourse relations.

Coarse-grained (CB) This bucketing strategy was the coarsest level of granularity. Under this strategy, the scenarios (MRs) are grouped using high-level argument names, which are at most two levels below the root node. For example, consider a second level argument such as date_time that may have multiple nested arguments in different combinations.

In Coarse-grained bucketing, all variations deeper than date_time were ignored. An example is shown in Table 3, where in both the INFORM_1 and INFORM_2 dialog acts, despite different sub-arguments for the parent argument date_time, variations are ignored. This strategy creates the smallest number of buckets. In spite of the high possible data efficiency using this method, models might exhibit worse performance due to limited MR coverage in the training data.

Medium-grained (MB) At this level of granularity, all sub-arguments were considered for creation of the bucket hashes. However, for certain pre-determined arguments/sub-arguments with small and finite variation, the argument name was replaced with its value. An example is the argument tense, which has 3 possible values; hence, when creating bucket hashes, we replace the tense argument with tense_past, tense_present, or tense_future. This led to an increase in the bucketing space by the number of possible values for each such argument.

In contrast to coarse-grained bucketing, the INFORM_2 and INFORM_3 dialog acts are grouped under different buckets as part of this strategy, since the date_time parent argument has different sub-arguments. Moreover, for the INFORM_3 dialog act, the value of sub-argument colloquial is retained. This implies that if there was another dialog act with the same shape as INFORM_3 dialog act but a different value for the colloquial sub-argument, it would have been grouped into a different bucket than INFORM_3. This strategy increased the number of buckets compared to the CB case, improving coverage of different response variations. An example of medium-grained bucket hash appears in Table 3.

Fine-grained (FB & FBQ) In this strategy, the goal was to group cases into the largest possible number of buckets in which the surface form of the sentence was independent of the argument values decided by linguists (FB). There were three major differences compared with the medium-grained approach: all argument values are considered, with partial delexicalization; argument values under the same argument name can be grouped; and uniqueness of argument values was tracked. For example, as shown in Table 3, all argument values are considered, where the todo values are delexicalized, while colloquial is not. In addition, if the value of `amount` or `amount_remaining` is 1, then the surface form of the response might change, since a plural form should be used for numbers more than 1. Therefore, there are two groups of these argument values, one for values greater than 1 and one for the value of 1. Finally, the `todo` argument values in `INFORM_1` and `INFORM_2` are the same. Therefore, they are both delexicalized to `todo__a`, which is to differentiate between cases where the `todos` are different, since the model was allowed to aggregate based on arguments values to limit verbosity and increase naturalness. (If the values of `todos` were different, they would have been delexicalized to `todo__a` and `todo__b`, resulting in a different bucket hash.)

Our production models receive as input a combination of query and MR, in order to enable the possibility of conditioning the surface form of the response based on the query. Therefore, an additional level of bucketing can be achieved by delexicalizing the query (FBQ). For example, in Table 3, the user has asked about a specific reminder, and the response confirms that by saying "Yes" at the beginning. (Saying "Yes" might have been unnecessary under a different query.) Since the queries in the datasets were generated synthetically, we could reliably delexicalize the query and consider the delexicalized query during bucket hash creation.

3.3 Metrics

We used various metrics to compare the performance of our proposed sampling and modeling approaches across experiments. Mainly, we focused on *Tree Accuracy*, which is a binary metric indicating whether the tree structure in the response is correct (Balakrishnan et al., 2019). This metric checks whether the structural tokens in the response are the same as those in the input MR, modulo reordering at the sibling level (see Balakrishnan et al.'s paper for complete details). Tree accuracy is also used in production to guard against hallucination: if tree accuracy fails, we fall back on templates to ensure correct response generation, even if it is less natural. In addition, we report *BLEU Score* (Papineni et al., 2002) for all of the experiments.

Tree Accuracy is a binary metric and can change from 1 to 0 even if one structural token is missing, as intended. We noticed that tree accuracy can fluctuate considerably due to the random initialization of the layer weights and the randomization in mini-batch creation, even if trained on the same dataset with the same training parameters. (This might be due to the fact that the models are trained to optimize for token-level likelihood, not correctness.) To track the effectiveness of the proposed approaches in reducing these fluctuations and increasing *Robustness*, we report the standard deviation of tree accuracy values based on 5 training instances for each experiment. The reported tree accuracy values for each experiment is the maximum one achieved in the same 5 runs.

Human evaluations were used as a qualitative method to raise red-flags in this study. For human evaluation, the authors rated the responses on Correctness and Grammaticality, defined as:

- **Correctness:** Evaluates semantic correctness of a response. Authors check for hallucinations, missing attributes, attribute aggregation and sentence structure.

- **Grammaticality:** Checks for grammatical correctness of a sentence, which includes subject-verb agreement, word order, completeness, etc.

We report an *Acceptability* metric, which is the proportion of correct and grammatical responses sent for human evaluation. Due to annotator constraints, we devised a method to select the top 150 most differentiating examples from each domain's test set, in order to provide an understanding of the performance of each approach on the most challenging MRs. First, we categorized all of the test samples using the fine-grained (FB) bucketing technique. Then, for each bucket, the sample with the least number of correct (tree accuracy) responses across all of the experiments was selected if at least one approach responded correctly. Finally, the top 150 buckets with the least correct response were selected.

In our experience, if a model output fails the tree accuracy check it has always been wrong, but passing tree accuracy does not guarantee acceptability. Nonetheless, it should be noted that the reported acceptability numbers are significantly worse than with our production models, as they are focused on the most challenging MRs. The production weather models have had very high acceptability, so we do not report acceptability for the Weather domain due to some bandwidth constraints.

To compare data-efficiency, we defined *Data Reduction Rate* as the percentage of the initial training examples that can be saved (not used for training) using any of the presented approaches.

3.4 Models

The model architectures used in this study are either a sequence-to-sequence one with stacked LSTMs (Bahdanau et al., 2014) or derivatives of BART (Lewis et al., 2019) with stacked transformers.

In the LSTM-based models, we use trainable $50d$ GloVe (Pennington et al., 2014) embeddings. Model weight are updated using an ADAM optimizer (Kingma and Ba, 2015). For each experiment, we start with a learning rate of 0.01 and reduce it by a factor of 0.1 if validation loss does not decrease for 2 epochs. Our loss function is label smoothed CrossEntropy, where the beta parameter is between [0.01, 1]. Each model was trained for 100 epochs with a batch size of 32 and terminated when the validation loss stopped decreasing for 5 epochs.

For BART, we use the 6 layer BART-Base model in fp16 mode. This helps avoid the memory issues, which were faced with using the 12 layer BART model. For each experiment, we use ADAM as our optimizer with 300 warm-up steps. The starting learning rate of 3e-5 is reduced by a factor of 0.5 if validation loss does not decrease for 5 epochs. Each model is trained for 100 epochs with a batch size of 4 and terminated when the validation loss stopped decreasing for 7 epochs. With all models we use a beam size of 1 to decrease latency.

LSTM-based Sequence-to-Sequence Model (S2S)   Our main LSTM-based model has a single-layer encoder and a single-layer decoder. The dimensions of both encoder and decoder hidden states are set to 128 with 0.2 dropout. The input to the model is a concatenation of the user query and the meaning representation produced by the dialog management system.

Joint-training (JT)   We experimented with a simple joint-training strategy for domains with similar responses, MRs, and semantics using the S2S architecture. The datasets were combined and a joint model was trained on them. Here, Alarm and Reminder are the two domains that are similar to each other and thus these were the domains we experimented with for joint-training.

Dynamic Data Augmentation (DDA)   To increase data efficiency, we carried out experiments using a limited number (1,3,5) of examples per bucket (coarse, medium, and fine) to determine at what training size the performance gains would plateau with more data collection. At very high data efficiency levels, we noticed that the model performance fluctuated significantly based on the argument values, which was unacceptable for a production system.

An initial idea was to pre-process the input and feed the delexicalized query and MR to the model. Although we could reliably delexicalize the user query during model training, it would have been very unstable to implement such a technique in production. In addition, there were concerns about added latency and higher complexity of the system. Therefore, we trained the model with the raw user query and with an MR in which argument values are lexicalized, which originally resulted in low data-efficiency in our production domains.

Epoch 1	**Augmented Query**	Do I have any reminder to go shopping ?

	Augmented MR	`INFORM_1[amount[ 8 ]]`
		`INFORM_2[todo[ go shopping ] date_time[time[ 10 AM ]]]`
		`INFORM_3[todo[ go shopping ] date_time[ colloquial[ tomorrow ]]]`
		`INFORM_4[amount_remaining[ 1 ]]`

Epoch 2	**Augmented Query**	Do I have any reminder to run ?

	Augmented MR	`INFORM_1[amount[ 4 ]]`
		`INFORM_2[todo[ run ] date_time[time[ 6 PM ]]]`
		`INFORM_3[todo[ run ] date_time[ colloquial[ tomorrow ]]]`
		`INFORM_4[amount_remaining[ 1 ]]`

Table 4: Two examples of how a single training example is augmented randomly at each epoch.

We devised Dynamic Data Augmentation (DDA) as a new technique to provide robust model response with respect to changes in argument values using only a fraction of human-annotated responses. The idea is to randomly replace pre-processed tokens in the leaf nodes such as `todo_a`, `time_a`, etc.—as shown in the fine-grained example in Table 3—with a value from a list of possible values, which are not expected to change the surface form of the sentence during mini-batch creation.

We used DDA to train on small datasets formed by sampling one or fewer examples per fine-grained bucket. In addition to higher data efficiency, such randomization should theoretically reduce the possibility of over-fitting. Similarly, DDA enables the 1PerBucket sampling technique in low-resource domains, resulting in a more uniform distribution of MR types during training. If the delexicalized query and MR shown in Table 3 are included in the training data, Table 4 demonstrates how DDA would augment the example differently at each epoch.

BART Data Augmentation (BART+DDA)   In BART auto-annotation, a small subset of data is sampled by selecting one example from each medium-grained bucket, followed by fine-tuning the BART model directly on this dataset. The fine-tuned BART model is then run on unlabelled scenario data, as part of the sequence-level knowledge distillation step described in the next section (S2S+KD), and the examples which match in tree structure with the input scenario are selected for training data augmentation. Sampling the small data using medium-grained bucketing introduces two issues. Firstly, although most response variations can be captured, the variations where words around argument slots change depending upon the argument value might be missed. Secondly, model performance is not robust to varying argument values.

DDA solves both the above issues. In the BART+DDA approach, instead of directly fine-tuning the BART model on a small data, we fine-tune it on the dynamically augmented data.

S2S+KD   BART+DDA suffers from high latency and model size. In an effort to create production-quality models, we run the BART+DDA model on unlabelled scenario inputs, and select examples which match in tree structure. To auto-annotate unlabelled scenarios, we run a beam search of following beam sizes [1, 5, 10], and select the first response which passes the tree accuracy check. With larger beam sizes, even if the lower responses pass the tree accuracy, they often tend to be incorrect.

We then combine the synthetically generated examples labelled by BART with the golden human-labelled small data, and train a S2S model on it. Using BART as a teacher model to train a smaller, faster S2S model is similar to Kim and Rush's (2016) sequence-level knowledge distillation (KD) approach.

S2S+KD+DDA   The S2S+KD model can make mistakes because the majority of its training data comes from synthetic data generated by the BART+DDA model. If the BART+DDA model makes a mistake on a particular scenario, these mistakes get amplified because it will be repeated when auto-annotating similar unlabelled scenarios. Even if golden human data has the correct response for these scenarios, it might not be enough to correct these mistakes. With S2S+KD+DDA, we solve this problem by fine-tuning the S2S+KD model using the DDA approach only on the gold human-labelled small data, as in recent self-training work for MT (He et al., 2020).

4   Results and Discussion

The results of selected experiments on Alarm, Time, Reminder and Weather domains are presented in Tables 5, 6, 7, and 8, respectively. More comprehensive experimental results can be found in the Appendix. In addition, Figure 1 demonstrates comparative plots of all experiments with more than 70.0% tree accuracy and a 70.0% data reduction rate. From a pure data reduction point of view, the results suggest that S2S+KD+DDA and S2S+KD performed the best followed by BART+DDA. S2S+DDA generally improved performance compared to S2S trained on the same data. It can be also observed that joint domain training can improve performance compared to training only on the in-domain data.

The methods proposed and applied in the paper vary significantly in term of complexity and engineering effort needed to execute them. Therefore, we will analyze the results in each domain considering ease of use and scalability, with the major focus still on data reduction while maintaining performance.

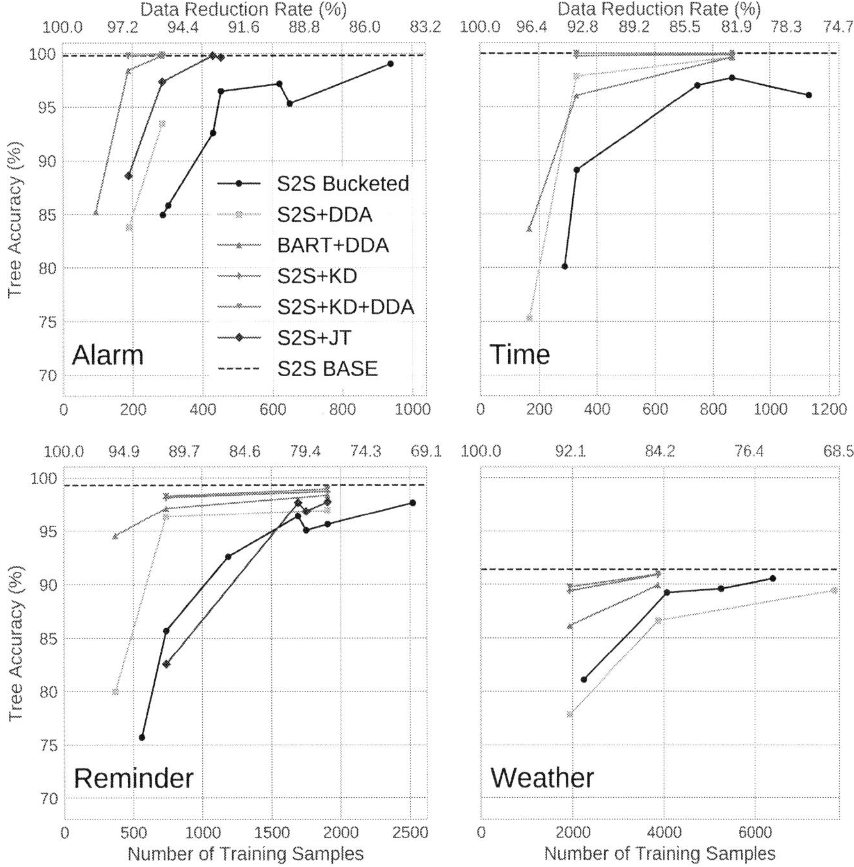

Figure 1: Change of tree accuracy vs. training data size and data reduction for the proposed approaches.

BART+DDA, S2S+KD and S2S+KD+DDA improved the performance in all of the domains. However, deploying them to production was not justified for all the domains due to higher development and maintenance resources required. Specifically, BART+DDA has very high latency. S2S+KD and S2S+KD+DDA provide similar latency as the S2S variants. However, they require multiple engineering steps including training 3 models sequentially: First, fine-tune a BART+DDA model on a small dataset, followed by auto-annotating large amounts of unlabelled data for augmentation. Finally, S2S+KD and S2S+KD+DDA are trained sequentially on the augmented dataset.

It is also not trivial to create non-annotated query and MR pairs for a new domain. Language expansion may also prove difficult as the cross-lingual mBART (Liu et al., 2020) is only available for 25 languages, and cross-lingual extension of the auto-annotation techniques should be verified. KD variants are mostly beneficial where the required resources for annotating more data are high. Moreover, the gap between KD variants and S2S+DDA might diminish with the addition of 500-1000 examples. The balance between the required data annotation resources and the required engineering resources should be considered during approach selection based on the domain complexity.

4.1 Alarm Domain

Alarm was the least complex domain studied here. There were only 286 fine-grained (1PerFBQ) buckets, which were reduced to 188 buckets after the variation in user query was ignored (1PerFB). As shown in Table 5 and Figure 1, S2S Bucketed (1PerCB, 1PerMB, 1PerFB, and 1PerFBQ) experiments did not perform as well as other approaches. Interestingly, S2S+DDA did not perform as well as in other domains, which was probably due to the extremely low training data size in Alarm. However, combining Alarm with Reminder data improved the performance considerably (S2S+JT). S2S+JT tree accuracy

Data	Approach	BLEU Score	Tree Accuracy	Acceptability	Data Reduction	TreeAcc STDev
ALL	S2S BASE	93.3	99.8	-	0.0	0.1
5PerMB+Reminder	S2S+JT	92.7	**99.6**	93.8	**93.7**	1.3
1PerFBQ+Reminder	S2S+JT	92.6	97.6	83.5	96.1	2.8
1PerFBQ	S2S	91.6	85.0	67.0	96.1	16.2
1PerFB	S2S	92.3	91.8	75.0	97.4	28.6
1PerFBQ	S2S+DDA	92.7	93.4	77.3	96.1	14.3
1PerFB	BART+DDA	92.8	98.4	90.7	97.4	10.0
1PerFB	S2S+KD	93.2	99.8	92.8	97.4	0.1
1PerFB	S2S+KD+DDA	93.2	99.8	93.8	97.4	0.1

Table 5: Results on selected Alarm domain experiments in percentage.

reached within 0.2% of the S2S BASE case with a data reduction rate of 93.7%. The KD variants had the highest performance but they required higher development and maintenance resources.

4.2 Time Domain

Time was the second simplest domain in this study. There were 860 fine-grained buckets, which were reduced to 330 buckets when the variation in user query was ignored. However, Time was unique in having tense as an argument which could result in errors that could pass tree accuracy.

S2S Bucketed (1PerCB, 1PerMB, 1PerFB, and 1PerFBQ) showed significantly lower performance both in terms of tree accuracy and acceptability compared to the S2S BASE experiment. S2S+DDA with 1PerFBQ data achieved tree accuracy of 99.6%, which was just 0.4% lower than S2S BASE (Figure 1). In addition, S2S+DDA represented a data reduction of 85.0%. Similar to Alarm, the KD variants perform the best but they require higher engineering resources.

4.3 Reminder Domain

Reminder was the second most complex domain with more than 1900 fine-grained buckets (1PerFBQ). As shown in Table 7 and Figure 1, S2S Bucketed experiments with limited data (1PerCB, 1PerMB, 1PerFB, and 1PerFBQ) significantly under performed compared to the S2S BASE case. S2S+DDA with 1PerFB achieve tree accuracy of 96.3% with data reduction of 92.5%. However, a specific issue with change of ordering was detected during the human evaluations, which resulted in considerably low acceptability. A more comprehensive implementation of tree accuracy will be worked on to solved this issue. While joint-training increased both tree accuracy and acceptability over the S2S Bucketed experiments, other methods still outperformed joint-training.

S2S+KD and S2S+KD+DDA performed higher than other methods. Specifically, S2S+KD+DDA with a data reduction of 92.5% achieved tree accuracy of 98.3%, which was within 1.0% of the S2S

Data	Approach	BLEU Score	Tree Accuracy	Acceptability	Data Reduction	TreeAcc STDev
ALL	S2S BASE	95.9	100	-	0.0	0.1
1PerFBQ	S2S	95.4	97.7	90.0	85.0	2.5
1PerFBQ	S2S+DDA	95.7	**99.6**	96.7	**85.0**	4.8
1PerFBQ	BART+DDA	95.5	99.6	98.0	85.0	0.2
1PerFBQ	S2S+KD	95.8	99.9	98.0	85.0	0.1
1PerFBQ	S2S+KD+DDA	95.8	100.0	99.3	85.0	0.1
1PerFB	S2S+KD+DDA	94.6	100.0	98.6	94.0	0.1

Table 6: Results on selected Time domain experiments in percentage.

Data	Approach	BLEU Score	Tree Accuracy	Acceptability	Data Reduction	TreeAcc STDev
ALL	S2S BASE	92.6	99.3	-	0.0	0.1
5PerMB+Alarm	S2S+JT	92.4	97.6	88.7	82.6	1.3
1PerFBQ+Alarm	S2S+JT	92.8	97.6	88.0	80.0	0.9
1PerFBQ	S2S	92.1	95.6	83.3	80.0	0.3
1PerFB	S2S	90.4	85.7	47.3	92.5	27.0
1PerFB	S2S+DDA	92.1	**96.3**	84.0	**92.5**	26.0
1PerFB	BART+DDA	91.5	97.1	86.7	92.5	1.6
1PerFB	S2S+KD	91.9	**98.1**	89.3	**92.5**	0.2
1PerFB	S2S+KD+DDA	91.9	**98.3**	94.0	**92.5**	0.2

Table 7: Results on selected Reminder domain experiments in percentage.

BASE experiment. Higher model maintenance resources will be required here as well, which might provide incentives for more data collection and ensuring higher data quality to improve the performance of S2S+DDA or S2S+JT to production levels.

4.4 Weather Domain

Weather was the most complex domain in this study. There were thousands of possible scenarios and the dataset size was considerably larger, accordingly. As demonstrated in Table 8, even a simple method such as S2S with only 1PerMB data achieved performance within 1.0% of the S2S BASE case with a data reduction rate of 74.8%. This is due to the high variety in the data that results in creation of more than 6400 medium-grained buckets, which was considerably higher than other domains. Therefore, we sub-sampled the buckets aggressively to examine the extent of possible data reduction.

Using only 1/4 of the fine-grained buckets to train the models in the S2S+KD and S2S+KD+DDA approaches resulted in tree accuracy values within 2.0% of the S2S BASE case. However, BART+DDA and S2S+DDA did not perform comparable to the KD variants. In addition, S2S+KD and S2S+KD+DDA provided low latency, which made the 92.5% data reduction very favorable. In complex domains such as Weather, deploying models trained with more complex approaches that require higher development and maintenance resources is justified by high data-efficiency gains (19,000 fewer training samples here).

Data	Approach	BLEU SCORE	TREE ACCURACY	DATA REDUCTION	TREEACC STDEV
ALL	S2S BASE	91.4	91.4	0.0	0.1
1PerMB	S2S	90.7	90.6	74.8	0.3
0.5PerFB	S2S+DDA	89.8	86.6	85.0	18.5
0.25PerFB	BART+DDA	89.2	86.2	92.5	1.8
0.25PerFB	S2S+KD	89.7	**89.4**	92.5	0.1
0.25PerFB	S2S+KD+DDA	89.8	**89.8**	92.5	0.1

Table 8: Results on selected Weather domain experiments in percentage.

5 Conclusions

Several considerations are necessary for deploying model-based task-oriented dialogue systems to production. While increasing data efficiency was the primary goal of our study, we also considered and balanced data efficiency gains with several other factors such as acceptability, latency, and the required development and maintenance resources. Focusing on four datasets for domains with varying level of complexity, we propose a sequential domain development run-book, where development of different domains can halt at different steps based on model performance evaluation. The steps are as follows:

- Bucketing MRs based on a structure (tree-based here) in the data to avoid unnecessary and imbalanced data collection. Collect 1-3 examples per bucket. Train a model and evaluate it.

- If data for domains with similar tasks and semantics (like Reminder and Time) are available, Perform joint-training possibly followed by in-domain fine-tuning. Evaluate the model performance.

- Implement Dynamic Data Augmentation (DDA) to reduce the dependency of responses on interchangeable argument values. Train with DDA and evaluate the model performance.

- First, use pre-trained models (e.g. BART) to generate responses for unlabelled data. Then, combine the augmentation data with human-annotated data and train a small model (KD). Finally, fine-tune the model using DDA with the small human-annotated data. Evaluate the model performance.

- If necessary, collect more examples per MR bucket and start from the beginning to deploy the model with the lowest required development and maintenance resources.

Acknowledgements

We would like to thank our reviewers for their helpful feedback. Many thanks to our linguistic engineering team (Anoop Sinha, Shiun-Zu Kuo, Catharine Youngs, Kirk LaBuda, Steliana Ivanova, Ceci Pompeo, and Briana Nettie) for their hard work and for being great partners in this effort. We would also like to thank Jinfeng Rao, Kartikeya Upasani, Ben Gauthier, and Fiona Yee for their contributions.

References

Dzmitry Bahdanau, Kyunghyun Cho, and Yoshua Bengio. 2014. Neural machine translation by jointly learning to align and translate. *arXiv preprint arXiv:1409.0473*.

Anusha Balakrishnan, Jinfeng Rao, Kartikeya Upasani, Michael White, and Rajen Subba. 2019. Constrained decoding for neural NLG from compositional representations in task-oriented dialogue. In *Proceedings of the 57th Annual Meeting of the Association for Computational Linguistics*, July. To appear.

Paweł Budzianowski, Tsung-Hsien Wen, Bo-Hsiang Tseng, Iñigo Casanueva, Stefan Ultes, Osman Ramadan, and Milica Gasic. 2018. Multiwoz-a large-scale multi-domain wizard-of-oz dataset for task-oriented dialogue modelling. In *Proceedings of the 2018 Conference on Empirical Methods in Natural Language Processing*, pages 5016–5026.

Zhiyu Chen, Harini Eavani, Wenhu Chen, Yinyin Liu, and William Yang Wang. 2020. Few-shot nlg with pre-trained language model. *Proceedings of the 58th Annual Meeting of the Association for Computational Linguistics*.

Kyunghyun Cho, Bart Van Merriënboer, Caglar Gulcehre, Dzmitry Bahdanau, Fethi Bougares, Holger Schwenk, and Yoshua Bengio. 2014. Learning phrase representations using rnn encoder-decoder for statistical machine translation. *arXiv preprint arXiv:1406.1078*.

Robert Dale. 2020. Natural language generation: The commercial state of the art in 2020. *Natural Language Engineering*. To appear.

Ondrej Dušek and Filip Jurcıcek. 2016. Sequence-to-sequence generation for spoken dialogue via deep syntax trees and strings. In *The 54th Annual Meeting of the Association for Computational Linguistics*, page 45.

Claire Gardent, Anastasia Shimorina, Shashi Narayan, and Laura Perez-Beltrachini. 2017. The WebNLG challenge: Generating text from RDF data. In *Proceedings of the 10th International Conference on Natural Language Generation*, pages 124–133, Santiago de Compostela, Spain, September. Association for Computational Linguistics.

Albert Gatt and Emiel Krahmer. 2018. Survey of the state of the art in natural language generation: Core tasks, applications and evaluation. *Journal of Artificial Intelligence Research*, 61:65–170.

Junxian He, Jiatao Gu, Jiajun Shen, and Marc'Aurelio Ranzato. 2020. Revisiting self-training for neural sequence generation. In *International Conference on Learning Representations*.

Chris Kedzie and Kathleen McKeown. 2019. A good sample is hard to find: Noise injection sampling and self-training for neural language generation models. In *Proceedings of the 12th International Conference on Natural Language Generation*, pages 584–593, Tokyo, Japan, October–November. Association for Computational Linguistics.

Yoon Kim and Alexander Rush. 2016. Sequence-level knowledge distillation. In *Proceedings of the 2016 Conference on Empirical Methods in Natural Language Processing*, pages 1317–1327.

Diederik P Kingma and Jimmy Ba. 2015. Adam: A method for stochastic optimization. *the 3rd International Conference for Learning Representations*.

Mike Lewis, Yinhan Liu, Naman Goyal, Marjan Ghazvininejad, Abdelrahman Mohamed, Omer Levy, Ves Stoyanov, and Luke Zettlemoyer. 2019. Bart: Denoising sequence-to-sequence pre-training for natural language generation, translation, and comprehension. *arXiv preprint arXiv:1910.13461*.

Yinhan Liu, Jiatao Gu, Naman Goyal, Xian Li, Sergey Edunov, Marjan Ghazvininejad, Mike Lewis, and Luke Zettlemoyer. 2020. Multilingual denoising pre-training for neural machine translation. In *arXiv preprint arXiv:2001.08210*.

Jekaterina Novikova, Ondřej Dušek, and Verena Rieser. 2017. The e2e dataset: New challenges for end-to-end generation. *arXiv preprint arXiv:1706.09254*.

Kishore Papineni, Salim Roukos, Todd Ward, and Wei Jing Zhu. 2002. Bleu: a method for automatic evaluation of machine translation. *In Proc. ACL-02*.

Baolin Peng, Chenguang Zhu, Chunyuan Li, Xiujun Li, Jinchao Li, Michael Zeng, and Jianfeng Gao. 2020. Few-shot natural language generation for task-oriented dialog. *arXiv preprint arXiv:2002.12328*.

Jeffrey Pennington, Richard Socher, and Christopher Manning. 2014. Glove: Global vectors for word representation. In *Proceedings of the 2014 conference on empirical methods in natural language processing (EMNLP)*, pages 1532–1543.

Alec Radford, Jeffrey Wu, Rewon Child, David Luan, Dario Amodei, and Ilya Sutskever. 2019. Language models are unsupervised multitask learners. *OpenAI Blog*, 1(8):9.

Jinfeng Rao, Kartikeya Upasani, Anusha Balakrishnan, Michael White, Anuj Kumar, and Rajen Subba. 2019. A tree-to-sequence model for neural nlg in task-oriented dialog. In *Proceedings of the 12th International Conference on Natural Language Generation*, pages 95–100.

Ehud Reiter and Robert Dale. 2000. *Building Natural-Language Generation Systems*. Cambridge University Press.

Pararth Shah, Dilek Hakkani-Tür, Bing Liu, and Gokhan Tür. 2018. Bootstrapping a neural conversational agent with dialogue self-play, crowdsourcing and on-line reinforcement learning. In *Proceedings of the 2018 Conference of the North American Chapter of the Association for Computational Linguistics: Human Language Technologies, Volume 3 (Industry Papers)*, pages 41–51, New Orleans - Louisiana, June. Association for Computational Linguistics.

Ilya Sutskever, Oriol Vinyals, and Quoc V Le. 2014. Sequence to sequence learning with neural networks. In *Advances in neural information processing systems*, pages 3104–3112.

Tsung-Hsien Wen, Milica Gasic, Nikola Mrkšić, Pei-Hao Su, David Vandyke, and Steve Young. 2015. Semantically conditioned LSTM-based natural language generation for spoken dialogue systems. In *Proceedings of the 2015 Conference on Empirical Methods in Natural Language Processing*, pages 1711–1721. Association for Computational Linguistics.

Tsung-Hsien Wen, Milica Gasic, Nikola Mrksic, Lina M. Rojas-Barahona, Pei-Hao Su, David Vandyke, and Steve Young. 2016. Multi-domain neural network language generation for spoken dialogue systems.

6 Appendix

6.1 Detailed Experimental Results

Data	Approach	BLEU SCORE	TREE ACCURACY	Acceptability	DATA REDUCTION	TREEACC STDEV
BASE	S2S	93.3	99.8	-	0.0	0.1
1PerCB	S2S	51.5	0.6	5.2	99.6	3.5
1PerMB	S2S	87.0	56.2	38.1	98.3	23.9
5PerMB+Reminder	S2S+JT	92.7	99.6	93.8	93.7	1.3
3PerFB+Reminder	S2S+JT	92.7	98.1	91.7	94.0	2.0
1PerFBQ+Reminder	S2S+JT	92.6	97.6	83.5	96.1	2.8
1PerFBQ	S2S	91.6	85.0	67.0	96.1	16.2
1PerFB	S2S	92.3	91.8	75.0	97.4	28.6
1PerFBQ	S2S+DDA	92.7	93.4	77.3	96.1	14.3
1PerFB	S2S+DDA	91.6	83.8	67.0	97.4	20.9
1PerFBQ	BART+DDA	92.5	99.8	93.8	96.1	1.3
1PerFB	BART+DDA	92.8	98.4	90.7	97.4	10.0
1PerFBQ	S2S+KD	92.9	99.9	94.8	96.1	0.1
1PerFB	S2S+KD	93.2	99.8	92.8	97.4	0.1
1PerFBQ	S2S+KD+DDA	92.9	99.9	94.8	96.1	0.05
1PerFB	S2S+KD+DDA	93.2	99.8	93.8	97.4	0.1

Table 9: Results on all Alarm domain experiments. All metrics are percentages.

Data	Approach	BLEU SCORE	TREE ACCURACY	Acceptability	DATA REDUCTION	TREEACC STDEV
ALL	S2S BASE	95.9	100	-	0.0	0.1
1PerCB	S2S	76.1	12.1	1.3	99.7	4.9
1PerMB	S2S	92.3	80.1	61.3	94.8	16.5
1PerFBQ	S2S	95.4	97.7	90.0	85.0	2.5
1PerFB	S2S	93.5	89.1	76.7	94.0	7.6
1PerFBQ	S2S+DDA	95.7	99.6	96.7	85.0	4.8
1PerFB	S2S+DDA	94.9	97.8	87.3	94.0	10.2
1PerFBQ	BART+DDA	95.5	99.6	98.0	85.0	0.2
1PerFB	BART+DDA	93.8	96.1	90.7	94.0	1.7
1PerFBQ	S2S+KD	95.8	99.9	98.0	85.0	0.1
1PerFB	S2S+KD	94.6	99.8	96.0	94.0	0.1
1PerFBQ	S2S+KD+DDA	95.8	100.0	99.3	85.0	0.1
1PerFB	S2S+KD+DDA	94.6	100.0	98.6	94.0	0.1

Table 10: Results on all Time domain experiments. All metrics are percentages.

Data	Approach	BLEU SCORE	TREE ACCURACY	Acceptability	DATA REDUCTION	TREEACC STDEV
ALL	S2S BASE	92.6	99.3	-	0.0	0.1
1PerCB	S2S	15.9	0.1	0.6	99.3	0.2
1PerMB	S2S	89.94	75.7	28.0	94.2	22.4
5PerMB+Alarm	S2S+JT	92.4	97.6	88.7	82.6	1.3
3PerFB+Alarm	S2S+JT	92.6	98.1	86.0	82.0	2.2
1PerFBQ+Alarm	S2S+JT	92.8	97.6	88.0	80.0	0.9
1PerFBQ	S2S	92.1	95.6	83.3	80.0	0.3
1PerFB	S2S	90.4	85.7	47.3	92.5	27.0
1PerFBQ	S2S+DDA	92.3	96.9	82.0	80.0	0.2
1PerFB	S2S+DDA	92.1	96.3	84.0	92.5	26.0
1PerFBQ	BART+DDA	92.1	98.3	93.3	80.0	0.2
1PerFB	BART+DDA	91.5	97.1	86.7	92.5	1.6
1PerFBQ	S2S+KD	92.6	98.7	92.0	80.0	0.2
1PerFB	S2S+KD	91.9	98.1	83.3	92.5	0.2
1PerFBQ	S2S+KD+DDA	92.6	98.9	96.0	80.0	0.2
1PerFB	S2S+KD+DDA	91.9	98.3	94.0	92.5	0.2

Table 11: Results on all Reminder domain experiments. All metrics are percentages.

Data	Approach	BLEU SCORE	TREE ACCURACY	DATA REDUCTION	TREEACC STDEV
ALL	S2S BASE	91.4	91.4	0.0	0.1
1PerCB	S2S	88.1	77.9	91.2	2.6
1PerMB	S2S	90.7	90.6	74.8	0.3
1PerFB	S2S	91.3	91.4	40.0	0.1
1PerFB	S2S+DDA	91.3	91.1	40.0	0.1
0.5PerFB	S2S+DDA	89.8	86.6	85.0	18.5
0.25PerFB	S2S+DDA	87.3	77.8	92.5	12.3
0.5PerFB	BART+DDA	90.2	89.9	85.0	1.7
0.25PerFB	BART+DDA	89.2	86.2	92.5	1.8
0.5PerFB	S2S+KD	90.8	90.9	85.0	0.1
0.25PerFB	S2S+KD	89.7	89.4	92.5	0.1
0.5PerFB	S2S+KD+DDA	90.8	91.0	85.0	0.1
0.25PerFB	S2S+KD+DDA	89.8	89.8	92.5	0.1

Table 12: Results on all Weather domain experiments. All metrics are percentages.

Interactive Question Clarification in Dialogue via Reinforcement Learning

Xiang Hu[†] Zujie Wen[†] Yafang Wang[†*] Xiaolong Li[†] Gerard de Melo[‡]

Ant Financial Services Group[†]
Hasso Plattner Institute, University of Potsdam[‡]

Abstract

Coping with ambiguous questions has been a perennial problem in real-world dialogue systems. Although clarification by asking questions is a common form of human interaction, it is hard to define appropriate questions to elicit more specific intents from a user. In this work, we propose a reinforcement model to clarify ambiguous questions by suggesting refinements of the original query. We first formulate a collection partitioning problem to select a set of labels enabling us to distinguish potential unambiguous intents. We list the chosen labels as intent phrases to the user for further confirmation. The selected label along with the original user query then serves as a refined query, for which a suitable response can more easily be identified. The model is trained using reinforcement learning with a deep policy network. We evaluate our model based on real-world user clicks and demonstrate significant improvements across several different experiments.

1 Introduction

In real-world dialogue systems, a substantial portion of all user queries are ambiguous ones for which the system is unable to precisely identify the underlying intent. We observed that many such queries in our question answering (QA) system exhibited one of the following two characteristics.

1. Lack of semantic elements such as subject, object, or predicate, e.g. "How to apply", "Credit card".
2. Ambiguous entities, e.g. "My health insurance" (because health insurance consists of numerous sub-categories).

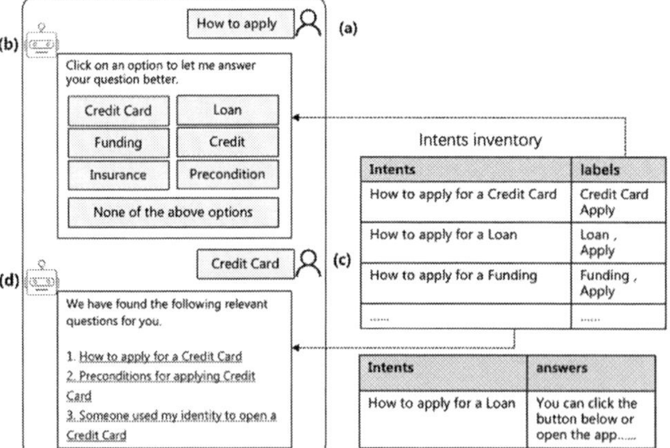

Figure 1: Interactive question clarification example. a) The user provides an incomplete or ambiguous question. b) The agent suggests pertinent labels. c) The user confirms by selecting one such label. d) The agent considers the label in conjunction with the original query as a refined query and responds to it.

*corresponding author, email: yafang.wyf@antfin.com
This work is licensed under a Creative Commons Attribution 4.0 International License. License details: http://creativecommons.org/licenses/by/4.0/.

Proceedings of the 28th International Conference on Computational Linguistics: Industry Track, pages 78–89
Barcelona, Spain (Online), December 12, 2020

Given such limited information, it is difficult for a system to accurately respond to a user's ambiguous queries, often resulting in that the user's needs cannot be addressed. For example, the specific intent underlying an utterance such as "How to apply?" remains obscure, because there are too many products related to the action of "applying". In practice, one often needs to fall back to human agents to assist with such requests, increasing the workload and cost. The main purpose of deployed automated systems is to reduce the human workload in scenarios such as customer service hotlines. The lack of an ability to deal with ambiguous questions may directly lead to these sessions being transferred to human agents. In our real-world customer service system, this affects up to 30% of sessions. Hence, it is valuable to find an effective solution to clarify such ambiguous questions automatically, greatly reducing the number of cases requiring human assistance.

Automated question clarification involves confirming a user's intent through interaction. Previous work has explored asking questions (Radlinski and Craswell, 2017; Quarteroni and Manandhar, 2009; Rao and Daumé, 2018; Rao and Daumé, 2019). Unfortunately, clarification by asking questions requires substantial customization for the specific dialogue setting. It is challenging to define appropriate questions to guide users towards providing more accurate information. Coarse questions may leave users confused, while overly specific ones may fail to account for the specific information a user wishes to convey.

In our work, we thus instead investigate interactive clarification by providing the user with specific choices as options, such as intent options (Tang et al., 2011). Unlike previous work, we propose an end-to-end model that suggests labels to clarify ambiguous questions. An example of this sort of approach is given in Figure 1. Here, we consider a closed-domain QA system, where a typical method is to build an intent inventory to address high-frequency requests. In this setting, the set of unambiguous candidate labels for an ambiguous user utterance corresponds to a set of frequently asked questions covered by the intent inventory. In a closed domain, we consider the candidate set to be finite. For example, in Figure 1, there are three specific intents corresponding to the ambiguous question "How to apply".

Our approach induces phrase tags as *labels* for each intent. Thus, we have a catalog of intents with corresponding labels that can be presented to the user. The challenge lies in selecting a suitable list of labels that can effectively clarify the ambiguous question. In our approach, the problem of finding the label sequence is formulated as a collection partitioning problem, where the objective is to cover as many elements as possible while distinguishing elements as clearly as possible. The task of question clarification thus amounts to obtaining a suitable set of labels.

The main contributions of our work are:

1. We formulate interactive clarification as a collection partitioning problem.
2. We propose a novel reward function to evaluate the clarification ability of phrase collections and an end-to-end sequential phrase recommendation model trained with reinforcement learning.
3. Both offline and online experiments confirm that our method outperforms pertinent baselines significantly.

2 Related Work

Query Refinement. Several works explore the use of clarification questions for query refinement (Kotov and Zhai, 2010; Sajjad et al., 2012; Zheng et al., 2011; Ma et al., 2010; Sadikov et al., 2010). For instance, Kotov and Zhai (2010) and Sajjad et al. (2012) use question templates to generate a list of clarification questions. Elgohary et al. (2019) rewrite questions using the dialogue context. Zhang et al. (2019) invoke graph edit distance for query refinement. Other studies rely on reinforcement learning to refine user queries (Nogueira and Cho, 2017; Buck et al., 2018; Liu et al., 2019), but consider queries that are unambiguous (though possibly ill-formed or non-standard). Accordingly, they seek to increase the recall, while in our setting, we consider ambiguous user queries, and our model primarily seeks to address the task of question clarification.

Dialogue. Boni and Manandhar (2003) developed an algorithm to recognize clarification dialogue, rather than for asking clarification questions. Varges et al. (2010) found that the use of clarification has a positive effect on concept precision in task-oriented dialogue. Li et al. (2017) focus on clarification in the specific circumstance of a bot not understanding a teacher because of spelling mistakes, which is a sub-problem of our setting. Zhang et al. (2018) generate clarification questions using language patterns with predicted aspect. They do not use reinforcement learning to optimize the order of the questions. Wang et al. (2018) devised soft and hard-typed decoders to generate good questions by capturing different roles of different word types. Aliannejadi et al. (2019) designed a two-stage retrieval and ranking model to rank clarification question candidates generated by human annotators, different from our end-to-end reinforcement learning approach. Korpusik and Glass (2019) construct clarification questions from a food attribute list (brand, fat, etc.). They rely on a hybrid reinforcement learning approach to select the order of clarification questions to ask, while we present an end-to-end reinforcement learning method.

Question Answering. Some studies focus on clarification questions in a community question answering setting (Braslavski et al., 2017; Rao and Daumé, 2018; Rao and Daumé, 2019). These share in common that they seek to rank or generate clarification questions, while our approach uses reinforcement learning to perform sequential label recommendation for question clarification. The key differences between our work and Tang et al. (2011) are three-fold. First, they rely on an ontology, which limits the applicability of their approach in real-world deployments and prevents us from being able to compare against their approach in our experiments, since each domain requires a custom ontology. Second, they cluster the keywords through the ontology, based on templates to achieve a refinement of questions, without using machine learning. Third, they rely on clustering to increase the keyword diversity, while we design a reward with an information gain term that automatically encourages diversity.

3 Preliminaries

System overview. In order to provide a more concrete picture of our approach, we first briefly describe our QA system, illustrated in Figure 2, as an example of how this approach can be instantiated.

When the conversation exceeds a certain number of rounds or the user explicitly requests human service, the conversation is transferred to a human customer service agent. In this setting, our clarification method chiefly serves to reduce the workload of those human agents. In our real system, there are two stages: label clarification and intent retrieval as illustrated in Figure 1. The label clarification stage provides 6 labels for the user to confirm. Upon selecting one of the suggested labels, the user question is concatenated with the selected label phrase as a new query input. The intent retrieval stage seeks to provide 3 relevant intents for the user to select according to the concatenated query. These additional labels can help clarify and improve the relevance.

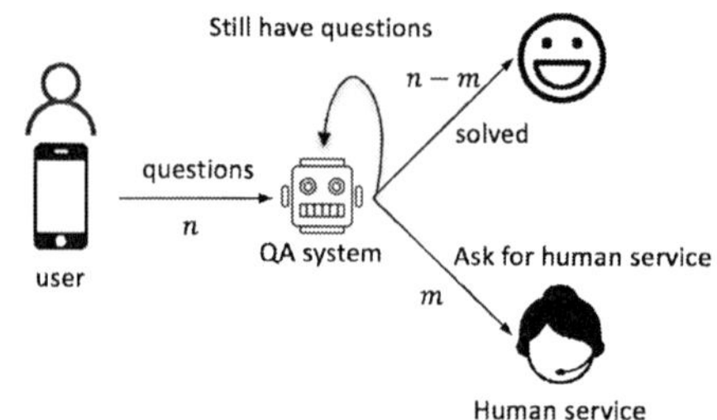

Figure 2: Pipeline of our QA system. $\frac{m}{n}$ is the rate of transferal to human agents (THA).

Intent and Label Inventory. Our system relies on a closed-domain intent and label inventory. The intents along with their corresponding answers are compiled by human experts. The set of labels is a collection of words or phrases that are manually constructed from intents by marking up keywords such as suitable predicates, subjects, or objects. As shown in Figure 3, there is a many-to-many relationship between intents and labels. Note that there is substantial synonymy among the set of labels, which may result in numerous repetitive recommendation results. Thus, ensuring the diversity of the results ought to be a factor in the design of the policy model.

Dataset Setup. In order to solve the cold start problem and evaluate the effectiveness of each model offline, we constructed a benchmark corpus. This annotated corpus consists of 40k ambiguous questions and their potential intents. For this, ten experts were divided into five teams. The two experts in each team annotate the same corpus. Data on which there are disagreements are

Recall	Valid
Can't transfer money using Alpha	No
How to apply for a Credit Card	Yes
How to apply for a Loan	Yes
...	...

Table 1: Example of related intent annotation for user question "How to apply".

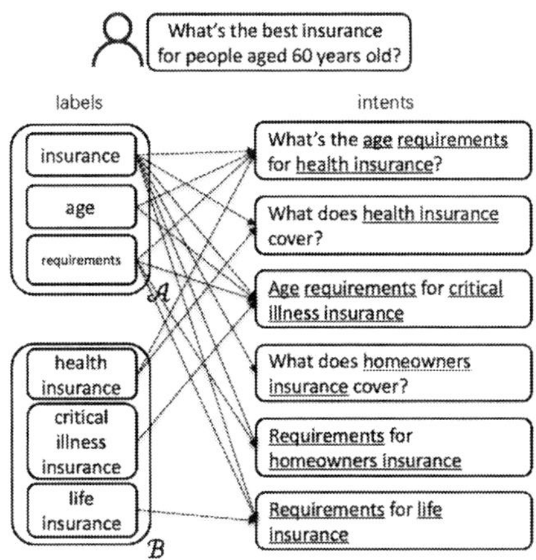

Figure 3: Example of relationship between labels and intents. A and B are different label groups to divide potential intents.

annotated anew, and only agreed-upon data is selected. To construct corpora at a relatively low cost, the annotation task is simplified so as to merely elicit a "yes" or "no" response. The whole annotation process is divided to two stages. At the first stage, we collect ambiguous questions by annotating online query logs. If a query lacks a predicate or the object of the predicate, it is annotated as ambiguous. At the second stage, we annotate potential intents for each ambiguous question. As Table 1 shows, for each ambiguous question ("How to apply"), the top 50 most relevant intent candidates are collected using the BERT (Devlin et al., 2019) semantic similarity model applied to the intent inventory. The human annotators are asked to decide whether an intent can possibly address a user's question.

4 Reinforcement Learning for Label Recommendation

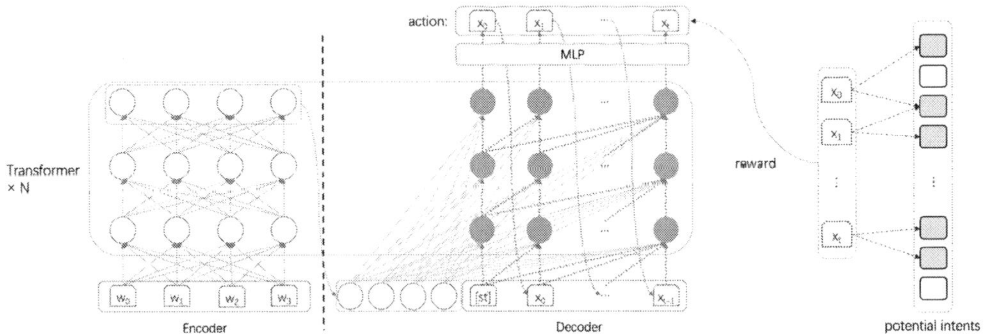

Figure 4: Label recommendation policy model architecture.

Label Recommendation as an RL problem. In order to train a model able to recommend labels one by one, we have two options: 1) Deduce a path reversely for supervised learning. 2) Create an environment for the model to explore. We believe that creating an environment for the model to explore different label sequences may lead to better generalization ability, which is confirmed in our comparative experiments. We can cast our label recommendation in the reinforcement learning paradigm as in Figure 4. Our model can be viewed as an *agent* that interacts with an *environment*, which consists of the user question and recommended labels. The action space consists of more than 1,000 candidate labels, out of which a suitable next label needs to be selected as a next action. In order to increase the diversity and reduce the number of synonymous labels, our model takes historical recommended labels into account. Upon having recommended N labels, the final reward (introduced later) is assigned and the parameters are updated.

Policy Model. As N labels to be recommended could be considered as a sequence, we use a seq2seq architecture to model the problem. As shown in Figure 4, in the encoder stage, the query is encoded by BERT and a vector representation is generated. In the decoder stage, the input at time step t is the action at step $t-1$ (step 0 is [st]). For each step, one-way multi-head attention (Vaswani et al., 2017) is applied on previously recommended labels and the vector representation of the input query. Finally, the action probability at each step is estimated.

Rewards. Intuitively, the chosen labels ought to maximize the recall of the intents with regard to the human-annotated potential intents. However, a trajectory with high recall may not be sufficient for clarification, as high recall can easily be achieved by suggesting labels such as in group A in Figure 3. Rather, a good label set should efficiently discriminate between potential intents as in group B in Figure 3. We recast this as a collection partition problem. Subsequently, inspired by the ID3 algorithm (Quinlan, 1986), we use Information Gain as a term to evaluate the final reward.

Formally, given a user query q, and the human-annotated potential intents $\mathcal{Q}(q)$, our policy model selects a list of labels $\tau_N = \{x_1, x_2, \ldots, x_N\}$. We map all the chosen labels τ to the retrieved potential intent set $S(\tau)$ with a many-to-many relationship between labels and intents:

$$S(\tau) = \bigcup_{x \in \tau} [\mathcal{M}(x) \cap \mathcal{Q}(q)] \tag{1}$$

$\mathcal{M}(x)$ denotes the intent set mapped from label x. $\mathcal{K}$ denotes the universe set of intents. An indicator vector $\mathbf{I}(q) = (\mathbf{I}_1, \mathbf{I}_2, \ldots, \mathbf{I}_{|\mathcal{K}|})$ indicates for each intent s^i in $\mathcal{K}$ whether it exists in the human-annotated intent set $\mathcal{Q}(q)$, as defined below.

$$\mathbf{I}_i = \begin{cases} 1 & s^i \in \mathcal{Q}(q) \\ 0 & s^i \notin \mathcal{Q}(q) \end{cases} \tag{2}$$

The probability that an intent is the answer to an ambiguous question is computed as

$$P(s^i \mid q) = \frac{\mathbf{I}_i}{|\mathcal{Q}(q)|}. \tag{3}$$

We define potential intents recalled at time step t as $S(\tau_t)$, the conditional entropy of $S(\tau_N)$ is $\mathcal{H}(\tau_N)$, defined as follows.

$$\mathcal{D}(x_t) = \mathcal{M}(x_t) \cap \mathcal{Q}(q) \setminus S(\tau_{t-1})$$
$$\widetilde{P}(s \mid q, \tau_t) = \frac{P(s \mid q)}{\sum\limits_{s' \in \mathcal{D}(x_t)} P(s' \mid q)} \tag{4}$$
$$\mathcal{H}(x_t) = -\sum_{s \in \mathcal{D}(x_t)} \widetilde{P}(s \mid q, \tau_t) \log \widetilde{P}(s \mid q, \tau_t)$$

Here, $\mathcal{M}(x_t)$ denotes the set of intents mapped from label x_t. $\mathcal{D}(x_t)$ is the marginal recall over the potential intent set $\mathcal{Q}(q)$ for label x_t. $\widetilde{P}(s \mid q, \tau_t)$ is the normalized probability of $P(s \mid q)$ for intents in $\mathcal{D}(x_t)$. The entropy at time step 0 is $\mathcal{H}_0$, defined as

$$\mathcal{H}_0 = -\sum_{s \in \mathcal{Q}(q)} P(s \mid q) \log P(s \mid q). \tag{5}$$

The Information Gain is defined as

$$\Delta(\tau_N) = \sum_{t=1}^{N} \frac{|\mathcal{D}(x_i)|}{|S(\tau_N)|} \mathcal{H}(x_t) - \mathcal{H}_0, \tag{6}$$

and the final reward is then defined as

$$R(\tau_N) = \sum_{s \in S(\tau_N)} P(s \mid q) + \beta \Delta(\tau_N). \tag{7}$$

In our experiments, β by default is set to 1.

Considering there are more than 1000 candidate labels, the size of the search space in MCTS may explode. To reduce its size, we only sample labels in $\{x | \mathcal{M}(x) \cap \mathcal{Q}(q) \neq \varnothing\}$ because only such labels have a relationship with candidate intents worth exploring. Thus, the size of the search space is drastically reduced.

Training. The policy model to suggest labels is trained from samples generated via a Monte-Carlo tree search (MCTS) (Coulom, 2006; Kocsis and Szepesvári, 2006; Browne et al., 2012). The MCTS starts from an empty label set and stops when the trajectory includes N labels, as in Figure 5.

Each simulation starts from the root state and iteratively selects a move with maximal $V(\cdot)$, which is computed according to the upper confidence bound for tree search (Kocsis and Szepesvári, 2006) as

$$V(v) = \frac{Q(v)}{N(v)} + \beta_{\mathrm{T}} \sqrt{\frac{2 \ln N(p_v)}{N(v)}}, \tag{8}$$

where p_v denotes the parent of v and β_{T} by default is set to 1. After a path has been sampled, the Q value of each node in the path is updated according to

$$Q(v) = \frac{\sum_{\tau \in T(v)} R(\tau)}{N(v)} \tag{9}$$

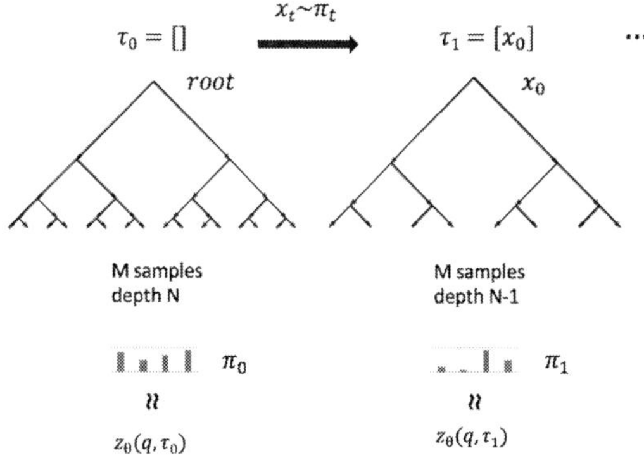

Figure 5: MCTS. At time step t, the sampling process keeps searching until it reaches depth $N - t$.

where $N(v)$ denotes the visiting time of v and $T(v)$ denotes the set of all trajectories containing v. Once the search is complete after M samples, probabilities π for the next action are estimated following Equation 10, where $N(\cdot)$ is the visit count of each move from the root state and T is a parameter controlling the temperature.

$$\pi(\cdot \mid v) = \frac{N(\cdot)^{1/T}}{\sum\limits_{v' \in C_v} N(v')^{1/T}} \tag{10}$$

Here, C_v denotes the children of node v. Additional exploration is achieved by adding Dirichlet noise $\mathrm{Dir}(\cdot)$ to the prior probabilities as in AlphaZero (Silver et al., 2017):

$$P(\cdot|v) \sim \frac{3}{4}\pi(\cdot \mid v) + \frac{1}{4}\mathrm{Dir}(0.03) \tag{11}$$

x_t is selected in a weighted round robin manner in accordance with $P(\cdot \mid v)$. The neural network $z_\theta(q, \tau_t)$ is adjusted to minimize the KL divergence D_{KL} of the neural network estimated probabilities to the search probabilities π as:

$$\mathcal{L}(\tau_N) = \sum_{t=1}^{N} D_{\mathrm{KL}} \big[z_\theta(\cdot|q, \tau_t) \,\|\, \pi(\cdot \mid v) \big]. \tag{12}$$

5   Experiments

Following standard practices in industry, we first conduct offline experiments to select reasonable models for which we subsequently perform an online evaluation. Only the best-performing model in the online tests is kept running online. We also perform an ablation study on the pipeline without label clarification. In order to verify whether the Information Gain can help to reduce the overlap between intents and the user question, we also perform experiments to evaluate the diversity and complementarity of the label recommendation method.

5.1   Experimental Settings

We first conduct offline experiments by using the 40k annotated ambiguous questions and their potential intents as explained in Section 3. The corpora are divided into training and test sets at a $9 : 1$ ratio. The parameters of our policy model are as follows. The sample count in MCTS is $M = 1,000$. We output $N = 6$ intents for each ambiguous question. The total number of training epochs is $E = 5$. We use a 12-layer pretrained BERT base model as the encoder for queries and the hyperparameters of the decoder are the same as for the encoder.

5.2   Evaluation Metrics

Evaluation metrics for offline experiments. The goal of our offline experiments is to evaluate the label recommendation methods, and select the most promising ones to perform online experiments. We evaluate them in terms of **Recall@N**, which reflects how many intents among all potential intents of q are retrieved among the N intents emitted by the model.

The key desideratum for label recommendation models is to cover as many potential questions as possible. It is relatively fair to compare the recall of potential intents recommended by different methods on the annotated data set. For label trajectory τ_N, the recall can be computed as

$$\text{recall}(q, \tau_N) = \frac{\sum_{x \in \tau_N} |\mathcal{M}(x) \cap \mathcal{Q}(q)|}{|\mathcal{Q}(q)|} \tag{13}$$

where $\mathcal{Q}(q)$ is the set of potential intents for ambiguous query q, and $\mathcal{M}(x)$ is the set of all intents mapped to intent x in the intent inventory. The upper bound is calculated inversely from the results of annotated corpora:

$$\tau_N^*(q) = \underset{\tau_N}{\text{argmax}} \sum_{x \in \tau_N} |\mathcal{M}(x) \cap \mathcal{Q}(q)| \tag{14}$$

$\tau_N^*(q)$ denotes the set of N best labels covering the potential intents. Thus, the upper bound recall of q would be $\text{recall}(\tau_N^*(q))$.

Evaluation metrics for online experiments. In our subsequent online experiments, our key metrics are the rate of transferal to human agents (THA) and the click through rate (CTR). In our experiments, every time a question is classified as an ambiguous question, six labels are provided to the user, who may select one of them or just ignore the selection. Given t as the number of times we output labels, and c as the number of times the user selected one of them, we define $\text{CTR} = \frac{c}{t}$. Note that the user may opt to select *none of the above options*. In this case, the pipeline equals intent retrieval without clarification. The CTR reflects how useful the recommended labels are to users.

Evaluation metrics for complementary experiments. We compare the repetition rate at the word piece level of labels generated by two methods as an experiment to evaluate the diversity. The diversity is quantified as:

$$\text{div}(\tau_N) = \frac{|\mathcal{W}(\tau_N)|}{\sum_{w \in \mathcal{W}(\tau_N)} C(w)}, \tag{15}$$

where $\mathcal{W}(\tau_N)$ is the set of word pieces tokenized from the labels, and $C(w)$ denotes the number of times word piece w appears among the labels. We also count the overlap rate:

$$\text{overlap}(\tau_N, q) = \frac{\sum_{x \in \tau_N} \sum_{t \in \mathcal{T}(x) \cap \mathcal{T}(q)} C(t)}{\sum_{x \in \tau_N} \sum_{t \in \mathcal{T}(x)} C(t)} \tag{16}$$

Here, $\mathcal{T}(x_t)$, $\mathcal{T}(q)$ denote the tokens sets of x_t and q, respectively. The overlap thus essentially reflects the number of tokens of labels appearing in a query.

5.3 Baselines

Several methods for label clarification serve as baselines for the offline experiments, while our method is denoted as *RL (ours)*.

5.3.1 Label Clarification Methods

Supervised. Given a query and a set of potential intents, there are limited labels related to the potential intents set. Traverse all possible label sequences over the limited labels set and choose the one with the highest rewards as the ground truth. If there are multiple sequences corresponding to the highest reward, pick one randomly.

Greedy. Given a user question, we train a classification model on the annotated corpus of ambiguous questions and the corresponding potential intents by minimizing the loss function

$$\mathcal{L} = \sum_q D_{\text{KL}}[f_\theta(\cdot|q) \,\|\, P(\cdot|q)] \tag{17}$$

The classification model f_θ is used to estimate the probability distribution $P(\cdot|q)$ of the potential intents. Through this greedy method, our goal is to find a set of intents for which the sum of the probabilities of intents they cover is as high as possible. The greedy rule is given by $\text{Score}(x_t) = \sum_{s \in \mathcal{D}(x_t)} f_\theta(s, q)$, where $\mathcal{D}(x_t)$ is the marginal recall of intents described in Section 4. At each time step t, we select the label with the highest score as x_t. Thus, the label set is generated by the rule.

RL (no state transition). As another baseline, we explore the implication of not taking recommended labels into account. This is a BERT classification model which outputs the intent with the highest probability at time step t and masks it at the next time step.

5.3.2 Ablation Study

Top-K intents. To contrast the truncated interface with the original, full interface, we retrieve the m most similar intents in terms of semantic similarity without interacting with users. The detail of intent retrieval is described below. (Note that for a label-oriented interface, after the user selects one label, the original query is concatenated with the label phrase as a new query and relevant intents are retrieved by the same model.)

Intent retrieval. For each query, a list of potential intents can be retrieved and ranked by BM25. We re-rank the candidates by applying BERT model to estimate the semantic similarity between query and each candidate. The model is a 12-layer BERT, which takes the concatenation of two sentences as input. Considering the display limitation of the dialogue bot environment, the top three results are presented to the user.

5.4 Results

Offline experiments. The experimental results in Table 2 show that our method significantly outperforms others. The greedy method has limited recall due to its reliance on the accuracy of its classification model. We observed that it is difficult to achieve a satisfactory recall by estimating potential intent probabilities through a classification model.

Our policy model also significantly outperforms the model without state transitions, confirming the need for considering the action history. The labels recommended by simple classification models do not yield sufficient diversity, resulting in very low recall. By modeling the problem as a seq2seq one, our model learns to recommend a next label that differs from previous ones, thereby improving the recall of potential intents.

It is worth noting that the supervised method outperforms all other baselines except ours. We believe that it does not explore the training data sufficiently. In most cases, there are multiple label sequences that can get similar rewards, and the supervised method can only consider one of them as the ground truth, remaining unable to explore equally good or second-best paths, which leads to insufficient exploration of labels. Thus, the search of the supervised method is not as exhaustive as our method's. Our results are close to the theoretical upper bound, which is further corroborates the effectiveness of our method.

	labels=3	labels=6
Greedy	19.47%	32.01%
Supervised	45.72%	51.53%
RL (no state transition)	17.23%	29.83%
RL (ours)	**52.45%**	**57.22%**
Upper bound	60.46%	67.34%

Table 2: Offline experimental results.

Online experiments. The offline experimental results show that *RL (no state transition)* and the *Greedy* method do not perform well, leaving only *RL (ours)* for the online experiments. Here we mainly compare the performance of two rewards: recall only and reward + entropy. We compare label recommendation methods and perform an ablation study using real online user clicks. For this, we collected data over a period of two weeks in our real deployment. The experimental results, illustrated in Table 3, show that the CTR of *RL (ours)* is significantly higher than for *RL (recall)*. We believe that this gap objectively

	THA	CTR
Top-K intents	15.40%	-
RL (recall)	14.51%	62.61%
RL (ours)	**14.20%**	**66.36%**

Table 3: Online experimental results.

reflects the importance of entropy to improve the quality of the label set. Furthermore, *RL (ours)* also outperforms *RL (recall)* with regard to the rate of transferal to human agents (THA). The Top-k intents method directly retrieves the most relevant three questions without interacting with users. The THA gap between Top-K intents and RL based methods reflects the contribution of label clarification. The experiments show that our method has a positive effect with regard to the system's ability to clarify ambiguous questions, reducing the workload of human agents.

5.5   Complementary Evaluation

How to apply	
RL (recall)	apply, register, credit card
RL (ours)	credit card, loan, QR code
How to claim insurance?	
RL (recall)	claim, health insurance, medical insurance
RL (ours)	health insurance, medical insurance, homeowners insurance
What was the payment just now?	
RL (recall)	transaction records, inquire, transfer money
RL (ours)	billing details, transition records, inquire records

Table 4: Excerpts of outputs from different methods. For simplicity, only the first three are displayed.

By inspecting specific cases, we find that the main difference between *RL (recall)* and *RL (ours)* is the complementarity with the user's question. Taking "How to apply" in Table 4 as an example, *RL (recall)* selects "apply", "register", which exhibit semantic overlap with the question itself. Though these may lead to improved recall of potential intents, they do not enable any further clarification. The results of *RL (ours)* include products that one can apply for, helping to establish the user's underlying intent. For a recall-only approach, the labels that yield the highest rewards must be the ones with the highest semantic overlap. Hence, it is inevitable that repetitive information will be chosen, thereby making a part of the label set redundant.

To verify our conjecture, we compare the diversity and complementarity using the indicators introduced in Section 5.2. Although the two indicators are not precise metrics for diversity and semantic overlap, they help to assess the gap of the models trained with the two different reward mechanisms. As we can see from Table 5, the reinforcement learning methods significantly surpass the *Greedy* method on diversity, but the two RL methods are comparable to each other. This illustrates that recall as a reward is a major contribution to diversity. On its own, the overlap indicator is not meaningful,

	Diversity	Overlap
Greedy	75.27%	6.39%
RL (recall)	79.92%	9.69%
RL (ours)	**80.10%**	**7.69%**

Table 5: Complementarity evaluation: The lower the overlap, the better the complementarity.

as it can be reduced to 0 by recommending irrelevant labels. But along with the recall, the difference in overlapping rate illustrates the effectiveness on reducing semantic repetition. Therefore, the proposed reward is superior to all other compared methods.

6   Conclusion

We present an end-to-end model to resolve ambiguous questions in dialogue by clarifying them using label suggestions. We cast the question clarification problem as a collection partition problem. In order to improve the quality of the interactive labels as well as reduce the semantic overlap of the labels and the user's question, we propose a novel reward based on recall of potential intents and information gain. We establish its effectiveness in a series of experiments, which suggest that this novel notion of clarification may as well be adopted for other kinds of disambiguation problems.

References

Mohammad Aliannejadi, Hamed Zamani, Fabio Crestani, and W. Bruce Croft. 2019. Asking clarifying questions in open-domain information-seeking conversations. In Benjamin Piwowarski, Max Chevalier, Éric Gaussier, Yoelle Maarek, Jian-Yun Nie, and Falk Scholer, editors, *Proceedings of the 42nd International ACM SIGIR Conference on Research and Development in Information Retrieval, SIGIR 2019, Paris, France, July 21-25, 2019*, pages 475–484. ACM.

Marco De Boni and Suresh Manandhar. 2003. An analysis of clarification dialogue for question answering. In Marti A. Hearst and Mari Ostendorf, editors, *Human Language Technology Conference of the North American Chapter of the Association for Computational Linguistics, HLT-NAACL 2003, Edmonton, Canada, May 27 - June 1, 2003*. The Association for Computational Linguistics.

Pavel Braslavski, Denis Savenkov, Eugene Agichtein, and Alina Dubatovka. 2017. What do you mean exactly?: Analyzing clarification questions in CQA. In Ragnar Nordlie, Nils Pharo, Luanne Freund, Birger Larsen, and Dan Russel, editors, *Proceedings of the 2017 Conference on Conference Human Information Interaction and Retrieval, CHIIR 2017, Oslo, Norway, March 7-11, 2017*, pages 345–348. ACM.

Cameron Browne, Edward Jack Powley, Daniel Whitehouse, Simon M. Lucas, Peter I. Cowling, Philipp Rohlfshagen, Stephen Tavener, Diego Perez Liebana, Spyridon Samothrakis, and Simon Colton. 2012. A survey of monte carlo tree search methods. *IEEE Trans. Comput. Intellig. and AI in Games*, 4(1):1–43.

Christian Buck, Jannis Bulian, Massimiliano Ciaramita, Wojciech Gajewski, Andrea Gesmundo, Neil Houlsby, and Wei Wang. 2018. Ask the right questions: Active question reformulation with reinforcement learning. In *6th International Conference on Learning Representations, ICLR 2018, Vancouver, BC, Canada, April 30 - May 3, 2018, Conference Track Proceedings*. OpenReview.net.

Rémi Coulom. 2006. Efficient selectivity and backup operators in monte-carlo tree search. In *Computers and Games, 5th International Conference, CG 2006, Turin, Italy, May 29-31, 2006. Revised Papers*, pages 72–83.

Jacob Devlin, Ming-Wei Chang, Kenton Lee, and Kristina Toutanova. 2019. BERT: pre-training of deep bidirectional transformers for language understanding. In *Proceedings of the 2019 Conference of the North American Chapter of the Association for Computational Linguistics: Human Language Technologies, NAACL-HLT 2019, Minneapolis, MN, USA, June 2-7, 2019, Volume 1 (Long and Short Papers)*, pages 4171–4186.

Ahmed Elgohary, Denis Peskov, and Jordan Boyd-Graber. 2019. Can you unpack that? learning to rewrite questions-in-context. In *Empirical Methods in Natural Language Processing*.

Levente Kocsis and Csaba Szepesvári. 2006. Bandit based monte-carlo planning. In *Machine Learning: ECML 2006, 17th European Conference on Machine Learning, Berlin, Germany, September 18-22, 2006, Proceedings*, pages 282–293.

Mandy Korpusik and James R. Glass. 2019. Deep learning for database mapping and asking clarification questions in dialogue systems. *IEEE/ACM Trans. Audio, Speech & Language Processing*, 27(8):1321–1334.

Alexander Kotov and ChengXiang Zhai. 2010. Towards natural question guided search. In Michael Rappa, Paul Jones, Juliana Freire, and Soumen Chakrabarti, editors, *Proceedings of the 19th International Conference on World Wide Web, WWW 2010, Raleigh, North Carolina, USA, April 26-30, 2010*, pages 541–550. ACM.

Jiwei Li, Alexander H. Miller, Sumit Chopra, Marc'Aurelio Ranzato, and Jason Weston. 2017. Learning through dialogue interactions by asking questions. In *5th International Conference on Learning Representations, ICLR 2017, Toulon, France, April 24-26, 2017, Conference Track Proceedings*. OpenReview.net.

Ye Liu, Chenwei Zhang, Xiaohui Yan, Yi Chang, and Philip S. Yu. 2019. Generative question refinement with deep reinforcement learning in retrieval-based QA system. In Wenwu Zhu, Dacheng Tao, Xueqi Cheng, Peng Cui, Elke A. Rundensteiner, David Carmel, Qi He, and Jeffrey Xu Yu, editors, *Proceedings of the 28th ACM International Conference on Information and Knowledge Management, CIKM 2019, Beijing, China, November 3-7, 2019*, pages 1643–1652. ACM.

Hao Ma, Michael R. Lyu, and Irwin King. 2010. Diversifying query suggestion results. In Maria Fox and David Poole, editors, *Proceedings of the Twenty-Fourth AAAI Conference on Artificial Intelligence, AAAI 2010, Atlanta, Georgia, USA, July 11-15, 2010*. AAAI Press.

Rodrigo Nogueira and Kyunghyun Cho. 2017. Task-oriented query reformulation with reinforcement learning. In Martha Palmer, Rebecca Hwa, and Sebastian Riedel, editors, *Proceedings of the 2017 Conference on Empirical Methods in Natural Language Processing, EMNLP 2017, Copenhagen, Denmark, September 9-11, 2017*, pages 574–583. Association for Computational Linguistics.

Silvia Quarteroni and Suresh Manandhar. 2009. Designing an interactive open-domain question answering system. *Natural Language Engineering*, 15(1):73–95.

J. Ross Quinlan. 1986. Induction of decision trees. *Machine Learning*, 1(1):81–106.

Filip Radlinski and Nick Craswell. 2017. A theoretical framework for conversational search. In Ragnar Nordlie, Nils Pharo, Luanne Freund, Birger Larsen, and Dan Russel, editors, *Proceedings of the 2017 Conference on Conference Human Information Interaction and Retrieval, CHIIR 2017, Oslo, Norway, March 7-11, 2017*, pages 117–126. ACM.

Sudha Rao and Hal Daumé. 2018. Learning to ask good questions: Ranking clarification questions using neural expected value of perfect information. In Iryna Gurevych and Yusuke Miyao, editors, *Proceedings of the 56th Annual Meeting of the Association for Computational Linguistics, ACL 2018, Melbourne, Australia, July 15-20, 2018, Volume 1: Long Papers*, pages 2737–2746. Association for Computational Linguistics.

Sudha Rao and Hal Daumé. 2019. Answer-based adversarial training for generating clarification questions. In Jill Burstein, Christy Doran, and Thamar Solorio, editors, *Proceedings of the 2019 Conference of the North American Chapter of the Association for Computational Linguistics: Human Language Technologies, NAACL-HLT 2019, Minneapolis, MN, USA, June 2-7, 2019, Volume 1 (Long and Short Papers)*, pages 143–155. Association for Computational Linguistics.

Eldar Sadikov, Jayant Madhavan, Lu Wang, and Alon Y. Halevy. 2010. Clustering query refinements by user intent. In Michael Rappa, Paul Jones, Juliana Freire, and Soumen Chakrabarti, editors, *Proceedings of the 19th International Conference on World Wide Web, WWW 2010, Raleigh, North Carolina, USA, April 26-30, 2010*, pages 841–850. ACM.

Hassan Sajjad, Patrick Pantel, and Michael Gamon. 2012. Underspecified query refinement via natural language question generation. In Martin Kay and Christian Boitet, editors, *COLING 2012, 24th International Conference on Computational Linguistics, Proceedings of the Conference: Technical Papers, 8-15 December 2012, Mumbai, India*, pages 2341–2356. Indian Institute of Technology Bombay.

David Silver, Julian Schrittwieser, Karen Simonyan, Ioannis Antonoglou, Aja Huang, Arthur Guez, Thomas Hubert, Lucas Baker, Matthew Lai, and Adrian Bolton. 2017. Mastering the game of go without human knowledge. *Nature*, 550(7676):354–359.

Yang Tang, Fan Bu, Zhicheng Zheng, and Xiaoyan Zhu. 2011. Towards interactive qa: suggesting refinement for questions. *Belkin et al.[2]*, pages 13–14.

Sebastian Varges, Silvia Quarteroni, Giuseppe Riccardi, and Alexei V. Ivanov. 2010. Investigating clarification strategies in a hybrid POMDP dialog manager. In Raquel Fernández, Yasuhiro Katagiri, Kazunori Komatani, Oliver Lemon, and Mikio Nakano, editors, *Proceedings of the SIGDIAL 2010 Conference, The 11th Annual Meeting of the Special Interest Group on Discourse and Dialogue, 24-15 September 2010, Tokyo, Japan*, pages 213–216. The Association for Computer Linguistics.

Ashish Vaswani, Noam Shazeer, Niki Parmar, Jakob Uszkoreit, Llion Jones, Aidan N. Gomez, Lukasz Kaiser, and Illia Polosukhin. 2017. Attention is all you need. In Isabelle Guyon, Ulrike von Luxburg, Samy Bengio, Hanna M. Wallach, Rob Fergus, S. V. N. Vishwanathan, and Roman Garnett, editors, *Advances in Neural Information Processing Systems 30: Annual Conference on Neural Information Processing Systems 2017, 4-9 December 2017, Long Beach, CA, USA*, pages 5998–6008.

Yansen Wang, Chenyi Liu, Minlie Huang, and Liqiang Nie. 2018. Learning to ask questions in open-domain conversational systems with typed decoders. In Iryna Gurevych and Yusuke Miyao, editors, *Proceedings of the 56th Annual Meeting of the Association for Computational Linguistics, ACL 2018, Melbourne, Australia, July 15-20, 2018, Volume 1: Long Papers*, pages 2193–2203. Association for Computational Linguistics.

Yongfeng Zhang, Xu Chen, Qingyao Ai, Liu Yang, and W. Bruce Croft. 2018. Towards conversational search and recommendation: System ask, user respond. In Alfredo Cuzzocrea, James Allan, Norman W. Paton, Divesh Srivastava, Rakesh Agrawal, Andrei Z. Broder, Mohammed J. Zaki, K. Selçuk Candan, Alexandros Labrinidis, Assaf Schuster, and Haixun Wang, editors, *Proceedings of the 27th ACM International Conference on Information and Knowledge Management, CIKM 2018, Torino, Italy, October 22-26, 2018*, pages 177–186. ACM.

Xinbo Zhang, Lei Zou, and Sen Hu. 2019. An interactive mechanism to improve question answering systems via feedback. In Wenwu Zhu, Dacheng Tao, Xueqi Cheng, Peng Cui, Elke A. Rundensteiner, David Carmel, Qi He, and Jeffrey Xu Yu, editors, *Proceedings of the 28th ACM International Conference on Information and Knowledge Management, CIKM 2019, Beijing, China, November 3-7, 2019*, pages 1381–1390. ACM.

Zhicheng Zheng, Xiance Si, Edward Y. Chang, and Xiaoyan Zhu. 2011. K2Q: generating natural language questions from keywords with user refinements. In *Fifth International Joint Conference on Natural Language Processing, IJCNLP 2011, Chiang Mai, Thailand, November 8-13, 2011*, pages 947–955. The Association for Computer Linguistics.

Towards building a Robust *Industry-scale* Question Answering System

Rishav Chakravarti,[*] Anthony Ferritto, Bhavani Iyer, Lin Pan
Radu Florian, Salim Roukos, Avirup Sil[†]
IBM Research AI
Yorktown Heights, NY
{panl, roukos, raduf, murdockj, bsiyer, avi}@us.ibm.com
aferritto@ibm.com
chakrris@amazon.com

Abstract

Industry-scale NLP systems necessitate two features. 1. Robustness: "zero-shot transfer learning" (ZSTL) performance has to be commendable and 2. Efficiency: systems have to train efficiently and respond instantaneously. In this paper, we introduce the development of a production model called GAAMA (Go Ahead Ask Me Anything) which possess the above two characteristics. For robustness, it trains on the recently introduced Natural Questions (NQ) dataset. NQ poses additional challenges over older datasets like SQuAD: (a) QA systems need to read and comprehend an entire Wikipedia article rather than a small passage, and (b) NQ does not suffer from observation bias during construction, resulting in less lexical overlap between the question and the article. GAAMA consists of Attention-over-Attention, diversity among attention heads, hierarchical transfer learning, and synthetic data augmentation while being computationally inexpensive. Building on top of the powerful BERT_{QA} model, GAAMA provides a ~2.0% absolute boost in F_1 over the industry-scale state-of-the-art (SOTA) system on NQ. Further, we show that GAAMA transfers zero-shot to unseen real life and important domains as it yields respectable performance on two benchmarks: the BioASQ and the newly introduced CovidQA datasets.

1 Introduction

A relatively new task in open domain question answering (QA) is machine reading comprehension (MRC), which aims to read and comprehend a given text and then answer questions based on it. Recent work on transfer learning, from large pre-trained language models like BERT (Devlin et al., 2019) and XLNet (Yang et al., 2019) has practically solved SQuAD (Rajpurkar et al., 2016; Rajpurkar et al., 2018), the most widely used MRC benchmark. This necessitates harder QA benchmarks for the field to advance. Additionally, SQuAD and other existing datasets like NarrativeQA (Kočiský et al., 2018) and HotpotQA (Yang et al., 2018) suffer from observation bias: annotators had read the passages before creating their questions.

In industry research, there is an urgent demand to build a usable MRC QA system that not only provides very good performance on academic benchmarks but also real life industry applications (Tang et al., 2020) in a ZSTL environment. In this paper, to build such a system, we first focus on Natural Questions (NQ) (Kwiatkowski et al., 2019): a MRC benchmark dataset over Wikipedia articles where questions (see Figure 1) were sampled from Google search logs. This key difference from past datasets eliminates annotator observation bias. Also, NQ requires systems to extract both a short (SA, one or more entities) and a long answer (LA, typically a paragraph that contains the short answer when both exist). The dataset shows human upper bounds of 76% and 87% on the short and long answer selection tasks respectively (for a "super-annotator" composed of 5 human annotators). The authors show that systems designed for past datasets perform poorly on NQ.

---

[*] Work completed while at IBM, author is currently at Amazon

[†] Corresponding author.

Proceedings of the 28th International Conference on Computational Linguistics: Industry Track, pages 90–101
Barcelona, Spain (Online), December 12, 2020

Example 1
Question: when did marley die in a christmas carol?
Wikipedia Page: Jacob Marley
Gold Long Answer: In A Christmas Carol, Marley is the first character mentioned in the first line of the story. Jacob Marley is said to have died seven years earlier on Christmas Eve (as the setting is Christmas Eve 1843, this would have made the date of his passing **December 24, 1836**)...
Gold Short Answer: December 24, 1836
$BERT_{QA}$: seven years earlier
Example 2
Question: who developed the concept of total quality management
Wikipedia Page: Total Quality Management
Gold Long Answer: The exact origin of the term "total quality management" is uncertain. It is almost certainly inspired by Armand V. Feigenbaum's multi-edition book Total Quality Control...
Gold Short Answer: *NULL*
$BERT_{QA}$: Armand V. Feigenbaum

Figure 1: Examples of questions in the NQ dataset. Example 1 contains the short answer in the long answer whereas Example 2 has none.

We propose GAAMA that possesses several MRC technologies that are necessary to perform well on NQ and achieve significant boosts over another industry setting competitor system (Alberti et al., 2019a) pre-trained on a large language model (LM) and then over millions of synthetic examples. Specifically, GAAMA builds on top of a large pre-trained LM and focusses on two broad dimensions:

1. **Improved Attention:** With the reduction of observation bias in NQ, we find a distinct lack of lexical and grammatical alignment between answer contexts and the questions. For example, here is a question to identify the date of an event from the SQuAD 2.0 dataset: *According to business journalist Kimberly Amadeo, when did the first signs of decline in real estate occur?* This question can be aligned almost perfectly with the text in the answering Wikipedia paragraph in order to extract the year *2006*: *Business journalist Kimberly Amadeo reports: "The first signs of decline in residential real estate occurred in 2006."* In contrast, as shown in Example 1 from Figure 1, a question from NQ to identify the date of *marley's death* requires parsing through a number of related sub clauses to extract the answer *December 24, 1836* from the context.

   This need for improved alignment leads us to explore two additional attention mechanisms.

   - **Attention-over-Attention (AoA)** (Cui et al., 2017): on top of BERT's existing layer stack, we introduce a *two-headed* AoA layer which combines *query-to-document* and *document-to-query* attention.
   - **Attention Diversity (AD)** Motivated by (Li et al., 2018), we explore a mechanism that maximizes diversity among BERT attention heads. Intuitively, we want different attention heads to capture information from different semantic subspaces, which BERT currently does not enforce. Finally, we experiment combining the two strategies, yielding a gain of ~1.5% for both short and long answers.

2. **Data Augmentation:** Given the data hungry nature of BERT-based models, we explore three strategies for data augmentation (DA). **Crowd-sourced DA** introduces human annotated Q&A pairs from prior MRC datasets. **Synthetic DA** introduces large amounts of machine generated QA pairs, inspired by the prior successes of (Alberti et al., 2019a; Dong et al., 2019). Unlike previous work, which predominantly relied on computationally expensive beam search decoding, we apply fast and diversity-promoting *nucleus* sampling (Holtzman et al., 2019) to generate 4M questions from a transformer-based question generator (Sultan et al., 2020). **Adversarial DA** performs a novel sentence-order-shuffling to perturb the native NQ data so as to tackle the inherent positional bias in Wikipedia-based MRC as shown by (Min et al., 2019; Kwiatkowski et al., 2019).

We find that, contrary to previous industry research SOTA (Alberti et al., 2019a) on NQ, it is not necessary to perform large scale synthetic DA. Instead we achieve better results with a well aligned Pre-Training (PT, a gain of 1.3–1.6%).

Most QA applications in an industry involve multiples domains e.g. Amazon Kendra[1] for Enterprise Search, Google Search, and IBM Watson Assistant[2] for Customer Service. Hence, there exists a need to develop *one* robust QA system that would work with ZSTL on a plethora of domains. Of course, one could futher fine-tune the system on the new domain to achieve better performance. However, the process is rather expensive as it demands manual human annotation which in real world applications is very scarce (Castelli et al., 2020). Hence, we explore GAAMA's ZSTL effectiveness on two publicly available benchmark bio-medical datasets: BioASQ (Tsatsaronis et al., 2015) and the newly introduced CoVIDQA (Tang et al., 2020). The former is an annual shared task for QA over biomedical documents involving factoid questions. The latter is built on top of the CORD-19 corpus (Wang et al., 2020) consisting of questions asked by humans about the Covid-19 disease. The COVID-19 pandemic has caused an abundance of research to be published on a daily basis. Providing the capability to ask questions on research is vital for ensuring that important and recent information is not overlooked and available to everyone. GAAMA consistently delivers competitive performance when compared to baselines either trained on the target domain or zero-shot transferred to the target.

Overall, our contributions can be summarized as follows: **1.** We propose a novel system that investigates several improved attention and enhanced data augmentation strategies, **2.** Outperforms the previous industry-scale QA system on NQ, **3.** Provides ZSTL capabilities on two unseen domains and **4.** Achieves competitive performance compared to the respective corresponding baselines.

2 Related Work

Most recent MRC systems either achieve SOTA by adding additional components on top of BERT (Devlin et al., 2019) such as syntax (Zhang et al., 2019) or perform attention fusion (Wang et al., 2018) without using BERT. However, we argue that additional attention mechanisms should be explored on top of BERT such as computing additional cross-attention between the question and the passage and maximizing the diversity among different attention heads in BERT. Our work is also generic enough to be applied on recently introduced transformer based language models such as ALBERT (Lan et al., 2019) and REFORMER (Kitaev et al., 2020).

Another common technique is DA (Zhang and Bansal, 2019) by artificially generating more questions to enhance the training data or in a MTL setup (Yatskar, 2018; Dhingra et al., 2018; Zhou et al., 2019). (Alberti et al., 2019a; Alberti et al., 2019b) combine models of question generation with answer extraction and filter results to ensure round-trip consistency to get the SOTA on NQ. Contrary to this, we explore several strategies for DA that either involve *diverse* question generation from a dynamic nucleus (Holtzman et al., 2019) of the probability distribution over question tokens or shuffling the existing dataset to produce adversarial examples.

Recently (Lee et al., 2019; Min et al., 2019) focus on "open" NQ, a modified version of the full NQ dataset for document retrieval QA that discards unanswerable questions. Contrary to that, we specifically focus on the full NQ dataset and believe there is room for improvement from a MRC research standpoint.

3 Model Architecture

In this section, we first describe $BERT_{QA}$, GAAMA's underlying QA model, and two additional attention layers on top of it. Figure 2 shows our overall model architecture with details explained below.

3.1 Underlying QA model: $BERT_{QA}$

Given a token sequence $\mathbf{X} = [x_1, x_2, \ldots, x_T]$: BERT, a deep Transformer (Vaswani et al., 2017) network, outputs a sequence of contextualized token representations $\mathbf{H}^L = [\mathbf{h}_1^L, \mathbf{h}_2^L, \ldots, \mathbf{h}_T^L]$.

$$\mathbf{h}_1^L, \ldots, \mathbf{h}_T^L = BERT(x_1, \ldots, x_T)$$

$BERT_{QA}$ adds three dense layers followed by a *softmax* on top of BERT for answer extraction: $\ell_b = softmax(\mathbf{W}_1\mathbf{H}^L)$, $\ell_e = softmax(\mathbf{W}_2\mathbf{H}^L)$, and $\ell_a = softmax(\mathbf{W}_3\mathbf{h}_{[CLS]}^L)$ — where $\mathbf{W}_1, \mathbf{W}_2 \in$

---

[1] https://www.onixnet.com/amazon-kendra
[2] www.ibm.com/watson/assistant

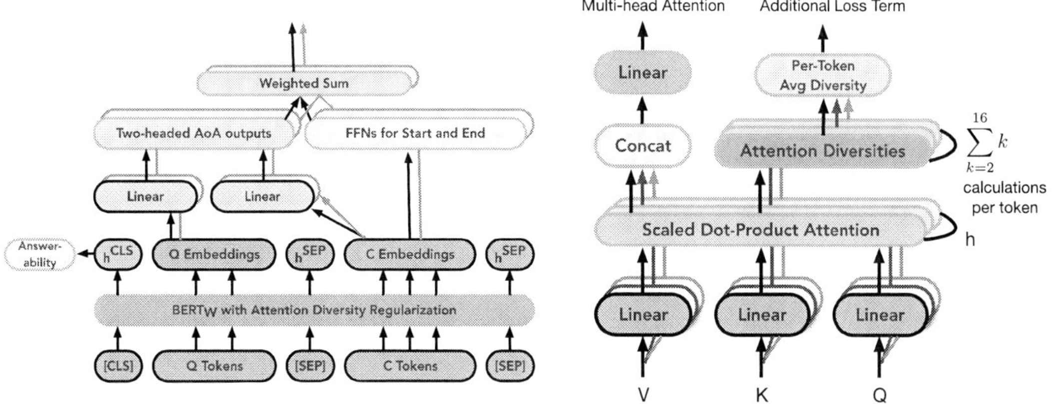

Figure 2: Overall Model Architecture
Figure 3: Our Attention Diversity Mechanism

$\mathbb{R}^{1\times 1024}$, $\mathbf{W}_3 \in \mathbb{R}^{5\times 1024}$, $\mathbf{H}^L \in \mathbb{R}^{N\times 1024}$, and $\mathbf{h}^L_{[CLS]} \in \mathbb{R}^{1024}$. ℓ^t_b and ℓ^t_e denote the probability of the tth token in the sequence being the answer beginning and end, respectively. These three layers are trained during the finetuning stage. The NQ task requires not only a prediction for short answer beginning/end offsets, but also a (containing) longer span of text that provides the necessary context for that short answer. Inspired by prior work from (Alberti et al., 2019b), we only optimize for short answer spans and then identify the bounds of the containing HTML span as the long answer prediction[3]. We use the hidden state of the [CLS] token (Devlin et al., 2019) to classify the answer type $\in [short, long, yes, no, null]$, so ℓ^y_a denotes the probability of the yth answer type being correct. Our loss function is the averaged cross entropy on the two answer pointers and the answer type classifier:

$$\mathcal{L}_{NQ} = -\frac{1}{3}\left(\sum_{t=1}^{T}(\mathbb{1}(\mathbf{b}_t)\log \ell^t_b + \mathbb{1}(\mathbf{e}_t)\log \ell^t_e) + \sum_{y=1}^{Y}\mathbb{1}(\mathbf{a}_y)\log \ell^y_a\right)$$

where $\mathbb{1}(\mathbf{b})$ and $\mathbb{1}(\mathbf{e})$ are one-hot vectors for the ground-truth beginning and end positions, and $\mathbb{1}(\mathbf{a})$ for the ground-truth answer type. During decoding, the span over *argmax* of ℓ_b and *argmax* of ℓ_e is picked as the predicted short answer.

3.2 Attention Strategies

In this section, we outline our investigation of the attention mechanisms on top of the above BERT$_{QA}$ model. Our main question: BERT already computes self-attention over the question and the passage in several layers—can we improve on top that?

3.2.1 Attention-over-Attention (AoA)

Our first approach is AoA: originally designed (Cui et al., 2017) for cloze-style question answering, where a phrase in a short passage of text is removed in forming a question. We seek to explore whether AoA helps in a more traditional MRC setting.

Let $\mathbf{Q}$ be a sequence of question tokens $[\mathbf{q}_1, \ldots, \mathbf{q}_m]$, and $\mathbf{C}$ a sequence of context tokens $[\mathbf{c}_1, \ldots, \mathbf{c}_n]$. AoA first computes an attention matrix:

$$\mathbf{M} = \mathbf{CQ}^T, \tag{1}$$

where $\mathbf{C} \in \mathbb{R}^{n\times h}$, $\mathbf{Q} \in \mathbb{R}^{m\times h}$, and $\mathbf{M} \in \mathbb{R}^{n\times m}$. In our case, the hidden dimension is $h = 1024$. Next, it separately performs on $\mathbf{M}$ a column-wise *softmax* $\alpha = softmax(\mathbf{M}^T)$ and a row-wise *softmax* $\beta = softmax(\mathbf{M})$. Each row i of matrix α represents the document-level attention regarding $\mathbf{q}_i$ (*query-to-document* attention), and each row j of matrix β represents the query-level attention regarding $\mathbf{c}_j$

---

[3]The candidate long answer HTML spans are provided as part of the preprocessed data for NQ.

(*document-to-query* attention). To combine the two attentions, β is first row-wise averaged:

$$\beta = \frac{1}{n} \sum_{j=1}^{n} \beta_j \tag{2}$$

The resulting vector can be viewed as the average importance of each $\mathbf{q}_i$ with respect to $\mathbf{C}$. This token-to-sequence attention encoded in AoA is a key difference from BERT attention. β is then used to weigh the document-level attention α.

$$\mathbf{s} = \alpha^T \beta^T \tag{3}$$

The final attention vector $\mathbf{s} \in \mathbb{R}^N$ represents document-level attention weighted by the importance of query words.

Since the output of AoA is a vector of document length, to use it for answer start and end prediction we add a *two-headed* AoA layer into the BERT_{QA} model and this layer is trained together with the answer extraction layer during the finetuning stage. Concretely, the combined question and context hidden representation $\mathbf{H}^L$ from BERT is first separated to $\mathbf{H}^Q$ and $\mathbf{H}^C$ [4], followed by *two* linear projections of $\mathbf{H}^Q$ and $\mathbf{H}^C$ respectively to $\mathbf{H}_i^Q$ and $\mathbf{H}_i^C$, $i \in \{1, 2\}$:

$$\mathbf{H}_i^Q = \mathbf{H}^Q \mathbf{W}_i^Q, \tag{4}$$
$$\mathbf{H}_i^C = \mathbf{H}^C \mathbf{W}_i^C, \tag{5}$$

where $\mathbf{H}^Q$, $\mathbf{H}_i^Q \in \mathbb{R}^{M \times 1024}$; $\mathbf{H}^C$, $\mathbf{H}_i^C \in \mathbb{R}^{N \times 1024}$; and $\mathbf{W}_i^Q, \mathbf{W}_i^C \in \mathbb{R}^{1024 \times 1024}$. Therefore, the AoA layer adds about 2.1 million parameters on top of BERT which already has 340 million. Next, we feed $\mathbf{H}_1^C$ and $\mathbf{H}_1^Q$ into the AoA calculation specified in Equations (1) - (3) to get the attention vector $\mathbf{s}_1$ for head 1. The same procedure is applied to $\mathbf{H}_2^Q$ and $\mathbf{H}_2^C$ to get $\mathbf{s}_2$ for head 2. Lastly, $\mathbf{s}_1$ and $\mathbf{s}_2$ are combined with ℓ_b and ℓ_e respectively via two weighted sum operations for answer extraction.

3.2.2 Attention Diversity (AD) layer

It has been shown through ablation studies (Kovaleva et al., 2019; Michel et al., 2019) that removing BERT attention heads can achieve comparable or better performance on some tasks. Our objective is to find out if we can diversify the information captured and train a better BERT model by enforcing diversity among the attention heads.

In a Transformer model, (Li et al., 2018) examine a few methods to enforce such diversity and see an improvement on machine translation tasks. Contrary to that we start with a pre-trained BERT model, take the attention output from scaled dot-product attention and compute the cosine similarity between all pairs of heads:

$$D = \sum_{i=1}^{Head} \sum_{j=1}^{Head} \frac{O^i \cdot O^j}{||O^i|| ||O^j||}.$$

We then average D for the per-token similarity and add it as an additional loss term. For each token, there are $16 + 15 + ... + 2$ total similarity calculations, 16 being the number of heads in BERT_{QA}. Figure 3 shows the modified structure of Multi-head Attention in the Transformer architecture. We apply this technique during finetuning on NQ and to the last layer of BERT only. It will be interesting to see how this additional training objective affects BERT pretraining, which we leave as future work.

4 Model Training

Our models follow the now common approach of starting with the pre-trained BERT language model and then finetune over the NQ dataset with an additional QA sequence prediction layer as described in section 3.1. Note that unless we specify otherwise, we are referring to the pre-trained "large" version of BERT with Whole Word Masking (BERT_W). BERT_W has the same model structure as the original BERT model, but masks whole words instead of word pieces for the Masked Language Model pre-training task and we empirically find this to be a better starting point for the NQ task.

---

[4]Superscript L is dropped here for notation convenience; we use the last layer $L = 24$ from the BERT output.

4.1 Data Augmentation (DA)

Model performance in MRC has benefited from training with labeled examples from human annotated or synthetic data augmentation from similar tasks. This includes the prior SOTA on NQ by (Alberti et al., 2019a) where 4 million synthetically generated QA pairs are introduced. In this paper, we similarly adapt and evaluate three different approaches for data augmentation: Crowd-sourced, Synthetic, and Adversarial.

Crowd-sourced DA: We leverage the previously released SQuAD 2.0 MRC dataset that obtained ~130k crowd-sourced question, answer training pairs over Wikipedia paragraphs. Note that we present results using a "pre-training" (PT) strategy where we first train on the augmentation data and, finally, perform fine-tuning exclusively on the NQ domain. We also experimented with a multi-task-learning setup as in (Ruder et al., 2019; Xu et al., 2018), but omit those experimental results for brevity since PT consistently proved to be a better augmentation strategy.

Synthetic DA: We also pre-train a model on 4M automatically generated QA examples. The generation works as follows: similar to (Dong et al., 2019), we first fine-tune a masked LM for question generation using SQuAD1.1 training examples—we choose RoBERTa (Liu et al., 2019) for its extended LM pre-training. Then a SQuAD MRC model trained on ten predefined question types—e.g. *what, how, when,* and *how many*, as opposed to full-length questions—is used to identify potential answer phrases in NQ training passages. Finally, we use diversity-promoting nucleus sampling (Holtzman et al., 2019) with a nucleus mass of .95 to sample questions from these passage-answer pairs, which has been shown to yield better QA training examples than standard beam search (Sultan et al., 2020).

Adversarial DA: Sentence Order Shuffling (SOS) The SOS strategy shuffles the ordering of sentences within paragraphs from the NQ training set. The strategy is based on an observation in the preliminary $BERT_{QA}$ model that predictions favored earlier rather than later text spans. As noted by (Kwiatkowski et al., 2019), this appears to reflect a natural bias in Wikipedia that earlier texts tend to be more informative for general questions (a default long answer classifier predicting the first paragraph gets a LA F1 of 27.8%). Hence, our perturbation of the sentence ordering is similar in spirit to the types of perturbations introduced by (Zhou et al., 2019) for SQuAD 2.0 based on observed biases in the dataset.

5 Experiments

5.1 Datasets

Source Domain We choose NQ as our source dataset. It provides 307,373 training queries, 7,830 development queries, and 7,842 test queries (with the test set only being accessible through a public leaderboard submission). For each question, crowd sourced annotators also provide start and end offsets for short answer spans[5] within the Wikipedia article, if available, as well as long answer spans (which is generally the most immediate HTML paragraph, table, or list span containing the short answer), if available. The dataset also forces models to make an attempt at "knowing what they don't know" (Rajpurkar et al., 2018) by requiring a confidence score with each prediction. For evaluation, we report the offset-based F1 overlap score. For additional details on the data and evaluation see (Kwiatkowski et al., 2019).

Target Domain To test GAAMA's ZSTL transfer capability, we choose two academic[6] benchmark datasets on a related domain: Bio-medical. The first one uses a subset of the questions and annotations from task 8b of the BioASQ competition (Tsatsaronis et al., 2015). Specifically, we extract 1,266 factoid biomedical questions for which exact answers can be extracted from one of the PubMED abstracts marked as relevant by the annotators. We report the Factoid Mean Reciprocal Rank (MRR) as the evaluation metric. Secondly, we choose the very recent CovidQA (Tang et al., 2020) benchmark to illustrate GAAMA's performance on a globally important transfer learning dataset. This is a QA dataset specifically designed for COVID-19 and manually annotated from knowledge gathered from Kaggle's

---

[5] ~1% of the questions are annotated with boolean Yes/No instead of short answers. We leave it as future work to detect and generate answers for these types of queries.

[6] Note, we have tested GAAMA's ZSTL successful transfer on several in-house datasets which we cannot publish due to license restrictions.

COVID-19 Open Research Dataset Challenge. It is the first publicly available QA resource on the pandemic intended as a stopgap measure for guiding research until more substantial evaluation resources become available. It consists of 124 question–article pairs (v0.1) and hence does not have sufficient examples for supervised machine learning. CovidQA evaluates the zero-shot transfer capabilities of existing models on topics specifically related to COVID-19. One difference of CovidQA from the other QA datasets we evaluate is that it requires systems to predict the correct *sentence* that answers the question. Hence we intuitively report the P@1, R@3, and MRR based on the official evaluation metric.

5.2 Competitors

We compare GAAMA against three strong competitors from the industry research: **1)** A hybrid of a decomposable attention model for Natural Language Inference (Parikh et al., 2016) and DrQA (Chen et al., 2017), a retrieve and rank QA model, which obtains commendable results on SQuAD. **2)** The NQ baseline system (Alberti et al., 2019b) and **3)** The current industry SOTA on NQ (Alberti et al., 2019a) which utilizes 4 million synthetic examples as pre-training. Architecturally, the latter is similar to us but we propose more technical novelty in terms of both improved attention and data augmentation. We note there is very recent academic work (Zheng et al., 2020)which we omit as GAAMA outperforms them on short answers and more importantly we compare against large scale industry SOTA for the scope of this paper. Since their work is more academic, their model enjoys being computationally more expensive for accuracy than GAAMA as they involve computing graph attentions that are typically more difficult to be run in parallel if we want to do whole graph propagation (Veličković et al., 2018).

6 Results:

Attention Strategies: Both the AoA and AD strategies provide a meaningful $(0.7 - 0.9\%)$ improvement over a baseline $BERT_W$ model as shown in Table 1. Note that our baseline $BERT_W$ already achieves a stronger baseline than previously published SOTA by (Alberti et al., 2019a) by relying on the stronger whole-word-masking pre-training mechanism for the underlying BERT model. Combining both attention strategies with the SQUAD 2 PT yields the best single model performance, though the improvements are primarily on LA performance rather than SA. Exploring why only LA improves is left as part of our future work once we start with even larger, better pre-trained models.

Data Augmentation: As seen in Table 2, using a (well aligned) crowd-sourced dataset (SQuAD 2) for pre-training proves to be quite effective. It provides the largest data augmentation gain in SA F1, ~1.6%, as well as a ~1% gain in LA F1. Employing 4 million synthetic question answer pairs also provide similar gains in SA F1 and an even better gain (~2.3%) in LA F1. From an efficiency perspective, however, SQuAD 2 PT only introduces 130K additional examples to the training process, whereas synthetic data augmentation requires training over 4M additional examples (on top of the training required for the data generator). We also find that it was unhelpful to combine SQUAD 2 PT with 4M synthetic examples for improving single model performance; so we evaluate our best performing model architectures only using the SQuAD 2 PT strategy.

	Short Answer F1	Long Answer F1
Human Performance		
Single human	57.5	73.4
Super-annotator	75.7	87.2
Prior Work (Industry Research on NQ)		
DecAtt + Doc Reader (Parikh et al., 2016)	31.4	54.8
$BERT_L$ w/ SQuAD 1.1 PT (Alberti et al., 2019b)	52.7	64.7
$BERT_L$ w/ 4M Synthetic (Alberti et al., 2019a)	55.1	65.9
This Work		
GAAMA: $BERT_W$ + AoA + AD + SQuAD 2 PT	**57.0**	**68.6**

Table 1: **Comparison of GAAMA vs prior work in the industry.** GAAMA clearly outperforms the competitors in both short and long answer F1.

Data Augmentation on BERT	Short Answer F1	Long Answer F1
BERT$_W$ + SOS	55.8	66.7
BERT$_W$ + 1M Synthetic	56.6	67.9
BERT$_W$ + 4M Synthetic	56.9	**68.3**
BERT$_W$ + SQuAD 2 PT	**57.0**	67.3
BERT$_W$ + SQuAD 2 PT + 4M Synthetic	56.8	67.6

Table 2: **Performance of various Data Augmentation strategies.** SQuAD helps short but synthetic helps long answers.

6.1 ZSTL Experiments

We create a random train (75%) and test split (25%) of the BioASQ 8b annotated questions in order to assess the performance of GAAMA with and without training. Comparison with more heavily fine-tuned prior art (Yoon et al., 2019) is left as part of future work and beyond the scope of this work as they focus on fine-tuned large language models e.g. BioBERT (Lee et al., 2020) with more extensive vocabularies. Note again, that our work focuses on minimizing these steps for new target domains. Hence, since our objective is not to keep retraining GAAMA for every new domain, we refrain from changing the underlying pre-trained LM. We observe that the GAAMA's ZSTL config performs competitively (0.56 lower on MRR) on BioASQ showing that there is hope of transferring models zero-shot to entirely unseen domains.

On CovidQA, we predict the sentence that contains our predicted answers. Table 6 shows the results. GAAMA performs quite competitively to a BioBERT baseline and outperforms it on all the three metrics. This amplifies the fact that it is not always necessary to start with a domain-specific LM. We note that GAAMA gets better P@1, slightly lower R@3, and the same MRR and hence it still gives a tough competition to a system trained on empirically a much better performing pre-trained LM than BERT: T5 (Raffel et al., 2019). We also note that both the T5 and BioBERT baselines are trained specifically to do sentence classification whereas GAAMA performs reading comprehension to extract answer spans and we predict the sentence that contains the spans. So no new "task-specific" training is involved in this process.

Components	SAF1	LA F1
BERT$_W$ + AoA + AD + SQuAD 2 PT	57.0	**68.6**
- AD	**57.2**	68.2
- AoA	57.0	68.5
- SQuAD 2 PT	56.7	67.5
Effects of Attention & Data Augmentation		
- AoA - SQuAD 2 PT	56.3	66.7
- AD - SQuAD 2 PT	56.1	67.3
- AoA - AD - SQuAD 2 PT	55.4	66.0

Table 3: Ablation study of GAAMA's various components.

Model	$F1$	T_{50}^G	T_{95}^G	T_{50}^C	T_{95}^C
Base	42.5	0.05	0.49	0.53	2.32
Large	50.8	0.10	0.66	1.51	6.00

Table 4: F1 and inference times for BERT base and large models running on GPU and CPU for a subset of the NQ dev set. T_K^D is the K-th percentile inference in seconds when running on device D (GPU or CPU).

GAAMA Configs	Factoid MRR
Trained on target domain	**24.93**
ZSTL	24.37

Table 5: Results on our test split of the BioASQ 8b dataset. GAAMA with ZSTL is highly competitive.

	P@1	R@3	MRR
Prior Work (Tang et al., 2020)			
BioBERT + MS MARCO	0.194	0.313	0.312
T5 + MS MARCO	0.282	**0.404**	**0.415**
This Work			
GAAMA (ZSTL)	**0.306**	0.377	0.414

Table 6: ZSTL performance of GAAMA vs. the prior work on the CovidQA dataset.

6.2 Efficiency

Inference: Inference efficiency is a crucial requirement of industry-scale systems. We investigate the inference times of both base and large models; while large models are ideal for academic benchmarks, the faster inference times of base models can be worth the reduction in accuracy in industrial settings. Measurements are carried out using a random sample of examples from the NQ dev set with a Nvidia® Tesla® P100 GPU and 8 threads from an Intel® Xeon® E5-2690 16-core CPU. In order to decrease inference time, we simulate passage retrieval to send the model the most relevant passage by selecting the first correct top level candidate if there is one and the first (incorrect) top level candidate if there is not. We find in Table 4 that switching from base to large yields an 8.3% absolute increase in F1 in exchange for 1.3x to 2.8x increases in inference time. When running the model on a GPU these result in manageable 95th percentile inference times of less than a second; whereas on the CPU the 95th percentile times are multiple seconds. We conclude that either of these models could be deployed in production environments on GPU only. In future work we intend to explore network pruning or knowledge distillation techniques for potential speedups with the large model.

Training: Efficient training is also an important component of industry-scale systems. To this end we consider both the number of model parameters and the amount of PT data. Our AoA implementation adds less than 1% to $BERT_W$'s parameters and AD does not add any as it is implemented in the loss. Similarly, by using a well-aligned PT dataset (SQuAD 2.0) we are able to rival the performance of the much larger 4M synthetically generated corpus (Alberti et al., 2019a) with only 130K examples as seen in Table 2.

7 Analysis of GAAMA's Components

Table 3 shows the ablation study of GAAMA's components. Note that our best model's performance on short answers (57.2) almost matches a single human performance[7]. When doing manual error analysis on a sample of the NQ dev set, we do observe patterns suggesting that each of GAAMA's components do bring different strengths over just the best final combination ($BERT_w$ + AoA + AD + SQuAD2 PT) e.g. the Wikipedia article for *Salary Cap* contains multiple sentences related to the query *"when did the nfl adopt a salary cap"*:

> The new Collective Bargaining Agreement (CBA) formulated in **2011** had an initial salary cap of $120 million...The cap was first introduced for the **1994** season and was initially $34.6 million. Both the cap and...

The later sentence contains the correct answer, *1994*, since the question is asking for when the salary cap was initially adopted. The SOS augmented model correctly makes this prediction whereas our SQUAD 2 augmented models predict *2011* from the earlier sentence. There are also cases where the correct answer span appears in the middle or later part of a paragraph and, though our SQUAD 2 augmented models predict the spans correctly, they assign a lower score (relative to its optimal threshold) than the SOS augmented model. The position bias, therefore, appears to hurt the performance of the system in certain situations where location of the answer span relative to the paragraph is not a useful signal of correctness.

On average, of course, the $BERT_W$+SQUAD2 PT + AoA + AD configuration performs the best and manual error analysis indicates some ability to better attend to supporting evidence when it is further out from the correct answer span. For example, the correct answer in example 1 from figure 1 is *December 24, 1836* which the AoA + AD model correctly identifies the answer span despite the question's and context's lack of lexical and grammatical alignment. While the base $BERT_W$ models fail at extracting the date (instead predicting a span more closely associated with the keywords in the query such as *seven years earlier*).

8 Conclusion

Although large pre-trained language models have shown super-human performance on benchmark datasets like SQuAD, we show that there is plenty of room to make improvements on top of $BERT_{QA}$. Specifically, we outline prior strategies that do not work on a real benchmark consisting of "natural

---

[7](Kwiatkowski et al., 2019) notes that human performance was measured on a random sample of NQ dev.

questions" showing the difficulty of the dataset and need for better algorithms. We introduce GAAMA and outline several strategies that are broadly classified under attention and data augmentation and show how effective it can be to attain competitive performance on NQ compared to other industry baselines. We also outline GAAMA's OOTB zero-shot transfer on two unseen datsets and show optimistic performance. Our future work will involve adding larger pre-trained language models like T5 and also exploring multi-lingual QA.

9 Acknowledgement

We would like to thank the multilingual NLP team at IBM Research AI and the anonymous reviewers for their helpful suggestions and feedback.

References

Chris Alberti, Daniel Andor, Emily Pitler, Jacob Devlin, and Michael Collins. 2019a. Synthetic QA corpora generation with roundtrip consistency. *CoRR*, abs/1906.05416.

Chris Alberti, Kenton Lee, and Michael Collins. 2019b. A BERT baseline for the natural questions. *arXiv preprint arXiv:1901.08634*, pages 1–4.

Vittorio Castelli, Rishav Chakravarti, Saswati Dana, Anthony Ferritto, Radu Florian, Martin Franz, Dinesh Garg, Dinesh Khandelwal, Scott McCarley, Mike McCawley, et al. 2020. The TechQA Dataset. *Association for Computational Linguistics (ACL)*.

Danqi Chen, Adam Fisch, Jason Weston, and Antoine Bordes. 2017. Reading wikipedia to answer open-domain questions. In *Proceedings of the 55th Annual Meeting of the Association for Computational Linguistics (Volume 1: Long Papers)*, pages 1870–1879.

Yiming Cui, Zhipeng Chen, Si Wei, Shijin Wang, Ting Liu, and Guoping Hu. 2017. Attention-over-attention neural networks for reading comprehension. In *Proc. of ACL (Volume 1: Long Papers)*, pages 593–602. ACL, July.

Jacob Devlin, Ming-Wei Chang, Kenton Lee, and Kristina Toutanova. 2019. BERT: Pre-training of deep bidirectional transformers for language understanding. In *NAACL-HLT*.

Bhuwan Dhingra, Danish Pruthi, and Dheeraj Rajagopal. 2018. Simple and effective semi-supervised question answering. *CoRR*, abs/1804.00720.

Li Dong, Nan Yang, Wenhui Wang, Furu Wei, Xiaodong Liu, Yu Wang, Jianfeng Gao, Ming Zhou, and Hsiao-Wuen Hon. 2019. Unified language model pre-training for natural language understanding and generation. In *NeurIPS*.

Ari Holtzman, Jan Buys, Maxwell Forbes, and Yejin Choi. 2019. The curious case of neural text degeneration. *arXiv preprint*.

Nikita Kitaev, Łukasz Kaiser, and Anselm Levskaya. 2020. Reformer: The efficient transformer.

Tomáš Kočiský, Jonathan Schwarz, Phil Blunsom, Chris Dyer, Karl Moritz Hermann, Gábor Melis, and Edward Grefenstette. 2018. The NarrativeQA reading comprehension challenge. *TACL*, 6:317–328.

Olga Kovaleva, Alexey Romanov, Anna Rogers, and Anna Rumshisky. 2019. Revealing the dark secrets of bert. In *EMNLP*, pages 4356–4365.

Tom Kwiatkowski, Jennimaria Palomaki, Olivia Redfield, Michael Collins, Ankur Parikh, Chris Alberti, Danielle Epstein, Illia Polosukhin, Matthew Kelcey, Jacob Devlin, Kenton Lee, Kristina N. Toutanova, Llion Jones, Ming-Wei Chang, Andrew Dai, Jakob Uszkoreit, Quoc Le, and Slav Petrov. 2019. Natural Questions: a benchmark for question answering research. *TACL*.

Zhenzhong Lan, Mingda Chen, Sebastian Goodman, Kevin Gimpel, Piyush Sharma, and Radu Soricut. 2019. Albert: A lite bert for self-supervised learning of language representations.

Kenton Lee, Ming-Wei Chang, and Kristina Toutanova. 2019. Latent retrieval for weakly supervised open domain question answering. *arXiv preprint arXiv:1906.00300*.

Jinhyuk Lee, Wonjin Yoon, Sungdong Kim, Donghyeon Kim, Sunkyu Kim, Chan Ho So, and Jaewoo Kang. 2020. Biobert: a pre-trained biomedical language representation model for biomedical text mining. *Bioinformatics*, 36(4):1234–1240.

Jian Li, Zhaopeng Tu, Baosong Yang, Michael R Lyu, and Tong Zhang. 2018. Multi-head attention with disagreement regularization. In *EMNLP*, pages 2897–2903.

Yinhan Liu, Myle Ott, Naman Goyal, Jingfei Du, Mandar Joshi, Danqi Chen, Omer Levy, Mike Lewis, Luke Zettlemoyer, and Veselin Stoyanov. 2019. RoBERTa: A robustly optimized BERT pretraining approach. *CoRR*, abs/1907.11692.

Paul Michel, Omer Levy, and Graham Neubig. 2019. Are sixteen heads really better than one? In *Advances in Neural Information Processing Systems 32*, pages 14014–14024. Curran Associates, Inc.

Sewon Min, Danqi Chen, Hannaneh Hajishirzi, and Luke Zettlemoyer. 2019. A discrete hard em approach for weakly supervised question answering. In *EMNLP*.

Ankur Parikh, Oscar Täckström, Dipanjan Das, and Jakob Uszkoreit. 2016. A decomposable attention model for natural language inference. *EMNLP*.

Colin Raffel, Noam Shazeer, Adam Roberts, Katherine Lee, Sharan Narang, Michael Matena, Yanqi Zhou, Wei Li, and Peter J Liu. 2019. Exploring the limits of transfer learning with a unified text-to-text transformer. *arXiv preprint arXiv:1910.10683*.

Pranav Rajpurkar, Jian Zhang, Konstantin Lopyrev, and Percy Liang. 2016. SQuAD: 100,000+ questions for machine comprehension of text. *EMNLP*.

Pranav Rajpurkar, Robin Jia, and Percy Liang. 2018. Know what you don't know: Unanswerable questions for SQuAD. *arXiv preprint arXiv:1806.03822*.

Sebastian Ruder, Matthew E. Peters, Swabha Swayamdipta, and Thomas Wolf. 2019. Transfer learning in natural language processing. In *Proc. of NAACL: Tutorials*, pages 15–18, Minneapolis, Minnesota, June. ACL.

Md Arafat Sultan, Shubham Chandel, Ramón Fernandez Astudillo, and Vittorio Castelli. 2020. On the importance of diversity in question generation for QA. In *Proceedings of the 58th Annual Meeting of the Association for Computational Linguistics*, pages 5651–5656, Online, July. Association for Computational Linguistics.

Raphael Tang, Rodrigo Nogueira, Edwin Zhang, Nikhil Gupta, Phuong Cam, Kyunghyun Cho, and Jimmy Lin. 2020. Rapidly Bootstrapping a Question Answering Dataset for COVID-19.

George Tsatsaronis, Georgios Balikas, Prodromos Malakasiotis, Ioannis Partalas, Matthias Zschunke, Michael R Alvers, Dirk Weissenborn, Anastasia Krithara, Sergios Petridis, Dimitris Polychronopoulos, et al. 2015. An overview of the bioasq large-scale biomedical semantic indexing and question answering competition. *BMC bioinformatics*, 16(1):138.

Ashish Vaswani, Noam Shazeer, Niki Parmar, Jakob Uszkoreit, Llion Jones, Aidan N Gomez, Ł ukasz Kaiser, and Illia Polosukhin. 2017. Attention is all you need. In *Advances in Neural Information Processing Systems*, pages 5998–6008. Curran Associates, Inc.

Petar Veličković, Guillem Cucurull, Arantxa Casanova, Adriana Romero, Pietro Liò, and Yoshua Bengio. 2018. Graph attention networks. In *International Conference on Learning Representations*.

Wei Wang, Ming Yan, and Chen Wu. 2018. Multi-granularity hierarchical attention fusion networks for reading comprehension and question answering. *ACL*.

Lucy Lu Wang, Kyle Lo, Yoganand Chandrasekhar, Russell Reas, Jiangjiang Yang, Darrin Eide, Kathryn Funk, Rodney Michael Kinney, Ziyang Liu, William. Merrill, Paul Mooney, Dewey A. Murdick, Devvret Rishi, Jerry Sheehan, Zhihong Shen, Brandon Stilson, Alex D. Wade, Kuansan Wang, Christopher Wilhelm, Boya Xie, Douglas M. Raymond, Daniel S. Weld, Oren Etzioni, and Sebastian Kohlmeier. 2020. Cord-19: The covid-19 open research dataset. *ArXiv*.

Yichong Xu, Xiaodong Liu, Yelong Shen, Jingjing Liu, and Jianfeng Gao. 2018. Multi-task learning for machine reading comprehension. *CoRR*, abs/1809.06963.

Zhilin Yang, Peng Qi, Saizheng Zhang, Yoshua Bengio, William W Cohen, Ruslan Salakhutdinov, and Christopher D Manning. 2018. HotpotQA: A dataset for diverse, explainable multi-hop question answering. *arXiv preprint arXiv:1809.09600*.

Zhilin Yang, Zihang Dai, Yiming Yang, Jaime G. Carbonell, Ruslan Salakhutdinov, and Quoc V. Le. 2019. XLNet: Generalized autoregressive pretraining for language understanding. *CoRR*, abs/1906.08237.

Mark Yatskar. 2018. A qualitative comparison of CoQA, SQuAD 2.0 and QuAC. *CoRR*, abs/1809.10735.

Wonjin Yoon, Jinhyuk Lee, Donghyeon Kim, Minbyul Jeong, and Jaewoo Kang. 2019. Pre-trained language model for biomedical question answering. In *Joint European Conference on Machine Learning and Knowledge Discovery in Databases*, pages 727–740. Springer.

Shiyue Zhang and Mohit Bansal. 2019. Addressing semantic drift in question generation for semi-supervised question answering. In *EMNLP*.

Zhuosheng Zhang, Yuwei Wu, Junru Zhou, Sufeng Duan, and Hai Zhao. 2019. SG-Net: Syntax-guided machine reading comprehension. *arXiv preprint arXiv:1908.05147*.

Bo Zheng, Haoyang Wen, Yaobo Liang, Nan Duan, Wanxiang Che, Daxin Jiang, Ming Zhou, and Ting Liu. 2020. Document modeling with graph attention networks for multi-grained machine reading comprehension. *ACL*.

Wen Zhou, Xianzhe Zhang, and Hang Jiang. 2019. Ensemble BERT with data augmentation and linguistic knowledge on SQuAD 2.0.

Delexicalized Paraphrase Generation

Boya Yu
Amazon Alexa AI
boyayu@amazon.com

Konstantine Arkoudas
Amazon Alexa AI
arkoudk@amazon.com

Wael Hamza
Amazon Alexa AI
waelhamz@amazon.com

Abstract

We present a neural model for paraphrasing and train it to generate delexicalized sentences. We achieve this by creating training data in which each input is paired with a number of reference paraphrases. These sets of reference paraphrases represent a weak type of semantic equivalence based on annotated slots and intents. To understand semantics from different types of slots, other than anonymizing slots, we apply convolutional neural networks (CNN) prior to pooling on slot values and use pointers to locate slots in the output. We show empirically that the generated paraphrases are of high quality, leading to an additional 1.29% exact match on live utterances. We also show that natural language understanding (NLU) tasks, such as intent classification and named entity recognition, can benefit from data augmentation using automatically generated paraphrases.

1 Introduction

Paraphrases provide additional ways in which the same semantic meaning can be communicated through text or voice. Automatic paraphrase generation can benefit various applications, including question answering (Fader et al., 2013), summarization (Barzilay and McKeown, 2005) and machine translation (Callison-Burch et al., 2006; Marton et al., 2009). Recently, neural paraphrasing methods have been proposed that utilize sequence-to-sequence models (Prakash et al., 2016) or generative models (Bowman et al., 2015; Gupta et al., 2018). Similar to other work (Sutskever et al., 2014; Mallinson et al., 2017), we apply an encoder-decoder model for paraphrasing, inspired by neural machine translation (NMT).

Delexicalization Unlike general paraphrases, which are typically reformulations of utterances, we paraphrase *delexicalized* sentences, in which named entities are replaced with generalized slot names. For example, "I want to listen to *Taylor Swift* 's *Shake It Off*" will be transformed into "I want to listen to {*Artist*}'s {*Music*}." As a result, it is expected that the paraphrasing model will learn more about syntactic variations rather than semantic similarities among words.

An example application of our paraphrasing model is third-party skill systems in digital voice assistants such as Amazon's Alexa. Users can extend Alexa's capabilities by "skills." These skills are built by third-party developers, using the Alexa Skills Kit (ASK), and may cover any specific domain—Starbucks orders, Uber reservations, Jeopardy quizzes, and so on. Developers can build skills on the Alexa Developer Console, and start by defining an interactive model including an intent schema, slot types, sample utterances, and an invocation phrase (Kumar et al., 2017). The sample utterances can be delexicalized, and include general slots that can be filled by provided slot values. Sample JSON for a developer-defined skill can be found below. Our paraphrasing model generates delexicalized utterances that help developers create sample utterances for Alexa Skills, augmenting the training data of NLU (Natural Language Understanding) models and improving the performance of such models.

Proceedings of the 28th International Conference on Computational Linguistics: Industry Track, pages 102–112
Barcelona, Spain (Online), December 12, 2020

Paraphrases?	Utterance	Delexicalized Utterance	Signature
Yes	Can you read me a book by Shakespear about romance	Can you read me a book by {author} about {topic}	Books, ReadBook, {author}, {topic}
	Could you find a comic book written by Mark Twain	Could you find a {topic} book written by {author}	
No	What are the movies on show near Seattle	What are the moves on show near {location}	Cinema, FindMovie, {location}
	Find movies in Chicago area on Saturday	Find movies in {location} area on {date}	Cinema, FindMovie, {location}, {date}

Table 1: Utterances with the same *signature* are considered paraphrases of one another. Slot names are in curly brackets. The *signature* of an utterance u consists of u's domain, intent, and set of slots.

Sample JSON of "play music" skill:

```
{"skill_name": "play music",
 "sample_utterances": [
   {"id": 0, "intent": "PlayMusicIntent", "text": "play {MusicName} please"},
   {"id": 1, "intent": "PlayMusicIntent", "text": "i want to listen to {MusicName}"},
   {"id": 2, "intent": "PlayMusicIntent", "text": "can you play {MusicName}"},
   {"id": 3, "intent": "PauseIntent", "text": "stop playing"},
   {"id": 4, "intent": "ResumeIntent", "text": "resume playing"}
 ],
 "slots": [{"name": MusicName, "values": ["shape_of_you", "frozen", "despacito"]}]
}
```

Equivalence sets of paraphrases. To train our neural paraphrase model, we use an internal dataset of spoken utterances and the external public dataset PPDB (Ganitkevitch et al., 2013). The internal data consists of a number of utterances in different domains and various skills that are manually annotated with intents and slots. Examples for intents and slots are shown in Table 1. We define two utterances as semantically equivalent if and only if they are annotated with the same domain or skill, intent, and *set* of slots; we then say that these utterances have the same *signature*. This equivalence relation is considerably weaker than full meaning identity (since, for example, it does not take slot order into account), but practically useful nevertheless.

Further, when creating training data for paraphrasing, we delexicalize utterances by replacing slot values with slot names; this allows us to focus on syntactic variations rather than on slot values. Grouping utterances by their *signature*, as well as delexicalizing the slots (as illustrated in Table 1), enables us to build large sets of paraphrases. In addition, since developers are required to add delexicalized grammar samples in ASK, our model can help to suggest possible utterances based on the examples developers provide during skill development stage.

The following are the main contributions of this paper:

- We use semantic equivalence classes based on the notion of *signatures*. This relaxation of strict semantic equivalence advances the prior paraphrasing paradigm.

- We generate paraphrases of delexicalized utterances, utilizing slot information from back-propagating through the values.

- We use pointers to copy slots which do not appear in the training data, thereby alleviating out-of-vocabulary problems during inference.

- We formally define various metrics to measure paraphrase quality, and use them to prove the effectiveness of the proposed sequence-of-sequence-of-sequence-to-sequence model and pointer network.

- We show that high-quality paraphrases that match live human utterances can improve downstream NLU tasks such as IC (intent classification) and NER (named entity recognition).

2   Related Work

To the best of knowledge, our research is the first to generate delexicalized paraphrases by leveraging entity information directly within a neural network. Malandrakis et al. (2019) introduce a similar notion of paraphrasing and apply variational autoencoders to control the quality of paraphrases. Sokolov and

Filimonov (2020) tackle a similar problem of paraphrasing utterances with entity types, but implement the slot copy mechanism via pre-processing and post-processing. In addition, Liu et al. (2013) apply paraphrases to improve natural understanding in an NLU system, both for augmenting rules and for enhancing features.

3   Model

We use the encoder-decoder sequence-to-sequence model (Sutskever et al., 2014). The encoder embeds an input sentence via transformers (Vaswani et al., 2017). The decoder is also a transformer model that generates output one token at a time, using information from the encoder and the previous time steps. An attention mechanism (Luong et al., 2015) helps the decoder to focus on appropriate regions of the input sentence while producing each output token. A good paraphrase should contain all the entity slots names from the source; some words remain the same in the paraphrase. To facilitate such copies, we use pointers that directly copy input tokens to the output (Rongali et al., 2020). As a result, in cases where an input token does not exist in the vocabulary, the model will learn to make the copy based on its embedding and context. Figure 1 depicts our proposed architecture.

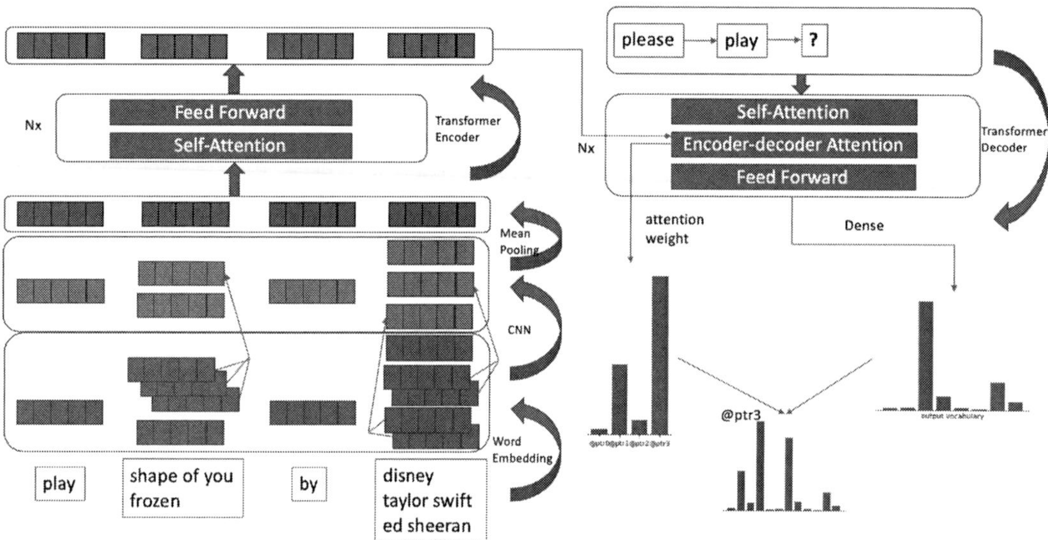

Figure 1: Sequence-of-Sequence-of-Sequence to Sequence Pointer Network to Generate Delexicalized Paraphrases

3.1   Input Embedding

One of the biggest challenges in our paraphrasing problem is how to deal with slots in sentences. Slots can come in a variety of flavors:

- Well-defined and popular slots (like music names, city names, or numbers).

- Partially defined slots, like a *Horoscope* slot that has a few samples (such as *Leo*, *Aquarius* and *Sagittarius*).

- Free-form slots that may include any random values.

Across different domains and skills, we might see slots from all three categories.

Similar to traditional sequence models for generation, we start with directly using delexicalized utterances in input and output, like "find movies in {location} on {date}" in the example above. Notice here that {location} and {date} define entity slots that may not have general semantics. We have observed that in the case of skills, each skill may have its own specific slots, and thus we may see millions of different tokens for slot values. There is little information to be gained by learning each slot value, and during inference we might see out-of-vocabulary tokens often. This model uses a direct sequence embedding layer, and we refer to it as S1. Also, at a later stage, in order to generate unseen slots during inference, we will need to anonymize the slot, and that will be referred to as AS. In this case, all slots with be replaced by tokens SLOT1, SLOT2, ... etc. in the order of their occurrence in the sequence.

We propose an S2 embedding layer (sequence-of-sequence) and an S3 embedding layer (sequence-of-sequence-of-sequence) for better handling of slots.

In S2, each token in the input sequence can also be treated as a sequence of words. For example, a delexicalized utterance such as "find movies in {location} on {date}" can be rewritten as "find movies in *boston,new york* on *tomorrow,march twenty first*". The embedding of each token will simply be the average word embedding from the sub-sequence.

However, S2 may not solve our problem in all cases. Any slot value itself can also be another sequence of multiple words, as in "find movies in *boston,new york* on *tomorrow,march twenty first*". Phrase embeddings can be used here instead of word embeddings, treating *new york* or *march twenty first* as single token. Alternatively, we add an extra convolutional layer on the sub-sub-sequence, and that will be S3. The 1D convolutional layer has a kernel size of 3, 512 channels and is followed by a dense layer to generate the phrase embedding.

In all cases, gradient descent will back-propagate all the way back to the average pooling layer and the convolutional layer. As a result, our model will learn to capture information from different slot values in any slot, and also to understand complex slot values.

3.2 Transformer Encoder and Decoder

We use the traditional transformer encoder and decoder for the seq2seq model. The embedding layer that maps input and output tokens to a vector is as defined in the previous section, while we have three different options to extract information from delexicalized sequences: AS, S2 and S3. Positional embedding will also be applied in the same way as in the original transformer model.

Afterwards, the encoder is composed of a stack of identical layers, where each layer has two sub-layers: a multi-head self-attention layer, and a simple, fully connected layer. A residual connection is employed around each of the two sub-layers, followed by layer normalization.

The decoder will be mostly similar to the encoder, including a multi-head self-attention layer and a fully connected layer, and also a third layer for multi-head attention over the encoder output.

3.3 Pointer Network

During the decoding stage, at each time step t the transformer decoder generates a hidden-state vector d_t. By multiplying that vector with the output word embedding, we get a score for each word in the vocabulary $[s_1, ..., s_{|V|}]$. A following softmax layer generates the probability for each word in vocabulary to be generated. Recall that in our case we are trying to paraphrase delexicalized utterances, where we sometimes need to generate slot names that might be out-of-vocabulary tokens. Previously, we applied a convolutional layer and mean pooling on the word embeddings, and managed to handle the problem in the encoder stage. However, similar technique cannot be directly applied in the decoder.

Alternatively, we use pointers to implement a copy mechanism that can directly copy tokens in the input to the output. From the attention over the encoder we can get a score for each token in the input, indicating the strength of the relationship between that input token and the next time step token in the decoder, $[a_1, ..., a_n]$. We concatenate the attention scores with the original unnormalized word scores, leading to a vector of $n + |V|$ dimensions $[a_1, ..., a_n, s_1, ..., s_{|V|}]$. The first n items represent @ptr$i$ ($i = 1, 2, .., n$) tokens as in Table 2, indicating scores for each input token to be copied, and the rest are scores for the output vocabulary. We then apply a softmax layer, and the model will learn that either an input token is copied or an in-vocabulary word is generated. The application of a pointer network along with AS, S2 and S3 input embeddings is referred to as ASP, S2P and S3P, respectively. And the AS embedding can be applicable even without points, because slots are anonymized.

Format	Input	Output	Slots
O	play {MusicName} by {ArtistName} please	i want to listen to {ArtistName} 's {MusicName}	MusicName:
AS	play SLOT1 by SLOT2 please	i want to listen to SLOT2 's SLOT1	frozen, shape of you
ASP	play SLOT1 by SLOT2 please	i want to listen to @ptr3 's @ptr1	ArtistName:
S2P/S3P	play frozen,shape_of_you by taylor_swift,disney please	i want to listen to @ptr3 's @ptr1	taylor swift, disney

Table 2: Different formats of training data
O: Original. AS: Anonymized Slots. ASP: Anonymized Slots with Pointers.
S2P: Sequence-of-Sequence with Pointers. S3P: Sequence-of-Sequence-of-Sequence with Pointers.

3.4 Reformat data

For implementing the model described above, we modify both source and target data to include necessary information. Within the output of models with pointers, we use token @ptr$n$ to indicate that this token is directly copied from the nth token in the input. You can find an example in Table 2.

4 Experimental Setup

In this section we introduce the training and evaluation datasets we used, and the deep sequence-to-sequence model training environment.

Dataset We train paraphrase models using data from 58,000 skills, live non-skill utterances from broader domains, and the public dataset PPDB. We then apply these models to the 88 most popular skill in order to obtain paraphrases and calculate evaluation metrics.

We generate 6.4 million paraphrase pairs from skills, which form the bulk of the training dataset. We also create another training set by appending an extra 500,000 non-skill paraphrase pairs, and two million pairs from PPDB. However, model performance here is not as remarkable. The public dataset PPDB we used only includes lexicalized paraphrase pairs, and those are generally sentences from the web and from various documents, which are a little different from our use case. In our task, including the public dataset does not seem to provide much extra gain. Thus, the discussion below focuses the analysis on results from the skill-only dataset.

Utterances are delexicalized, and each *signature* (as defined in Section 1) corresponds to a set of delexicalized utterances. We create two source-target pairs for each utterance, by randomly sampling its target from the same set. When training the model with pointers, slots in the target are replaced by respective pointers. We also cleaned up noisy data, so that utterances have reasonable length and contain enough contextual words around entities.

As described in Section 3.4, the training dataset is reformatted into four different types, with various paraphrasing models trained on each of them.

Training and Inference We implemented the special input embedding layer and transformers with pointers in MXnet 1.5.0 (Gluon API). All models are trained with the same hyperparameters for fair comparison. Both the transformer encoder and the decoder include 8 heads, 6 layers, a hidden size of 512, and a 0.1 dropout (Srivastava et al., 2014) ratio. The Adam optimizer (Kingma and Ba, 2014) and Noam learning rate scheduler are used, with an initial learning rate of 0.35 and 4000 warm-up steps. The model is trained for 40 epochs with a batch size of 1400 and with 8 batches per update. Inference is performed with a beam-search decoder. The beam size is 5 and 3-best paraphrases are kept for each input.

5 Evaluation

There are numerous evaluation metrics for sequence generation problems, such as BLEU (Papineni et al., 2002) and ROUGE (Lin, 2004). However, in our case we do not have ground truth for paraphrases and thus it would be hard to directly apply these metrics. We now describe how to evaluate paraphrase generation for the use case of data augmentation, and propose several intrinsic metrics that emphasize different characteristics. We hypothesize that paraphrases which benefit downstream models should have the following properties: divesity, novelty, and good coverage of test data. We describe each of these in detail below.

5.1 Intrinsic Metrics

We use $\mathcal{D}$ to denote the set of delexicalized utterances available at training time, and $G(\mathcal{D})$ to denote the set of generated paraphrases.

Slot Copy Error Rate calculates the ratio of slot copy misalignment in the generation. In some cases, not all slots in the input are copied into the output. To calculate this metric, all sample utterances in our 88-skill dataset are run through the paraphrasing model, generating paraphrased utterances for each; we then measure the fraction of generated utterances that don't match the source utterance slots. This metric indicates how well the model is able to identify and copy all slots in the source sequence.

Novelty is the proportion of generated utterances which are not in original paraphrase sets. This metric should give an indication of how much paraphrasing can be expected to help in augmenting grammar samples and training data:

$$\frac{|G(\mathcal{D}) \setminus \mathcal{D}|}{|G(\mathcal{D})|}$$

Diversity is the number of unique generated utterances:

$$|G(\mathcal{D})|$$

Trigram Novelty and Trigram Diversity We notice that many generated paraphrases are minor modifications of existing utterances, e.g., obtained by inserting or removing stopwords like "the" or "please." To gauge the ability of the paraphrasing model to generate sequences with larger structural differences (like creating a passive voice from an active voice), in addition to metrics at utterance level we also evaluate novelty and diversity at trigram level. This metric is similar to an inverse ROUGE-3 metric between input sequences and paraphrase outputs.

5.2 Extrinsic Metrics

In this paper we also consider downstream NLU applications, including IC and NER. We use the Alexa Skills Kit base pipeline (Kumar et al., 2017), which builds NLU models from delexicalized utterances and slots. The model includes Finite-State Transducers (FSTs) for capturing exact matches and a DNN statistical model on joint IC/NER tasks. The network consists of shared bi-LSTM layers from pre-training, skill-specific bi-LSTM layers, and on top of those two individual branches it features a dense layer and a softmax for IC, along with a dense layer and a CRF layer for NER.

For each skill, the FST is constructed from delexicalized samples and slot value samples. For the statistical model, training data is sampled from delexicalized utterances. During lexicalization, each slot is replaced with a word or phrase uniformly sampled from its entity list. We apply paraphrasing models to delexicalized samples, and augment both the FST and the DNN model training data. The added samples will first go through an intent classification filter by filling the slots and predicting the intent using the original model, and then only samples which retain the intent are added for data augmentation.

Finally, each model is applied on test data and we calculate the following metrics:

Intent Filter Rate evaluates the proportion of paraphrases which belong to the same intent.

FST New Rules is the total number of delexicalized samples added in all skills. The samples serve both as additional FST rules and as extra training data for statistical models.

FST New Matches is the percentage of live utterances in the test data that are matched by FSTs. This metric measures whether the generated paraphrases capture what users say exactly.

Intent Error Rate measures accuracy in the intent classification model. It is the proportion of utterances where the model makes an intent error.

Slot Error Rate is a metric for evaluating NER. It is defined as

$$\text{SER} = \frac{S + I + D}{\text{Total number of slots}}$$

where S, I and D are the numbers of substituted, inserted, and deleted slots, respectively.

Model	Slot Copy Rate	Novelty	Diversity	Trigram Novelty	Trigram Diversity
AS	99.98%	72.21%	33408	59.27%	39429
ASP	92.22%	53.70%	36824	48.35%	41614
S2P	84.90%	53.42%	35315	45.95%	39470
S3P	87.47%	54.16%	35706	47.88%	36779

Table 3: Intrinsic metrics from different models

		FST		NLU		
	Intent Filter Rate	New Rules	New Matches	Intent Error	Slot Error	Semantic Error
AS	54.31%	13103	1528	-2.75%	-7.97%	-3.65%
ASP	61.87%	12235	1669	-2.58%	-0.74%	-2.28%
S2P	58.21%	10982	1376	-0.20%	-0.93%	-0.83%
S3P	60.04%	11610	1438	-1.60%	-3.02%	-0.78%

Table 4: Extrinsic metrics from different models
Note: All NLU metrics are relative numbers because we cannot disclose absolute numbers

Semantic Error Rate (Makhoul et al., 1999) is a joint metric for both IC and NER. It is defined as

$$\text{SEMER} = \frac{S + I + D + IE}{\text{Total number of slots} + 1}$$

where S, I and D are again the numbers of substituted, inserted, and deleted slots, respectively. IE is 1 if there is an intent error and 0 if the model predicts the correct intent.

6 Results

The intrinsic and extrinsic results are presented in Table 3 and Table 4. In Table 5 you can find examples of paraphrases from three different skills.

Intrinsic Metrics The usual sequence-to-sequence model achieves the highest novelty, while all models with pointers have similar numbers. We also investigate how likely it is that the paraphrase has the same set of slots with the source, which aligns to our definition of *signature*. (Note that utterances with no slots are not included when calculating this metric.) Overall, using pointers in the decoder stage does not benefit slot copying: When all slots are anonymized, a usual sequence decoder gives near perfect slot copy rate, because anonymized slot names like SLOT1 and SLOT2 provide direct strong signals indicating that this token is extremely likely to be copied, both in the encoder and in the decoder. The pointer decoder gives 92.22%, and we find in most misalignment cases the output sequence misses a pointer to a slot in the input. Pointers compete with the vocabulary from the final softmax in the decoder and they rely on context (encoder state) to identify the logit, which may bring much noise, and hence it's reasonable to see the relatively lower copy rate in the AS case of simply generating very frequent SLOT1, SLOT2 output tokens.

For S2P and S3P, the tokens to be copied are unknown and have embeddings originating from extra layers. We still see over 80% copy rate, and the chance of perfectly copying all the slots reduces as the number of slots increases. As is shown in Figure 2, the exact copy rate is greater than 90% for all pointer models if there is only one slot in the input, while the number for vanilla seq2seq model is 100.0%. The proportion of exact slot copy falls drastically as the number of slots increases, especially for the S2P and S3P models. For the ASP model, the explicit token SLOTX in the input provides an indication for it to be copied, but in S2P and S3P the token could be from the pooling of embeddings from various words and makes it hard for the pointer to locate all slots, thus we see a sharper decrease of copy rate. In future work, in order to improve the copy rate of pointer models, we can try to add extra signals to the input, indicating whether each token is a slot, as well as an extra connection between the input sequence and the decoder.

For the novelty and diversity metrics, both at utterance level and trigram level, there is not much difference among models with pointers. Vanilla seq2seq model with anonymized slots generates the most unique utterances. However, since no information on slot values is provided, some of the generations

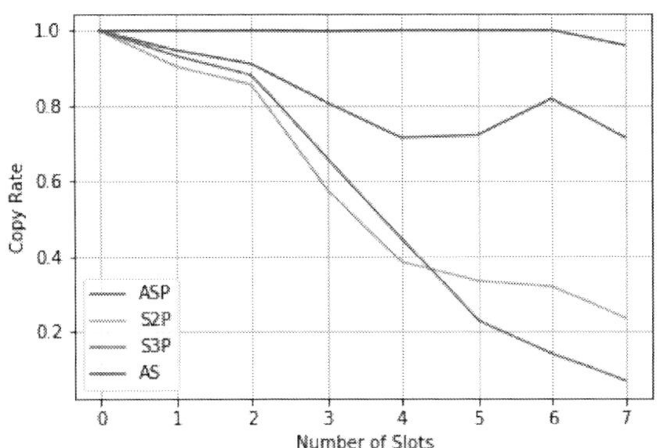

Figure 2: Variation of Slot Copy Rate by Number of Slots

may not be proper paraphrases. As in our definition of paraphrases, the generated utterance must belong to the same intent. In the next section on extrinsic metrics, we can see that vanilla seq2seq is least likely to retain the intent.

From the internal metrics, we might not see benefits from pointer decoders, as they limit the span of generation and do not copy as much slots. However, novel generated utterances might be just random and do not possess similar semantics, even if same slots are included. In addition, for models with anonymized slots, since the slot tokens do not convey any information about semantics, we expect to see more natural and proper generation from the S2P and S3P models.

Extrinsic Metrics Overall, our paraphrasing models generate utterances that help both FST matching and NLU models. Within 129,599 test utterances, we see 1,669 new FST matches in the best model. Paraphrasing as data augmentation also benefits both IC and NER, leading to a reduction in slot error rate, intent error rate and semantic error rate.

Models with pointers all show higher intent filter rate, suggesting that the direct connection to encoder output helps the decoder to locate appropriate slots in the input, and consequently the context words learn from the generated pointer and eventually generate a sequence with more similar semantics.

The number of new FST matches is an essential metric for evaluating the quality of paraphrases, as they demonstrate whether the model can learn what humans are likely to say. From various data sources, especially enormous numbers of diversified skills, our model learns to gather information from similar skills and also adapts to what people usually say when using a virtual assistant. All models generate considerable numbers of new FST matches: Out of 40,109 utterances that were not matched by the original FSTs, the number of new matches from AS, ASP, S2P and S3P models are 1,528, 1,669, 1,376 and 1,438, respectively. Anonymized slots with pointers achieve the highest number of exact matches, which further highlights the effectiveness of pointers.

We also see improvements of downstream NLU tasks by applying paraphrases to data augmentation. After lexicalizing generated paraphrases, those are filtered by intent and then added to the training data for IC and NER, and evaluated on a multi-task DNN model with bi-LSTM encoders and decoders. We calculate evaluation metrics mentioned in section 4.2 for all 88 skills, and report the average.

Adding extra paraphrases improves both IC and NER for all our proposed paraphrasing models. AS, the most naive model which anonymizes slots and does not use pointers, achieves the highest performance. We see a 2.75% relative reduction in intent error rate, 7.97% reduction in slot error rate and 3.65% reduction in semantic error rate.

Skill Analysis When using paraphrases for data augmentation using the AS model, among all 88 skills, 44 see improvement in SEMER, with 15 improving by more than 2%; 34 see degradation, with 7 of them degrading by more than 2%. We want to understand what kind of skills benefit most from paraphrases. For investigating such skill characteristics, we calculate Spearman's rank-order correlation coefficient between SEMER relative improvements and skill features including number of intents, number of slots,

Original Utterances	Paraphrases from both AS and S3P	Paraphrases from AS only	Paraphrases from S3P only
{comedian} show play {comedian} stand up {comedian} performance {comedian} to play {comedian} search for {comedian} about {comedian} stand up	find {comedian} tell me about {comedian} the {comedian} show	what is {comedian} a {comedian} standup comedy {comedian} up play {comedian} game i think it is {comedian} play a standup of {comedian} play the {comedian}	i want to hear {comedian} listen to {comedian} play {comedian} standup comedy to play {comedian} podcast what is the performance of {comedian} what is the status of {comedian} what is {comedian} doing
play noise {item} play {item} play sound {item} play {item} sounds play song {item} play the song {item}	play {item} song play {item} sound	make the {item} screensaver make the {item} sound take the sound number {item} {item} sounds	play ambient sound {item} play {item} please sing song {item}
i'd rather {answer} i would rather {answer} probably {answer} i choose {answer} maybe {answer} i would {answer}	i think it's {answer} i think it is {answer} i would like to try {answer}	i {answer} is it {answer}	a {answer} i want {answer}
{answer}	N/A	i think it is {answer}	the {answer}

Table 5: Paraphrase Examples

number of unique delexicalized utterances, number of unique lexicalized utterances, number of unique delexicalized utterances per intent, and number of lexicalized utterances per intent. The highest correlation is between SEMER improvement and the number of unique delexicalized utterances, with Spearman correlation coefficient -0.240 and p-value of 0.024, indicating that our paraphrasing model will benefit more for skills with scarce delexicalized samples.

Paraphrase Examples Among the three paraphrasing examples shown in Table 5, each behaves differently on the SEMER evaluation metric. The first row is from the skill where data augmentation from all models outperform the baseline, and the S3P model greatly outperforms the AS model. The second row is from the skill where AS greatly outperforms S3P. The third and fourth rows are utterances of two different intents from a skill where all data augmentation techniques degrade NLU performance.

The first example is from a skill for comedian shows. Alexa users can ask to play a comedian's show or to search for comedians. As is shown in the examples, the S3P model learns from the CNN and embeddings of artists' names, and understands that {comedian} is a person, thus generates utterances like "i want to hear {comedian}" and "what is {comedian} doing." In contrast, the model with anonymized slots treats {comedian} as a general slot without any extra information, and as a result generates paraphrases that are not appropriate for this skill, like "what is {comedian}" and "play {comedian} game."

The second example is from a skill for playing different kinds of sounds. From the examples, it is apparent that S3P is generating better paraphrases. However, downstream NLU tasks perform better with paraphrases from AS. The shown examples are sample utterances for PlaySoundIntent, however, there is another PlayAmbientSoundIntent in the skill. Notice that S3P generates a paraphrase "play ambient sound {item}" and probably due to a defect of intent filtering, the utterance is not filtered out. After the paraphrase is added to the training data, the statistical model may get confused on similar utterances for playing ambient sounds.

The third example shows utterances for two different intents, AnswerIntent and AnswerOnlyIntent. The skill intends to create a class for {answer} without any carrier phrases. However, the paraphrasing models have no knowledge of this objective and generate utterances by adding context words. The original intent classfication cannot filter out all of these cases. And afterwards, adding these samples to the FST and training data will further confuse the NLU model.

Overall, downstream NLU tasks may not be best indicators for paraphrase quality. S3P models show the effectiveness of incorporating entity values knowledge in paraphrase generation, which may or may not lead to an accuracy gain on downstream NLU tasks. Some heavy manual evaluations might provide a more accurate overview for comparison among different paraphrasing models.

7 Conclusion

We trained and evaluated multiple types of models for paraphrasing delexicalized utterances, motivated to assist skill developers and ultimately to improve the user experience of virtual assistant customers. We experimented with anonymizing entity slots in utterances, applying CNNs and pooling on slot entities, and using pointers to locate slots in the output. The generated paraphrases bring about 1,669 exact matches with human utterances in the best model, and also improve NLU tasks, especially for those skills with insufficient training samples. In addition, we showed the benefit of including slot value information in paraphrasing for some skills.

References

Regina Barzilay and Kathleen R McKeown. 2005. Sentence fusion for multidocument news summarization. *Computational Linguistics*, 31(3):297–328.

Samuel R Bowman, Luke Vilnis, Oriol Vinyals, Andrew M Dai, Rafal Jozefowicz, and Samy Bengio. 2015. Generating sentences from a continuous space. *arXiv preprint arXiv:1511.06349*.

Chris Callison-Burch, Philipp Koehn, and Miles Osborne. 2006. Improved statistical machine translation using paraphrases. In *Proceedings of the main conference on Human Language Technology Conference of the North American Chapter of the Association of Computational Linguistics*, pages 17–24. Association for Computational Linguistics.

Anthony Fader, Luke Zettlemoyer, and Oren Etzioni. 2013. Paraphrase-driven learning for open question answering. In *Proceedings of the 51st Annual Meeting of the Association for Computational Linguistics (Volume 1: Long Papers)*, volume 1, pages 1608–1618.

Juri Ganitkevitch, Benjamin Van Durme, and Chris Callison-Burch. 2013. Ppdb: The paraphrase database. In *Proceedings of the 2013 Conference of the North American Chapter of the Association for Computational Linguistics: Human Language Technologies*, pages 758–764.

Ankush Gupta, Arvind Agarwal, Prawaan Singh, and Piyush Rai. 2018. A deep generative framework for paraphrase generation. In *Thirty-Second AAAI Conference on Artificial Intelligence*.

Diederik P Kingma and Jimmy Ba. 2014. Adam: A method for stochastic optimization. *arXiv preprint arXiv:1412.6980*.

Anjishnu Kumar, Arpit Gupta, Julian Chan, Sam Tucker, Bjorn Hoffmeister, Markus Dreyer, Stanislav Peshterliev, Ankur Gandhe, Denis Filiminov, Ariya Rastrow, et al. 2017. Just ask: building an architecture for extensible self-service spoken language understanding. *arXiv preprint arXiv:1711.00549*.

Chin-Yew Lin. 2004. Rouge: A package for automatic evaluation of summaries. In *Text summarization branches out*, pages 74–81.

Xiaohu Liu, Ruhi Sarikaya, Chris Brockett, Chris Quirk, William B Dolan, and Bill Dolan. 2013. Paraphrase features to improve natural language understanding. In *INTERSPEECH*, pages 3776–3779.

Minh-Thang Luong, Hieu Pham, and Christopher D Manning. 2015. Effective approaches to attention-based neural machine translation. *arXiv preprint arXiv:1508.04025*.

John Makhoul, Francis Kubala, Richard Schwartz, Ralph Weischedel, et al. 1999. Performance measures for information extraction. In *Proceedings of DARPA broadcast news workshop*, pages 249–252. Herndon, VA.

Nikolaos Malandrakis, Minmin Shen, Anuj Goyal, Shuyang Gao, Abhishek Sethi, and Angeliki Metallinou. 2019. Controlled text generation for data augmentation in intelligent artificial agents. *arXiv preprint arXiv:1910.03487*.

Jonathan Mallinson, Rico Sennrich, and Mirella Lapata. 2017. Paraphrasing revisited with neural machine translation. In *Proceedings of the 15th Conference of the European Chapter of the Association for Computational Linguistics: Volume 1, Long Papers*, volume 1, pages 881–893.

Yuval Marton, Chris Callison-Burch, and Philip Resnik. 2009. Improved statistical machine translation using monolingually-derived paraphrases. In *Proceedings of the 2009 Conference on Empirical Methods in Natural Language Processing: Volume 1-Volume 1*, pages 381–390. Association for Computational Linguistics.

Kishore Papineni, Salim Roukos, Todd Ward, and Wei-Jing Zhu. 2002. Bleu: a method for automatic evaluation of machine translation. In *Proceedings of the 40th annual meeting on association for computational linguistics*, pages 311–318. Association for Computational Linguistics.

Aaditya Prakash, Sadid A Hasan, Kathy Lee, Vivek Datla, Ashequl Qadir, Joey Liu, and Oladimeji Farri. 2016. Neural paraphrase generation with stacked residual lstm networks. *arXiv preprint arXiv:1610.03098*.

Subendhu Rongali, Luca Soldaini, Emilio Monti, and Wael Hamza. 2020. Don't parse, generate! a sequence to sequence architecture for task-oriented semantic parsing. *arXiv preprint arXiv:2001.11458*.

Alex Sokolov and Denis Filimonov. 2020. Neural machine translation for paraphrase generation. *arXiv preprint arXiv:2006.14223*.

Nitish Srivastava, Geoffrey Hinton, Alex Krizhevsky, Ilya Sutskever, and Ruslan Salakhutdinov. 2014. Dropout: a simple way to prevent neural networks from overfitting. *The Journal of Machine Learning Research*, 15(1):1929–1958.

Ilya Sutskever, Oriol Vinyals, and Quoc V Le. 2014. Sequence to sequence learning with neural networks. In *Advances in neural information processing systems*, pages 3104–3112.

Ashish Vaswani, Noam Shazeer, Niki Parmar, Jakob Uszkoreit, Llion Jones, Aidan N Gomez, Łukasz Kaiser, and Illia Polosukhin. 2017. Attention is all you need. In *Advances in neural information processing systems*, pages 5998–6008.

Multi-task Learning of Spoken Language Understanding by Integrating N-Best Hypotheses with Hierarchical Attention

Mingda Li   Xinyue Liu   Weitong Ruan   Luca Soldaini   Wael Hamza   Chengwei Su

Amazon Alexa AI, Cambridge, USA

`{mingda, luxnyu, weiton, lssoldai, waelhamz, chengwes}@amazon.com`

Abstract

Currently, in spoken language understanding (SLU) systems, the automatic speech recognition (ASR) module produces multiple interpretations (or hypotheses) for the input audio signal and the natural language understanding (NLU) module takes the one with the highest confidence score for domain or intent classification. However, the interpretations can be noisy, and solely relying on one interpretation can cause information loss. To address the problem, many research works attempt to rerank the interpretations for a better choice while some recent works get better performance by integrating all the hypotheses during prediction. In this paper, we follow the way of integrating hypotheses but strengthen the training mode by involving more tasks, some of which may be not in existing tasks of NLU but relevant, via multi-task learning or transfer learning. Moreover, we propose the Hierarchical Attention Mechanism (HAM) to further improve the performance with the acoustic-model features like confidence scores, which are ignored in the current hypotheses integration models. The experimental results show that compared to the standard estimation with one hypothesis, the multi-task learning with HAM can improve the domain and intent classification by relatively 19% and 37%, which are much higher than improvements with current integration or reranking methods. To illustrate the cause of improvements brought by our model, we decode the hidden representations of some utterance examples and compare the generated texts with hypotheses and transcripts. The comparison shows that our model could recover the transcription by integrating the fragmented information among hypotheses and identifying the frequent error patterns of the ASR module, and even rewrite the query for a better understanding, which reveals the characteristic of multi-task learning of broadcasting knowledge.

1   Introduction

In an SLU system (Tur and De Mori, 2011), the domains and intents are usually inferred by natural language understanding (NLU) modules with the hypotheses mapped from input speech by ASR module. For each speech audio, the transferred hypothesis is the one with the highest recognition score. However, due to the unsatisfactory ASR accuracy (Xiong et al., 2018; Barker et al., 2018), the 1-best hypothesis may contain errors. To solve the problem, there are some research works rescoring (reranking) the n-best hypotheses[1] to reduce the word error rate (WER) by dual comparison with a discriminative language model (Ogawa et al., 2018; Ogawa et al., 2019); or involving morphological, lexical, syntactic or confidence score features for reranking (Sak et al., 2011; Collins et al., 2005; Chan and Woodland, 2004; Peng et al., 2013; Morbini et al., 2012).

In contrast to the reranking models, which predict only one hypothesis with the lowest WER and transfer that hypothesis to NLU modules, there is recently another attempt to integrate the fragmented information among the n-best hypotheses by feeding all the hypotheses together to NLU modules (Li et al., 2020; Li, 2020). The proposed approaches to integrating hypotheses include hypothesized text

---

[1]We use ASR *n-best hypotheses* or n-bests to denote the top n interpretations of a speech and the 1-best or 5-best stands for the top 1 or 5 hypotheses. The hypotheses are ranked by the associated confidence scores.

Proceedings of the 28th International Conference on Computational Linguistics: Industry Track, pages 113–123
Barcelona, Spain (Online), December 12, 2020

concatenation (Combined Sentence) and hypotheses embedding concatenation (PoolingAvg and Pooling-Max). Compared to the accuracy on the oracle reranking results (i.e., picking the hypothesis most similar to transcription), the PoolingAvg achieves much higher improvements for the NLU tasks. However, the integration framework can be further improved by introducing more tasks with Multi-Task Learning (MTL) or Transfer Learning and involving more features to optimize the integration process.

MTL (Zhang and Yang, 2017; Liu et al., 2019; Caruana, 1997) is a widely used machine learning paradigm for simultaneously training related tasks. In the MTL training, one task can apply the knowledge learned from others. MTL can improve the generalization of the trained model by avoiding overfitting to a single task and make full use of all the labeled data from all tasks to solve the issue of insufficient training data. The MTL has been shown efficient for some natural language processing tasks outside the SLU system like text similarity, pairwise text classification (Liu et al., 2019). In contrast to multi-task learning, by transfer learning or domain adaption (Pan and Yang, 2009; Howard and Ruder, 2018; Torrey and Shavlik, 2010), some tasks (source tasks) can be trained in the first stage knowing nothing about the other tasks (target tasks). While in the second stage, the embeddings from pre-trained model are fine-tuned according to the target mission. The transfer learning cares more about the target tasks. Some popular fine-tunable pre-trained models like BERT (Devlin et al., 2018), ELMO (Peters et al., 2018) nail down the transfer learning in NLP.

The rest of the paper is organized as follows. Sec. 2 presents various models and training paradigms explored in this work. Sec. 3 describes our experimental details, results and analysis. Sec. 4 concludes our findings and discusses the future directions.

2   Models

We start by reviewing different categories of SLU system designs in Sec. 2.1. Those designs have achieved great success, but they are trained solely on one task and cannot borrow the knowledge from some relevant tasks like transcription reconstruction. To involve more tasks during training, we explore two paradigms to: 1) train them simultaneously in a single stage (Sec. 2.2), which is actually multi-task learning; 2) train them asynchronously (Sec. 2.3) in multiple stages, which includes two ways of using the pre-trained model from the first stage (transfer learning or text generation). In Sec. 2.4, we illustrate the importance of acoustic-model features and the way of utilizing them hierarchically.

2.1   The Standard SLU, Reranking, Integration And Oracle

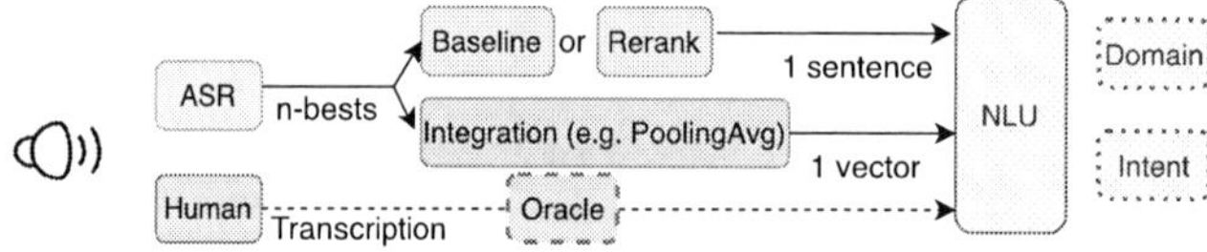

Figure 1: The pipelines of current SLU systems with various ways to exploit hypotheses (with the Oracle).

We firstly review the current designs for the SLU system in Figure 1, which include the standard pipeline (Baseline), Reranking and Integration models. In production, the input audio is transcribed by ASR to get n-best hypotheses. Then, the Baseline model will take the one with the highest confidence score for NLU tasks. Nevertheless, the Reranking models do not solely rely on the confidence scores generated by the ASR module. They prefer to rescore the interpretations based on more features like semantic information and choose the most reliable one. Both Baseline and Reranking models transfer one sentence to the NLU module for classification. However, some recent works like (Li et al., 2020) indicate this causes information loss and attempt to use all the hypotheses during classification. They embed each hypothesis to one vector and unify the vectors to one by a pooling layer, which becomes the input to the NLU task. Ideally, we can make the hypothesis close to the transcribed sentence by humans. To know the ceiling point of performance, there is always the Oracle model predicting with human transcriptions.

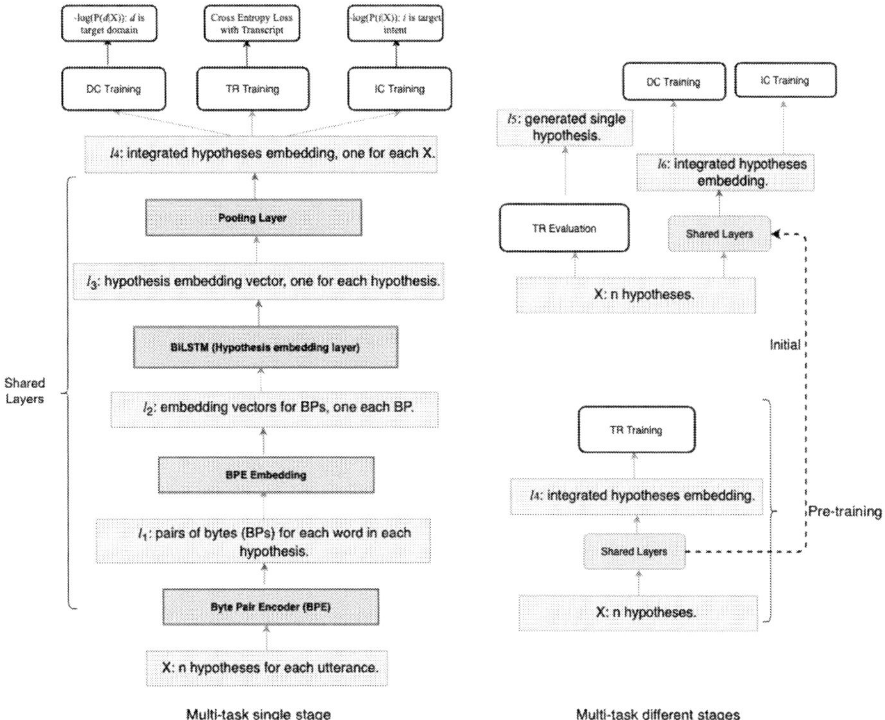

Figure 2: The architecture of multi-task training in a single stage or different stages. The left side is training all tasks (TR, DC, IC) in the same stage while the right side is to train TR firstly and fine-tune or generate texts base on the pre-trained TR model for DC and IC.

2.2 Multi-task Learning: Training Tasks Simultaneously in A Single Stage (MT_S)

Although the current approaches have gained a large improvement, their training is exclusive for one task each time and overlooks the knowledge from other tasks, which can be improved by considering more relevant tasks simultaneously with MTL. The left side of Figure 2 shows the design of training multiple tasks (transcription reconstruction, domain classification and intent classification) simultaneously for integrating n-bests. The lower layers are shared and the top two layers are task-specific.

Shared Layers: In shared layers, the input $X = \{x_1, ...x_n\}$, are n hypotheses generated by the ASR module for one speech. To decrease the embedded vocabulary size, the hypothesis is split to subword units (byte of pairs or BPs) in l_1 by a byte pair encoder (Sennrich et al., 2015) and each BP is embedded to a vector in l_2. Then, the BiLSTM encoder gets contextualized representations for the BPs ($bp_{H_i,1}...bp_{H_i,j}$) of the hypothesis (H_i) containing j byte pairs as follow:

$$(h_{H_i,1}, ..., h_{H_i,j}) \leftarrow BiLSTM_\theta(bp_{H_i,1}, ..., bp_{H_i,j}). \tag{1}$$

Each hidden state is the concatenation of the forward and backward directions, e.g. $[h_{H_i,1f}, h_{H_i,1b}]$, where f means forward and b means backward. The finally utilized output state for H_i is the concatenation of the last hidden state of the forward and backward LSTM, i.e. $h_{output_i} = [h_{H_i,1b}, h_{H_i,jf}]$. To integrate the output states of all hypotheses, we follow the empirically best approach in Li et al. (2020), PoolingAvg, which firstly pads into the output state of the first best hypothesis by $n - r$ times when the amount of hypotheses, r is smaller than n. Then, a unified representation $h_{unified}$ can be achieved by average pooling (n by 1 sliding window and stride 1) for the n output states in layer l_4. In the PoolingAvg, the unified representation is used to predict the domain or intent and all the parameters are trained by the cross entropy loss for the classification task. While in our method, we introduce a new task and train tasks simultaneously. Below, we discuss the task specific layers and the training objective.

Transcription Reconstruction (TR): For all the natural language understanding tasks, it is important to obtain a high-quality unified representation of the incoming utterance. To assure the quality of $h_{unified}$, we consider the task to reconstruct transcription by an LSTM decoder adopting $h_{unified}$ as the initial state of its first recurrent layer. Once the decoder's output is close to transcription, it shows the representation contains the high-quality information of transcription. The task is trained based on cross entropy loss:

$$\mathcal{L}_{CE-TR} = \sum_{bp=1}^{|S|} \sum_{e=1}^{|V|} y_{bp,e} log(1/\hat{y}_{bp,e}). \tag{2}$$

The S is the transcription while the bp represents the bp^{th} byte pair inside S. The e represents the eth byte pair in the vocabulary. Each time, $y_{bp,e}$ is 1 when the bp^{th} byte pair is the eth entry of vocabulary and 0 otherwise. $\hat{y}_{bp,e}$ is the predicted probability that the eth byte pair should appear at bp^{th} position. With the transcription reconstruction, the model can learn some erroneous patterns between the n best hypotheses and target transcriptions and recover accordingly. For example, one phrase may always be mis-recognized as another phrase by an ASR module. During our evaluation, with a set of utterance examples, we decode the hidden states and show the recovering capability.

Domain Classification (DC): With the same output hidden state, we could as well predict the domains (e.g. music, weather or knowledge) by a multilayer perceptron (MLP) (Mather and Tso, 2016) module. The loss for the DC task is:

$$\mathcal{L}_{CE-DC} = \sum_{d=1}^{|D|} y_{u,d} log(1/\hat{y}_{u,d}). \tag{3}$$

The $y_{u,d}$ is the indicator function which equals to 1 when the utterance belongs to the dth domain of the candidates set D. The $\hat{y}_{u,d}$ is the predicated probability, $\hat{y}_{u,d} = softmax(f_{MLP-DC}(h_{unified}))$, where the f_{MLP-DC} contains the parameters to be trained in DC task.

Intent Classification (IC): Then, we could further utilize $h_{unified}$ for domain-specific intent prediction with another MLP module. For an incoming utterance, it is usually firstly classified to one domain and the intent classification will be domain-specific (Tur and De Mori, 2011). The loss of the IC task is:

$$\mathcal{L}_{CE-IC} = \sum_{i=1}^{|I|} y_{u,i} log(1/\hat{y}_{u,i}), \tag{4}$$

where the $y_{u,i}$ is 1 when the utterance should be classified to the ith intent. The $\hat{y}_{u,i} = softmax(f_{MLP-IC}(h_{unified}))$, where $\hat{y}_{u,i}$ is the predicted probability of the utterance belonging to the ith intent and f_{MLP-IC} contains the task-specific parameters.

Training Objective: For the PoolingAvg method, the objective is to minimize the $\mathcal{L}_{CE-IC}$ or $\mathcal{L}_{CE-DC}$, while for our MTL framework, the objective is minimizing

$$\mathcal{L} = \lambda_{TR} \mathcal{L}_{CE-TR}/|S| + \lambda_{IC} \mathcal{L}_{CE-IC} + \lambda_{DC} \mathcal{L}_{CE-DC}, \tag{5}$$

where the λ_{TR}, λ_{DC} and λ_{IC} are the weights of the loss functions associated with corresponding tasks. Since for one utterance, the target transcription contains multiple words and the $\mathcal{L}_{CE-TR}$ is the sum of loss for all the words, we utilize the normalized version of the transcription reconstruction loss.

The Language Model: During our experiments, we also tried the multi-layer transformer (Vaswani et al., 2017) for the encoder. We find it costs more for training or evaluation while bringing no improvements. In addition, since the length of hypotheses varies, it is hard to align variant-length output states of different n-best hypotheses and exploit the attention between encoder and decoder (if we also use the Transformer's decoder) for the TR task. Thus, we exploit the BiLSTM encoder and LSTM decoder.

2.3 Multi-task Training in Multiple Stages (MT_M) with Transfer Learning or Text Generation

Another way to train the above-mentioned tasks is in different stages as shown in the right part of Figure 2. Inasmuch as for all the NLU tasks, it is necessary to obtain a high-quality hypothesis representation. We prioritize the training of TR in the first step and let all NLU models share the same pre-trained TR model. The approaches of exploiting the pre-trained model are introduced as follows.

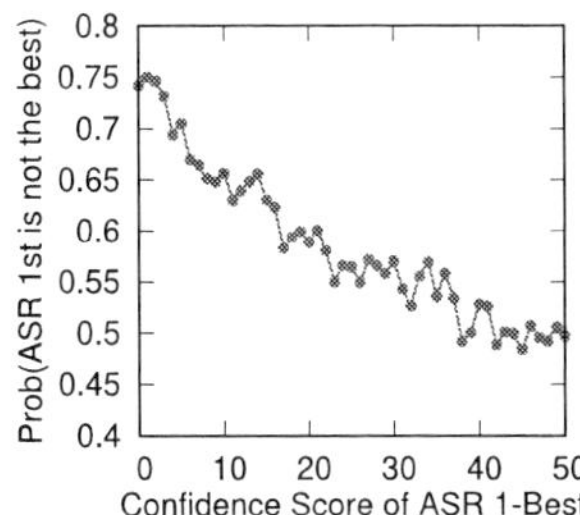

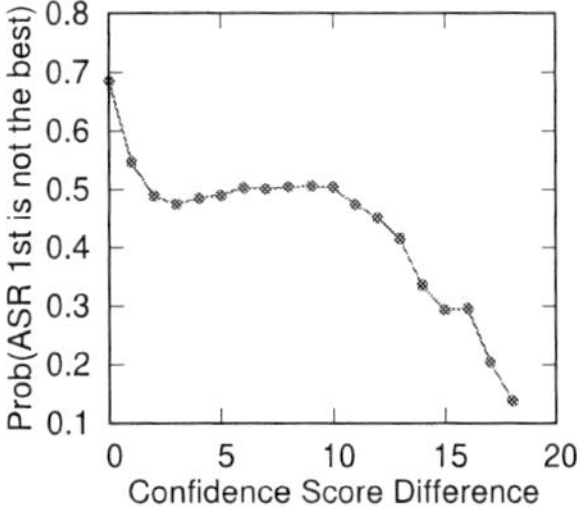

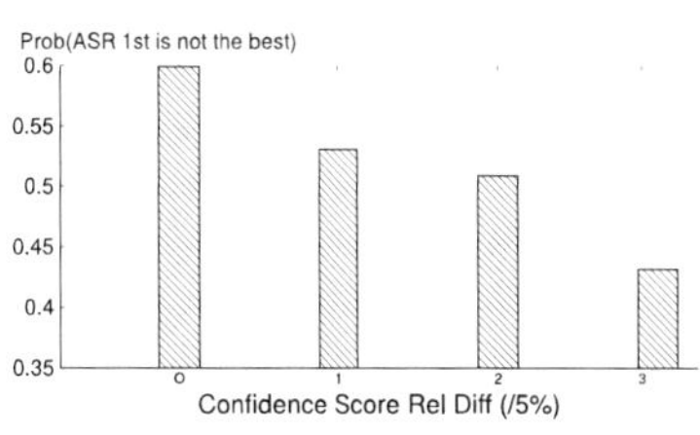

Figure 3: Confidence score of ASR 1-Best (bin size 10‰).

Figure 4: Confidence score difference (bin size 5‰).

Figure 5: Confidence score relative difference (bin size 5%)

Transfer Learning: One way to use the TR task from the first step is transfer learning, where we regard the TR as the pre-training step and let the DC, IC tasks adapt the knowledge by fine-tuning. We call the method following this idea as Transfer Learning (TL). The parameters of the pre-trained TR's shared layers, including the embedding of byte pairs and the BiLSTM encoder, are used as the initial value. The TR task-specific parameters like the decoder part's are discarded. Then, the shared layers' parameters and task-specific layer's parameters, in f_{MLP-DC} or f_{MLP-IC}, are all trained during the fine-tuning step. Although DC and IC share the same initialization parameters, their fine-tuned models are separate. The benefit of the two-step training is that the model and knowledge from pre-training step can serve multiple downstream tasks. In addition, with the well-initialized parameters, it saves much time for fine-tuning.

MT_M with Text Generation: Since the TR model has been tuned to recover the errors contained in the ASR n-bests, we can firstly evaluate it to generate the text closer to transcription. Then, the domain or intent can be predicted based on the generated text. This method is called Multi-task Multi-stage with Text Generation (MMTG). At this moment, the input to DC or IC is only one generated hypothesis instead of n-bests. To predict with one hypothesis, we can exploit the IC or DC models pre-trained on transcription or 1-best, which only expect one sentence as the input.

2.4 Hierarchical Attention on Byte Pair Embedding and Hypothesis Integration Layer

All the above algorithms treat the input hypotheses as normal natural language to process but ignore that the hypotheses are generated by ASR and associated with more acoustic-model information than the text itself. For example, the position information (whether the hypothesis is the first best or the last best), the difference of confidence score associated with the first best and second best hypothesis, etc. The acoustic-model features have been proven to be valuable for many applications including: 1) the arbitration task to select the best among client and service recognition results (Kumar et al., 2015), 2) the Recognizer Output Voting Error Reduction (ROVER) (Fiscus, 1997), which takes the outputs generated by multiple ASR systems to generate one output with reduced error rate, 3) confidence normalization (Kumar et al., 2014), etc. In this section, we would like to introduce those features, why they can be helpful, and how they can hierarchically take part in the shared layers in the left side of Figure 2.

2.4.1 Acoustic-model Information

Those features can be divided into three categories including confidence-score features, positional information and confusibility. We illustrate their close relationship with the hypothesis quality as following.

(a) Confidence-score Features: The confidence scores quantitatively represent the correctness of recognized hypotheses and words in a [0‰,1000‰] range. Plenty of previous research works have proven the effectiveness of those features. Here, we take the confidence score of hypothesis as an example to show the valuable information contained in confidence scores. For each utterance in the training set, we evaluate the probability that ASR 1-best is not the best for different scales of the ASR 1-best confidence score. A hypothesis is the best when it is the most similar one to the transcription considering the edit distance. In Figure 3, it is obvious that a higher confidence score means a higher probability that the ASR 1-best is the best one among hypotheses.

(b) Positional Information: The ranking position of the hypothesis is another important information. To show its significance, we gain the distribution of exact matchings, i.e. the hypothesis is the same as the transcription, between different ranking positions and the transcription. Among all the exact matching cases, 50% appear at the first best hypothesis while 19%, 13%, 10% and 6% occur at the 2nd, 3rd, 4th, and 5th best hypothesis. Hence, a more forward position does indicate a higher recognition quality.

(c) Confusibility: The features of the confusibility category include the difference ($confidence_{H_1} - confidence_{H_i}$) and relative difference ($difference/confidence_{H_1}$) of confidence score between the ASR 1-best and the others. The larger difference implies the lower confusibility to choose the first hypothesis as the best. As the confidence score of the first best should be larger or equal to the others, the difference and relative difference are non-negative values measuring the degree of outperforming. In the Figure 4 and 5, there is a trend that the larger difference (between ASR first and second best) implies the lower probability that ASR 1-best is not the best, which means it is easier to determine the ASR 1-best as the best. Here, we only show the difference to the second best as an example. While in later designs, the features will be formed based on the difference between each i-best's confidence score and the 1-best's.

2.4.2   Hierarchical Attention Mechanism (HAM)

We have shown that the acoustic-model information reveals the quality of recognition and to exploit them, we add them into shared layers hierarchically. The HAM is proposed by the hierarchical structure of the n-bests (BPs from a hypothesis, a hypothesis from n-bests). Similar hierarchical structures are realized in different areas, where various kinds of information like documentation (Yang et al., 2016), knowledge graphs (Hu et al., 2015), Internet network (Li et al., 2018), or voice queries (Rao et al., 2017) are encoded. While integrating n-bests, the process is building representation for one hypothesis from BPs and then aggregating them into an n-bests representation. We likewise exploit the acoustic-model information hierarchically to BPs embedding (HAM_BP) and then to the aggregation of hypotheses (HAM_H). The HAM_ALL exploits the information in both layers.

Byte Pair Embedding Layer (HAM_BP): In Figure 6 right side, we show the way of involving the byte pair acoustic-model information in the byte pair embedding layer of Figure 2 left side. Instead of concatenating the last hidden state of forward and backward LSTM for hypothesis embedding (Figure 6 left side), we would like to consider the quality of each byte pair and take into account the entire sequence of hidden states. To exploit the information, we firstly need to figure out the problem of missing acoustic-model information for byte pairs because we only have the confidence scores associated with words. Since it can be ensured that each byte pair only belongs to one word, we can assign the confidence score for a byte pair according to its parent, i.e. the word. For example, in Figure 6, the "low" and "-er" are two byte pairs of the word "lower", so they share the same confidence score of the word "lower", i.e. 0.9. To use the confidence scores as attention scores, we can normalize them by Softmax or convert them to bin value or logarithmic scale, etc (shown by $f(x)$ in Figure 6). The attention score matrix is multiplied with the hidden vectors matrix of the BiLSTM embedding, where each hidden vector concatenates its forward and backward states. The mean (from pooling) of weighted hidden state vectors forms a single vector for each hypothesis and the vector will participate in the following hypotheses integration layer.

Hypotheses Integration Layer (HAM_H): Figure 7 illustrates the integration of hypotheses with their associated acoustic-model information. The left side of the dotted line in Figure 7 is the way to integrate without the acoustic-model features in Figure 2 layer l_4, where hypotheses embeddings transferred from the l_3 layer are combined by the pooling operation. The problem is that the normal pooling layer treats hypotheses equally, although the quality of the n-best hypotheses actually varies. We add a Multiple Layer Perceptron (MLP), i.e. Feedforward (FFW), to synthesize all the features revealing the quality of each hypothesis, including the positional information, confidence score, confidence score difference and confidence score relative difference. The output of FFW is normalized via Softmax and works as the attention scores or weights. In MatMul, we multiply the attention score matrix and the hypothesis embedding matrix. Finally, the weighted embeddings are combined through pooling.

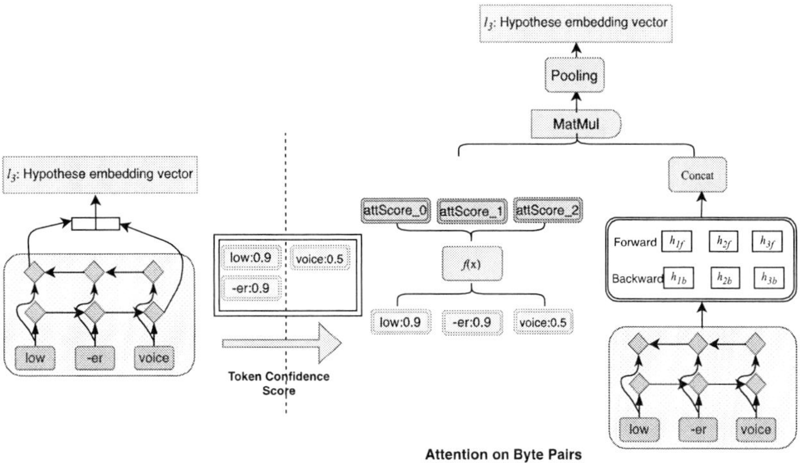

Figure 6: Attention on byte pair embedding.

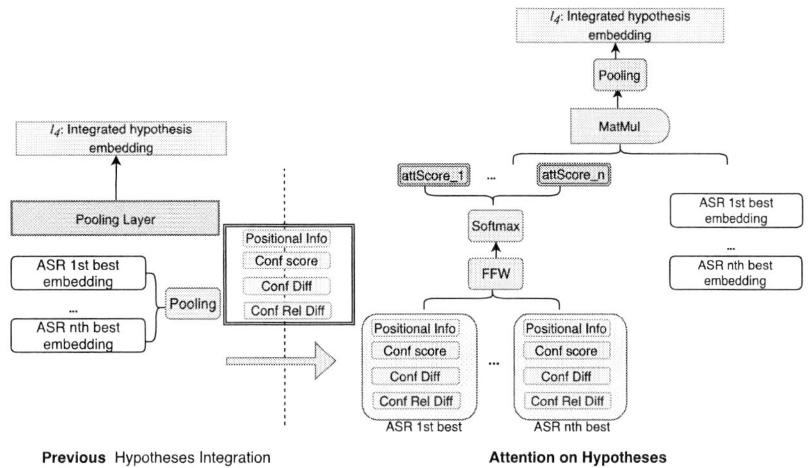

Figure 7: Attention on hypotheses integration.

3 Experiments

3.1 Dataset and Models

Our data consists of ~ 9M anonymized English utterances. The utterances are divided into training, development and testing parts with 8:1:1 ratio. They are annotated with 23 domains and further classified into different intents for each domain. The transcripts are hand-transcribed by humans.

The compared approaches include the Baseline model and Oracle model mentioned in Sec. 2.1, PoolingAvg, Oracle of Reranking Model and the approaches mentioned in this paper. The PoolingAvg is the foremost one among all the models integrating n-best hypotheses (Li et al., 2020). The Oracle of Reranking Model makes prediction by the hypothesis most similar to the transcription each time. As for the models in this paper, they include the multi-task training in a single stage (MTL, Sec. 2.2), or in different stages (TL and MMTG, Sec. 2.3) and the HAM (Sec. 2.4). The HAM actually modifies the shared layers and is not task-specific, so it is possible to combine it with the MTL or transfer learning mechanism. For example, MTL_{HAM} means using HAM to modify shared layers and training with mode of MTL. For all the models, the byte pairs are embedded to a 128-dimensional space. The hidden states in the BiLSTM encoder of the shared layers and the LSTM decoder of task TR are both 512-dimensional. The training iterator is a fixed mini-batch iterator with size 128 and each model is trained for ten epochs, while the model providing the highest performance for the development data is selected.

3.2 Domain Classification

		Entire test set	Agree Part	Disagree Part
Category	Model	RErr(%)	RErr(%)	RErr(%)
Standard	Baseline	0.00	0.00	0.00
Rerank	Oracle	3.71	0.00	7.25
Integration	PoolingAvg	14.29	3.56	24.67
MT_S	**MTL**	**17.99**	**7.67**	**28.26**
MT_M	TL	17.34	7.32	27.37
	MMTG	9.16	1.88	16.20
HAM	MTL_{HAM_H}	18.10	7.88	28.22
	MTL_{HAM_BP}	18.10	8.07	28.05
	$\textbf{MTL}_{HAM\_ALL}$	**19.30**	**9.94**	**28.68**
Oracle		27.04	0.00	53.02

Table 1: Relative error reduction (RErr) for domain classification.

Table 1 compares the domain classification performance of all the models. As seen from the results of the entire test set, the transfer learning, multi-task learning and the improved versions with HAM are all better than the existing methods. Among the ways of training multiple tasks synchronously or asychronously, the MTL works the best. In our experiments, we have tried different hyperparametric values in formula 5. Since the predictions of IC is based on the specific domain predicted in DC, we only have two tasks (DC, TR) and associated hyperparametrics ($\lambda_{DC}, \lambda_{TR}$) for MTL in the domain classification. We tried ratios of $\lambda_{TR} : \lambda_{DC}$ with $1 : i, i \in 1...10$. Here, we assign the weight for DC as a larger one because we care more about the DC task performance, while the TR is actually an auxillary task. Through experiments, we find the performance for ratio $1 : i, i \in 1...3$ is comparable to each other and better than the rests and we show the results for ratio $1 : 1$ in Table 1. With the acoustic-model information, the performance of MTL is further improved. Exploiting the acoustic-model information hierarchically on both hypotheses and byte pairs layers, i.e. HAM_ALL, is better than on one layer (HAM_H, HAM_BP).

To reveal the reason of improvements, we split the entire test set into two parts by whether the 1-bests agree with transcriptions or not and evaluate respectively. Comparing the Agree and Disagree part, we find that the gained improvements of models in MTL, TL and MTL with HAM mainly come from the disagreed part. This indicates that integrating more hypotheses could help more when 1-best differs from transcription. Later, we will illustrate the reasons more visually with some utterance examples.

3.3 Real Effect of MTL: Analysis of Utterance Examples

Domain Estimation Result			Generated Text (decoded hidden representation), ASR n-bests and transcription				
Baseline	MTL	Real	Transcription	Generated Text by MTL	ASR-1st	ASR-2nd	ASR-3rd
Daily	Music	Music	play muse	play muse	play news	play muse	play mus
Knowledge	Video	Video	harry porter	harry porter	how do you porter	how do you patter	harry power
Communication	Help	Help	how the **call** service work	how the **remote** service work	how the call service work	how the cost service work	None

Table 2: Comparison among the decoded hidden representations, hypotheses and transcriptions.

We use the well-trained MTL on some utterance examples to predict their domains and decode the integrated hypotheses embedding (hidden representations) with Beam Search Decoder (beam size 1) to compare the generated text with the ASR hypotheses, transcription. In Table 2, the first three columns are the predicted domains of Baseline model , MTL model (predicted by the hidden representation) and the Real domain. The other columns compare the transcriptions, the decoder's generated text in MTL and the n-bests. Due to space limit, we only choose three typical example with their top 3 hypotheses. The number of hypotheses varies, so we use None for the missing one.

Why are we better than Baseline on Disagree Part? The reasons MTL can outperform the Baseline model's prediction on Disagree Part can be categorized into two as follows. 1) **Choose the best from ASR 2-n bests** (e.g. the third row in Table 2): In this condition, there is a high-quality hypothesis ("play

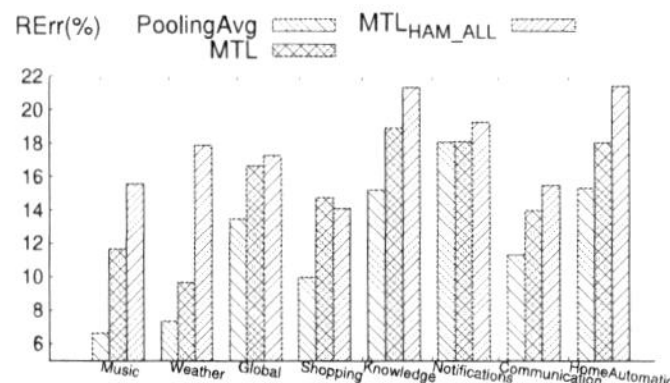

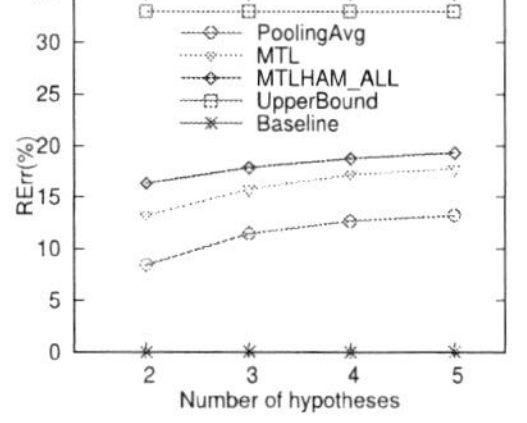

Domain	Shopping	Knowledge	Comm
Baseline	0.0	0.0	0.0
Oracle	47.63	40.28	32.89
PoolingAvg	25.55	25.00	11.92
MTL	35.02	36.11	12.36
MTL_{HAM_ALL}	36.91	30.56	12.58

Figure 8: Improvements on 8 important domains.

Figure 9: Comparison under different amount of n-bests.

Table 3: Intent classification: relative error reduction versus Baseline.

muse") within the n-bests. The position of the hypothesis is not the first one but we can correctly identify it in the generated text. 2) **Integrate fragmented information** (e.g. the forth row in Table 2): In this condition, the transcription "harry porter" spread out over hypotheses. The "harry" is in the third best while the "porter" is in the first best. We can collect the information and recover the "harry porter" in the generated text. The ability of integration can thus been shown. The ability can be obtained by learning the error patterns between ASR hypotheses and transcriptions during the TR task.

Why are we even better than Baseline on Agree Part? The transcriptions should be the golden information but we can still outperform the Baseline's prediction from ASR 1-best when ASR 1-best agrees with the transcription. The reason is **Query rewriting** (e.g. the fifth row): We find the trained model attempt to rewrite transcription when it may cause misunderstanding. In the fifth row, while the transcription is "how the call service work", the trained model replaces the sensitive word "call" with another word "remote" with similar meaning or embedding position. The word "call" is a sensitive word because it always occurs in the Communication domain, which can make the predictor mis-classify it. However, the word "remote" is not sensitive but semantically similar to the word "call". This example is also a perfect demo to show the effect of multi-task learning. The multi-task learning here is to find the balance point between the domain classification and transcription reconstruction. Considering both tasks will propel the model to rewrite a query with a similar semantic meaning and avoid misunderstanding.

We summarize the different causes of improvements by some utterance examples here to offer an insight of the model's real effect. However, we do not show the numerical analysis like WER because it is hard to evaluate whether the decode generation is high-quality considering the query rewriting.

3.4 Improvements on Different Domains and Different Numbers of Hypotheses

Now, we compare more specifically the MTL, MTL_{HAM_ALL} and PoolingAvg on 8 important domains out of the whole 23 domains in Figure 8. The performance of each of the three models will be compared to the baseline model and the relative error reduction (RErr) is shown. This result shows that the MTL gains more improvements than the best integration model PoolingAvg for all the 8 domains while the HAM can enhance the performance on almost all 8 domains (except an acceptable decay for Shopping).

All the previous results of models based on n-best actually utilize 5-best hypotheses and we also want to see the performance with different number of hypotheses. In Figure 9, we could find the best model is always MTL_{HAM_ALL} for different numbers of utilized hypotheses. There is also a trend that after 4 hypotheses are utilized the growth become more gentle. The lines for Baseline and UpperBound are flatten because they are only based on ASR 1-bests and transcriptions. We only show the performance until 5 hypotheses are utilized because: 1) Most of our ASR recognition results only contain at most 5-bests; 2) In production, the more hypotheses are utilized, the slower it will be for training and testing. We only want to afford up to 5 hypotheses considering response delay.

3.5 Intent Classification on Three Important Domains

Another task, intent classification, is domain specific and we show the IC of 3 important domains. Table 3 shows the relative error reduction compared to Baseline model. The multi-task learning for intent classification considers both the intent classification and transcription reconstruction. The result showed is under the loss ratio $\lambda_{TR} : \lambda_{IC} = 1:1$ for the two tasks. We can find the MTL_{HAM_ALL} and MTL outperforms the foremost PoolingAvg for all three domains' domain-specific intent classification.

4 Conclusion and Future Work

This work is motivated by introducing multi-task learning (MTL), transfer learning (TL) and acoustic-model information into the framework of integrating n-best hypotheses for spoken language understanding. Among those algorithms, we find the MTL results in higher performance compared to the TL. For the acoustic-model information, we illustrate their close relationship with the hypothesis quality and utilize the hierarchical attention mechanism to include the information for byte pair embedding and hypothesis integration layer within the shared layers, which can further enhance the MTL. The relative error reduction is 19.3% for domain classification and 36.9% for intent classification. We also use some utterances to analyze the real cause of the improvements. By decoding the hidden representations and comparing with transcription, we find by the MTL, the model attempts to find a balance point and do some reasonable query rewriting. In the future, we will explore more by introducing more tasks, improving the efficiency and utilizing more abundant information like word lattice.

References

Jon Barker, Shinji Watanabe, Emmanuel Vincent, and Jan Trmal. 2018. The fifth'chime'speech separation and recognition challenge: dataset, task and baselines. *arXiv preprint arXiv:1803.10609*.

Rich Caruana. 1997. Multitask learning. *Machine learning*, 28(1):41–75.

Ho Yin Chan and Phil Woodland. 2004. Improving broadcast news transcription by lightly supervised discriminative training. In *2004 IEEE International Conference on Acoustics, Speech, and Signal Processing*, volume 1, pages I–737. IEEE.

Michael Collins, Brian Roark, and Murat Saraclar. 2005. Discriminative syntactic language modeling for speech recognition. In *Proceedings of the 43rd Annual Meeting on Association for Computational Linguistics*, pages 507–514. Association for Computational Linguistics.

Jacob Devlin, Ming-Wei Chang, Kenton Lee, and Kristina Toutanova. 2018. Bert: Pre-training of deep bidirectional transformers for language understanding. *arXiv preprint arXiv:1810.04805*.

Jonathan G Fiscus. 1997. A post-processing system to yield reduced word error rates: Recognizer output voting error reduction (rover). In *1997 IEEE Workshop on Automatic Speech Recognition and Understanding Proceedings*, pages 347–354. IEEE.

Jeremy Howard and Sebastian Ruder. 2018. Universal language model fine-tuning for text classification. *arXiv preprint arXiv:1801.06146*.

Zhiting Hu, Poyao Huang, Yuntian Deng, Yingkai Gao, and Eric Xing. 2015. Entity hierarchy embedding. In *Proceedings of the 53rd Annual Meeting of the Association for Computational Linguistics and the 7th International Joint Conference on Natural Language Processing (Volume 1: Long Papers)*, pages 1292–1300.

Kshitiz Kumar, Chaojun Liu, and Yifan Gong. 2014. Normalization of asr confidence classifier scores via confidence mapping. In *Fifteenth Annual Conference of the International Speech Communication Association*.

Kshitiz Kumar, Ziad Al Bawab, Yong Zhao, Chaojun Liu, Benoît Dumoulin, and Yifan Gong. 2015. Confidence-features and confidence-scores for asr applications in arbitration and dnn speaker adaptation. In *INTERSPEECH*.

Mingda Li, Cristian Lumezanu, Bo Zong, and Haifeng Chen. 2018. Deep learning ip network representations. In *Proceedings of the 2018 Workshop on Big Data Analytics and Machine Learning for Data Communication Networks*, pages 33–39.

Mingda Li, Weitong Ruan, Xinyue Liu, Luca Soldaini, Wael Hamza, and Chengwei Su. 2020. Improving spoken language understanding by exploiting asr n-best hypotheses. *arXiv preprint arXiv:2001.05284*.

Mingda Li. 2020. *Efficient Latent Semantic Extraction from Cross Domain Data with Declarative Language*. Ph.D. thesis, UCLA.

Xiaodong Liu, Pengcheng He, Weizhu Chen, and Jianfeng Gao. 2019. Multi-task deep neural networks for natural language understanding. *arXiv preprint arXiv:1901.11504*.

Paul Mather and Brandt Tso. 2016. *Classification methods for remotely sensed data*. CRC press.

Fabrizio Morbini, Kartik Audhkhasi, Ron Artstein, Maarten Van Segbroeck, Kenji Sagae, Panayiotis Georgiou, David R Traum, and Shri Narayanan. 2012. A reranking approach for recognition and classification of speech input in conversational dialogue systems. In *2012 IEEE Spoken Language Technology Workshop (SLT)*, pages 49–54. IEEE.

Atsunori Ogawa, Marc Delcroix, Shigeki Karita, and Tomohiro Nakatani. 2018. Rescoring n-best speech recognition list based on one-on-one hypothesis comparison using encoder-classifier model. In *2018 IEEE International Conference on Acoustics, Speech and Signal Processing (ICASSP)*, pages 6099–6103. IEEE.

Atsunori Ogawa, Marc Delcroix, Shigeki Karita, and Tomohiro Nakatani. 2019. Improved Deep Duel Model for Rescoring N-Best Speech Recognition List Using Backward LSTMLM and Ensemble Encoders. In *Proc. Interspeech 2019*, pages 3900–3904.

Sinno Jialin Pan and Qiang Yang. 2009. A survey on transfer learning. *IEEE Transactions on knowledge and data engineering*, 22(10):1345–1359.

Fuchun Peng, Scott Roy, Ben Shahshahani, and Françoise Beaufays. 2013. Search results based n-best hypothesis rescoring with maximum entropy classification. In *2013 IEEE Workshop on Automatic Speech Recognition and Understanding*, pages 422–427. IEEE.

Matthew E. Peters, Mark Neumann, Mohit Iyyer, Matt Gardner, Christopher Clark, Kenton Lee, and Luke Zettlemoyer. 2018. Deep contextualized word representations. In *Proc. of NAACL*.

Jinfeng Rao, Ferhan Ture, Hua He, Oliver Jojic, and Jimmy Lin. 2017. Talking to your tv: Context-aware voice search with hierarchical recurrent neural networks. In *Proceedings of the 2017 ACM on Conference on Information and Knowledge Management*, pages 557–566.

Hasim Sak, Murat Saraclar, and Tunga Gungor. 2011. Discriminative reranking of ASR hypotheses with morpholexical and n-best-list features. In *2011 IEEE Workshop on Automatic Speech Recognition & Understanding, ASRU 2011, Waikoloa, HI, USA, December 11-15, 2011*, pages 202–207.

Rico Sennrich, Barry Haddow, and Alexandra Birch. 2015. Neural machine translation of rare words with subword units. *arXiv preprint arXiv:1508.07909*.

Lisa Torrey and Jude Shavlik. 2010. Transfer learning. In *Handbook of research on machine learning applications and trends: algorithms, methods, and techniques*, pages 242–264. IGI Global.

Gokhan Tur and Renato De Mori. 2011. *Spoken language understanding: Systems for extracting semantic information from speech*. John Wiley & Sons.

Ashish Vaswani, Noam Shazeer, Niki Parmar, Jakob Uszkoreit, Llion Jones, Aidan N Gomez, Łukasz Kaiser, and Illia Polosukhin. 2017. Attention is all you need. In *Advances in neural information processing systems*, pages 5998–6008.

Wayne Xiong, Lingfeng Wu, Fil Alleva, Jasha Droppo, Xuedong Huang, and Andreas Stolcke. 2018. The microsoft 2017 conversational speech recognition system. In *2018 IEEE international conference on acoustics, speech and signal processing (ICASSP)*, pages 5934–5938. IEEE.

Zichao Yang, Diyi Yang, Chris Dyer, Xiaodong He, Alex Smola, and Eduard Hovy. 2016. Hierarchical attention networks for document classification. In *Proceedings of the 2016 conference of the North American chapter of the association for computational linguistics: human language technologies*, pages 1480–1489.

Yu Zhang and Qiang Yang. 2017. A survey on multi-task learning.

Misspelling Detection from Noisy Product Images

Varun Nagaraj Rao, Mingwei Shen
Product Assurance, Risk, and Security (PARS)
Amazon.com
{varao, mingweis}@amazon.com

Abstract

Misspellings are introduced on products either due to negligence or as an attempt to deliberately deceive stakeholders. This leads to a revenue loss for online sellers and fosters customer mistrust. Existing spelling research has primarily focused on advancement in misspelling correction and the approach for misspelling detection has remained the use of a large dictionary. The dictionary lookup results in the incorrect detection of several non-dictionary words as misspellings. In this paper, we propose a method to automatically detect misspellings from product images in an attempt to reduce false positive detections. We curate a large scale corpus, define a rich set of features and propose a novel model that leverages importance weighting to account for within class distributional variance. Finally, we experimentally validate this approach on both the curated corpus and an out-of-domain public dataset and show that it leads to a relative improvement of up to 20% in F1 score. The approach thus creates a more robust, generalized deployable solution and reduces reliance on large scale custom dictionaries used today.

1 Introduction

Misspellings often occur on printed descriptions, warranty cards and advertisements associated with products despite the ubiquitous presence of spell checkers. Although these misspellings are often due to human typographical errors (Kukich, 1992), or by non-native writers who are confused by language intricacies, they may also be deliberately introduced by malicious elements to deceive stakeholders (Gong et al., 2019). A single inadvertent or intentional misspelling can propagate to large amounts of inventory. As a consequence and much to the chagrin of sellers, misspellings cost millions in lost online sales (Coughlan, 2011) and breaks customer trust.

This paper aims to automatically and accurately identify misspellings from product images in order to improve customer experience. We loosely *define* a misspelling as "incorrectly spelled ubiquitous words and proper nouns which are very similar to their correct forms". Example images and words are present in Figure 1 and Table 1 respectively. As can be seen, product images predominantly contain many

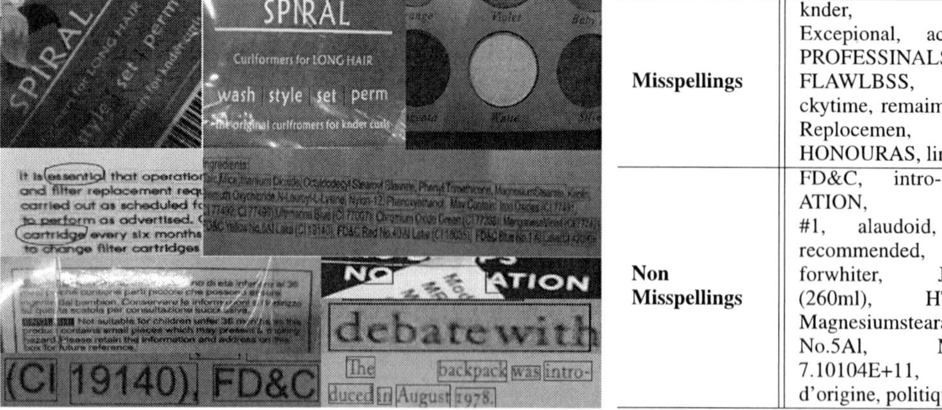

<table>
<tr><td rowspan="2">Misspellings</td><td>knder, Wnite, Excepional, accommodat, PROFESSINALS, FLAWLBSS, harmfiil, ckytime, remaimin, ELOW, Replocemen, favoeite, HONOURAS, limietd</td></tr>
</table>

Misspellings	knder, Wnite, Excepional, accommodat, PROFESSINALS, FLAWLBSS, harmfiil, ckytime, remaimin, ELOW, Replocemen, favoeite, HONOURAS, limietd
Non Misspellings	FD&C, intro-, duced, ATION, HSOOMS, #1, alaudoid, yeqioos, recommended, forwhiter, JavaPresse., (260ml), HT1S1A10d, Magnesiumstearate, No.5Al, MICHAEL, 7.10104E+11, Fabrique, d'origine, politique

Figure 1: Product Images after OCR processing   Table 1: Sample Product Image Instances

Proceedings of the 28th International Conference on Computational Linguistics: Industry Track, pages 124–135
Barcelona, Spain (Online), December 12, 2020

non-dictionary words including quantities, identification numbers, ingredients and other proper nouns, which should not be detected as misspellings. Further, text extraction from these noisy images is challenging since they often suffer from lighting, orientation, text occlusion and font dissimilarities issues. As a result, the class distribution is skewed with a very small number of misspellings amidst a large set of non misspellings. For instance, in Figure 1, "knder" and "Wnite" (present in the top row images) are the only two misspellings that are to be detected among several other words.

Leveraging existing approaches for misspelling detection from product images is beset with a number of challenges. First, although spelling research has intrigued the NLP community for long (Damerau, 1964; Kukich, 1992), misspelling detection research (Zamora et al., 1981; Dalkiliç and Çebi, 2009; Attia et al., 2012; Yu and Li, 2014) is very sparse, language specific and the primary approach has remained a dictionary lookup. This approach does not scale or generalize to billions of product images leading to a large number of false positive detections. Second, unlike most language modeling tasks, the use of contextual cues is ineffective. As a misspelling might be deliberate, its occurrence is unlikely to be influenced by its neighbouring words. Further, due to varied image quality and orientation, the extracted words may be scattered and not in the order they appear on the image. And third, to the best of our knowledge, there is no publicly available large scale corpus of product images annotated for misspellings. To address these deficiencies we make the following contributions.

- We curate Image-MisSpell [1], the first large scale corpus of product images and novel language agnostic misspelling features, explicitly annotated for misspellings and augmented with publicly available misspelling data. (Section 4.1, 4.2)
- We propose a weakly supervised cost sensitive weighted SVM model that leverages importance weighting of instances to handle within class distributional variance. The model can scale and generalize well to unseen examples. The small model size and low inference latency make it ideal to be used in a production environment. (Section 4.3)
- Finally, we present extensive experiments, results and discussions of the model and observe an improvement in F1-score of up to 20% over the dictionary lookup baseline. This result is promising because curating a custom set of non-dictionary words to filter for billions of products is prohibitively expensive and our model achieves better results with significantly lower cost. (Section 5, 6).

The remaining sections contain an overview of spelling related literature (Section 2), problem formulation (Section 3) and finally our conclusions and plans for further research (Section 7).

2 Related Work

Misspelling detection research is very limited, small scale and often on domain specific private data (Zamora et al., 1981). Approaches for misspelling detection primarily involve use of a predefined dictionary of n-grams (Zamora et al., 1981) and words (Dalkiliç and Çebi, 2009; Yu and Li, 2014; Attia et al., 2012). Additionally, dictionaries used are limited to specific languages like Chinese (Yu and Li, 2014), Turkish (Dalkiliç and Çebi, 2009) and Arabic (Attia et al., 2012).

Most existing work on spelling has focused on spelling error correction (Kukich, 1992; Ng et al., 2014; Chollampatt and Ng, 2018; Nagata et al., 2017; Hagen et al., 2017; Flor et al., 2019; Flor, 2012; Toutanova and Moore, 2002; Brill and Moore, 2000; Hasan et al., 2015). Initial approaches for correcting misspelling include those that compute edit distance and phonetic similarity between misspelling and candidate correction. Consequently, Flor (2012) introduced an approach to combine ranking candidate corrections using contextual cues with edit distance and phonetic similarity. Although several datasets exist for spelling correction research, many of these are small and proprietary corpora. Flor et al. (2019) proposed TOEFL-Spell as the first large scale corpus to benchmark spelling correction performance.

Spelling research is transitioning to leverage word embeddings with the advent of deep learning. Since pretrained word embeddings like Word2Vec (Mikolov et al., 2013b; Mikolov et al., 2013a) and GloVe (Pennington et al., 2014) do not support Out-Of-Vocabulary (OOV) words such as a misspelling, Bojanowski et al. (2017) and Piktus et al. (2019) introduced approaches for obtaining word embeddings resilient to misspellings. However, misspelling embeddings leverage context during training and have

---

[1]`https://github.com/amzn/image-misspell-coling2020`

been designed to be close to their correct variants. This is counter intuitive to our task where we would like to disentangle misspellings from non misspellings and the occurrence of a misspelling is unlikely to be influenced by its neighbouring words present on product images.

3 Problem Formulation

Given an image I consisting of n words, and an OCR Engine O which extracts words w_i from the image not necessarily in the order they appear:

$$O(I) = \{w_1, w_2, ..., w_n\} \tag{1}$$

we learn a model f such that for each word w_i and feature extractor g

$$(f \circ g)(w_i) = \begin{cases} 1 & w_i \text{ is a misspelling} \\ 0 & w_i \text{ is a non misspelling} \end{cases} \tag{2}$$

A word w is characterized as a *misspelling* if it loosely satisfies one or more of the following conditions:
- Is *not* present in a dictionary of *any* language
- Differs from its correctly spelled word form in only *very few characters*
- In most cases, does *not* contain punctuation, digits and special characters
- In most cases, contains only alphabets

An important distinction to our problem formulation is that a word w is a non misspelling, not only if it is present in the dictionary, but also if it doesn't satisfy any of the other conditions for a misspelling outlined above. This implies there could be words which are not present in the dictionary but are non misspellings. Further, our focus is on modelling words to detect misspellings *after* they have been extracted from images. We do not make any changes to either the existing OCR pipeline *before* word extraction or any potential misspelling correction approaches *after* misspelling detection.

4 Proposed Approach

We now describe the process of data curation, feature extraction and model learning.

4.1 Data Curation

To detect misspellings from product images, we create the Image-MisSpell Corpus curated from two distinct sources (1) Bin Check Images and (2) Public Corpora of Misspellings (Mitton, 2007).

4.1.1 Bin Check Images

Products are stored in large containers or *bins*. Based on requests investigators perform a bin check and capture product images. These images may include external packaging, internal product accessories, and documentation. Investigators may augment the captured images with product and brand images found online. As seen in Figure 1, these product images are very noisy. They contain diverse font styles and suffer from illumination issues, blurriness, rotation and occlusions making the process of extracting text using an OCR system, annotating the misspellings and detecting misspellings by avoiding false positives, a very challenging task. Once the product images were collected, words were extracted using AWS Textract (Amazon-AWS, 2019) and annotated for misspellings. Samples are present in Table 1.

As is evident from both Figure 1 and Table 1, the images contain a lot of non-dictionary instances such as quantities, punctuation, special characters, identification numbers, dates, zipcodes, ingredient lists and proper nouns that should be flagged as a non misspelling. Further adding to the challenge is that although the images predominantly contain English text, they occasionally do also contain multilingual non-English text. The Bin Check Images dataset is summarized by category in Table 2. The dataset is very skewed and contains only 0.5% misspelled words in relation to 99.5% of non misspelled words. As the dataset grows over time, the skew is only expected to get worse. This could lead to a large number of false positive detections by a classifier. To ensure our corpus is adequately balanced and representative, rather than waiting on the time-consuming and expensive process of using human investigators, we

# Misspelled Words	57 (0.5%)
# Non Misspelled Words	10617 (99.5%)

Table 2: Bin Check Images Dataset Summary

leverage a large public corpus of misspellings (Mitton, 2007) in a *weakly supervised* manner. Although the misspellings present in (Mitton, 2007) were not obtained from product images, their features are similar to those extracted from the Bin Check Images dataset (see Figure 2a) and can thus be used to correct class imbalance.

4.1.2 Public Corpora of Misspellings

The corpus has been curated by Mitton (2007), as an amalgamation of four datasets, to promote spellchecking research. It has a single correctly spelled English word which is present in a dictionary and is mapped to one or more spelling errors which may or may not be present in a dictionary. The constituent datasets are described below.

(1) birkbeck : It contains 36,133 misspellings of 6,136 words. It includes results of handwritten spelling tests run on students. Correct spellings are given in Oxford English form and misspellings due to American forms have been explicitly excluded.

(2) holbrook : It contains 1791 misspellings of 1200 target words (including 20 of unknown targets represented as '?'). The passages are taken from (Holbrook, 1964). They are extracts from the writings of secondary-school children, in their next-to-last year of schooling.

(3) aspell : It contains 531 misspellings of 450 words for testing the GNU Aspell Spellchecker.

(4) wikipedia : It contains 2,455 misspellings of 1,922 words made by Wikipedia editors.

To curate a single corpus we performed the following steps:

- Removed redundancy by mapping unique correct words to unique misspellings across the datasets.
- Removed words with unknown targets.
- Removed misspellings that are present in a dictionary and corresponding correct words if they do not have any misspellings associated with it after deletion. For instance, we noticed that "here" was a misspelling of "there" whereas by our problem formulation, "here" is not a misspelling as it is present in the dictionary.
- Replace the underscore by a space. Spaces are represented by an underscore in these datasets.

Sample examples from the dataset categorized by class is present in Table 3.

Misspellings	acomedation,acruied, expaine, exterordenary, heven, inconviencence, leaft, misstake
Non Misspellings	accommodation, accrued, explained, extraordinary, heaven, inconvenience, left, mistake

Table 3: Public Corpus Sample Instances

In contrast to the samples from the Bin Check Images in Table 1, these words are very clean, predominantly in English, contain very few proper nouns and have almost no punctuation and special characters other than a space. After performing the above mentioned steps, we ended up with a single dataset which we henceforth term as the "public corpus". The public corpus' summary statistics are summarized in Table 4. Since the distribution of samples is skewed towards more misspellings than non misspellings, it serves to complement the Bin Check Images dataset well.

# Misspelled Words	32051 (80%)
# Non Misspelled Words	8179 (20%)

Table 4: Public Corpus Dataset Summary

4.1.3 Image-MisSpell Corpus

We created the Image-MisSpell Corpus from both the Bin Check Images Dataset and the Public Corpus. We used all the samples of the Bin Check Images and randomly sampled instances from the Public Corpus

127

so that the class distribution is balanced. Consequently, we used a stratified sampling strategy to create a 90:10 train/test split that preserved the class balance in both the splits and ensured the distributions are similar. These splits can be used to build models for automatic detection of misspellings. The Image-MisSpell Corpus is summarized in Table 5.

Class	#Train Words	#Test Words
Misspelling	15027	1600
Non Misspelling	15064	1600

Table 5: Image-MisSpell Corpus Dataset Summary

4.2 Feature Extraction

The performance and success of machine learning models is heavily dependent on the features chosen. Different representations can hide or reveal the diverse factors that explain the variation in the data. Although automatic feature representation and transfer learning has shown promising results on several NLP benchmark tasks, it is not directly applicable for the task of misspelling detection since (1) context does not affect misspellings on product images and (2) pretrained misspelling embeddings (Piktus et al., 2019) are designed to be close to their correct variants. Thus, we chose to perform traditional feature engineering relying on domain knowledge and generic priors. A blend of language specific and language agnostic features are chosen. We define the features below.

4.2.1 Standalone Features

These features are extracted from a single word and do not require any additional information.

(1) `textract_score`: The AWS Textract Word Recognizer produces a confidence score associated with each recognized word from the image (Litman et al., 2020). Textract can detect Latin-script characters from the standard English alphabet and ASCII symbols. The prediction confidence score is calculated as the average of the CTC decoder probabilities until the end-of-sequence token. The score is bounded in the range [0,1] with higher scores for more confident predictions. Since the Public Corpus does not have an associated confidence score, we simulate the score using a uniform sampling from the 95% confidence interval (in Table 6) of the textract scores of the Bin Check Images Corpus. This ensures a non zero variance across all samples and preserves the features characteristics. Ignoring the values completely or filling in with order statistics or mean/median/mode is not appropriate when number of missing values is very high. This feature is included as we are interested in words that have mostly been correctly recognized by the OCR system.

Stats \ Class	Misspelling	Non Misspelling
Mean	0.97	0.90
Max	1.00	1.00
Min	0.39	0.01
95% Conf.Int.	[0.95, 0.99]	[0.89, 0.90]

Table 6: Bin Check Images `textract_score` distribution

(2) `ner_score`: We obtain the probability of each word being a named entity from AWS Comprehend (Amazon-AWS, 2017). The decoder probability predicted for each token is averaged. This basically tells us given confidence score of each token, how likely the whole span will be an entity (Shen et al., 2017). We default to the English language model of Comprehend. Using this feature, the model would thus have the ability to exclude named entities as misspellings while still being able to classify their variants as misspellings.

(3) `pos_score`: We obtain the probability of each word being a proper noun (PROPN) from AWS Comprehend's Part-Of-Speech (POS) Tagger (Amazon-AWS, 2017). We default to the English language model of Comprehend. Using this feature, the model would have the ability to exclude proper nouns as misspellings while being able to classify their variants as misspellings.

(4) `gibb_score`: We calculate the probability of a word being gibberish using a first order markov chain. The model should exclude gibberish from the predicted misspellings. We pretrain a 27 x 27 matrix of bigram probabilities (26 lowercase characters and a space) using a text file [2] of a million English words. It is a concatenation of public domain book excerpts from Project Gutenberg and lists of most frequent words from Wiktionary and the British National Corpus. For each word encountered, we use the matrix to calculate the joint probability of occurrence of all possible bigrams formed from the chosen character set. OOV words are expected to have a low probability of occurrence. Further, long gibberish words are also expected to have a low joint probability due to the product of several low probability bigrams. In the practical application, the gibberish score can also help with OCR errors. For instance, a gated structure on an image may be incorrectly recognized as a series of alphabets (l's or x's) even though it does not actually contain any letters and is only a graphic resembling text. The joint probability in these cases is also expected to be low. Given a matrix M of bigram probabilities, and ordered sequence of n characters $[c_1, ..., c_n] \in M$, the gibberish score of word w is calculated as follows:

$$\text{gibb\_score}(w) = \text{gibb\_score}([c_1, ..., c_n]) = \prod_{i=1}^{n-1} (M[c_i, c_{i+1}]) \tag{3}$$

(5) `word_length`: Integer length of a word.

(6) `contains_nonalpha`: Boolean value that indicates whether word w contains non alphabetical characters. Misspellings usually do not contain punctuation, special characters and digits.

$$\text{contains\_nonalpha} = \begin{cases} 1, & w \text{ contains non alpha} \\ 0, & \text{otherwise} \end{cases} \tag{4}$$

(7) `dict_presence`: Boolean value for whether the word w is present in a dictionary. We make use of the Hunspell dictionary (Németh, 2010) with its Python bindings (Latinier, 2014). We leverage dictionaries of prevalent languages [en_us, en_gb, en_au, en_ca, en_za, es, de, fr, pt, it, ru] from (Wormer, 2018) since product images occasionally contain multilingual text. In addition to checking for dictionary presence of the word in its recognized form, we also check for presence of its stemmed and lowercase forms. PyHunspell provides flexibility to add in new words to the dictionary at runtime. We insert a set of about 100 product specific words. Words present in a dictionary of any language should not be misspellings. This feature ensures the model is less sensitive to a specific language.

$$\text{dict presence} = \begin{cases} 1, & w \text{ present in a dict} \\ 0, & \text{otherwise} \end{cases} \tag{5}$$

4.2.2 String Similarity Features

In order to leverage a weak context, we obtain string similarity metrics using the autocorrected form of the word with least edit distance. For the Bin Check Images Dataset we use the PyHunspell module to suggest the closest autocorrect word. The autocorrected form of the word may be from any of the language dictionaries. Ties are broken based on the order of the listed languages in the dict_presence feature. The Public Corpus Dataset already has a word mapped to its correct form.

(1) `editdistance`: We calculate the Levenshtein distance (Hyyrö, 2001) with equal weight for insertion, deletion and substitution. This is further normalized by dividing by the maximum of the lengths of the two words ensuring the value obtained is bounded in the range [0,1].

(2) `jaccard_similarity`: Jaccard Similarity is another well-known measure of the similarity of a pair of strings. It captures information orthogonal to edit distance. Given two *sets* of unique lowercase characters w_1, w_2 the jaccard similarity is defined in Equation 6.

$$\text{jaccard\_similarity} = |w_1 \cap w_2| / |w_1 \cup w_2| \tag{6}$$

---

[2] `https://norvig.com/big.txt`

(3) `string_containment`: Sometimes an indicator of a match is that the letters in one string are entirely or partially contained in the other string. String containment captures this notion. Given two *sets* of unique lowercase characters w_1, w_2 the string containment is defined in Equation 7.

$$\text{string\_containment} = |w_1 \cap w_2|/min(|w_1|, |w_2|) \tag{7}$$

(4) `char_intersection_count`: This is simply the number of unique lowercase intersecting characters given two sets of characters w_1, w_2.

$$\text{char\_intersection\_count} = |w_1 \cap w_2| \tag{8}$$

4.3 Importance Weighting and Learning Using Privileged Information:

Once we have represented the Image-MisSpell corpus using the features described, we are able to build models for automatic detection of misspellings. However, we must keep in mind the data and class distributions before modeling. Most machine learning models perform poorly when there is a skew in the class distribution. With a greater class imbalance ratio, the decision function usually favours the majority class. Two strategies for handling the class imbalance include (1) over sampling the minority class using approaches like SMOTE (Chawla et al., 2002) and ADASYN (He et al., 2008) and (2) under sampling the majority class. Given the abundance of data due to the augmentation with the Public Corpus, we were able to generate a class balanced corpus by under sampling the majority class.

Now, although the classes are balanced, we noticed that the distributions within each class varied. The Public Corpus non misspellings are very clean and contain words present in a dictionary whereas the Bin Check Images non misspellings class is very noisy and contains words not present in the dictionary. Further, the actual number of misspellings from the Bin Check Images is very small. An approach to correct the sampling bias, used in active learning (Beygelzimer et al., 2009) and weighted SVMs (Lapin et al., 2014), is called *importance weighting*. Lapin et al. (2014) state that "prior knowledge expressible with privileged features can be encoded by weights associated with every training example". Higher the weight, more emphasis the classifier puts on that instance to classify correctly. The Instance Weighted or Cost Sensitive SVM (He and Ma, 2013; Yang et al., 2007) is able to implicitly incorporate importance weighting into its objective. We now discuss SVM optimization formulation incorporating the instance weighting.

Given n, d dimensional training instances $x_i \in \mathbb{R}^d, \forall i \in [1, n]$, binary labels $y \in \{1, -1\}^n$, a kernel function ϕ, the SVM algorithm obtains $w \in \mathbb{R}^d, b \in \mathbb{R}$ such that the prediction $sign(w^T \phi(x_i) + b)$ is correct in most cases. The primal objective is:

$$\min_{w,b,\zeta} \frac{1}{2} w^T w + C \sum_{i=1}^{n} \zeta_i, \text{ subject to } y_i(w^T \phi(x_i) + b) \geq 1 - \zeta_i, \text{ where } \zeta_i \geq 0, i = 1, ..., n \tag{9}$$

Since data is not always perfectly separable by a hyperplane, few samples are allowed to be at a distance of ζ_i from their correct margin boundary. The C controls the strength of this penalty. As each example in the training dataset has its own weight, the instance C_i can be calculated as a weighting of the global C such that $C \in \mathbb{R}^n$. A larger weighting is used for lesser representative instances allowing the margin to be softer and preventing misclassified examples. In other words, the modified SVM algorithm would *not* skew the hyperplane towards the distribution with larger samples since the minority samples are assigned a higher misclassification cost. The weights are inversely proportional to the number of samples that satisfy the condition, i.e, smaller the number of samples, higher is the weight.

$$C_i = \text{instance\_weight}_i * C \tag{10}$$

5 Experimental Setup

In this section, we describe the experimental set up used for training, the model used and feature ablations.
Datasets. We use the Image-MisSpell and an out-of-domain publicly available dataset TOEFL-Spell

Rule	Weight
Initial Weight for All samples	= 1
'filename' == 'bin_check'	= 2
'contains_nonalpha' == 1 && 'is_error' == 0	= 5
'filename' == 'bin_check' && 'is_error' == 1	= 10
'filename' == 'bin_check' && 'is_error' == 0	= 15
'filename' == 'bin_check' && 'is_error' == 0 && 'dict_presence' == 0	= 20
'textract_score' $\geq$ 0.95 && 'is_error' == 1	+2
'textract_score' $<$ 0.1	-1

Table 7: Instance Weight values. Each instance initially has a weight of 1. The weights are then modified sequentially in the order of the rules listed.

(Flor et al., 2019) for our experiments. The Image-MisSpell dataset includes about 30K train samples and 3.2K test samples. Both the train and test splits are class balanced. More details have been described in Section 4.1. The TOEFL-Spell is a corpus of learner essays, annotated for spelling errors. We preprocess and extract out features from the TOEFL-Spell dataset similar to the Public Corpus and obtain 3699 misspellings and 2343 non misspellings. All models have been trained using the Image-MisSpell trainset. For evaluation, we use both the Image-MisSpell and the TOEFL-Spell testsets.

Models. We present two baselines that involve table lookups and thresholds that *do not* include a learning component (1) Hunspell dictionary presence lookup and (2) heuristics model. The machine learning model we used is a Cost Sensitive / Weighted SVM (WSVM) with linear and RBF kernels chosen due to the implicit ability to allow importance weighting and interpretability using linear feature weights. We also present feature ablations using the standalone and string similarity features in isolation.

Implementation details. For the heuristics model, the features and conditions chosen empirically by human annotators include [textract_score $<$ 0.93, ner_score $\geq$ 0.1, pos_score $\geq$ 0.99, gibb_score $\leq$ 0.01, word_length $\leq$ 2, contains_nonalpha == 1, dict_presence == 1]. If any of the conditions are satisfied, the word is classified as a non misspelling, else it is a misspelling. The importance weight heuristic values are present in Table 7. Both absolute and relative values are used. The SVM parameters are RBF kernel coefficient $\gamma = 1/(num\_features * \sigma^2(train\_set))$ and a vector C as described in Table 7 and Equation 10.

6 Results and Discussion

	Experiment	Image-MisSpell			TOEFL-Spell		
		P	R	F1	P	R	F1
Baseline	Hunspell Dictionary Lookup	0.61	0.99	0.76	0.94	1.00	0.97
	Heuristics with Thresholds	0.89	0.70	0.79	0.99	0.73	0.84
Model	SVM + Linear Kernel	0.74	1.00	0.85	0.98	1.00	0.99
	SVM + RBF Kernel	0.78	1.00	0.87	0.99	1.00	1.00
	WSVM + Linear Kernel	0.87	0.96	0.91	0.98	0.96	0.97
	WSVM + RBF Kernel	0.86	0.97	0.91	0.99	0.96	0.98
Ablation	WSVM + Linear (only standalone features)	0.85	0.97	0.90	0.98	0.96	0.97
	WSVM + Linear (only string similarity features.)	0.68	0.75	0.71	0.98	0.60	0.74

Table 8: Experimental Results on the Image-MisSpell and TOEFL-Spell datasets.

We report results using standard classification metrics of precision, recall and F1-score in Table 8. On the Image-MisSpell corpus, which contains many non-dictionary words as non misspellings, the WSVM models indicate up to 20% relative improvement in F1-scores. As expected, this behaviour is not observed on the TOEFL-Spell dataset which does not have any non-dictionary words as non misspellings. However, results are comparable to a dictionary lookup. Without using instance weighting, which is tailored to the Image-MisSpell distribution, we get near perfect detection on the TOEFL-Spell dataset. In most cases and across the two datasets, the SVM and WSVM models perform better than the baselines. The choice of kernel (linear or RBF) does not alter performance significantly. The performance of the WSVM is better than the SVM on the Image-MisSpell, but not so on TOEFL-Spell. This indicates that the importance weighting utilized by the WSVM helps improve performance when the underlying distributions vary, unlike the TOEFL-Spell dataset which is very clean and without a within class distributional variance. Feature ablations indicate that the exclusion of either standalone or string similarity features causes a reduction in performance.

Benefits of Hand Crafted Features. There are finer distinctions to the type of misspellings and non misspellings that may occur. In Table 9 we detail the form of word encountered and the most prominent corresponding features which help disentangle them.

Form of Word	Classification	Prominent Feature(s)
Not present in any dictionary and differs from the correct form in few edit distances	Misspelling	Standalone and String Similarity Features
Not in any dictionary but is a correctly spelled domain word (entities, terminology)	Non Misspelling	dict_presence, ner_score, pos_score
Misspelled domain word (entities, terminology)	Misspelling	String Similarity Features, dict_presence, ner_score, pos_score
Random collection of alphabets or alpha-numeric characters	Non Misspelling	gibb_score, contains_nonalpha

Table 9: Details about the type of misspellings that may occur and corresponding features that help accurately detect them.

Weak Supervision. Given a small set of labeled data, we can express functional invariances as weak label distributions. In this way we view techniques such as data augmentation as a form of weak supervision (Ratner et al., 2017). Data augmentation was necessary due to the skewed class distribution on the Bin Check Images Dataset as shown in Table 2. As the Bin Check Images dataset matures, the skewness is expected to get worse and a means to correct for this imbalance is required. Without augmentation, the classifer could choose to ignore the misspelling class entirely and still lead to a 99.5% accuracy. Although data augmentation helped correct the class imbalance, the Public Corpus misspelling class needed to have a similar distribution to that of the Bin Check Images misspellings. This distributional similarity of the misspellings is evident in the 2-dimensional TSNE plot of the Image-MisSpell trainset is depicted in Figure 2a. Since the distribution of misspellings of the public corpus was similar to the Bin Check Images the data augmentation was a reasonable choice.

Interpretability and Explainability. Machine learning systems are increasingly making or informing several critical decisions. However, they are often opaque black boxes that are not explainable. A key requirement in this study was to have a model whose decision can be *explained* by a human when required. The WSVM + Linear model decision can be easily interpreted by examining the learned feature weights (Figure 2b). Positive weighted features contribute to the misspelling labels and negative weighted features contribute to non misspelling labels. We notice that the weights learned are inline with human interpretations and the models decision can be held accountable.

Model Deployment. The WSVM + Linear model takes up only a few kilobytes of spaces and has very low inference latency. In addition, the instance weights provided a useful toggle to tweak the feature importance based on runtime performance, thus making this model suitable for a production environment.

Use of Word Embeddings. Although techniques such as Word2Vec (Mikolov et al., 2013b; Mikolov et al., 2013a) and GloVe (Pennington et al., 2014) have been extensively used, they cannot provide embeddings for OOV words such as misspellings. FastText by Bojanowski et al. (2017) and Misspelling Oblivious Embeddings (MOE) by Piktus et al. (2019) introduced approaches for obtaining word embeddings for OOV words. Although FastText can capture morphological aspects of text, it may not be particularly resistant to misspellings which can occur also within the dominant morphemes. MOE on the other hand combines the FastText loss with a spell correction loss giving explicit importance to misspelled words. However, these are supervised tasks which embed misspellings close to their correct variants. Since our task involves disentangling misspellings from their correct variants, the direct use of these embeddings without the use of hand crafted features may not be ideal. Further, pretrained MOE have not been released publicly at the time of writing this paper. An interesting experiment, which we leave as future work, is to augment the string similarity features with MOE since both are expected to capture

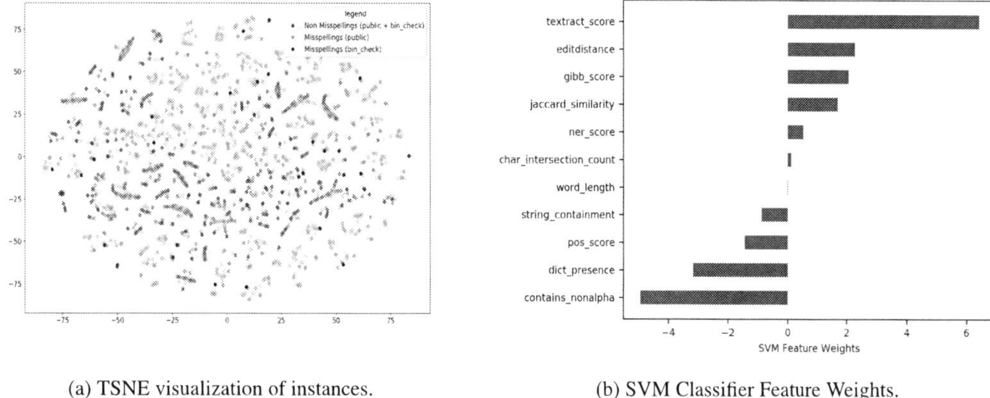

(a) TSNE visualization of instances.   (b) SVM Classifier Feature Weights.

Figure 2: The misspelling features of the bin_check images are *mostly* distributed amongst the public misspellings features as seen in (a). Feature weights are in line with human interpretation in (b).

similarity between a misspelling and its closely related correctly spelled word form, complimenting the feature space.

Error Analysis. We perform an error analysis of the WSVM+Linear model used in production. Qualitative examples are present in Table 10. Words present in the dictionary of popular languages ("environment", "bonjour"), proper nouns ("Microsoft", "Amazon"), gibberish ("jncjnvuhebvioheosv env") and words with special characters/digits ("(njcwjncp3e9r") are rightly classified as non misspellings. Words which mostly satisfy the conditions in Section 3 such as "mroning", "Micorsoft", and "precison", are rightly classified as misspellings. However, the model does occasionally make mistakes. Even though "jncjnvuhebvioheosv" is gibberish, and "Amazn", "environmen" differs in only a few characters from its correct form the model incorrectly classifies them as non misspellings. A character level model may be able to accurately disentangle correct words like "environment" from many more of its incorrect forms like "environmnt" and "environemnt" by better learning about similar character patterns. We must also note that in certain cases this behaviour is due to the insufficient representative samples in the trainset that the importance weighting is unable to correct for. For instance, we noticed that long words with no meaning are extremely rare ($<0.5\%$) and hence the gibberish detector mostly does not fire on them. Additional samples, representative of the system's use case in practice can correct for these errors.

Misspellings	mroning, environmnt, Micorsoft, Facebdok, precison, bonjuor, jncjnvuhebvioheosv, helli, helo
Non Misspellings	jncjnvuhebvioheosv env, environment, environmen, Amazon, Amazn, Microsoft, (njcwjncp3e9r, bonjour, #4tg%ju, lake union, marketplace, he\$\$o, 10/23/2019, 50oz, MagnesiumStearate

Table 10: Qualitative Example Results Produced by the WSVM+Linear Model

7   Conclusion and Future Directions

This paper addressed the problem of automatic detection of misspellings from product images. We presented Image-MisSpell, a large dataset of product images augmented with public corpora, exhaustively annotated for misspelling detection. We also defined a rich set of features that can be extracted from words without context. Further, we proposed a cost sensitive weighted SVM model that leverages importance weighting to account for the within class distributional variation. Finally through experiments we demonstrated the enhanced performance of this model in relation to baseline approaches. The approach is promising since it achieves better results with a lower time, monetary and human capital investment. Future directions include leveraging deep learning where character level language modeling could be used to learn embeddings that disentangle misspellings from their correct form. Visual features like Pyramidal Histogram of Characters (PHOC) (Almazán et al., 2014) can also provide important cues for OCR errors and deliberate misspellings.

133

Acknowledgments

We thank Srikar Appalaraju for scoping out this problem. We also thank Karen Hovsepian, Shuping Ji and Thi Nhat Anh Nguyen for providing constructive feedback about this work. We also extend our gratitude to the reviewers who provided us with very constructive and detailed comments. Finally, we'd like to thank Qingzhou Yu, Ananth Kasturirangan, Kirsty Bolden, Will Lewis and others from tech and business for their support.

References

Jon Almazán, Albert Gordo, Alicia Fornés, and Ernest Valveny. 2014. Word spotting and recognition with embedded attributes. *IEEE transactions on pattern analysis and machine intelligence*, 36(12):2552–2566.

Amazon-AWS. 2017. Comprehend. `https://aws.amazon.com/comprehend/`.

Amazon-AWS. 2019. Textract. `https://aws.amazon.com/textract/`.

Mohammed Attia, Pavel Pecina, Younes Samih, Khaled Shaalan, and Josef Van Genabith. 2012. Improved spelling error detection and correction for arabic. In *Proceedings of COLING 2012: Posters*, pages 103–112.

Alina Beygelzimer, Sanjoy Dasgupta, and John Langford. 2009. Importance weighted active learning. In *Proceedings of the 26th annual international conference on machine learning*, pages 49–56.

Piotr Bojanowski, Edouard Grave, Armand Joulin, and Tomas Mikolov. 2017. Enriching word vectors with subword information. *Transactions of the Association for Computational Linguistics*, 5:135–146.

Eric Brill and Robert C Moore. 2000. An improved error model for noisy channel spelling correction. In *Proceedings of the 38th annual meeting on association for computational linguistics*, pages 286–293. Association for Computational Linguistics.

Nitesh V Chawla, Kevin W Bowyer, Lawrence O Hall, and W Philip Kegelmeyer. 2002. Smote: synthetic minority over-sampling technique. *Journal of artificial intelligence research*, 16:321–357.

Shamil Chollampatt and Hwee Tou Ng. 2018. A multilayer convolutional encoder-decoder neural network for grammatical error correction. In *Thirty-Second AAAI Conference on Artificial Intelligence*.

Sean Coughlan. 2011. Spelling mistakes 'cost millions' in lost online sales, `https://www.bbc.com/news/education-14130854`. *BBC News*.

Gökhan Dalkiliç and Yalçin Çebi. 2009. Turkish spelling error detection and correction by using word n-grams. In *2009 Fifth International Conference on Soft Computing, Computing with Words and Perceptions in System Analysis, Decision and Control*, pages 1–4. IEEE.

Fred J Damerau. 1964. A technique for computer detection and correction of spelling errors. *Communications of the ACM*, 7(3):171–176.

Michael Flor, Michael Fried, and Alla Rozovskaya. 2019. A benchmark corpus of english misspellings and a minimally-supervised model for spelling correction. In *Proceedings of the Fourteenth Workshop on Innovative Use of NLP for Building Educational Applications*, pages 76–86.

Michael Flor. 2012. Four types of context for automatic spelling correction. *TAL*, 53(3):61–99.

Hongyu Gong, Yuchen Li, Suma Bhat, and Pramod Viswanath. 2019. Context-sensitive malicious spelling error correction. In *The World Wide Web Conference*, pages 2771–2777.

Matthias Hagen, Martin Potthast, Marcel Gohsen, Anja Rathgeber, and Benno Stein. 2017. A large-scale query spelling correction corpus. In *Proceedings of the 40th International ACM SIGIR Conference on Research and Development in Information Retrieval*, pages 1261–1264.

Saša Hasan, Carmen Heger, and Saab Mansour. 2015. Spelling correction of user search queries through statistical machine translation. In *Proceedings of the 2015 Conference on Empirical Methods in Natural Language Processing*, pages 451–460.

Haibo He and Yunqian Ma. 2013. *Imbalanced learning: foundations, algorithms, and applications*. John Wiley & Sons.

Haibo He, Yang Bai, Edwardo A Garcia, and Shutao Li. 2008. Adasyn: Adaptive synthetic sampling approach for imbalanced learning. In *2008 IEEE international joint conference on neural networks (IEEE world congress on computational intelligence)*, pages 1322–1328. IEEE.

David Holbrook. 1964. English for the rejected: Training literacy in the lower streams of the secondary school.

Heikki Hyyrö. 2001. Explaining and extending the bit-parallel approximate string matching algorithm of myers. Technical report, Citeseer.

Karen Kukich. 1992. Techniques for automatically correcting words in text. *Acm Computing Surveys (CSUR)*, 24(4):377–439.

Maksim Lapin, Matthias Hein, and Bernt Schiele. 2014. Learning using privileged information: Svm+ and weighted svm. *Neural Networks*, 53:95–108.

Benoit Latinier. 2014. PyHunspell. https://github.com/blatinier/pyhunspell.

Ron Litman, Oron Anschel, Shahar Tsiper, Roee Litman, Shai Mazor, and R Manmatha. 2020. Scatter: selective context attentional scene text recognizer. *arXiv preprint arXiv:2003.11288*.

Tomas Mikolov, Kai Chen, Greg Corrado, and Jeffrey Dean. 2013a. Efficient estimation of word representations in vector space. *arXiv preprint arXiv:1301.3781*.

Tomas Mikolov, Ilya Sutskever, Kai Chen, Greg S Corrado, and Jeff Dean. 2013b. Distributed representations of words and phrases and their compositionality. In *Advances in neural information processing systems*, pages 3111–3119.

Roger Mitton. 2007. Corpora of misspellings for download. https://www.dcs.bbk.ac.uk/~ROGER/corpora.html.

Ryo Nagata, Hiroya Takamura, and Graham Neubig. 2017. Adaptive spelling error correction models for learner english. *Procedia Computer Science*, 112(C):474–483.

Hwee Tou Ng, Siew Mei Wu, Ted Briscoe, Christian Hadiwinoto, Raymond Hendy Susanto, and Christopher Bryant. 2014. The conll-2014 shared task on grammatical error correction. In *Proceedings of the Eighteenth Conference on Computational Natural Language Learning: Shared Task*, pages 1–14.

László Németh. 2010. Hunspell. https://github.com/hunspell/hunspell.

Jeffrey Pennington, Richard Socher, and Christopher D Manning. 2014. Glove: Global vectors for word representation. In *Proceedings of the 2014 conference on empirical methods in natural language processing (EMNLP)*, pages 1532–1543.

Aleksandra Piktus, Necati Bora Edizel, Piotr Bojanowski, Édouard Grave, Rui Ferreira, and Fabrizio Silvestri. 2019. Misspelling oblivious word embeddings. In *Proceedings of the 2019 Conference of the North American Chapter of the Association for Computational Linguistics: Human Language Technologies, Volume 1 (Long and Short Papers)*, pages 3226–3234.

Alex Ratner, Stephen Bach, Paroma Varma, and Chris Ré. 2017. Weak Supervision: The New Programming Paradigm for Machine Learning. https://dawn.cs.stanford.edu/2017/07/16/weak-supervision.

Yanyao Shen, Hyokun Yun, Zachary C Lipton, Yakov Kronrod, and Animashree Anandkumar. 2017. Deep active learning for named entity recognition. *arXiv preprint arXiv:1707.05928*.

Kristina Toutanova and Robert C Moore. 2002. Pronunciation modeling for improved spelling correction.

Titus Wormer. 2018. Hunspell Dictionaries. https://github.com/wooorm/dictionaries.

Xulei Yang, Qing Song, and Yue Wang. 2007. A weighted support vector machine for data classification. *International Journal of Pattern Recognition and Artificial Intelligence*, 21(05):961–976.

Junjie Yu and Zhenghua Li. 2014. Chinese spelling error detection and correction based on language model, pronunciation, and shape. In *Proceedings of The Third CIPS-SIGHAN Joint Conference on Chinese Language Processing*, pages 220–223.

EM Zamora, Joseph J Pollock, and Antonio Zamora. 1981. The use of trigram analysis for spelling error detection. *Information Processing & Management*, 17(6):305–316.

hinglishNorm - A Corpus of Hindi-English Code Mixed Sentences for Text Normalization

Piyush Makhija
piyush@vahan.co

Ankit Kumar
ankit@vahan.co

Anuj Gupta
anuj@vahan.co

Abstract

We present *hinglishNorm* - a human annotated corpus of Hindi-English code-mixed sentences for text normalization task. Each sentence in the corpus is aligned to its corresponding human annotated normalized form. To the best of our knowledge, there is no corpus of Hindi-English code-mixed sentences for text normalization task that is publicly available. Our work is the first attempt in this direction. The corpus contains 13494 segments annotated for text normalization. Further, we present baseline normalization results on this corpus. We obtain a Word Error Rate (WER) of 15.55, BiLingual Evaluation Understudy (BLEU) score of 71.2, and Metric for Evaluation of Translation with Explicit ORdering (METEOR) score of 0.50.

1 Introduction

Hindi is the fourth most-spoken first language in the world[1]. According to one estimate, nearly 0.615 billion people speak Hindi as their first language[2]. Of these people, most of the speakers are in India. The second most spoken language in India is English[3]. Hindi and English are the official languages of the Indian Commonwealth[4]. A large number of these people have joined the Internet recently. As a matter of fact, Next Billion Users (NBU) is a term commonly used in tech and business circles to refer to the large number of people from India, Brazil, China and South-East Asia who joined the Internet in the last decade[5]. This phenomena is primarily attributed to ubiquitous highly affordable phone and internet plans[6]. A large fraction of NBU users come from India and speak Hindi as either their first or second language. A large number of these people use a blend of Hindi and English in their daily informal communication. This hybrid language is also known as Hinglish[7].

These users extensively use Internet platforms which heavily rely on User Generated Content (UGC) - social media platforms such as Facebook or Twitter; messaging platforms such as WhatsApp or Facebook messenger; user reviews aggregators such as the Google play store or Amazon. A key characteristic of their behaviour on such platforms is their use of Hinglish. Thus, building any Natural Language Processing (NLP) based Internet applications for these users necessitates the ability to process this 'new' language. Further, these UGC platforms are notoriously noisy. This means there is an additional challenge of non-canonical text. Therefore, a key step in building applications for such text data is *text normalization*. Intuitively, it is transforming text to a form where written text aligned to its normalized spoken form (Sproat and Jaitly, 2016). More formally, *it is the task of mapping non-canonical language,*

---

[1]https://en.wikipedia.org/wiki/List_of_languages_by_number_of_native_speakers
[2]https://blog.busuu.com/most-spoken-languagesintheworld/
[3]https://en.wikipedia.org/wiki/List_of_languages_by_number_of_native_speakers_in_India
[4]https://en.wikipedia.org/wiki/Hindi
[5]https://www.blog.google/technology/nextbillionusers/nextbillionusersarefutureinternet/
[6]https://www.hup.harvard.edu/catalog.php?isbn=9780674983786
[7]https://en.wikipedia.org/wiki/Hinglish

Proceedings of the 28th International Conference on Computational Linguistics: Industry Track, pages 136–145
Barcelona, Spain (Online), December 12, 2020

typical of speech transcription and computer-mediated communication, to standardized writing (Lusetti et al., 2018).

Separately, there has been a lot of work in the two areas of normalization and building corpora of Hindi-English code mix text data, not much has been done at the intersection of the two(refer to section 2). To the best of our knowledge, there does not exist a corpus of Hindi-English Code Mixed sentences for normalization where the normalizations are human annotated. This work is an effort to release such a corpus

This work is motivated from our business use case where we are building a conversational system over WhatsApp to screen candidates for blue-collar jobs. Our candidate user base often comes from tier-2 and tier-3 cities of India. Their responses to our conversational bot are mostly a code mix of Hindi and English coupled with non-canonical text (ex: typos, non-standard syntactic constructions, spelling variations, phonetic substitutions, foreign language words in non-native script, grammatically incorrect text, colloquialisms, abbreviations, etc). The raw text our system gets is far from clean well formatted text and text normalization becomes a necessity to process it any further.

The main contributions of this work are two-fold, viz. (i) creating a human annotated corpus for text normalization of Hindi-English code mix sentences; and (ii) reporting baseline metrics on the corpus. Further, we release the corpus and annotations under a Creative Commons Attribution-NonCommercial-ShareAlike License[8].

2   Related Work

In this section, we present relevant work in the following areas viz.(1) Text Normalization (2) Normalization and UGC Datasets (3) Code-mixed Datasets, (4) Hindi-English Datasets.

Text Normalization: Text normalization, sometimes also called lexical normalization, is the task of translating/transforming a non-standard text to a standard format. Using text normalization on noisy data, one can provide cleaner text data to downstream NLP tasks and improve the overall system performance (Liu et al., 2012), (Satapathy et al., 2017). Some of the early work used a rule-based spell-checker approach to generate a list of corrections for any misspelled word, ranked by corresponding posterior probabilities (Church and Gale, 1991) (Mays et al., 1991) (Brill and Moore, 2000). However, this approach did not factor in any context while normalizing words. (Choudhury et al., 2007) used a Hidden Markov Model (HMM), where they modeled each standard English word as a HMM and calculated the probability of observing the noisy token. "Moses", a well known Statistical Machine Translation (SMT) tool, provided significant improvements in comparison to previous solutions (Koehn et al., 2007). (Aw et al., 2006) adapted a phrase-based Machine Translation (MT) model for normalizing SMS and achieved significant gain in performance. In the past few years, Neural network based approaches for text normalization have become increasingly popular and have shown competitive performance in shared tasks (Chrupała, 2014), (Min and Mott, 2015). (Lusetti et al., 2018), (Liu et al., 2012) and (Satapathy et al., 2017) provide excellent literature covering the landscape on this topic.

Normalization and UGC Datasets: (Han and Baldwin, 2011) introduced a text normalization approach for twitter data using a variety of supervised & unsupervised learning techniques. This study resulted in 'lexNorm'[9], an open-source dataset containing 549 tweets. (Baldwin et al., 2015) subsequently released lexNorm15[10]. This new dataset contained 2950/1967 annotated tweets in train/test sets. (Michel and Neubig, 2018) created the MTNT dataset[11] containing translations of Reddit comments from the English language to French/ Japanese and vice versa, containing 7k~37K data points per language pair. This dataset contains user-generated text with different kinds of noise, e.g., typos, grammatical errors, emojis, spoken languages, etc. for two language pairs. (van der Goot and van Noord, 2017) introduced 'MoNoise', a general purpose model for normalizing UGC text data. This model utilizes Aspell spell checker, an n-gram based language model and word embeddings trained on a few million tweets. It

---

[8]http://creativecommons.org/licenses/by-nc-sa/4.0/

[9]http://people.eng.unimelb.edu.au/tbaldwin/etc/lexnorm_v1.2.tgz

[10]https://github.com/noisy-text/noisy-text.github.io/blob/master/2015/files/lexnorm2015.tgz

[11]https://www.cs.cmu.edu/ pmichel1/mtnt/

Dataset	Task	Size
IITB English-Hindi Parallel Corpus (Anoop et al., 2018)	Machine Translation	Train - 1,561,840 Dev - 520 Test - 2,507
HindiEnCorp 0.5 (Dhariya et al., 2017)	Machine Translation	132,300 sentences
Xlit-Crowd: Hindi-English Transliteration Corpus (Khapra et al., 2014)	Machine Translation	14,919 words
IIITH Codemixed Sentiment Dataset (Prabhu et al., 2016)	Sentiment Analysis	4,981 sentences

Table 1: indicnlp_catalog Hindi-English Datasets

gave significant improvement in State-Of-The-Art (SOTA) normalization performance on the lexNorm15 dataset. (Muller et al., 2019) focused on enhancing BERT model on UGC by applying lexical normalization.

Code-Mixed Datasets: Since the launch of EMNLP Shared Tasks of Language identification in Code-Switched Data[12], there has been an increased focus on analyzing the nature of code-mixed data, language identification approaches and how to carry out NLP tasks like POS tagging and Text normalization on such text data. For the first shared task, code-switched data was collected for language pairs such as Spanish-English (ES-EN), Mandarin-English (MAN-EN), Nepali-English(NEP-EN) and Modern Standard Arabic - Dialectal Arabic(MSA-DA) (Solorio et al., 2014). Subsequently more language pairs were added with primary focus on language identification task (Molina et al., 2019). (Aguilar et al., 2019) introduced Named Entity Recognition on Code-Switched Data. (Mandal et al., 2018) introduced Bengali-English code-mixed corpus for sentiment analysis. More recently, normalization of code mixed data has been receiving a lot of attention. (Barik et al., 2019) worked on normalizing Indonesian-English code-mixed noisy social media data. Further, they released 825 annotated tweets from this corpus[13]. (Phadte and Thakkar, 2017) focused on normalization of Konkani-English code-mixed text data from social media. (Adouane et al., 2019) worked on normalizing algerian code-switched UGC utilizing encoder-decoder network and showed promising results.

Hindi-English Datasets: (Vyas et al., 2014) was one of the earliest work to focus on creating a Hindi-English code-mixed corpus from social media content for POS tagging. The same year (Bali et al., 2014) analyzed Facebook English-Hindi posts to show a significant amount of code-mixing. (Bhat et al., 2018) worked with similar English-Hindi code-mixed tweets in roman script for dependency parsing. (Patra et al., 2018) worked on sentiment analysis of code mixed Hindi-English & Bengali-English language pairs. (Singh et al., 2018) focused on normalization of code-mixed text using pipeline processing to improve the performance on POS Tagging task. indicnlp_catalog[14] is a effort to consolidate resources on Indian languages. Table 1 presents the most relevant Hindi-English datasets from this effort.

While there exists extensive work in each of these areas, for some reason normalization of Hindi-English (which is at intersection of these areas) hasn't received its due attention. This may be partly due to unavailability of a comprehensive data set and baseline. We believe our work will address this lacuna.

3 Corpus Preparation

While preparing this corpus, we carry out the following steps.

1. **Data Collection**: collecting Hindi-English sentences.

2. **Data Filtering & Cleaning**: standard pre-processing of raw sentences.

---

[12]http://emnlp2014.org/workshops/CodeSwitch/call.html

[13]https://github.com/seelenbrecher/code-mixed-normalization/tree/master/data

[14]https://github.com/anoopkunchukuttan/indic_nlp_library

3. **Data Annotation**: sentence-level text normalization by human annotators.

3.1 Data Collection

We collected data in two phases: In the first phase we built and deployed general chit-chat bots on social media platforms. User responses were randomly sampled and pooled to create the dataset. In the second phase, we collected data from our platform. Here too the responses were chosen randomly to be added to the dataset.

3.2 Data Filtering & Cleaning

The raw text data we collected was then preprocessed and cleaned. Following were the key steps:

1. Drop all messages that were forwarded messages or consisted of only emojis.

2. Hindi words were written in both scripts - Devanagari and Roman. All words in Devanagari were converted into roman script.

3. Removed all characters other than alpha-numeric or white space.

4. All sentences containing profane words or phrases were dropped.

5. All sentences containing any Personal Identification Information (PII) were dropped.

The exact steps followed can be found here[15]. Steps (4) and (5) were done manually.

3.3 Data Annotation

The preprocessed data was sent to human annotators for text normalization annotation. Each word in the input sentence was tagged for the type of non-canonical variation & its phonetically standard transliteration[16]. The annotators chosen were native speakers of Hindi and had bilingual proficiency in English. The dataset was annotated by three annotators while maintaining an average error rate of less than 5% on the dataset.

Based on the context in which the word appears in the input sentence, annotators provide the corresponding normalized word. Further, to better capture the process used by the annotators to arrive at the normalized text, the annotators provide a unique *tag* for each word. This tag describes the transformation applied by annotators to arrive at the corresponding normalized word. The corpus along with normalized text also contains these tags. (van der Goot et al., 2018) proposes a taxonomy to annotate normalization of UGC in parallel sentences. We follow a similar but independent approach. Below we describe various tags used in the corpus, the scenario in which a given tag is used and explain the transformation applied with example(s):

1. **Looks Good**: The word under consideration is already an English word with proper spelling. No corrective action is required here. e.g. *"yes"*, *"hello"*, *"friend"*.

2. **Merge**: A word is mistakenly split into two or more consecutive words by uncautious white spaces. In such cases, the corrective action is to merge such words. e.g. *"ye s"* → *"yes"*, *"hell oo"* → *"hello"*, *"fri en dd"* → *"friend"*.

3. **Split**: Two words get conjoined or when a user uses a contraction of two words. In such cases, the corrective action is to split the words with correct spelling. e.g. *"yeshellofriend"* → *"yes hello friend"*, *"isn't"* → *"is not"*, *"should've"* → *"should have"*

4. **Short Form**: The word is a short form (phonetically or colloquially). In such cases the corrective action is to replace the word with the corresponding full form. e.g. *"u"* → *"you"*, *"y"* → *"why"*, *"doc"* → *"doctor"*.

5. **Acronym**: The word is an acronym or abbreviation. In such cases, the corrective action is to replace with their full form. e.g. *"fb"* → *"facebook"*, *"brb"* → *"be right back"*

---

[15] https://github.com/piyushmakhija5/normalizationDataset/blob/master/dataPreprocessing.py
[16] https://www.iso.org/standard/28333.html

6. **Typo**: The word is a typo/spelling mistake if its spelling is incorrect. This is an unintentional error (due to haste, fat-finger error[17] or low attention to details) made while typing. In such cases the corrective action is to undo the typing error. e.g *"yess"* → *"yes"*, *"helllo00o"* → *"hello"*, *"frieendd"* → *"friend"*

7. **Wordplay**: User has deliberately modified the word for creative purposes. In such cases, the corrective action is to undo the creativity and replace with correct spellings. e.g. *"hiiiii"* → *"hi"*, *"I 8t mahh food"* → *"I ate my food"*

8. **Profanity**: The word is a profane word. In such cases, no corrective action is taken. e,g *"f**k"*, *"ba*tard"*.

9. **Hindi**: The word is a Hindi language word in Roman script. In case the spelling is incorrect, replace the word with the corresponding phonetically correct transliteration. e.g. *"haaan"* → *"haan"*[18], *"namskar"* → *"namaskaar"*[19]

10. **Unrecognizable or Other Language (UOL)**: Default tag to catch words from any language other than English and Hindi or any other type of error/variation that is not covered by any of the previously mentioned tags such as gibberish. In such cases, no corrective action is taken. e.g. *"asgjhsad is my name"*, *"n233s is cool"*, *"call maadi"*[20]

3.4 Corpus Examples

To facilitate better understanding, we list out two examples from our dataset to illustrate the input text and corresponding normalized text along with annotations:

1. **id:** 5089
   inputText: *"pakka lisenc nahin hai but ll hai"*
   tags: ['Hindi', 'Typo', 'Hindi', 'Hindi', 'Looks Good', 'Acronym', 'Hindi']
   normalizedText: *"pakka license nahi hai but learning licence hai"*[21]

   Here, the word 'pakka' is a Hindi word that means 'confirmed'. 'lisenc' is a typo for 'license' and refers to driving license. 'nahin' in hindi means 'no', so on and so forth.

2. **id**: 13427
   inputText: *"hiii mjhe jab chaiye"*
   tags: ['Wordplay', 'Hindi', 'Typo', 'Hindi']
   normalizedText: *"hi mujhe job chaahie"*[22]

   Here, the word 'hiii' is a wordplay for 'hi', 'mjhe' is a typo for hindi word 'mujhe' which means 'I'. 'jab' is a typo for 'job' and 'chaiye' is typo for hindi word 'chaahie' which means 'want'.

4   Corpus Analysis

After the preprocessing and manual annotation as described in Section 3, we refer to the data set obtained as *hinglishNorm*. It contains 13494 sentences along with their text normalized form. Table 2 presents some basic statistics of the *hinglishNorm* corpus. Each data point in the corpus is a sentence pair consisting of an *inputText* and *normalizedText*. *inputText* is the text as given by the user after preprocessing and *normalizedText* is the corresponding human annotated text. Table 3 gives corpus level statistics of

---

[17]https://en.wikipedia.org/wiki/Fat-finger_error
[18]Hindi word corresponding to *"yes"* in English
[19]Hindi greeting corresponding to *"hi"* in English
[20]Slang that means *"call me"*
[21]Corresponding English translation: "don't have a permanent license, but I have learning licence"
[22]Corresponding English translation: *"hi, I want a job"*

Attribute	Value
# Datapoints	13494
# Train	10795
# Test	2699
% Sentences Modified after Annotation	80.08%
% Hindi-English Code-Mixing Sentences	52.69%
% Non-English/Non-Hindi words	5.41%
% Normalized Words in Corpus	54.25%
% Hindi Words in Corpus	41.48%
Code-Mixing Index (CMI) (Das and Gambäck, 2014)	88.40

Table 2: Basic Statistics *hinglishNorm* Corpus

Features	*inputText*	*normalizedText*
# Sentence	13494	13494
# Unique Sentences	13066	12547
# Unique Words	9326	7465
# Unique Characters	37	37
Most Common Sentence	"whats ur name"	"what is your name"
# Most Common Sentence	12	38
Mean Character Length	22.06	25.25
Std Var of Character Length	16.97	19.00
Median Character Length	18	21
Mean Word Length	4.96	5.13
Std Var of Word Length	3.53	3.66
Median Word Length	4	4

Table 3: Statistics for *inputText* vs *normalizedText*

inputText and *normalizedText*. Each of these data points is also annotated with *tags* which denotes the transformation applied to obtain the text normalized form of *inputText*. Figure 1 gives us distribution of tags within the dataset.

An important aspect of this corpus is that the correct normalized equivalent of an input word can vary. Based on the context in which the the input word appears in the sentence, the misspelled words might require different corrections. For e.g.

- *"hii, I have a bike" (inputText)* → *"hi, I have a bike" (normalizedText)*

    – Input text provided by the user is an English language sentence with misspelled *"hi"*. Annotators understand that the word belongs to English language and correct spelling, in this case, should be *"hi"*

- *"mere pass bike hii" (inputText)* → *"mere pass bike hai" (normalizedText)*

    – Input text is a romanized version of a Hindi sentence that means *"I have a bike"*. Annotators understand that the word belongs to Hindi language and correct spelling, in this case, should be *"hai"*

5   Benchmark Baseline

It is common to model the text normalization problem as a Machine Translation problem (Mansfield et al., 2019) (Lusetti et al., 2018) (Filip et al., 2006) (Zhang et al., 2019). Given that Bidirectional LSTM with attention is a popular baseline model for machine translation task, we built a text normalization model using the same on the lines of work by (Bahdanau et al., 2014). We evaluated our system using

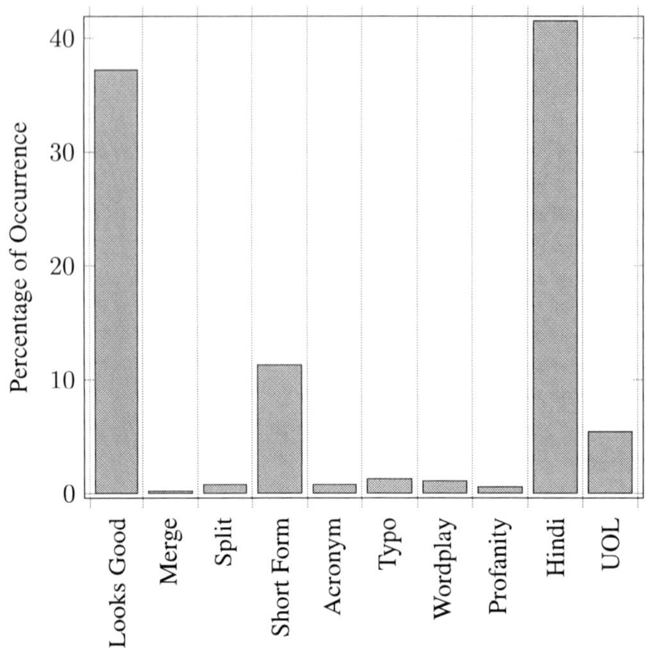

Figure 1: Distribution of tags in hinglishNorm Dataset

Evaluation Metric	Baseline
WER	15.55
BLEU	71.21
METEOR	0.50

Table 4: Baseline Performance on *hinglishNorm*

well established metrics - Word-Error Rate (WER) (Nießen et al., 2000), BiLingual Evaluation Understudy (BLEU) (Papineni et al., 2002) and Metric for Evaluation of Translation with Explicit ORdering (METEOR) (Banerjee and Lavie, 2005). Table 4 shows the results of our experiments over *hinglishNorm*.

6 Availability

The homepage for the dataset can be accessed here[23].

The new corpora we release are available for research and non-commercial use under a Creative Commons Attribution-NonCommercial-ShareAlike License[24].

7 Conclusion & Future Work

We presented *hinglishNorm* version 1.0, a corpus of Hindi-English code mix sentences for text normalization task. Thereby, filling a much needed gap. The purpose of this corpus is to serve as a benchmark dataset for evaluation of Hindi-English code mixed text normalization model performance. We have also provided our benchmark baseline results on this corpus for comparison. As future work, we plan to build stronger baselines using SOTA models such as BERT (Devlin et al., 2018), DistilBERT (Sanh et al., 2019), RoBERTa (Liu et al., 2019), etc.

---

[23] https://github.com/piyushmakhija5/hinglishNorm
[24] http://creativecommons.org/licenses/by-nc-sa/4.0/

References

Wafia Adouane, Jean-Philippe Bernardy, and Simon Dobnik. 2019. Normalising non-standardised orthography in Algerian code-switched user-generated data. In *Proceedings of the 5th Workshop on Noisy User-generated Text (W-NUT 2019)*, pages 131–140, Hong Kong, China, November. Association for Computational Linguistics.

Gustavo Aguilar, Fahad AlGhamdi, Victor Soto, Mona Diab, Julia Hirschberg, and Thamar Solorio. 2019. Named entity recognition on code-switched data: Overview of the calcs 2018 shared task. *arXiv preprint arXiv:1906.04138*.

Kunchukuttan Anoop, Mehta Pratik, and Bhattacharyya Pushpak. 2018. The iit bombay englishhindi parallel corpus. LREC.

AiTi Aw, Min Zhang, Juan Xiao, and Jian Su. 2006. A phrase-based statistical model for sms text normalization. In *Proceedings of the COLING/ACL on Main conference poster sessions*, pages 33–40. Association for Computational Linguistics.

Dzmitry Bahdanau, Kyunghyun Cho, and Yoshua Bengio. 2014. Neural machine translation by jointly learning to align and translate. *arXiv preprint arXiv:1409.0473*.

Timothy Baldwin, Marie-Catherine de Marneffe, Bo Han, Young-Bum Kim, Alan Ritter, and Wei Xu. 2015. Shared tasks of the 2015 workshop on noisy user-generated text: Twitter lexical normalization and named entity recognition. In *Proceedings of the Workshop on Noisy User-generated Text*, pages 126–135.

Kalika Bali, Jatin Sharma, Monojit Choudhury, and Yogarshi Vyas. 2014. "i am borrowing ya mixing?" an analysis of english-hindi code mixing in facebook. In *Proceedings of the First Workshop on Computational Approaches to Code Switching*, pages 116–126.

Satanjeev Banerjee and Alon Lavie. 2005. Meteor: An automatic metric for mt evaluation with improved correlation with human judgments. In *Proceedings of the acl workshop on intrinsic and extrinsic evaluation measures for machine translation and/or summarization*, pages 65–72.

Anab Maulana Barik, Rahmad Mahendra, and Mirna Adriani. 2019. Normalization of indonesian-english code-mixed twitter data. In *Proceedings of the 5th Workshop on Noisy User-generated Text (W-NUT 2019)*, pages 417–424.

Irshad Ahmad Bhat, Riyaz Ahmad Bhat, Manish Shrivastava, and Dipti Misra Sharma. 2018. Universal dependency parsing for hindi-english code-switching. *arXiv preprint arXiv:1804.05868*.

Eric Brill and Robert C Moore. 2000. An improved error model for noisy channel spelling correction. In *Proceedings of the 38th annual meeting on association for computational linguistics*, pages 286–293. Association for Computational Linguistics.

Monojit Choudhury, Rahul Saraf, Vijit Jain, Animesh Mukherjee, Sudeshna Sarkar, and Anupam Basu. 2007. Investigation and modeling of the structure of texting language. *International Journal of Document Analysis and Recognition (IJDAR)*, 10(3-4):157–174.

Grzegorz Chrupała. 2014. Normalizing tweets with edit scripts and recurrent neural embeddings. In *Proceedings of the 52nd Annual Meeting of the Association for Computational Linguistics (Volume 2: Short Papers)*, pages 680–686.

Kenneth W Church and William A Gale. 1991. Probability scoring for spelling correction. *Statistics and Computing*, 1(2):93–103.

Amitava Das and Björn Gambäck. 2014. Identifying languages at the word level in code-mixed indian social media text.

Jacob Devlin, Ming-Wei Chang, Kenton Lee, and Kristina Toutanova. 2018. Bert: Pre-training of deep bidirectional transformers for language understanding. *arXiv preprint arXiv:1810.04805*.

Omkar Dhariya, Shrikant Malviya, and Uma Shanker Tiwary. 2017. A hybrid approach for hindi-english machine translation. In *2017 International Conference on Information Networking (ICOIN)*, pages 389–394. IEEE.

Gralinski Filip, Jassem Krzysztof, Wagner Agnieszka, and W Mikolaj. 2006. Text normalization as a special case of machine translation. In *Proceedings of the International Multiconference on Computer Science and Information Technology*, pages 51–56.

Bo Han and Timothy Baldwin. 2011. Lexical normalisation of short text messages: Makn sens a# twitter. In *Proceedings of the 49th Annual Meeting of the Association for Computational Linguistics: Human Language Technologies-Volume 1*, pages 368–378. Association for Computational Linguistics.

Mitesh M Khapra, Ananthakrishnan Ramanathan, Anoop Kunchukuttan, Karthik Visweswariah, and Pushpak Bhattacharyya. 2014. When transliteration met crowdsourcing: An empirical study of transliteration via crowdsourcing using efficient, non-redundant and fair quality control. In *LREC*, pages 196–202. Citeseer.

Philipp Koehn, Hieu Hoang, Alexandra Birch, Chris Callison-Burch, Marcello Federico, Nicola Bertoldi, Brooke Cowan, Wade Shen, Christine Moran, Richard Zens, et al. 2007. Moses: Open source toolkit for statistical machine translation. In *Proceedings of the 45th annual meeting of the association for computational linguistics companion volume proceedings of the demo and poster sessions*, pages 177–180.

Fei Liu, Fuliang Weng, and Xiao Jiang. 2012. A broad-coverage normalization system for social media language. In *Proceedings of the 50th Annual Meeting of the Association for Computational Linguistics: Long Papers-Volume 1*, pages 1035–1044. Association for Computational Linguistics.

Yinhan Liu, Myle Ott, Naman Goyal, Jingfei Du, Mandar Joshi, Danqi Chen, Omer Levy, Mike Lewis, Luke Zettlemoyer, and Veselin Stoyanov. 2019. Roberta: A robustly optimized bert pretraining approach. *arXiv preprint arXiv:1907.11692*.

Massimo Lusetti, Tatyana Ruzsics, Anne Göhring, Tanja Samardžić, and Elisabeth Stark. 2018. Encoder-decoder methods for text normalization. Association for Computational Linguistics.

Soumil Mandal, Sainik Kumar Mahata, and Dipankar Das. 2018. Preparing bengali-english code-mixed corpus for sentiment analysis of indian languages. *arXiv preprint arXiv:1803.04000*.

Courtney Mansfield, Ming Sun, Yuzong Liu, Ankur Gandhe, and Björn Hoffmeister. 2019. Neural text normalization with subword units. In *Proceedings of the 2019 Conference of the North American Chapter of the Association for Computational Linguistics: Human Language Technologies, Volume 2 (Industry Papers)*, pages 190–196.

Eric Mays, Fred J Damerau, and Robert L Mercer. 1991. Context based spelling correction. *Information Processing & Management*, 27(5):517–522.

Paul Michel and Graham Neubig. 2018. Mtnt: A testbed for machine translation of noisy text. *arXiv preprint arXiv:1809.00388*.

Wookhee Min and Bradford Mott. 2015. Ncsu_sas_wookhee: A deep contextual long-short term memory model for text normalization. In *Proceedings of the Workshop on Noisy User-generated Text*, pages 111–119.

Giovanni Molina, Fahad AlGhamdi, Mahmoud Ghoneim, Abdelati Hawwari, Nicolas Rey-Villamizar, Mona Diab, and Thamar Solorio. 2019. Overview for the second shared task on language identification in code-switched data. *arXiv preprint arXiv:1909.13016*.

Benjamin Muller, Benoît Sagot, and Djamé Seddah. 2019. Enhancing bert for lexical normalization. In *Proceedings of the 5th Workshop on Noisy User-generated Text (W-NUT 2019)*, pages 297–306.

Sonja Nießen, Franz Josef Och, Gregor Leusch, Hermann Ney, et al. 2000. An evaluation tool for machine translation: Fast evaluation for mt research. In *LREC*.

Kishore Papineni, Salim Roukos, Todd Ward, and Wei-Jing Zhu. 2002. Bleu: a method for automatic evaluation of machine translation. In *Proceedings of the 40th annual meeting on association for computational linguistics*, pages 311–318. Association for Computational Linguistics.

Braja Gopal Patra, Dipankar Das, and Amitava Das. 2018. Sentiment analysis of code-mixed indian languages: An overview of sail_code-mixed shared task@ icon-2017. *arXiv preprint arXiv:1803.06745*.

Akshata Phadte and Gaurish Thakkar. 2017. Towards normalising konkani-english code-mixed social media text. In *Proceedings of the 14th International Conference on Natural Language Processing (ICON-2017)*, pages 85–94.

Ameya Prabhu, Aditya Joshi, Manish Shrivastava, and Vasudeva Varma. 2016. Towards sub-word level compositions for sentiment analysis of hindi-english code mixed text. *arXiv preprint arXiv:1611.00472*.

Victor Sanh, Lysandre Debut, Julien Chaumond, and Thomas Wolf. 2019. Distilbert, a distilled version of bert: smaller, faster, cheaper and lighter. *arXiv preprint arXiv:1910.01108*.

Ranjan Satapathy, Claudia Guerreiro, Iti Chaturvedi, and Erik Cambria. 2017. Phonetic-based microtext normalization for twitter sentiment analysis. In *2017 IEEE International Conference on Data Mining Workshops (ICDMW)*, pages 407–413. IEEE.

Rajat Singh, Nurendra Choudhary, and Manish Shrivastava. 2018. Automatic normalization of word variations in code-mixed social media text. *arXiv preprint arXiv:1804.00804*.

Thamar Solorio, Elizabeth Blair, Suraj Maharjan, Steven Bethard, Mona Diab, Mahmoud Ghoneim, Abdelati Hawwari, Fahad AlGhamdi, Julia Hirschberg, Alison Chang, et al. 2014. Overview for the first shared task on language identification in code-switched data. In *Proceedings of the First Workshop on Computational Approaches to Code Switching*, pages 62–72.

Richard Sproat and Navdeep Jaitly. 2016. Rnn approaches to text normalization: A challenge. *arXiv preprint arXiv:1611.00068*.

Rob van der Goot and Gertjan van Noord. 2017. Monoise: Modeling noise using a modular normalization system. *arXiv preprint arXiv:1710.03476*.

Rob van der Goot, Rik van Noord, and Gertjan van Noord. 2018. A taxonomy for in-depth evaluation of normalization for user generated content. In *Proceedings of the Eleventh International Conference on Language Resources and Evaluation (LREC 2018)*, Miyazaki, Japan, May. European Language Resources Association (ELRA).

Yogarshi Vyas, Spandana Gella, Jatin Sharma, Kalika Bali, and Monojit Choudhury. 2014. Pos tagging of english-hindi code-mixed social media content. In *Proceedings of the 2014 Conference on Empirical Methods in Natural Language Processing (EMNLP)*, pages 974–979.

Hao Zhang, Richard Sproat, Axel H Ng, Felix Stahlberg, Xiaochang Peng, Kyle Gorman, and Brian Roark. 2019. Neural models of text normalization for speech applications. *Computational Linguistics*, 45(2):293–337.

Assessing Social License to Operate
from the Public Discourse on Social Media

Chang Xu
University of Melbourne
xu.c3@unimelb.edu.au

Cécile Paris
CSIRO Data61
cecile.paris@data61.csiro.au

Ross Sparks
CSIRO Data61
ross.sparks@data61.csiro.au

Surya Nepal
CSIRO Data61
surya.nepal@data61.csiro.au

Keith VanderLinden
Calvin University
kvlinden@calvin.edu

Abstract

Organisations are monitoring their Social License to Operate (SLO) with increasing regularity. SLO, the level of support organisations gain from the public, is typically assessed through surveys or focus groups, which require expensive manual efforts and yield quickly-outdated results. In this paper, we present SIRTA (Social Insight via **R**eal-**T**ime **T**ext **A**nalytics), a novel real-time text analytics system for assessing and monitoring organisations' SLO levels by analysing the public discourse from social posts. To assess SLO levels, our insight is to extract and transform peoples' *stances* towards an organisation into SLO levels. SIRTA achieves this by performing a chain of three text classification tasks, where it identifies task-relevant social posts, discovers key SLO risks discussed in the posts, and infers stances specific to the SLO risks. We leverage recent language understanding techniques (e.g., BERT) for building our classifiers. To monitor SLO levels over time, SIRTA employs quality control mechanisms to reliably identify SLO trends and variations of multiple organisations in a market. These are derived from the smoothed time series of their SLO levels based on exponentially-weighted moving average (EWMA) calculation. Our experimental results show that SIRTA is highly effective in distilling stances from social posts for SLO level assessment, and that the continuous monitoring of SLO levels afforded by SIRTA enables the early detection of critical SLO changes.

1 Introduction

Social License to Operate (SLO) represents the ongoing acceptance (or lack thereof) of an organisation's standard business practices or operating procedures by the general public (or the society at large) (Moffat and Zhang, 2014; Gunningham et al., 2004; Moffat et al., 2016). It captures the opinion of the public towards a business. Low SLO levels can increase business risks significantly, and, in the worst case scenarios, prevent the operation of an organisation. To obtain a high SLO level, organisations typically need to build trust with the community and then work to maintain that trust. Traditionally, the SLO of an organisation is evaluated using surveys and focus groups (Moffat and Zhang, 2014), during which a diversity of opinions is collected and the results then quantified. These effective techniques provide in-depth analysis. They are, however, manual practices and thus expensive to do on a frequent basis (Moffat and Zhang, 2014). In addition, the samples of a survey are often limited, and, as the time intervals between consecutive surveys are usually long, an organisation might not detect critical changes in its SLO levels in a timely fashion, leading to exposure to potential risks. The public discussions continuously taking place on social media, where people are not shy about expressing their opinions about a number of topics, including companies and specific projects, provide an opportunity to monitor SLO in real-time, on a continuous basis and at scale. This is what we aim to do in this work.

We first determined the possible facets of SLO for our domain, specifically *economic* (e.g., the public is in favor of a project because it will create jobs), *environmental* (e.g., the public believes the company has a good/bad environmental record) and *social* (e.g., the public believes the company addresses - or not - its social responsibilities). We then built SIRTA (Social Insight via **R**eal-**T**ime **T**ext **A**nalytics), a

Proceedings of the 28th International Conference on Computational Linguistics: Industry Track, pages 146–159
Barcelona, Spain (Online), December 12, 2020

novel automated system that combines advanced text analytics with real-time monitoring techniques to assess and monitor the SLO levels of a collection of organisations (in the same industry) over time. By taking the "pulse" of the public towards an organisation in real time, through the lens of social media, this tool complements the in-depth analysis done through surveys and focus groups, providing an early indication of trends, and potentially informing the design of in-depth surveys.

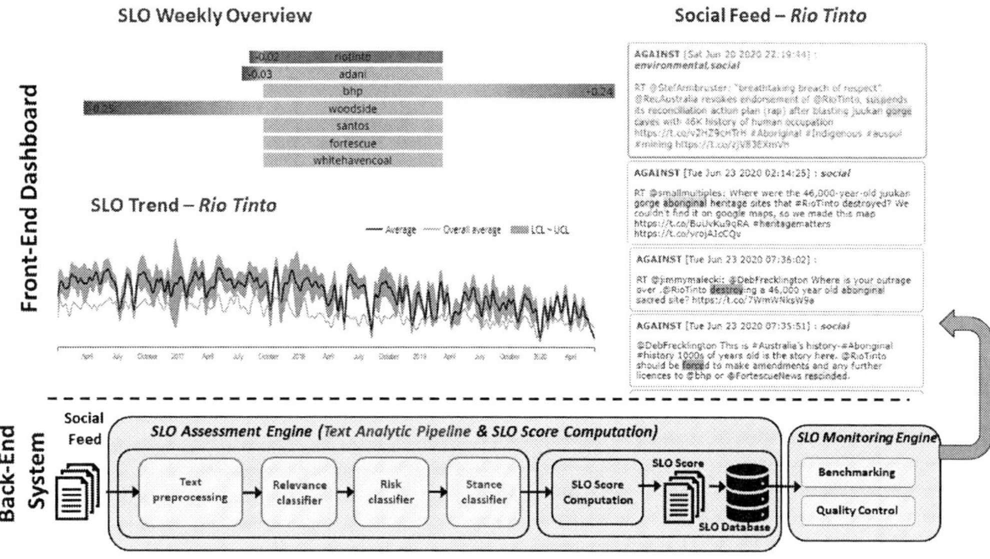

Figure 1: The dashboard of SIRTA for SLO assessment and monitoring plus the SIRTA architecture.

Figure 1 shows the dashboard of SIRTA for monitoring several major mining companies in the country. Its main functionality is demonstrated in three panels: 1) the *SLO Weekly Overview*, a list of real-time (weekly) numerical scores representing the SLO levels for the organisations under consideration, 2) the *SLO Trend*, which plots the long-term trend of the SLO level of a selected organisation (here, Rio Tinto), compared with the general trend of the market (all the organisations together), and 3) the *Social Feed*, with the most recent social media posts (e.g., tweets) about the selected organisation, with both the stances and SLO risk categories (i.e., *environment*, *social*, and *economic*) identified.

To carry out the SLO assessment, SIRTA extracts opinion information from posts published on social media (Twitter), along the different SLO facets, and then transforms that information into SLO scores. In contrast to many opinion mining systems that rely primarily on sentiment analysis, e.g., (Pang et al., 2008), we focus on *stance detection* (Mohammad et al., 2016a), which is more suitable for our task because it indicates whether someone is *for*, *neutral* or *against* a specific company, not just whether the surface sentiment of their posts is positive or negative. The novel aspect of SIRTA's SLO assessment engine includes a specialised text classification pipeline (see the Text Analytic Pipeline on the bottom of Figure 1), where three chained text classification tasks are performed for opinion extraction: 1) *relevance classification*, for finding posts contributing to the SLO assessment, 2) *risk classification*, for identifying the different facet(s), or *SLO risk(s)*, being discussed in the posts, and 3) *risk-aware stance classification*, for detecting stances in the posts that are specific to each SLO risk. The outcome from text analytic pipeline is fed into the SLO score computation component for converting the stances into numerical SLO scores. To train and evaluate the classifiers for each task above, we created both a silver standard and a gold standard dataset and employed state-of-the-art language understanding models such as BERT (Devlin et al., 2019). To monitor the derived SLO scores, a monitoring engine keeps track of the time series of the SLO scores of multiple organisations operating in a market. Specifically, it leverages Control Charts (Kan, 2002), a powerful tool for statistical process control. The monitoring engine discovers if an organisation is experiencing significant changes in its SLO score by contrasting its time series with a benchmark of the market.

147

We conduct several quantitative experiments to evaluate the performance of our classifiers, and thus the effectiveness of our text analysis pipeline. We then present a case study, which suggests that SIRTA can identify periods of unusual changes early. This confirms our original hypothesis that we could harness social media to monitor SLO in real-time and at scale, in a relatively inexpensive manner, reserving the more expensive, traditional methods for circumstances where a more detailed assessment is required.

2 SIRTA: Real-Time Text Analytics for SLO Assessment and Monitoring

2.1 System Overview

The bottom part of Figure 1 illustrates the architecture of SIRTA, which consists of two processing modules: the *SLO assessment engine* and the *SLO monitoring engine*. The *assessment engine* takes social feeds as inputs and generates SLO scores by first extracting opinions from social feeds via text analytics. Specifically, it performs the three text classification tasks mentioned earlier to extract, in real-time, opinions from a stream of posts, and then calculates the SLO scores.

To enable appropriate monitoring (the detection of a significant change), the opinions are aggregated regularly in different time frames (e.g., weekly). These are computed and stored in a dedicated database.

The *monitoring engine* keeps track of the time series of different organisations' scores as well as that of the overall market over time. It first computes a benchmark SLO time series representing the context (market) where those organisations operate. This allows one to see when an organisation's score departs significantly from the benchmark. To identify such a departure, the monitoring engine applies quality control techniques (Kan, 2002) to compute control limits for bounding an organisation's time series and a departure occurs when the benchmark falls out of the bound.

2.2 SLO Assessment Engine

The assessment engine transforms social posts into an organisation's SLO score with two modules: a text analytic pipeline and the SLO score computation. In the text analytic pipeline, three sequential tasks are performed: *relevance classification*, *risk classification*, and *risk-aware stance classification*.

2.2.1 Relevance Classification: Finding Task-Relevant Posts

SIRTA uses the Twitter API to collect all tweets containing the names of the organisations under consideration. It is, of course, inevitable that posts irrelevant to our task are also collected by our system. We thus need to discard these irrelevant posts and keep only the posts that can contribute to the SLO assessment. This is done through the relevance classification task, and a binary *relevance classifier* C_r was trained for this task. The classifier C_r reads a post $\mathbf{x}_i$ and assigns it a relevance label $\hat{\mathbf{y}}_r$. To train C_r, we minimised the negative log-likelihood of the ground truth label: $\mathcal{L}_r = -\sum_{i=1}^{N_r} \mathbf{y}_r \log \hat{\mathbf{y}}_r$, where $\mathbf{y}_r$ is $\mathbf{x}_i$'s true relevance label, and N_r the training data size. To facilitate discussion, we use R_o to denote the set of all relevant posts discussing organisation o detected by C_r.

2.2.2 Risk Classification: Discovering Key SLO Risks Mentioned in a Post

As mentioned earlier, SLO can have many facets, or, put differently, SLO poses risks along various dimensions. In turn, an individual post can relate to different SLO risks. Consider, for example, the following two posts about mining companies. The first one is solely expressing an opinion about the company's handling of environmental concerns, thus contributing (negatively) to the SLO risk of environment for this company. In contrast, the second negatively mentions a company's actions with respect to both environmental and social concerns, thus contributing (again negatively) to the SLO risks of both environment and social for this company.

- *They don't even know which aquifer is the source of the Doongmabulla Springs, but <u>Adani</u>* [**the company name**] *is belittling crucial environmental studies as "paperwork".* (SLO risk factor: **environmental**)

- *We are at <u>BHP</u>* [**the company name**] *HQ protesting against their toxic Olympic Dam uranium mine that fuels war and breaches land rights #uprootthesystem #nonukes #KeepItInTheGround* (SLO risk factors: **environmental** and **social**)

Being able to identify the specific SLO risks discussed in the public discourse allows an organisation to better identify and manage them. We took a two-step approach to detecting the risk factors mentioned in a post. First, we identified the SLO risks for our domain (mining), based on knowledge from domain experts and a literature survey. They are *economic*, *social* and *environment*. We note that, while these risks are fairly general, SLO risks might be different in different domains. Let K be the set of these risks: $K = \{economic, environmental, social\}$.

We then trained a *multi-label risk classifier* C_k to find all potential risk factors mentioned in a post $\mathbf{x}_i \in R_o$. The training involved minimising the *one-vs-all* loss, a commonly-used objective for multi-label classification (Tsoumakas and Katakis, 2007). Formally, we calculated a binary cross entropy between the logits and ground-truth labels of the same training example,

$$\mathcal{L}_k = \mathbf{y}_i^k \cdot \log C_k(\mathbf{x}_i) + (1 - \mathbf{y}_i^k) \cdot \log(1 - C_k(\mathbf{x}_i)) \tag{1}$$

where $C_k(\mathbf{x}_i)$ produces the logits. $\mathbf{y}_i^k$ is the corresponding risk label of $\mathbf{x}_i$, which is multi-hot encoded; $\mathbf{y}_{ij}^k = 1$ as long as $\mathbf{x}_i$ belongs to the jth risk, otherwise $\mathbf{y}_{ij}^k = 0$.

2.2.3 Stance Classification: Revealing Risk-Specific Stances

The first two classifiers identified the overall relevance of a post to our task, and to which specific SLO risk the post is relevant. In the final text analytics task, we extract the opinion of a post. Sentiment analysis (Liu, 2012) is a common opinion mining technique, but recent studies have shown that one's sentiment may not always reflect one's attitude towards a target (Sobhani et al., 2016; Mohammad et al., 2017). For example, consider the following post about a mining company, "This is huge! Our momentum is unstoppable. Every day we're closer to stopping Adani and saving our Reef". Although the sentiment here is positive ("This is huge!"), the author's attitude towards the mining company (Adani) is negative. Therefore, instead of extracting the sentiment of the post, we propose to extract the *stance* of the author implied in their posts (Mohammad et al., 2016a; Augenstein et al., 2016; Sun et al., 2018), which could be *for*, *against*, or *neutral* towards a target (an organisation). The stance could be extracted in two ways. We could employ a general stance classifier (to obtain the stance of any relevant post) or a *risk-aware stance classifier*, that is a classifier specifically designed to detect the stance in posts discussing a specific risk factor. We posit that the language used to express stances vary with different risk factors (e.g., "create jobs" for *economic* vs. "destroy the reef" for *environmental*), and thus a risk-aware stance classifier would be more effective. Our experiments show that training a stance classifier for each risk factor indeed allows us to capture the stance more accurately ($\sim$4% boost) than training a generic stance classifier to work across the classes (see Section 3.3 below).

To train these classifiers, we minimised the negative log-likelihood of the ground truth label: $\mathcal{L}_s^j = -\sum_{i=1}^N \mathbf{y}_s^j \log C_s^j(\mathbf{x}_i)$, where $\mathbf{y}_s^j$ is the true stance label of the post $\mathbf{x}_i$ for the jth risk factor.

2.2.4 SLO Score Computation: Transforming Stances into SLO Scores

The final step in the assessment engine is to quantify the stances derived from the text analytic pipeline to obtain an SLO score, based on the degree of the opinion expressed in each post for an organisation o using the set of relevant posts R_o. With all the stance classifiers $\{C_s^j\}_{j=1}^{|K|}$ developed (one for each risk factor), given a post, $\mathbf{x}$, its overall SLO score is derived by averaging over the stances across all risk factors: $s = \frac{1}{|K|} \sum_{j=1}^{|K|} C_s^j(\mathbf{x})^1$. To produce the final SLO score for an organisation o, we aggregate the SLO scores of all relevant posts R_o via averaging: $s_o = \frac{1}{|R_o|} \sum_{\mathbf{x}_i \in R_o} s_i$.

2.3 SLO Monitoring Engine

The changing nature of an organisation's operational context can impact its SLO score. Changes could be due, for example, to a change of a company's CEO, changes in the general trend of the overall market, or a major event. Assessing such changes thus requires that we keep track of not only the time series of a company's SLO scores but also the time series of scores of other companies operating in that market sector. This allows us to see when a company's score departs significantly from the average score across similar organisations, which can be seen as a benchmark of the context/market. Such information can drive strategic action at critical points in time. SIRTA's SLO monitoring engine is

---

[1] The stance of an absent risk factor will not be included in the summation.

designed to track a comparable set of organisations across time. To achieve this, it first obtains the market benchmark by averaging over all organisations' SLO time series. This ensures that the larger or more topical organisations (i.e., the ones that are discussed more often) do not dominate in the comparison. All organisations are thus comparable as they have faced the same market conditions over the same period. Then, the engine seeks to monitor the departure of each organisation's time series from the benchmark over a period of time (e.g., one week), which is computed as follows.

Let $s_{o,i}^t$ be the ith SLO score of organisation o in period t, and n_o^t the number of its SLO scores in t, the average SLO score of o in t is then given by $\bar{s}_o^t = \sum_{i=1}^{n_o^t} s_{o,i}^t / n_o^t$ and standard deviation $\sigma_o^t = \sum_{i=1}^{n_o^t} (s_{o,i}^t - \bar{s}_o^t)^2 / n_o^t$. For organisations with sufficient observations in t, the Shewhart chart (Kan, 2002) with upper control limit (UCL) and lower control limit (UCL) is given by

$$UCL_o = \bar{s}_o^t + 3\sigma_o^t/\sqrt{n_o^t} \quad \text{and} \quad LCL_o = \bar{s}_o^t - 3\sigma_o^t/\sqrt{n_o^t} \tag{2}$$

Then a departure of the organisation o from the benchmark in t occurs if the benchmark is below LCL_o or above UCL_o. For organisations with zero observations in t, we use the exponentially-weighted moving average (EWMA) for the monitoring. Specifically, in period t, we compute the moving average as $a_o^t = 0.05\bar{s}_o^t + 0.95a_o^{t-1}$ if $\bar{s}_o^t$ exists, otherwise $a_o^t = a_o^{t-1}$. Similarly the moving standard deviation is defined as $v_o^t = 0.05\sigma_o^t + 0.95v_o^{t-1}$ if σ_o^t exists, otherwise $v_o^t = v_o^{t-1}$. Then the control charts for this case is given by $UCL_o = a_o^t + 3v_o^t/\sqrt{39}$ and $LCL_o = a_o^t - 3v_o^t/\sqrt{39}$.

3   Training and Evaluating the SLO Assessment Engine

We now present how we developed, trained and evaluated the classifiers for the SLO assessment engine. We first created training and test data sets for each task in the text classification pipeline. We used these data sets to train a number of modules, experimenting with several state-of-the-art techniques. Finally, we evaluated the classifiers, in order to choose the best ones to incorporate into SIRTA.

3.1   Data sets

Data sets for stance classification. We collected tweets about different mining organisations posted in the country from January 1, 2016 up to 23 October, 2019. We obtained *silver* standard labels for these tweets with rules that automatically determine the stance labels based on specific meta signals such as hashtags and Twitter account names. While the full set of rules is presented in Appendix, some examples are: 1) *favour* - a tweet by a mining company-owned account, e.g., *adaniaustralia*; 2) *against* - a tweet contains disapproving hashtags, e.g., *#stopadani*; and 3) *neutral* - a tweet from known mining-related news sources, e.g., *MiningNewsNet*. We

	#train	#test
Favour	24,255	111
Against	19,311	103
Neutral	19,317	60
Total	62,883	274

Table 1: Statistics summary of the datasets for SLO stance classification.

do not rely on the content of a tweet to determine its label. To test the accuracy of the auto-coding, we randomly sampled 24 tweets from the resulting training set and asked three coders to manually code them as stance for, against or neutral. The coding had a Fleiss Kappa score of 0.71, in the "substantial agreement" range, and the majority code from this manual coding matched the auto-coding in all cases. We took this as evidence that the auto-coder based on the simple rules listed above provided largely accurate codings. We note that such silver training set would inevitably contain noise (e.g., a news source account may occasionally post a positive news report about a mining company), but we suspect that this would not harm the performance much (as shown later in our experiments) due to the large scale of the training set. To prepare the test set, we manually created a *gold* standard dataset by asking three human coders to annotate 274 tweets[2] using specific annotating guidelines (see Appendix). The statistics summary of the training/test sets for this task are shown in Table 1.

Data sets for risk classification. The training set for this task shares the same tweets as in the above task, except that each tweet is now associated with one or more SLO risk labels. As already mentioned, our risk labels were: *social*, *economic*, and *environmental*. We again obtained *silver* risk labels by using

---

[2] A Fleiss Kappa score of 0.88.

rules on matching the tweet contents with specific keywords (e.g., "community" for *social*, "environment" and "greatbarrierreef" for *environment*, and 'jobs' for *economic*). For the test set, we asked three human coders to annotate 300 tweets. Table 2 shows the statistics summary[3] of the training/test sets.

	Social	Economic	Environmental	Other	One-Label	Two-Label	Three-Label	Total
Train	12,960	13,540	7,405	35,878	56,605	5,654	624	62,883
Test	140	72	61	101	207	84	9	300

Table 2: Statistics summary of the datasets for SLO category classification.

Data set for relevance classification. Finally, we built the training/test sets for the relevance classification task. For the training set, we considered all the tweets used in the stance classification task as relevant, as they were collected with rules for ensuring they were mining-related and informative to stance determination. Then, to get the irrelevant tweets and a balanced data set, we randomly sampled the Twitter stream[4] to obtain the same number of tweets (62,883). The resulting training set contains 125,764 tweets in total (50% *relevant* and 50% *irrelevant*). For the test set, as we lacked a gold standard set, 5-fold cross-validation was used instead.

3.2 Classifiers and Training Details

We pre-processed the data in the above data sets as follows. For each tweet, tokenisation was done via the CMU Tweet Tagger (Owoputi et al., 2013), and character elongations were shrunk (e.g., "yeees" → "yes"). We removed all hashtags and mentions[5]. We also replaced all URLs, and year, time, cash with place holders (e.g., "slo_url"). All text were down-cased. Stop words were retained, because of the stance-indicative information they can contain (e.g., "not").

We followed the best practice of training text classification models by implementing four classifiers with state-of-the-art neural network models as the baselines: 1) **fastText** (Joulin et al., 2017): an efficient classification model trained on word vectors created with subword information; 2) **BiLSTM** (Augenstein et al., 2016): a bidirectional LSTM trained on word vectors pretrained with GloVe word embeddings (Pennington et al., 2014) (glove.twitter.27B, 200d); 3) **CNN** (Kim, 2014): a convolutional neural network for sentence classification; 4) **BERT** (Devlin et al., 2019): a general-purpose pre-training contextual model for sentence encoding and classification.

The following configurations were used for training the classifiers: 1) **fastText**: learning rate of 0.1 was used, and the training did not stop until 10 epochs had passed; 2) **BiLSTM**: the hidden sizes of both LSTM and the followed dense layer were set to 256. A step learning rate scheduler was used, where the learning rate was set to 0.5 initially and then decayed by 10% after each epoch. A dropout layer was placed after the dense layer with a dropout rate of 0.3; 3) **CNN**: four 1D convolutional layers of 256 filters were chained as the sentence encoder, with the sequential filter sizes as 2, 3, 4, and 5. The same learning rate scheduler and dropout layer as those in BiLSTM were used; 4) **BERT**: the $\text{BERT}_{\text{BASE}}$ (uncased) was used. The learning rate was set to 10^{-5}. The maximum number of wordpieces was set to 128. The batch size for each training step was 16 for BERT (due to GPU memory limits) and 128 for others. Early stopping was applied with a patience of 3.

3.3 Experimental Results

We now report the results of all the text classifiers in SIRTA's SLO assessment engine.

Relevance Classification All the classifiers achieved reasonable results on this task, as shown in Table 3, suggesting the distributions of the relevant and irrelevant tweets are easily separable. Among the classifiers, fastText and BiLSTM obtained the highest scores in different training set settings, while BERT, as a cutting-edge modelling tool for text, surprisingly failed to show its potential on this task.

---

[3] More details of the rules/guidelines for the silver/gold label acquisition are in Appendix.

[4] https://developer.twitter.com/en/docs/labs/sampled-stream/api-reference/get-tweets-stream-sample-v1

[5] The removal of all hashtags/mentions allows us to train models that generalise and are not specific to the seen hashtags/mentions in the training data. The removal of the hashtags is also because some of them were already used for obtaining the silver standard labels of the training data.

% Train	fastText	BiLSTM	CNN	BERT
25%	95.9±0.9	94.5±1.0	93.5±1.5	89.7±1.0
50%	96.0±0.9	94.9±2.4	93.9±1.5	91.3±1.4
75%	96.1±0.9	96.0±1.1	93.9±1.5	92.9±2.1
100%	96.2±0.9	96.2±1.1	94.3±1.4	93.2±1.7

Table 3: Accuracy on relevance classification.

This could be caused by the small batch size (16) used for BERT training in order to avoid the out-of-GPU-memory issue; a small batch size usually makes SGD updates less effective on each batch. Another reason behind this could be that the BERT model is over-complex for such an easy task (the classes are easily separable), potentially leading to overfitting.

Risk Classification Table 4 shows the classification results. This task is more challenging than the previous one, as evidenced by the generally lower accuracy attained by all classifiers. BERT performed the best across all risk factors, exhibiting its superiority on this more demanding modelling task. However, considering its complexity, the improvements gained by BERT were not proportionally outstanding ($2\%\sim2.9\%$). fastText also performed well, better than both BiLSTM and CNN, demonstrating that it is also a cost-effective choice for this task.

The performance on the *Environmental* risk factor was better than all other factors, which may suggest that it is easier to recognise a post discussing the environmental than one discussing social or economic issues. The performance on the *Social* risk was the worst. We found that *Social* samples dominate the multi-label samples in the test set (88.2%); such multi-label posts are harder to classify. As a result, the classifiers make more mistakes on the *Social* samples.

Risk Factor	fastText	BiLSTM	CNN	BERT
Social	57.7±0.3	57.3±0.2	55.2±0.4	60.7±2.0
Economic	64.3±0.2	63.9±0.6	64.3±0.3	64.5±0.3
Environmental	68.3±0.4	67.3±0.5	68.6±0.3	70.9±0.3
Other	71.1±0.5	68.9±1.4	69.7±0.8	73.2±0.7
Average	65.4±0.4	64.4±0.7	64.4±0.5	67.3±0.8

Table 4: Accuracy on risk classification.

Stance Classification To validate the hypothesis that a risk-aware classifier is more accurate than a generic stance classifier, we compared two experiments: 1) we trained four individual risk-specific stance classifiers using data from the corresponding risk ($\mathcal{R}$), and 2) we trained a single generic stance classifier using data on all risks (not differentiating the risk labels). For both experiments, we split the test set into subsets on different risks. For each risk-specific classifier, we tested it on the respective risk subset. The generic stance classifier was tested on all risk subsets. The results are shown in Table 5, where we observe the risk-aware stance classifiers provided performance gains across all risk-classifier

SLO Risk	fastText	BiLSTM	CNN	BERT
Social	70.8±1.3	76.1±1.3	75.9±0.9	74.7±2.0
Social ($\mathcal{R}$)	71.3±2.6 (**0.5**)	76.9±3.7 (**0.8**)	77.7±2.6 (**1.8**)	76.2±2.2 (**1.5***)
Economic	59.6±2.6	63.1±2.5	62.2±2.4	66.3±3.8
Economic ($\mathcal{R}$)	62.2±2.5 (**2.6**)	68.4±2.0 (**5.3***)	66.5±2.7 (**4.3**)	71.2±1.5 (**4.9**)
Environmental	61.5±2.2	67.0±4.0	67.5±4.5	69.4±2.7
Environmental ($\mathcal{R}$)	68.0±2.9 (**6.5***)	68.4±1.2 (**1.4**)	68.0±4.0 (**0.5**)	72.5±1.6 (**3.2**)
Other	49.1±2.7	53.0±3.4	55.9±1.7	58.1±1.0
Other ($\mathcal{R}$)	56.7±1.4 (**7.6***)	57.5±2.7 (**4.5***)	56.3±1.3 (**0.4**)	61.1±4.9 (**3.0**)
Overall	58.5±1.5	64.8±2.8	65.4±2.4	67.2±1.9
Overall ($\mathcal{R}$)	64.3±2.0 (**5.8***)	67.8±2.4 (**3.0**)	67.1±2.7 (**1.7**)	71.7±4.0 (**4.5**)

(Two-tailed t-test: *** $p < 0.01$; ** $p < 0.05$; * $p < 0.1$)

Table 5: Accuracy on stance classification. Performance gains of the risk-aware methods over the corresponding non-risk ones are shown in the parentheses.

combinations, although the gains are not necessarily statistically significant in all cases. This validates our hypothesis that the language used to express stances generally varies when people discuss different SLO risk factors, and training specialised stance classifiers for different risks could better capture the underlying risk-specific language variations.

3.4 Implementation and Deployment of SIRTA

SIRTA was built by using Apache Kafka and ELK stack (Elasticsearch, Logstash, and Kibana) for constructing the real-time text classification pipeline in SIRTA's SLO assessment engine. It continuously obtains streaming tweets, which are then fed into the analytics pipeline. For the classifier configuration, based on our evaluation in the previous subsection (§3.3), we deployed fastText for the relevance classification task and BERT for both the risk and stance classification tasks. The monitoring dashboard was implemented with NodeJS and D3. SIRTA was deployed on a web server with a dockerised form.

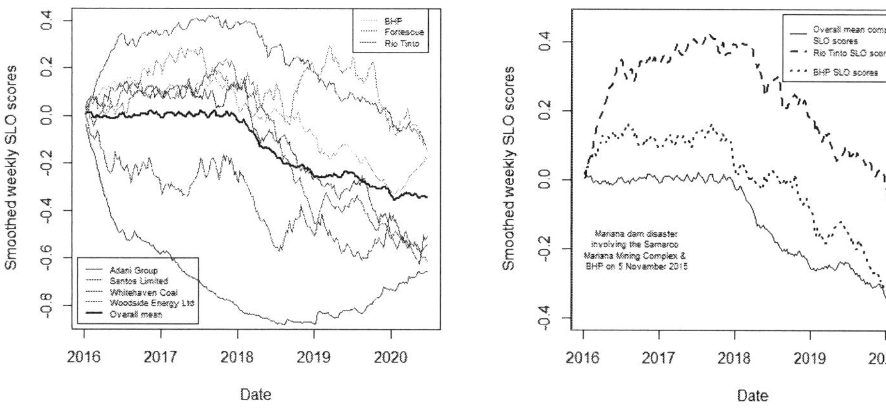

(a) SLO trends and variations of the monitored mining companies

(b) A case study of detection of SLO score changes in relation to BHP and Rio Tinto

Figure 2: The monitoring of SLO scores of seven major mining companies in the country.

3.5 Monitoring in Practice

We have been using SIRTA to monitor a number of major mining companies in the country. Figure 2a shows the chart of the trends and variations of their (EWMA[6]) SLO scores over a four-year span, from 2016 to 2020, on a weekly basis (averaging over a one-week window). Among these companies, Adani has had consistently the lowest score over time. This is aligned with our observations on Twitter of the numerous campaigns against the company.[7] SIRTA captured these negative opinions and trend over time. Rio Tinto, at the other extreme, had maintained a generally higher SLO profile until very recently, when it destroyed the Juukan Gorge, an ancient Aboriginal sacred site in Australia.[8] BHP also started with a high SLO, on par with Rio Tinto, but we then see a big departure from Rio Tinto in early 2016. This is likely due to the Mariana dam disaster[9] in South America late 2015.[10] Overall, the mean time series of SLO scores (black) was essentially steady until 2018 (although there is a decrease in early 2016, also probably due to the dam disaster), and then decreased significantly, indicating the general public in the country has become more negative about the mining sector overall. This is likely due to increased

---

[6]Exponentially-Weighted Moving Average, as a measure to account for data scarcity cases.

[7]These campaigns often have the textual prefix "StopAdani" in their Twitter account names.

[8]See news articles: www.business-humanrights.org/en/australia-rio-tinto-mining-blast-destroys-ancient-aboriginal-sacred-site and www.ft.com/content/6db79b46-8e46-4e89-8688-97064effbc61 – accessed June 24th, 2020.

[9]https://en.wikipedia.org/wiki/Mariana_dam_disaster

[10]Unfortunately, we lack the data before 1st Jan, 2016.

concerns about the environment and the public awareness of a major project by Adani, with the 'stop adani' movement becoming very active in early 2018.

An advantage of SIRTA is its ability to detect SLO changes, thus allowing for prompt mitigating actions being taken. To demonstrate this, we look at two companies, BHP and Rio Tinto. Both experienced significant changes in SLO scores during the monitoring period - See Figure 2b. We again observe the drop in the sector's SLO in 2018. With respect to BHP, there is a sharp departure from Rio Tinto in early 2016, most likely from the Mariana dam disaster, as mentioned above. Another point of particular interest is the sharp decline in Rio Tinto's SLO score in 2020, probably due to the destruction of the sacred site. After that, Rio Tinto and BHP appear converging in their scores, while Rio Tinto was performing much higher earlier. We notice a recent rise in BHP's SLO, potentially because of an announcement to postpone the destruction of other ancient caves until they had a chance to discuss with the community. We note that BHP, Rio Tinto, and Fortescue are essentially Iron Ore companies and have moved out of fossil fuels, while the other companies are related to fossil fuels. The figure shows that Iron Ore companies generally do better than mining companies (when no major event like the destruction of ancient sites or a dam disaster occurs), reinforcing the hypothesis that the downward trend in the mean SLO score is due to climate change concerns about using fossil fuels.

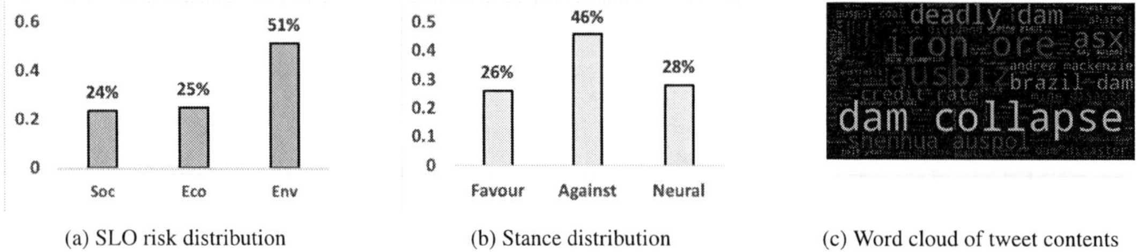

(a) SLO risk distribution   (b) Stance distribution   (c) Word cloud of tweet contents

Figure 3: Further analysis on the tweets posted between Jan and March 2016 about BHP.

To verify our hypothesis that the departure from Rio Tinto in early 2016 is due to the dam collapse, we did a further text analysis on all the tweets about BHP in our database between Jan and March of 2016. The results are shown in Figure 3. We found that most of those tweets were discussing environmental issues (51%, as opposed to about 25% for both economic and social issues in Figure 3a) and holding an against stance towards the company (46% in Figure 3b). We also drew a word cloud of the contents of those tweets (Figure 3c), which shows the frequent use of words such as "deadly", "dam", and "collapse'. All the findings above clearly suggest the occurrence of the negative change of BHP's SLO scores during that period was related (at least partly) to the dam collapsing event.

3.6 Cross-Validation with Survey-based Approaches

We contacted Voconiq[11], a company focused on measuring social license to operate with mining companies in Australia and overseas. Voconiq has pioneered the development of social science tools to provide insights for their clients on their social license to operate. Voconiq employs survey data, unstructured qualitative data, workshops and interviews with community members and company employees living in mining communities. Voconiq collects data about a similar set of companies as SIRTA. We shared our results with the CEO and Co-Founder, Dr Moffat. He told us he believed our work "added an important piece of research and technical development to the field of SLO research and practice". Dr Moffat also made some observations about the insights gained from SIRTA, compared to the patterns Voconiq observed. The first observation was the results in response to the Juukan Gorge incident, evident in the Twitter data in Quarter 2, 2020 (Figure 2a). The patterns observed through SIRTA in terms of company specific patterns of community responding were similar to those observed in his own work utilising data collected from monthly community surveys. Publicly available data regarding community sentiment toward Rio Tinto in Pilbara communities showed a drop in community sentiment corresponding with a similar drop in the SLO scores in SIRTA.

---

[11]https://voconiq.com/

Dr Moffat's second observation pointed to the fact that SIRTA and Voconiq "listen to different voices", reinforcing our hypothesis that looking at SLO from a social media perspective can provide complementary information to other methods. While large events like the San Marco dam collapse or the Juukan Gorge incident are of a magnitude that affect community sentiment within local mining communities and at a larger societal scale in similar ways, typically the sentiment of community members at these two scales are different. Local communities are more supportive of mining companies typically (often because of the jobs they provide), and they have more realistic understanding of both the benefits and impacts of mining operations. In contrast, data collected at a societal level (e.g., from social media) often reflects a different set of issues and agendas. These differences are evident in divergences Dr Moffat observed when looking at the insights from the Twitter data through SIRTA. He emphasised, however, that this was not a problem but rather a strength of our work. Data from social media provides a unique, and often leading, indicator of community sentiment, allowing companies and other stakeholders to combine these perspectives with those of local community residents for a more three-dimensional (and accurate) understanding of SLO at multiple scales.

4   Related Work

Traditionally, organisations determine SLO using surveys and focus groups (Moffat and Zhang, 2014), which are effective but also expensive to run. Our work seeks to complement these in-depth qualitative methods, harnessing social media to provide a real-time view of social license for organisations and/or specific projects, with early detection of changes - especially downward changes which might need to be addressed through immediate action. It can also inform the design of the focus groups and surveys, by providing information as to current concerns of the public.

Social media monitoring systems have been built to cover social phenomena (Wan and Paris, 2015; Larsen et al., 2015; Joshi et al., 2019), but none has focused on social license. Yet, this is potentially a very important application of social media analytics, as, increasingly, companies need to ensure they have such license, either as an organisation as a whole, or for specific projects they intend to carry out. In addition, an important aspect of our work is to couple the text analytics with a statistical monitoring engine to ensure insights from the text are appropriately put into an overall historical and sector contexts.

Stance detection in social media has gained much attention in recent years. The SemEval-2016 Task 6 challenge (Mohammad et al., 2016b) focused on stance classification of tweets discussing controversial political positions (e.g., abortion and climate change) and opposing political candidates (e.g., Clinton and Trump) (Mohammad et al., 2016b). Following this work, we focus on stance and code tweet instances as stance-for, against and neutral with respect to target companies. Note that, in our application domain, the zero-sum context inherent in the political domain used for SemEval-2016 does not apply; rejection of one company doesn't necessarily imply support of other companies. Indeed, in our specific case, tweet authors with environmentalist inclinations tend to reject all mining companies.

5   Conclusion

In this paper, we present SIRTA, a novel real-time text analytic system coupled with sophisticated monitoring techniques to help organisations manage their social license to operate (SLO) over time. Our experimental results and a case study show its effectiveness and applicability. The work could be furthered in a number of directions. First, our multi-label risk classifier currently does not consider the potential correlations among the risk factors mentioned in a post. It might be helpful to examine whether these correlations exist, and, if they do, refine the model. Second, our current strategy for aggregating the SLO scores of individual posts treats each post equally. We are considering employing a weighting function instead. Third, over time, the underlying distributions of the social media posts may shift, and our text classification models may need to be updated requiring a retraining policy. Finally, we plan to extend SIRTA to other organisations, sector or technology and extend our text analytics to support languages other than English (such as Korean and Japanese).

References

Isabelle Augenstein, Tim Rocktäschel, Andreas Vlachos, and Kalina Bontcheva. 2016. Stance detection with bidirectional conditional encoding. *arXiv preprint arXiv:1606.05464*.

Jacob Devlin, Ming-Wei Chang, Kenton Lee, and Kristina Toutanova. 2019. BERT: Pre-training of deep bidirectional transformers for language understanding. In *Proceedings of the 2019 Conference of the North American Chapter of the Association for Computational Linguistics: Human Language Technologies, Volume 1 (Long and Short Papers)*, pages 4171–4186, Minneapolis, Minnesota, June. Association for Computational Linguistics.

Neil Gunningham, Robert A. Kagan, and Dorothy Thornton. 2004. Social License and Environmental Protection: Why Businesses Go beyond Compliance. *Journal of the American Bar Foundation*, 39(2):307–341.

Aditya Joshi, Ross Sparks, James McHugh, Sarvnaz Karimi, Cecile Paris, and Raina MacIntyre. 2019. Harnessing tweets for early detection of an acute disease event. *Epidemiology*, 31:90 – 97.

Armand Joulin, Edouard Grave, Piotr Bojanowski, and Tomas Mikolov. 2017. Bag of tricks for efficient text classification. In *Proceedings of the 15th Conference of the European Chapter of the Association for Computational Linguistics: Volume 2, Short Papers*, pages 427–431. Association for Computational Linguistics, April.

Stephen H Kan. 2002. *Metrics and models in software quality engineering*. Addison-Wesley Longman Publishing Co., Inc.

Yoon Kim. 2014. Convolutional neural networks for sentence classification. In *Proceedings of the 2014 Conference on Empirical Methods in Natural Language Processing (EMNLP)*, pages 1746–1751, Doha, Qatar, October. Association for Computational Linguistics.

M. Larsen, T. T. Boonstra, P. Batterham, B. B. O'Dea, C.Paris, and H. Christensen. 2015. We feel: Mapping emotions on Twitter. *IEEE Journal of Biomedical and Health Informatics (JBHI)*, 9:1246 – 1252.

Bing Liu. 2012. Sentiment analysis and opinion mining. *Synthesis lectures on human language technologies*, 5(1):1–167.

Kieren Moffat and Airong Zhang. 2014. The paths to social licence to operate: An integrative model explaining community acceptance of mining. *Resources Policy*, 39(1):61–70.

Kieren Moffat, Justine Lacey, Airong Zhang, and Sina Leipold. 2016. The social licence to operate: a critical review. *Forestry*, 89:477–488.

Saif Mohammad, Svetlana Kiritchenko, Parinaz Sobhani, Xiaodan Zhu, and Colin Cherry. 2016a. Semeval-2016 task 6: Detecting stance in tweets. In *Proceedings of the 10th International Workshop on Semantic Evaluation (SemEval-2016)*, pages 31–41.

Saif M. Mohammad, Swetlana Kiritchenko, Parinaz Sobhani, Xiaodan Zhu, and Colin Cherry. 2016b. SemEval-2016 Task 6: Detecting stance in tweets. In *Proceedings of the International Workshop on Semantic Evaluation*, pages 31–41. ACM, jun. https://www.aclweb.org/anthology/S/S16/S16-1003.pdf.

Saif M Mohammad, Parinaz Sobhani, and Svetlana Kiritchenko. 2017. Stance and sentiment in tweets. *ACM Transactions on Internet Technology (TOIT)*, 17(3):26.

Olutobi Owoputi, Brendan O'Connor, Chris Dyer, Kevin Gimpel, Nathan Schneider, and Noah A. Smith. 2013. Improved part-of-speech tagging for online conversational text with word clusters. In *Proceedings of NAACL-HLT 2013*, pages 380–390. ACL.

Bo Pang, Lillian Lee, et al. 2008. Opinion mining and sentiment analysis. *Foundations and Trends® in Information Retrieval*, 2(1–2):1–135.

Jeffrey Pennington, Richard Socher, and Christopher D. Manning. 2014. Glove: Global vectors for word representation. In *Empirical Methods in Natural Language Processing (EMNLP)*, pages 1532–1543.

Parinaz Sobhani, Saif Mohammad, and Svetlana Kiritchenko. 2016. Detecting stance in tweets and analyzing its interaction with sentiment. In *Proceedings of the Fifth Joint Conference on Lexical and Computational Semantics*, pages 159–169.

Qingying Sun, Zhongqing Wang, Qiaoming Zhu, and Guodong Zhou. 2018. Stance detection with hierarchical attention network. In *Proceedings of the 27th International Conference on Computational Linguistics*, pages 2399–2409.

Grigorios Tsoumakas and Ioannis Katakis. 2007. Multi-label classification: An overview. *International Journal of Data Warehousing and Mining (IJDWM)*, 3(3):1–13.

Stephen Wan and Cécile Paris. 2015. Understanding public emotional reactions on Twitter. In *Proceedings of the Ninth International AAAI Conference on Web and Social Media*, pages 715–716. AAAI.

A   Appendix

A.1   Datasets

A.1.1   Query Terms for SLO Relevance Annotation

Type	Query Terms
Hashtag	#StopAdani, #GoAdani, #StopBHP, #StopRioTinto, #StopFortescue, #StopSantos, #nonewcoal, #NoNewCoalMines
Username	StopAdani, StopAdaniNoon, StopAdaniMelbs, StopAdaniK, StopadaniB, stopadanieltham, StopAdaniTSV, stopadanisydney, StopadaniGC, StopAdaniCairns, StopadaniW, StopAdaniGTown, stopadaninoosa, stopadanibowen, adani_stop, StopBHP, AdaniOnline, bhp, RioTinto, SantosLtd, FortescueNews, kennecottutah, NSWMC, CMEWA, QRCouncil, WoodsideEnergy, MiningNewsNet, ozmining, miningcomau, Mining_EnergySA, AUMiningMonthly, MineralsCouncil, Austmine, MiningWeeklyAUS, AuMiningReview
Text	stopadani, adani, goadani, santosltd, santos, bhpbilliton, bhp, riotinto, rio tinto, woodside, woodsideenergy, woodside petroleum, woodside energy, fortescuenews, fortescue, metals, fortescue, whitehaven, whitehavencoal, iluka, ilukaresources, iluka resources, oilsearchltd, oil search, cuestacoal, cuesta coal, cuesta, cqc, newmont, newmont mining

A.1.2   SLO Risk Annotation

Query Terms for Automatic Training Set Annotation:

Category	Instances	Query Terms
Social	12960	culture, support, live, land, public, approve, traditional, humanity, licence, human, labor, moral, national, land, donate, local, farm, vote, trust, life, multinational, regional, party, generation
Economic	13540	fund, financial, business, work, economic, import, money, job, employ, invest, spend, pay, market, cost, productivity, deposit, donation, asset
Environmental	7405	environment, destroy, approve, reef, insanity, enviro, climate, danger, greatbarrierreef, climatechange, reefnotcoal, flood, renewable, river, groundwater, poison, agriculture, save, protect, threaten

Guidelines for Manual Test Set Annotation:

(1) Select *Economic* if the message is about the economic value of the company or its production, about shareholders, or about any employment/staff related issues (hiring, firing, Health and Safety). Examples:

- share price movements, or an indication that the company is doing well/bad.

- jobs (new hires(+ve) and cuts(-ve)). (e.g., "[company]" is recruiting/laying off")

- big economic wins.

- Positive or negative movement in terms of commodity price (e.g., iron price per ton).

- Positive/negative economic forecasts for the industry/company.

- Mentions of shareholders.

- Health and safety matters or working conditions.

(2) Select Social and cultural if the focus of the message is about how the company interacts with the community and how its activity affects the community. Sample topics include: health and education, community support services, social engagement with government, the cultural value of a site (e.g., sacred sites) used by the organisation. Any protest activity or activity trying rally for a cause is taken as "Social and Cultura" (this does not include shareholders revolt, which would be "Economic and Employment"). Examples:

- Government calls for a company to be investigated.

- Wining and dining government officials.

- Any interactions between the government and the mining company.

- Company partnerships with schools, hospitals, communities, that relates to funded programs or infrastructure.

- Any danger to valued sacred sites or cultural artefacts, e.g., art.

- Any dangers to the cultural way of life for local inhabitants.

- Any community issue that surfaces in relation to mine operations or management.

- Protests.

(3) Select *Environmental* if the message is related to natural environment, including fauna, flora, water, air, climate, etc. Examples:

- Discussions about the impact on the natural environment.

- Comments on environmental impact of the company, its decisions and actions.

A.1.3   SLO Stance Annotation

Query Terms:

Stance	Instances	Query Terms
Favour	24255	GoAdani, AdaniOnline, bhp, RioTinto, SantosLtd, FortescueNews, kennecottutah, NSWMC, CMEWA, QRCouncil, WoodsideEnergy
Against	19311	#StopAdani, #StopBHP, #StopRioTinto, #StopFortescue, #StopSantos, #nonewcoal, #NoNew-CoalMines, StopAdani, StopAdaniNoon, StopAdaniMelbs, StopAdaniK, StopadaniB, stopadanieltham, StopAdaniTSV, stopadanisydney, StopadaniGC, StopAdaniCairns, StopadaniW, StopAdaniGTown, stopadaninoosa, stopadanibowen, adani_stop, StopBHP
Neutral	19317	MiningNewsNet, ozmining, miningcomau, MiningEnergySA, AUMiningMonthly, MineralsCouncil, Austmine, MiningWeeklyAUS, AuMiningReview

Guidelines for Manual Test Set Annotation:

for: The coder infers from the tweet and its context that the author supports the target either because:

- the tweet explicitly supports the target.

- the tweet supports something/someone else aligned with or supporting the target or rejects something/someone else not aligned with or supporting the target.

- the tweet can be seen, in context, to support the target, either because:

  - the tweet author's profile lists positions consistent with support of the target.
  - the tweet discourse context places the tweet in support the target either by echoing support for the target in other tweets or by opposing rejection for the target in other tweets.

against: The coder infers from the tweet and its context that the author rejects the target.
neutral: The coder infers from the tweet or its context that the author neither supports nor rejects the target because:

- the tweet states no position consistent with support or rejection of the target.

- the tweet re-posts information only, with no clear hint as to the author's stance.

- the tweet context gives no hints as to the tweet author's stance.

Extreme Model Compression for On-device
Natural Language Understanding

Kanthashree Mysore Sathyendra **Samridhi Choudhary** **Leah Nicolich-Henkin**
Amazon Alexa   Amazon Alexa   Amazon Alexa
ksathyen@amazon.com   samridhc@amazon.com   nicolich@amazon.com

Abstract

In this paper, we propose and experiment with techniques for extreme compression of neural natural language understanding (NLU) models, making them suitable for execution on resource-constrained devices. We propose a task-aware, end-to-end compression approach that performs word-embedding compression jointly with NLU task learning. We show our results on a large-scale, commercial NLU system trained on a varied set of intents with huge vocabulary sizes. Our approach outperforms a range of baselines and achieves a compression rate of 97.4% with less than 3.7% degradation in predictive performance. Our analysis indicates that the signal from the downstream task is important for effective compression with minimal degradation in performance.

1 Introduction

Spoken Language Understanding (SLU) is the task of extracting meaning from a spoken utterance. A typical approach to SLU consists of two modules: an automatic speech recognition (ASR) module that transcribes the audio into a text transcript, followed by a Natural Language Understanding (NLU) module that predicts the semantics (domain, intent and slots) from the ASR transcript. The last few years have seen an increasing application of deep learning approaches to both ASR (Mohamed et al., 2011; Hinton et al., 2012; Graves et al., 2013; Bahdanau et al., 2016) and NLU (Xu and Sarikaya, 2014; Yao et al., 2013; Ravuri and Stolcke, 2015; Sarikaya et al., 2014), making them more reliable, accurate and efficient. This has led to an increasing popularity of feature-rich commercial voice assistants (VAs) – like Amazon Alexa, Google Assistant, Apple's Siri and Microsoft's Cortana. VAs were used in over 3 billion devices in the world in 2019, and are estimated to reach 8 billion devices by 2023[1]. With a growing number of users relying on VAs for their day-to-day activities, voice interfaces have become ubiquitous, and are employed in a range of devices, including smart TVs, mobile phones, smart appliances, home assistants and wearable devices.

The SLU processing for VAs is often offloaded to the cloud, where high-performance, compute-rich hardware is used to serve complex machine learning models. However, on-device SLU is growing in popularity due to its wide applicability and attractive benefits (Coucke et al., 2018; McGraw et al., 2016; Saade et al., 2018). First, it enables VAs to work offline, without an active internet connection, allowing their use in remote areas and on devices with poor or intermittent internet connectivity, for eg. in automobiles. Second, on-device processing reduces latency by eliminating communication over the network, and results in an improved user experience. And third, processing utterances on the edge decreases the load on cloud-services, resulting in reduced cloud hardware requirements and associated costs.

NLU is the task of extracting intents and semantics from user queries. NLU in VAs typically consists of the following sub-tasks - domain classification (DC), intent classification (IC) and named entity recognition (NER). Prior work has shown the effectiveness of recurrent neural models, that jointly model

---

[1]https://www.statista.com/statistics/973815/worldwide-digital-voice-assistant-in-use/

Proceedings of the 28th International Conference on Computational Linguistics: Industry Track, pages 160–171
Barcelona, Spain (Online), December 12, 2020

these tasks in a multi-task setup (Kim et al., 2017; Hakkani-Tr et al., 2016; Liu and Lane, 2016a). These models typically are made up of large word embeddings, sometimes accounting for more than 90% of the model parameters, and hence require compression for their deployment on resource constrained devices. Generic model compression approaches such as quantization (Hubara et al., 2017) are ineffective for compressing large word-embeddings, as they do not achieve the required performance at high compression rates. Prior approaches for word-embedding compression (Raunak, 2017; Shu and Nakayama, 2017) tackle comparatively smaller vocabulary sizes and are typically post-processing approaches, where compression is performed after the downstream task models are trained. Post-processing compression for large vocabulary sizes is not effective as the compression is lossy and task-agnostic. Under higher compression rates, post-processing word embedding compression can lead to a significant degradation in downstream performance.

In this paper, we present a principled approach for compressing neural models targeted to perform NLU on resource-constrained devices. We tackle a large number of intents and huge vocabularies ($\sim 200K$), which are typical in a large-scale, commercial NLU system. To overcome the limitations of prior task-agnostic embedding compression approaches, we propose an end-to-end compression technique, where the compression layers are jointly trained with the downstream task (NLU) model. Joint training allows for both *task-aware compression* and *compression-aware task learning*. *Task-aware compression* enables the compression model to learn better reconstructions for words that are more important to the downstream task. At the same time, *compression-aware task learning* enables the downstream task model to adapt itself to the errors in embedding reconstructions. We further combine word embedding compression with recurrent layer compression using quantization to compress our model to just a few MB, achieving a compression rate $>97\%$ with $<4\%$ drop in predictive performance.

2 Related Work

Joint Modeling and Multi-Tasking for NLU: Joint modeling of component NLU tasks, such as IC and NER, has been an extensive area of research. Jeong and Lee (2008) propose a triangular conditional random field (CRF) as a unified probabilistic model combining IC and NER. This is further extended by Xu and Sarikaya (2013), where convolutional neural network based triangular CRFs are used. Other neural network architectures like recursive neural networks (RNNs) (Guo et al., 2014) and their variants (Zhang and Wang, 2016; Liu and Lane, 2016a; Hakkani-Tr et al., 2016; Liu and Lane, 2016b) have also been well explored. However, all these approaches propose to build domain specific models and produce multiple models, one for each domain. Work by Kim et al. (2017) explores a unified, multi-domain, multi-task neural model using RNNs (MT-RNN) and was shown to be effective in sharing knowlege across the component tasks and domains. In contrast, the authors in (Hakkani-Tr et al., 2016) use a sequence-to-sequence model to output the complete semantic interpretation of an utterance (DC, IC, NER). In our work, we adapt the multi-task architecture from Kim et al. (2017), and demonstrate its effectiveness in meeting strict device constraints on compression.

Neural Model Compression: Due to its many practical applications, research on neural model compression has received massive interest in recent years. Existing approaches for general neural model compression include low-precision computation (Vanhoucke et al., 2011; Hwang and Sung, 2014; Anwar et al., 2015), quantization (Chen et al., 2015; Zhou et al., 2017), network pruning (Wen et al., 2016; Han et al., 2015), SVD-based weight matrix decomposition (Xue et al., 2013) and knowledge distillation (Hinton et al., 2015). For neural NLP models, however, larger focus has been on compressing huge word embedding matrices. Embedding compression approaches include quantization (Hubara et al., 2017), binarization (Tissier et al., 2019), dimensionality reduction and matrix factorization methods such as PCA (Raunak, 2017) and SVD (Acharya et al., 2019). An alternative post-training compression approach using deep compositional code learning (DCCL) was also proposed by Shu and Nakayama (2017). This approach learns compressed embedding representations based on additive quantization (Babenko and Lempitsky, 2014) and forms the basis of our task-aware compression approach. In contrast to Shu and Nakayama (2017), we propose a task-aware compression approach, where embedding compression is performed during the task model training, instead of as a post-processing step.

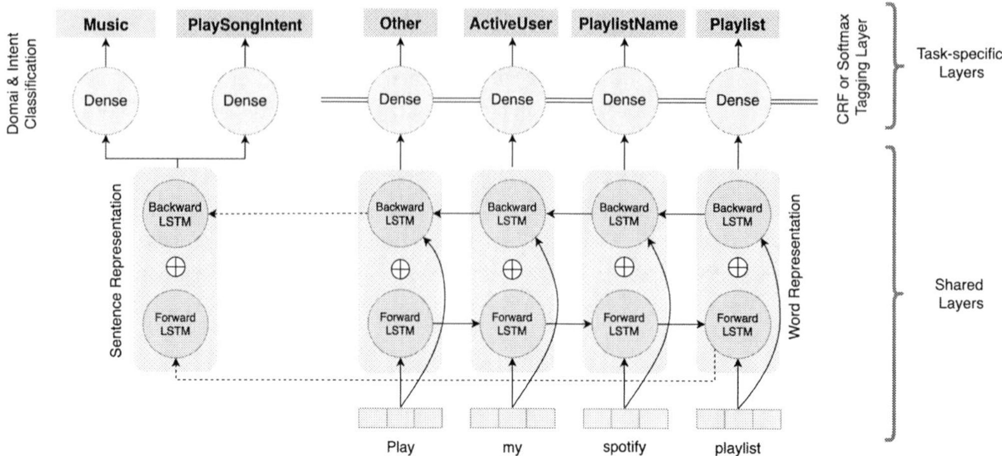

Figure 1: Multi-Domain, Multi-Task Recurrent Architecture for on-device NLU.

3   Method

Problem Setup: NLU consists of three component tasks - Domain Classification (DC), Intent Classification (IC) and Named Entity Recognition (NER). DC and IC are sentence classification tasks and determine the domain (e.g. Music) and the intent (e.g. PlayMusic) of the input utterance. NER is a sequence tagging task, where each word in the utterance is assigned a slot tag (e.g. AlbumName, SongName etc). The combination of the domain, intent and slots represents the semantic interpretation for the given utterance and is passed on to the downstream application. Our goal is to compress the NLU models, to fit within extreme disk space constraints with minimal degradation in predictive performance. Furthermore, low-latency and inference support for the models are desirable.

3.1   NLU Task Model Architecture

Model Architectural Constraints: Our choice of a suitable on-device NLU architecture is largely driven by hardware resource constraints. First, on-device systems come with a strict memory budget, restricting our choices to architectures with fewer parameters. Second, the architectures chosen should not only be amenable to model compression, but should result in *minimal* degradation in performance on compression. Third, on-device models have rigorous latency targets, requiring fast inference. This restricts our choices to simpler, seasoned architectures, like LSTMs and GRUs, that require fewer layers and FLOPs as opposed to the newer computationally intensive transformer-based architectures like BERT. Moreover, on-device inference engines often lack support for sophisticated layers such as self-attention layers. Driven by these constraints and relying on the considerable effectiveness of recurrent architectures (Hakkani-Tr et al., 2016; Liu and Lane, 2016a; Zhang and Wang, 2016), we use a multi-domain, multi-task RNN model (MT-RNN), built using bi-directional LSTMs (Figure 1) for performing NLU. We train a single neural model that can jointly perform DC, IC and NER for a given input utterance. Furthermore, in order to reduce inference latency, we use word-level LSTMs as opposed to character or sub-word based models.

Architecture Details - Our task model, which we call the MT-RNN model, is shown in Figure 1. It consists of a *shared* bi-directional LSTM (Bi-LSTM) to extract features shared by all tasks, and *task-specific* layers for the classification and tagging tasks. The input to the recurrent layers are pretrained embeddings and are fine-tuned during training. The input to each of the classification components is a sentence representation, obtained by concatenating the final states of the forward- and the backward-LSTM. This is passed on to a fully-connected dense layer with a softmax to predict the domain and intent for the utterance. The tagging layer produces a slot tag for each word in the utterance. The input at each time step consists of the forward- and backward-LSTM states for each word and the output is the slot tag. We choose the popularly used *Conditional Random Fields (CRF)* layer for NER. The network is trained to minimize a joint NLU loss defined as the sum of the cross-entropy losses for IC and DC and the CRF loss for NER:

$$\mathcal{L}_{NLU} = \mathcal{L}_{DC} + \mathcal{L}_{IC} + \mathcal{L}_{NER}$$

In the following sections, we describe our approach for compressing the word embeddings and the recurrent components of our MT-RNN model.

3.2 Word Embedding Compression

Word embeddings have been shown to be the largest components in an NLP model, owing to large vocabulary sizes and floating point parameters, accounting for $>90\%$ of the model sizes (Shu and Nakayama, 2017). Hence, compressing embeddings is crucial for reducing NLP model sizes. Our approach is based on additive quantization (Babenko and Lempitsky, 2014), which has shown great success in compressing word embeddings, achieving high compression rates (Shu and Nakayama, 2017).

3.2.1 Additive Quantization using Deep Compositional Code Learning

Additive quantization (Babenko and Lempitsky, 2014) aims to approximate vectors by representing them as a sum of basis vectors, called codewords. Originally proposed for image compression and approximate nearest neighbor search, this method has recently been used for post-processing word embedding compression (Chen et al., 2018; Shu and Nakayama, 2017) achieving high compression rates, upwards of 90%, on modest vocabulary sizes.

Let $W \in \mathcal{R}^{V \times D}$ be the original word embedding matrix, where V denotes the vocabulary size and D denotes the embedding size. Using additive quantization, the original word embedding matrix is compressed into a matrix of integer codes as $W_c \in \mathcal{Z_K}^{V \times M}$, where $\mathcal{Z_K}$ denotes the set of integers from 1 to K, $\mathcal{Z_K} = \{1, 2, \ldots, K\}$. This is achieved using a set of M codebooks, C_1 through C_M, $C_m \in \mathcal{R}^{K \times D}$, each containing K codewords of size D. C_m^k is the kth codeword in the mth codebook. For each word embedding w_i in W, the compressed codes can be w_{ci}, where

$$w_{ci} = [z_1^i, z_2^i, \ldots, z_M^i] \qquad \text{where } z_m^i \in \mathcal{Z_K}, \forall m \in \{1, 2, \ldots, M\}$$

The original word embedding w_i is approximated from the codes and codebooks as w_i' by summing the $(z_m^i)^{\text{th}}$ codeword in the mth codebook over all codebooks:

$$w_i' = \sum_{m=1}^{M} C_m^{z_m^i}$$

Shu and Nakayama (2017) propose the deep compositional code learning (DCCL) architecture to learn discrete codes and codebooks for a given word embedding matrix through an unsupervised autoencoding task. In this model, a continuous word vector input, $w_i \in \mathcal{R}^D$ is first projected into a lower dimensional space using a linear transformation. This is projected through a second linear layer into M different K-dimensional vectors. Each of these M vectors is passed through a gumbel-softmax activation to get M one-hot vectors, $r_m^i \in \mathcal{R}^{1 \times K}$:

$$r_m^i = \sigma_G(f_L(w_i)) \qquad \forall m \in \{1, 2, \ldots, M\}$$

where f_L denotes the linear transformations and σ_G denotes the gumbel-softmax activation. The gumbel-softmax activation allows the network to learn discrete codes via gumbel-sampling, while also making the network differentiable, enabling the backpropagation of gradients (Jang et al., 2016).

These one-hot vectors are converted to integer codes corresponding to the input word embedding. In order to reconstruct the word embedding, the following operations are performed:

$$w_i' = \sum_{m=1}^{M} r_m^i * C_m \qquad \text{where } r_m^i \in \mathcal{R}^{1 \times K}, C_m \in \mathcal{R}^{K \times D}, w_i' \in \mathcal{R}^{1 \times D} \tag{1}$$

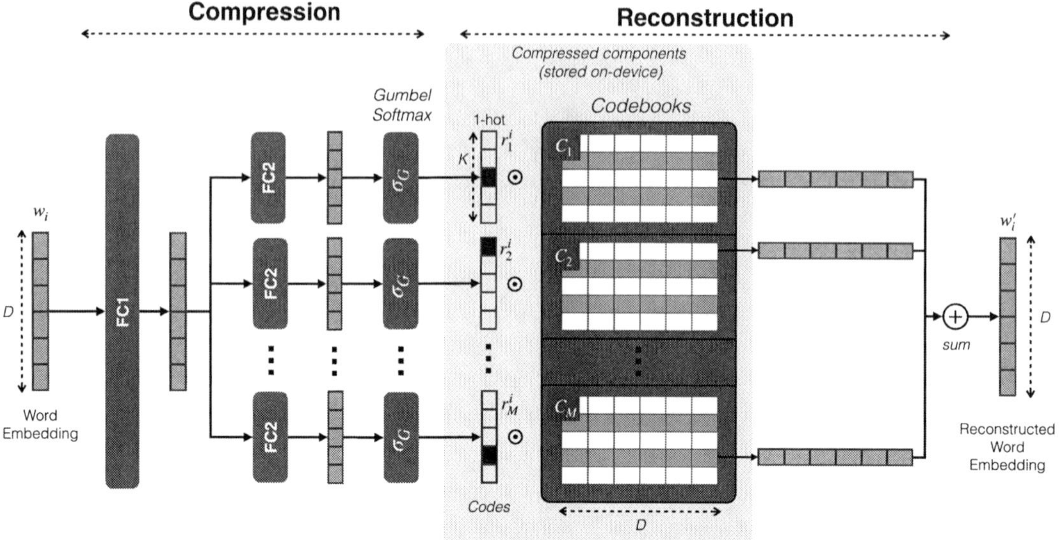

Figure 2: Deep Compositional Code Learning Architecture.

Figure 2 provides an overview of the DCCL model. Since the word embedding matrix W can be reconstructed using just the codes W_c and the codebooks $C = [C_i \ldots C_m]$, the original embedding matrix W with $V \times D$ floating point values need not be stored on-device, thus achieving the required compression. Furthermore, W_c would be an integer matrix requiring only $M \log_2 K$ bits per embedding and the codebook C requires just $M * K * D * 32$ bits on disk, where each floating point element takes 32 bits. By choosing M and $K \ll V$, the size of the codes and codebooks can be greatly reduced when compared to the original embedding matrix.

3.2.2 Task-agnostic Post-Processing Compression

Shu and Nakayama (2017) propose to use the DCCL architecture to perform post-processing embedding compression, where embeddings are compressed after the downstream task model has been trained. The task model is first initialized with pretrained word embeddings that are fine-tuned during task model training to obtain task-specific embeddings. These are compressed using the DCCL architecture trained on an unsupervised autoencoding task. The input to the autoencoder is the embedding matrix $W \in \mathcal{R}^{V \times D}$ and the model is trained to minimize the average embedding reconstruction loss (denoted by $l(W, W')$) for words in the embedding matrix:

$$l(W, W') = \frac{1}{V} \sum_{i=1}^{V} (w_i - w_i')^2$$

DCCL is shown to outperform other approaches such as parameter pruning and product quantization on sentence classification and machine translation tasks.

Since compression is performed as a post-processing step after the task model is trained, the compression algorithm has no information about the downstream task, making the compression task-agnostic and results in several drawbacks. First, unsupervised post-processing compression treats all words equally for compression. However, in practice, some words may be more important than others for the downstream task. Hence, better reconstructions of more important words may benefit the downstream task. Second, post-processing compression typically is lossy resulting in a degradation in downstream performance since the task model is not adapted to the compression error. We propose a task-aware end-to-end compression approach which aims to address these issues.

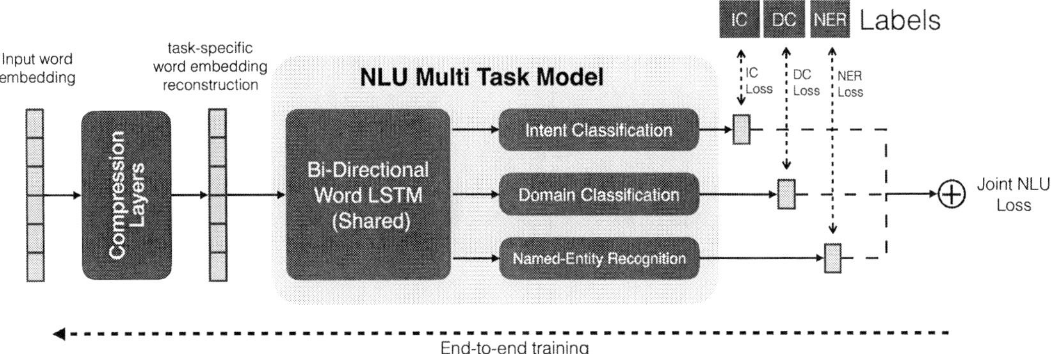

Figure 3: Task-aware end-to-end compression with the MT-RNN model.

3.2.3 Task-aware End-to-End Compression

Our algorithm improves on the above said approach, by training the DCCL a.k.a. the compression model, jointly with the downstream task model (Figure 3). End-to-end training allows the compression model to receive signals about the downstream task, thus adapting the compression to the downstream task. Intuitively, since the compression model now has the information about how the words are used in the downstream task (via the downstream loss), it can spend more network capacity in achieving better reconstructions for more important words. At the same time, the downstream task model also adapts to the lossy reconstructions learned by the compression model, thus improving on the downstream performance. We call this *task-aware end-to-end compression*, where the compression algorithm takes the downstream task loss into account during embedding compression.

In order to perform task-aware compression with a DCCL model, we replace the original embedding lookup operations in the task model with layers from the DCCL model a.k.a. the compression layers. The input to our model is now a sequence of L word embeddings corresponding to words from the input text utterances. These are passed through the compression layers and are reconstructed, as shown in equation 1, to obtain a sequence of D dimensional word representations corresponding to each word in the input. The word representation is then fed to the recurrent layers in the task model and the remaining network is unchanged. The entire setup is trained end-to-end to minimize the downstream task loss and the gradients are back-propagated through the entire network, including the compression layers. Further, the compression layers can be initialized with pretrained model parameters from the task-agnostic DCCL model, and the NLU layers can be initialized from a trained NLU model.

Training an end-to-end DCCL model is tricky, especially when the number and size of codebooks is large. The stochasticity introduced by gumbel-sampling can easily stray off the training, leading to sub-optimal convergence. For these cases, we ground the training by adding the word embedding reconstruction loss to the downstream task loss as follows:

$$\mathcal{L} = \mathcal{L}_{NLU} + \mathcal{L}_e \text{ where } \mathcal{L}_e = \frac{1}{N} \sum_{i=1}^{N} \left(w_i - w_i' \right)^2$$

Adding the embedding reconstruction loss not only stabilizes the training, but also provides stronger gradients to the compression layers. Note that unlike task-agnostic compression where all words are treated equally for compression, the embedding reconstruction loss term in task-aware compression considers only the words appearing the in the input batch. This ensures that the words that are more frequent in the training data have better reconstructions, resulting in better downstream performance.

3.3 Recurrent Layer Compression

Quantization (Hubara et al., 2017) is a simple and effective technique for model compression. Quantization maps each floating point model paramater to its closest representative from a pre-chosen set of floating-point values. More concretely, the model parameter range is divided into B equally spaced bins (or buckets), and each parameter is assigned its closest bin. The bins can be represented by integer indices and require at most $\log_2 B$ bits. For instance, with 256 bins, a 32-bit floating point parameter can represented by an integer bin index occupying just 8 bits.

We apply post-training 8-bit linear quantization to quantize the recurrent layers of the model. Since 32-bit floating point model parameters are now represented by 8-bit integers, this results in an instant $4\times$ compression. Furthermore, quantization improves model latency, as all the floating point operations are performed using integers. While more sophisticated compression techniques exist for compressing recurrent layers, we found that quantization was extremely effective and resulted in no degradation in performance.

4 Experiments

In this section we describe the datasets used and our experimental setup for model compression. While our approach is generically applicable to any NLP task that uses word embeddings, we show the effectiveness of our approach on the three NLU tasks – DC, IC, and NER. We show our results on a large scale commercial NLU system trained across a large number of intents with huge vocabularies.

Dataset. We use annotated live traffic data of a large-scale, cloud based, commercial VA system to train our NLU models. Utterances from the live traffic are randomly sampled and anonymized to remove any customer specific information. They are then annotated by skilled annotators for the NLU labels corresponding to the domain, intent and slot labels for each utterance. The training set chosen for our experiments contains millions of utterances spanning 5 domains, and over 150 intents and slots. One of these domains is the 'Out of domain' (or OOD) domain, consisting of utterances not supported by the NLU system. The intent for these utterances is labeled as the 'OODIntent' and the words are given the 'Other' slot tag. Our held-out test set is prepared by randomly sampling 1 million utterances from the live-production traffic, following a similar process. In order to facilitate optimization and early stopping, we also use a validation set of a similar scale.

Evaluation Metrics. We use the following metrics for evaluating the performance on the NLU tasks:

Intent Recognition Error Rate (IRER): This is the ratio of number of incorrect interpretations to the total number of utterances. A correct interpretation is when the predicted domain, intent and all slots for an utterances are correct. We compute the *IRER* only on non-OOD utterances.

Intent Classification Error Rate (ICER): This is the ratio of number of incorrect intent predictions to the total number of utterances.

Domain Classification Error Rate (DCER): This is the ratio of number of incorrect domain predictions to the total number of utterances.

Slot Error Rate (SER): This is the ratio of number of incorrect slot predictions to the total number of slots.

False Accept Rate (FAR): This is the ratio of number of out-of-domain utterances falsely accepted as a supported utterance to the total number of out-of-domain utterances. This metric is mainly used to evaluate the effectiveness of the model in rejecting out-of-domain (or unsupported) utterances.

Along with the above metrics we also compute the sizes of the word embeddings and the MT-RNN task model. We only report relative changes in the above metrics compared to the baseline.

NLU Model Training. We train the NLU task model (the MT-RNN model) described in Section 3.1 using the prepared training dataset (Section 4). We initialize the embeddings with FastText (Joulin et al., 2016) embeddings that have been pretrained on a large corpus of unannotated, anonymized, live utterances. The model is trained to minimize the NLU loss $\mathcal{L}_{NLU}$ as described in Section 3.1 and the embeddings are fine-tuned during training. The models are trained for a total of 25 epochs, with early stopping on the validation loss, using Adam optimizer with a learning rate of 0.0001. We further perform a grid search on a range of hyperparameter values for dropout and variational dropout and select the best performing model as our candidate model for compression. This model also serves as our uncompressed baseline.

Model	Type	Word Embedding Compression Rate			
		15×	30×	60×	120×
SVD	TAg.	+786.94	+794.11	+794.43	+794.42
DCCL	TAg.	+12.14	+81.67	+280.89	+530.54
DCCL + NLU Fine-tuning	TAg.	+1.49	+3.78	+6.13	+8.84
SVD	TAw.	+82.20	+106.06	+161.70	+235.68
Ours	TAw.	**+0.84**	**+2.45**	+4.87	+8.85
Ours – w.o. recons. loss	TAw.	+5.91	+3.79	**+3.72**	**+5.53**
Ours – w.o. pretraining	TAw.	+7.23	+5.39	+6.30	+8.71

Table 1: Relative percentage IRER change for different word embedding compression rates.

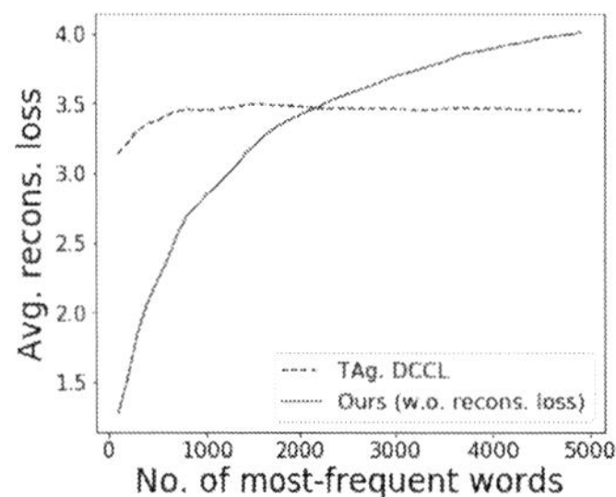

Figure 4: Average Reconstruction loss for top frequent words.

Baselines. We compare our proposed approach with the following baselines. We use the abbreviations 'TAg.' for 'Task Agnostic' and 'TAw.' for 'Task Aware'.

TAg. SVD: In this approach, large embedding matrices are factorized into matrices of much smaller sizes to produce low-rank approximations of the original embedding matrix, using Singular Value Decomposition (SVD). This is applied as an offline compression method where the embedding matrices are compressed as a post-processing step.

TAw. SVD: Acharya et al. (2019) propose a task-aware SVD-based embedding compression approach, where the embedding matrix is first factorized into lower dimensional matrices using SVD. The factors are then used to initialize a smaller word embedding layer followed by a linear layer, and jointly fine-tuned with the downstream task model. Stochastic Gradient Descent (SGD) with a learning rate of 0.001 as presented in Acharya et al. (2019) is used for the optimizer.

TAg. DCCL: Task-agnostic compression method proposed by Shu and Nakayama (2017) where the code learning autoencoder described in Section 3.2 is used to compress word-embeddings from the trained NLU model. Since it does not perform joint training of the compression layers with the downstream task, this serves as an ablation test for our proposed task-aware compression approach.

TAg. DCCL + NLU Finetuning: This is another ablation test for our proposed task-aware compression approach. In this approach, task-agnostic compression is performed as in the previous baseline. Once compressed in a task-agnostic way, the embeddings are kept frozen and the downstream task model is fine-tuned to minimize the downstream NLU loss. NLU model fine-tuning is performed with a learning rate of 0.0001 for 5 epochs.

For all SVD-based approaches, we run experiments over a range of values for n where n is the fraction of components retrained in the low-rank SVD approximation. This produces models of different sizes. For all DCCL-based baselines, we train the task-agnostic autoencoder model for 300 epochs (approximately 800k iterations) with a learning rate of 0.0001 using the Adam optimizer. We experiment with a range of values for hyperparameters M and K where M is the number of codebooks and K is the number of basis vectors per codebook. Different values of M and K produce models of different sizes.

Implementation details. Our approach is essentially a task-aware version of DCCL (*TAw. DCCL*). In our method, the compression layers are initialized with the parameters from the trained autoencoder model, obtained as a result of task-agnostic post-processing compression. Similarly, the NLU specific layers are initialized from the trained NLU model. The entire compression model is then trained end-to-end to minimize the loss function as mentioned in Section 3.2.3. The model is trained with a learning rate of 0.0001 for 5 epochs. Similar to the above task-agnostic setups, we experiment with a range of values for M and K. We further explore the following additional setups:

Without pretraining: In this setup, the compression layers and the task model are jointly trained from scratch and are not initialized from pretrained components. The model is trained to minimize the joint NLU loss without the embedding reconstruction loss. We use the Adam optimizer with a learning rate

Method		Compression		Performance				
	Type	Model Compr. Rate	WE Compr. Rate	Rel. IRER Change (%)	Rel. ICER Change (%)	Rel. DCER Change (%)	Rel. SER Change (%)	Rel. FAR Change (%)
Uncompressed	NA	1×	1×	0	0	0	0	0
SVD	TAg.	17.4×	60×	+794.43	+1929.50	+2387.46	+1107.66	+2.78
DCCL	TAg.	17.6×	64×	+280.89	+257.63	+282.29	+291.10	**-0.28**
DCCL + NLU Finetuning	TAg.	17.6×	64×	**+6.13**	**+5.53**	**+5.93**	**+7.77**	+0.06
SVD	TAw.	17.4×	60×	+161.70	+190.05	+180.76	+169.53	+0.94
Ours	TAw.	17.6×	64×	+4.87	+4.50	+5.57	+6.13	**+0.07**
Ours – w.o. Reconstruction Loss	TAw.	17.6×	64×	**+3.72**	**+3.66**	**+4.23**	**+4.86**	+0.08
Ours – w.o. Pretraining	TAw.	17.6×	64×	+6.30	+6.08	+6.70	+7.50	+0.08
Ours + NLU LSTM Quantization	TAw.	39.5×	64×	**+3.69**	**+3.67**	**+4.27**	**+4.91**	**+0.08**

Table 2: This table shows relative performance metrics and model sizes for different baselines and our proposed approaches. The best models in each category are highlighed in bold.

of 0.0001 and train the model for 25 epochs.

Without embedding reconstruction loss: In this approach, we do not add the embedding reconstruction loss to the downstream task loss. The models are, however, initialized from pretrained components, and trained end-to-end for 5 epochs.

5   Results and Analysis

Table 1 summarizes the impact of various word embedding compression approaches on the downstream IRER metric for a range of compression rates. *Compression rate* is determined by dividing the uncompressed embedding (or model) size by the compressed embedding (or model) size. We report percentage relative changes[2] to the IRER when compared to the uncompressed baseline. The results presented are for 300 dimensional embeddings. However, similar trends were observed for 100 dimensional embeddings as well.

In general, we find that task-aware approaches perform better than task-agnostic post-processing approaches. This is because the task-aware end-to-end compression tunes the compression to the downstream task, while also adjusting the task model parameters to recover performance due to lossy reconstructions. From Table 1 we also find that for any given compression rate, our proposed task-aware DCCL approach has the least degradation in predictive performance when compared to other methods.

Task-aware DCCL outperforms even the best task-agnostic compression baseline (TAg. DCCL + NLU Fine-tuning) by 39-44% at each of the different compression rates. This shows that the loss signal from the downstream task helps performance by not only adapting the task model to the compression, but also by improving compression quality. Moreover, our model at 120× compression rate performs better than the best baseline even at 60× compression rate. In other words, our models are 2× smaller than even the best baseline for a similar performance. We also find that the embedding reconstruction loss added to the downstream task loss helps improve the downstream performance, especially when the compression rate is lower i.e. when the gumbel-sampling layers are larger or more in number.

In order to understand the importance of task-aware compression, we plot the word embedding reconstruction loss (Figure 4) for the top most frequent words in our dataset. As seen in Figure 4, the average reconstruction loss for task-agnostic DCCL remains approximately constant irrespective of frequency of the words, indicating that all words are treated equally. In contrast, task-aware compression reduces the average reconstruction loss for more frequent words indicating that the network capacity is spent to learn better reconstructions for words more important for the downstream task. Note that the model used for the graph is the task-aware DCCL model without the reconstruction loss term.

We also find that DCCL-based approaches consistently performed better than their SVD counterparts, in both task-aware and task-agnostic variants. SVD-based approaches do not perform well beyond a

---

[2]Absolute numbers are not provided due to commercial confidentiality requirements.

specific compression rate (+7.99% for 1.7× compression). On investigating, we found that word embeddings were full rank matrices, with high singular values for all components, indicating that these components captured high variance.

Table 2 presents a summary of the performance of the best models for each of the approaches at around 60× embedding compression rate. 8-bit Bi-LSTM quantization helps reduce the size of the recurrent layers in the models, resulting in a net model compression ratio of 39.5× with a minimal performance degradation of 3.69% when compared to the uncompressed baseline.

6 Conclusion

In this paper, we present approaches for extreme model compression for performing natural language understanding on resource-constrained device. We use a unified multi-domain, multi-task neural model that performs DC, IC and NER for all supported domains. We discuss model compression approaches to compress the bulkiest components of our models - the word embeddings, and propose a task-aware end-to-end compression method based on deep compositional code learning where we jointly train the compression layers with the downstream task. This approach reduced word embeddings sizes to just a few MB, achieving a word-embedding compression rate of 98.4% and outperforms all other task-agnostic and task-aware embedding compression baselines. We further apply post-training 8-bit linear quantization to compress the recurrent layers of the model. These approaches together result in a net model compression rate of 97.5%, with a minimal performance degradation of 3.64% when compared to the uncompressed model baseline.

DCCL approaches are complementary to other compression approaches such as knowledge distillation and model pruning. While our work demonstrates the effectiveness of task-aware DCCL on the classification and tagging tasks in NLU, the approach itself is generic and can be applied to other NLP tasks that rely on large word-embeddings. As part of future work, we would like to explore the effectiveness of task-aware DCCL on NLP tasks such as machine translation and language modeling. We would also like to explore compression of models with advanced architectures using contextual embeddings.

References

Anish Acharya, Rahul Goel, Angeliki Metallinou, and Inderjit Dhillon. 2019. Online embedding compression for text classification using low rank matrix factorization. In *Proceedings of the AAAI Conference on Artificial Intelligence*, volume 33, pages 6196–6203.

Sajid Anwar, Kyuyeon Hwang, and Wonyong Sung. 2015. Fixed point optimization of deep convolutional neural networks for object recognition. In *2015 IEEE International Conference on Acoustics, Speech and Signal Processing (ICASSP)*, pages 1131–1135. IEEE.

Artem Babenko and Victor Lempitsky. 2014. Additive quantization for extreme vector compression. In *Proceedings of the IEEE Conference on Computer Vision and Pattern Recognition*, pages 931–938.

Dzmitry Bahdanau, Jan Chorowski, Dmitriy Serdyuk, Philemon Brakel, and Yoshua Bengio. 2016. End-to-end attention-based large vocabulary speech recognition. In *2016 IEEE international conference on acoustics, speech and signal processing (ICASSP)*, pages 4945–4949. IEEE.

Wenlin Chen, James Wilson, Stephen Tyree, Kilian Weinberger, and Yixin Chen. 2015. Compressing neural networks with the hashing trick. In *International conference on machine learning*, pages 2285–2294.

Ting Chen, Martin Renqiang Min, and Yizhou Sun. 2018. Learning k-way d-dimensional discrete codes for compact embedding representations. *arXiv preprint arXiv:1806.09464*.

Alice Coucke, Alaa Saade, Adrien Ball, Théodore Bluche, Alexandre Caulier, David Leroy, Clément Doumouro, Thibault Gisselbrecht, Francesco Caltagirone, Thibaut Lavril, et al. 2018. Snips voice platform: an embedded spoken language understanding system for private-by-design voice interfaces. *arXiv preprint arXiv:1805.10190*.

Alex Graves, Abdel-rahman Mohamed, and Geoffrey Hinton. 2013. Speech recognition with deep recurrent neural networks. In *2013 IEEE international conference on acoustics, speech and signal processing*, pages 6645–6649. IEEE.

Daniel Guo, Gokhan Tur, Wen-tau Yih, and Geoffrey Zweig. 2014. Joint semantic utterance classification and slot filling with recursive neural networks. In *2014 IEEE Spoken Language Technology Workshop (SLT)*, pages 554–559. IEEE.

Dilek Hakkani-Tr, Gokhan Tur, Asli Celikyilmaz, Yun-Nung Vivian Chen, Jianfeng Gao, Li Deng, and Ye-Yi Wang. 2016. Multi-domain joint semantic frame parsing using bi-directional rnn-lstm. In *Proceedings of The 17th Annual Meeting of the International Speech Communication Association (INTERSPEECH 2016)*. ISCA, June.

Song Han, Jeff Pool, John Tran, and William Dally. 2015. Learning both weights and connections for efficient neural network. In *Advances in neural information processing systems*, pages 1135–1143.

Geoffrey Hinton, Li Deng, Dong Yu, George E Dahl, Abdel-rahman Mohamed, Navdeep Jaitly, Andrew Senior, Vincent Vanhoucke, Patrick Nguyen, Tara N Sainath, et al. 2012. Deep neural networks for acoustic modeling in speech recognition: The shared views of four research groups. *IEEE Signal processing magazine*, 29(6):82–97.

Geoffrey Hinton, Oriol Vinyals, and Jeff Dean. 2015. Distilling the knowledge in a neural network. *arXiv preprint arXiv:1503.02531*.

Itay Hubara, Matthieu Courbariaux, Daniel Soudry, Ran El-Yaniv, and Yoshua Bengio. 2017. Quantized neural networks: Training neural networks with low precision weights and activations. *The Journal of Machine Learning Research*, 18(1):6869–6898.

Kyuyeon Hwang and Wonyong Sung. 2014. Fixed-point feedforward deep neural network design using weights+ 1, 0, and- 1. In *2014 IEEE Workshop on Signal Processing Systems (SiPS)*, pages 1–6. IEEE.

Eric Jang, Shixiang Gu, and Ben Poole. 2016. Categorical reparameterization with gumbel-softmax. *arXiv preprint arXiv:1611.01144*.

Minwoo Jeong and Gary Geunbae Lee. 2008. Triangular-chain conditional random fields. *IEEE Transactions on Audio, Speech, and Language Processing*, 16(7):1287–1302.

Armand Joulin, Edouard Grave, Piotr Bojanowski, Matthijs Douze, Hérve Jégou, and Tomas Mikolov. 2016. Fasttext.zip: Compressing text classification models. *arXiv preprint arXiv:1612.03651*.

Young-Bum Kim, Sungjin Lee, and Karl Stratos. 2017. Onenet: Joint domain, intent, slot prediction for spoken language understanding. In *2017 IEEE Automatic Speech Recognition and Understanding Workshop (ASRU)*, pages 547–553. IEEE.

Bing Liu and Ian Lane. 2016a. Attention-based recurrent neural network models for joint intent detection and slot filling. *Interspeech 2016*, Sep.

Bing Liu and Ian Lane. 2016b. Joint online spoken language understanding and language modeling with recurrent neural networks. *arXiv preprint arXiv:1609.01462*.

Ian McGraw, Rohit Prabhavalkar, Raziel Alvarez, Montse Gonzalez Arenas, Kanishka Rao, David Rybach, Ouais Alsharif, Haşim Sak, Alexander Gruenstein, Françoise Beaufays, et al. 2016. Personalized speech recognition on mobile devices. In *2016 IEEE International Conference on Acoustics, Speech and Signal Processing (ICASSP)*, pages 5955–5959. IEEE.

Abdel-rahman Mohamed, George E Dahl, and Geoffrey Hinton. 2011. Acoustic modeling using deep belief networks. *IEEE transactions on audio, speech, and language processing*, 20(1):14–22.

Vikas Raunak. 2017. Simple and effective dimensionality reduction for word embeddings. *arXiv preprint arXiv:1708.03629*.

Suman Ravuri and Andreas Stolcke. 2015. Recurrent neural network and lstm models for lexical utterance classification. In *Sixteenth Annual Conference of the International Speech Communication Association*.

Alaa Saade, Alice Coucke, Alexandre Caulier, Joseph Dureau, Adrien Ball, Théodore Bluche, David Leroy, Clément Doumouro, Thibault Gisselbrecht, Francesco Caltagirone, et al. 2018. Spoken language understanding on the edge. *arXiv preprint arXiv:1810.12735*.

Ruhi Sarikaya, Geoffrey E Hinton, and Anoop Deoras. 2014. Application of deep belief networks for natural language understanding. *IEEE/ACM Transactions on Audio, Speech, and Language Processing*, 22(4):778–784.

Raphael Shu and Hideki Nakayama. 2017. Compressing word embeddings via deep compositional code learning. *arXiv preprint arXiv:1711.01068*.

Julien Tissier, Christophe Gravier, and Amaury Habrard. 2019. Near-lossless binarization of word embeddings. In *Proceedings of the AAAI Conference on Artificial Intelligence*, volume 33, pages 7104–7111.

Vincent Vanhoucke, Andrew Senior, and Mark Z Mao. 2011. Improving the speed of neural networks on cpus.

Wei Wen, Chunpeng Wu, Yandan Wang, Yiran Chen, and Hai Li. 2016. Learning structured sparsity in deep neural networks. In *Advances in neural information processing systems*, pages 2074–2082.

Puyang Xu and Ruhi Sarikaya. 2013. Convolutional neural network based triangular crf for joint intent detection and slot filling. In *2013 ieee workshop on automatic speech recognition and understanding*, pages 78–83. IEEE.

Puyang Xu and Ruhi Sarikaya. 2014. Contextual domain classification in spoken language understanding systems using recurrent neural network. In *2014 IEEE International Conference on Acoustics, Speech and Signal Processing (ICASSP)*, pages 136–140. IEEE.

Jian Xue, Jinyu Li, and Yifan Gong. 2013. Restructuring of deep neural network acoustic models with singular value decomposition. In *Interspeech*, pages 2365–2369.

Kaisheng Yao, Geoffrey Zweig, Mei-Yuh Hwang, Yangyang Shi, and Dong Yu. 2013. Recurrent neural networks for language understanding. In *Interspeech*, pages 2524–2528.

Xiaodong Zhang and Houfeng Wang. 2016. A joint model of intent determination and slot filling for spoken language understanding. In *Proceedings of the Twenty-Fifth International Joint Conference on Artificial Intelligence*, IJCAI16, page 29932999. AAAI Press.

Aojun Zhou, Anbang Yao, Yiwen Guo, Lin Xu, and Yurong Chen. 2017. Incremental network quantization: Towards lossless cnns with low-precision weights. *arXiv preprint arXiv:1702.03044*.

Scalable Cross-lingual Treebank Synthesis for Improved Production Dependency Parsers

Yousef El-Kurdi, Hiroshi Kanayama, Efsun Sarioglu Kayi*,
Todd Ward, Vittorio Castelli, Hans Florian
IBM Research
`yousefelk@us.ibm.com, hkana@jp.ibm.com, efsun@gwu.edu`
`toddward@us.ibm.com, vittorio@us.ibm.com, raduf@us.ibm.com`

Abstract

We present scalable Universal Dependency (UD) treebank synthesis techniques that exploit advances in language representation modeling which leverage vast amounts of unlabeled general-purpose multilingual text. We introduce a data augmentation technique that uses synthetic treebanks to improve production-grade parsers. The synthetic treebanks are generated using a state-of-the-art biaffine parser adapted with pretrained Transformer models, such as Multilingual BERT (M-BERT). The new parser improves LAS by up to two points on seven languages. The production models' LAS performance improves as the augmented treebanks scale in size, surpassing performance of production models trained on originally annotated UD treebanks.

1 Introduction

Dependency parsers are important components in many NLP systems, such as language understanding, semantic role labeling and relation extraction (Marcheggiani and Titov, 2017; Zhang et al., 2018). Universal Dependencies (UD) (Nivre et al., 2020; Zeman et al., 2018) are becoming a widely accepted standard among many NLP practitioners for definition of syntactic structures and treebanks. However, production parsers require custom tokenization policies and Part of Speech (PoS) tagging, mostly dictated by supported downstream applications. In addition, parsers in production environments require fine balancing of demands for model accuracy, service performance, response time and constraints on hardware resources, making the design of an industrial-grade parser a challenge. Hereby, we introduce data augmentation techniques to improve production parsers without violating their architectural constraints.

Since their early inception, advances in language representation modeling lead to major improvements in many NLP tasks (Wang et al., 2018; Moon et al., 2019). Representations trained on various language modeling objectives, ranging from context free embeddings (Pennington et al., 2014; Mikolov et al., 2013), to deep context aware representations (Peters et al., 2018; Le and Mikolov, 2014; Devlin et al., 2018), were trained on massive amounts of unlabeled multilingual text, greatly enabling transfer learning opportunities for NLP tasks. Particularly, models such as BERT (Devlin et al., 2018), ALBERT (Lan et al., 2020), RoBERTa (Liu et al., 2019) and XLM (Lample and Conneau, 2019) employ a masked language modeling objective (Taylor, 1953) on a bidirectional self-attention encoder (Vaswani et al., 2017) enabling such models to utilize both left and right context for each word representation. Pretrained multilingual BERT (M-BERT) was used for dependency parsing in (Kondratyuk and Straka, 2019) aiming to create a single multilingual model. This work, in contrast, shows that parsing performance for a particular language can considerably be improved when adapting the biaffine-attention parser (Qi et al., 2018) with a selected set of pretrained Transformer models while training on multilingual subsets of selected language family treebanks. We then use this novel parser to project synthetic treebanks, which are used in a teacher-student technique to improve the accuracy of a fast production parser.

Our approach can generally be described as a form of model compression which was introduced by (Bucilu et al., 2006), and later reformulated and generalized as neural network knowledge distillation by

---

* Work done during AI Residency at IBM Research.

Proceedings of the 28th International Conference on Computational Linguistics: Industry Track, pages 172–178
Barcelona, Spain (Online), December 12, 2020

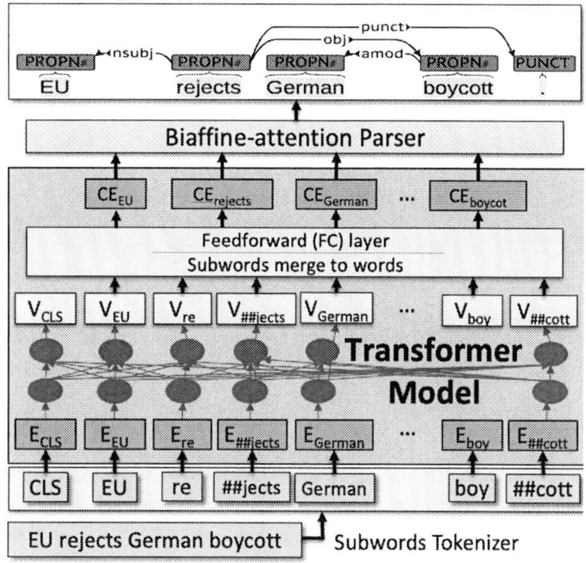

Figure 1: Transformer enhanced biaffine-attention Parser (TBAP).

(Hinton et al., 2015). However, instead of using a large number of ensemble for a teacher model, we use a deep neural network parser augmented with a large transformer-based pretrained model creating a new parser that advances the current state of the art. Since the pretrained transformer model can be trained on large amounts of unlabeled monolingual and multilingual data of various domains and languages, the teacher model gains improved generalization performance that is facilitated by both cross-lingual and cross-domain transfer learning. Our student model is a non-neural net based model that is designed to be fast and efficient in production environments.

Conventionally, parsers are trained on human annotated treebanks, which can be both costly and limited in quantity. Certain languages may not have enough annotation resources, have very small amount of data, or data that carries non-commercial licenses. In other cases, the data may be available in a specific topical domain resulting in models that perform poorly on unrelated domains. In addition, annotation errors can be common in some treebanks. To address these data challenges, we use cross-lingual transfer learning and pretrained deep contextualized representations to create a novel parser that helps generate synthetic data. We describe a production parser trained on these data, whose performance increases as the synthetic data size surpasses that of human annotated data.

2 System Description

The aim of our system is to produce synthetically labeled treebanks in order to significantly improve the accuracy of a production parser. The synthetic data will be generated using a different parser that is higher in quality. We create a new parser using two key components: the deep biaffine-attention parser (Qi et al., 2018) and a pretrained Transformer model. Not only does such a setup improve the parsing accuracy, as shown in Section 3, the incorporation of Transformer models facilitates greater degree of generalization and domain adaptation. In the sections below, we detail the training data augmentation process as well as the new parser architecture.

2.1 Transformer Enhanced Biaffine-Attention Parser

Figure 1 shows the architecture of the Transformer enhanced Biaffine-Attention Parser (TBAP). The Transformer provides contextualized word representations for each input sentence to the BiLSTM layer of the biaffine parser. First, a tokenized input sentence is passed through the Transformer. The Transformer further breaks word tokens into subword tokens. This is done in order to significantly reduce the size of the fixed vocabulary representation in the output prediction layer (Sennrich et al., 2016) overcom-

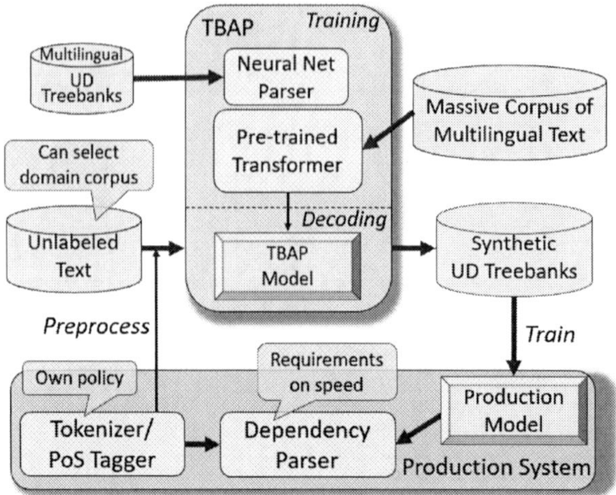

Figure 2: The data augumentation process for training a production parser.

ing the open-vocabulary problem. We then take the sum of the last four encoder layers of the Transformer as the output representation, which is comprised of the contextualized subword representations of the input sentence. Afterwords, two operations are performed on the Transformer's output. Subword token representations (also referred to as WordPiece tokens for BERT) are merged back into word-based representations. Merging the subword representations can either be done by averaging, maxpooling, or simply taking the first subword of each word. A forward Fully Connected (FC) layer is then applied to the merged subword representations, resulting in a sequence of representations aligned for each word of the tokenized input sequence.

The TBAP is trained on available treebanks. This is a process where the Transformer itself is fine-tuned by allowing backpropagation to flow through it during training. Alternatively, freezing the Transformer layers while training can help in speeding up the training process with some drop in performance.

2.2 Data Augmentation Process

Figure 2 outlines the stages of multilingual treebank generation. Initially, the TBAP is trained with available treebanks. Depending on the type of Transformer model used, two training approaches can be followed, monolingual and multilingual. Monolingual training can be applied when monolingual Transformer models are used. Pretrained monolingual Transformer models are available for certain languages, such as English, German, French, Chinese, Japanese as well as others. Performance can particularly be improved for these languages due to both the abundance and specialization of their monolingual data. Multilingual Transformer models, such as Multilingual-BERT (M-BERT) are trained on more than 100 languages. When using M-BERT, both monolingual as well as multilingual treebanks can be used to train the parser. Low resource languages can particularly benefit from cross-lingual transfer learning.

2.3 Fast Production Parser

Our production parser should meet rigid criteria regarding runtime speed; thus, we choose the arc-eager algorithm (Nivre, 2004) trained with features similar to those used by Chen and Manning (2014). To maintain UD compatability for existing downstream tasks, the tokenization and PoS tagging should not be modified even if they do not completely follow the definitions from UD. As shown in Figure 2, the dependency parser takes the tokenizer and PoS tagger's results as input in order to produce UD-based syntactic structures.

UD	Parser	Transformer Model	LAS
en_ewt	SNLP		89.50
	TBAP	BERT-base-en	91.36
		BERT-large-en	**92.38**
		Multilingual-BERT	91.14
		Albert-xxlarge	92.12
		Roberta-large	91.02
		XLM	91.56
de_gsd	SNLP		86.16
	TBAP	BERT-base-de	**87.92**
		Multilingual-BERT	87.35

Table 1: LAS results for monolingual and multilingual Transformer models.

UD	SNLP	M-BERT TBAP	Multilingual Treebanks
nl_alpino	93.76	94.01	de_gsd, en_ewt
fr_gsd	92.13	93.54	
it_isdt	92.61	94.66	es_gsd, pt_bosque
pt_bosque	90.49	91.08	it_isdt, es_gsd
es_gsd	89.94	91.72	it_vit, pt_bosque

Table 2: LAS comparison SNLP and TBAP.

UD	Tags	No-Tags
fr_gsd	72.30	84.90
pt_bosque	62.59	75.47

Table 3: TBAB LAS for unmatched tags.

3 Experiments

In this section, we show results demonstrating the improved performance of the new TBAP architecture on seven languages. We also show the effectiveness of the treebank synthesis technique when used in the augmented training of a production parser.

3.1 Transformer Enhanced Biaffine-Attention Parser (TBAP)

The TBAP is implemented by combining two key components, a pretrained Transformer model and the Biaffine-attention parser. The interface to the pretrained Transformer models was obtained from the Hugging Face's Transformers library (Wolf et al., 2019). The implementation of the biaffine-attention parser was obtained from the open-source StanfordNLP (SNLP) library (Qi et al., 2018). The FC and the subwords merge layers were added between the Transformer and the biaffine parser. We have adapted the dependency parser component to be connected to the pretrained transformers and left other components of the SNLP pipeline unchanged. In fact, since the synthetic data is being preprocessed by the production parser's tokenizer and tagger, we only needed to adapt the UD parser and disable the other modules in the pipeline. Other modifications were performed on the UD parser to make it more suitable for our task such as changing the internal dimensions of the embeddings layers, adjusting the vocabulary data structures to make them suitable for multilingual training, and controlling which UD features can be used when training the UD parser. The PyTorch[1] library is used to implement the TBAP code.

We use the standard UD treebanks v2.6 in our evaluations of the TBAP models. The UD v2.6 designated devset of each treebank is used as a tune-set for early stopping criterion during training. The UD v2.6 testset of each treebank is used for Labeled Attachment Score (LAS) results in the tables below. All models generated from UDs are for evaluation purposes. In most cases, we re-trained the SNLP (unmodified) parser in order to obtain improved baseline scores over the existing pretrained models.

Table 1 shows the LAS results of TBAP with various Tranformer models compared with the baseline SNLP parser. Since we only modified the dependency parser, we compute scores based on gold sentences, tokens and tags. Table 1 shows that TBAP with any of the used Transformer models improves LAS over the baseline parser. Also the best results are observed when using a Transformer model trained monolingually on the corresponding language. This can be attributed to the larger amount of monolingual text used to train the monolingual Transformer. Also in monolingual language models, the subword splitting models are improved, which results in less splitting and consequently improved contextual representations. For English, BERT large outperforms the base one. Table 2 shows LAS results for training on different language UDs using M-BERT TBAP. M-BERT TBAP consistently outperforms the baseline SNLP parser.

In the typical case where the synthetic data will be used to train a different production parser, it will be first preprocessed by the production parser; that is sentence segmented, tokenized, and PoS tagged by the

---

[1] https://pytorch.org

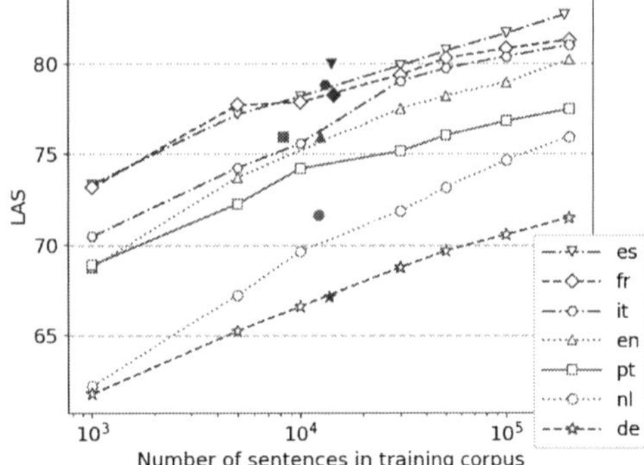

UD	UD Corpus		Synthetic	
	Size	**LAS**	**Size**	**LAS**
es_gsd	14.2k	80.0	190k	82.7
fr_gsd	14.4k	78.3	200k	81.3
it_isdt	13.0k	78.8	300k	81.6
en_ewt	12.5k	75.9	200k	80.2
pt_bosque	8.3k	75.9	300k	77.5
nl_alpino	12.3k	71.7	300k	76.7
de_gsd	13.8k	67.2	200k	71.5

Figure 3: LAS against the size of synthetic training corpora. The filled symbols (*e.g.* ▲, ★) denote the results with the corresponding UD corpora.

Table 4: Results of the production parser for seven languages on UD 2.6 testsets. Comparing training data by number of sentences and LAS (F1) for both the original UD and the larger synthetic corpora.

production parser's own pipeline. This preprocessing is required so that the parser's output is compatible with other downstream NLP tasks. This means that the preprocessing will not necessarily be consistent with the treebank from its corresponding language. In order to improve the robustness of the synthetic data under different preprocessing requirements, the M-BERT TBAP must be trained without relying on such predicted tags. Table 3 shows the effect of removing the tags while training the M-BERT TBAP for synthetic data generation. As expected the overall LAS consequently drops; however, the no-tags model's scores shows less of an impact for the preprocessed testset.

3.2 Augmented Training of the Production Parser

We retrained the production parser using the synthetic data generated by the methods above. Table 4 shows the results of seven language parsers, evaluated on the testsets of the UD corpus (v2.6) of the corresponding language. Parsers trained with the larger synthetic data showed higher LAS than those trained with the smaller manually created UD corpus data.

Figure 3 shows LAS against the size of training corpora. All languages show similar trends between parsing accuracy and corpus size; larger synthetic corpora compensate for the smaller size of the UD corpora, except for English, French and German in which the synthetic data performs nearly equally with the same size of the original UD training data.

4 Conclusion and Future Work

We presented a data augmentation approach for UD parsing that improves fast production parsers accuracy and overcomes critical treebank limitations. A new Transformer enhanced biaffine parser is used to generate scalable synthetic data. We showed that utilizing deep contextualized representations pretrained on massive multilingual corpora can be used to considerably improve parsing accuracy. In the future, we plan to extending our method to generate synthetic data for additional languages.

References

Cristian Bucilu, Rich Caruana, and Alexandru Niculescu-Mizil. 2006. Model compression. In *Proceedings of the 12th ACM SIGKDD international conference on Knowledge discovery and data mining*, pages 535–541.

Danqi Chen and Christopher D Manning. 2014. A fast and accurate dependency parser using neural networks. In *Proceedings of the 2014 conference on empirical methods in natural language processing (EMNLP)*, pages 740–750.

Jacob Devlin, Ming-Wei Chang, Kenton Lee, and Kristina Toutanova. 2018. BERT: pre-training of deep bidirectional transformers for language understanding. *CoRR*, abs/1810.04805.

Geoffrey Hinton, Oriol Vinyals, and Jeff Dean. 2015. Distilling the knowledge in a neural network.

Dan Kondratyuk and Milan Straka. 2019. 75 languages, 1 model: Parsing universal dependencies universally. In *Proceedings of the 2019 Conference on Empirical Methods in Natural Language Processing and the 9th International Joint Conference on Natural Language Processing (EMNLP-IJCNLP)*, pages 2779–2795, Hong Kong, China, November. Association for Computational Linguistics.

Guillaume Lample and Alexis Conneau. 2019. Cross-lingual language model pretraining. *CoRR*, abs/1901.07291.

Zhenzhong Lan, Mingda Chen, Sebastian Goodman, Kevin Gimpel, Piyush Sharma, and Radu Soricut. 2020. Albert: A lite bert for self-supervised learning of language representations. *ArXiv*, abs/1909.11942.

Quoc Le and Tomas Mikolov. 2014. Distributed representations of sentences and documents. In Eric P. Xing and Tony Jebara, editors, *Proceedings of the 31st International Conference on Machine Learning*, volume 32 of *Proceedings of Machine Learning Research*, pages 1188–1196, Bejing, China, 22–24 Jun. PMLR.

Yinhan Liu, Myle Ott, Naman Goyal, Jingfei Du, Mandar Joshi, Danqi Chen, Omer Levy, Mike Lewis, Luke Zettlemoyer, and Veselin Stoyanov. 2019. Roberta: A robustly optimized BERT pretraining approach. *CoRR*, abs/1907.11692.

Diego Marcheggiani and Ivan Titov. 2017. Encoding sentences with graph convolutional networks for semantic role labeling. In *Proceedings of the 2017 Conference on Empirical Methods in Natural Language Processing*, pages 1506–1515, Copenhagen, Denmark, September. Association for Computational Linguistics.

Tomas Mikolov, Ilya Sutskever, Kai Chen, Greg S Corrado, and Jeff Dean. 2013. Distributed representations of words and phrases and their compositionality. In C. J. C. Burges, L. Bottou, M. Welling, Z. Ghahramani, and K. Q. Weinberger, editors, *Advances in Neural Information Processing Systems 26*, pages 3111–3119. Curran Associates, Inc.

Taesun Moon, Parul Awasthy, Jian Ni, and Radu Florian. 2019. Towards lingua franca named entity recognition with bert. *ArXiv*, abs/1912.01389.

Joakim Nivre, Marie-Catherine de Marneffe, Filip Ginter, Jan Hajič, Christopher D. Manning, Sampo Pyysalo, Sebastian Schuster, Francis Tyers, and Daniel Zeman. 2020. Universal Dependencies v2: An evergrowing multilingual treebank collection. In *Proceedings of The 12th Language Resources and Evaluation Conference*, pages 4034–4043, Marseille, France, May. European Language Resources Association.

Joakim Nivre. 2004. Incrementality in deterministic dependency parsing. In *Proceedings of the workshop on incremental parsing: Bringing engineering and cognition together*, pages 50–57.

Jeffrey Pennington, Richard Socher, and Christopher D. Manning. 2014. Glove: Global vectors for word representation. In *Empirical Methods in Natural Language Processing (EMNLP)*, pages 1532–1543.

Matthew Peters, Mark Neumann, Mohit Iyyer, Matt Gardner, Christopher Clark, Kenton Lee, and Luke Zettlemoyer. 2018. Deep contextualized word representations. In *Proceedings of the 2018 Conference of the North American Chapter of the Association for Computational Linguistics: Human Language Technologies, Volume 1 (Long Papers)*, pages 2227–2237, New Orleans, Louisiana, June. Association for Computational Linguistics.

Peng Qi, Timothy Dozat, Yuhao Zhang, and Christopher D. Manning. 2018. Universal dependency parsing from scratch. In *Proceedings of the CoNLL 2018 Shared Task: Multilingual Parsing from Raw Text to Universal Dependencies*, pages 160–170, Brussels, Belgium, October. Association for Computational Linguistics.

Rico Sennrich, Barry Haddow, and Alexandra Birch. 2016. Neural machine translation of rare words with subword units. In *Proceedings of the 54th Annual Meeting of the Association for Computational Linguistics (Volume 1: Long Papers)*, pages 1715–1725, Berlin, Germany, August. Association for Computational Linguistics.

Wilson L. Taylor. 1953. "cloze procedure": a new tool for measuring readability. *Journalism & Mass Communication Quarterly*, 30:415–433.

Ashish Vaswani, Noam Shazeer, Niki Parmar, Jakob Uszkoreit, Llion Jones, Aidan N Gomez, Ł ukasz Kaiser, and Illia Polosukhin. 2017. Attention is all you need. In I. Guyon, U. V. Luxburg, S. Bengio, H. Wallach, R. Fergus, S. Vishwanathan, and R. Garnett, editors, *Advances in Neural Information Processing Systems 30*, pages 5998–6008. Curran Associates, Inc.

Alex Wang, Amanpreet Singh, Julian Michael, Felix Hill, Omer Levy, and Samuel Bowman. 2018. GLUE: A multi-task benchmark and analysis platform for natural language understanding. In *Proceedings of the 2018 EMNLP Workshop BlackboxNLP: Analyzing and Interpreting Neural Networks for NLP*, pages 353–355, Brussels, Belgium, November. Association for Computational Linguistics.

Thomas Wolf, Lysandre Debut, Victor Sanh, Julien Chaumond, Clement Delangue, Anthony Moi, Pierric Cistac, Tim Rault, R'emi Louf, Morgan Funtowicz, and Jamie Brew. 2019. Huggingface's transformers: State-of-the-art natural language processing. *ArXiv*, abs/1910.03771.

Daniel Zeman, Filip Ginter, Jan Hajič, Joakim Nivre, Martin Popel, and Milan Straka. 2018. CoNLL 2018 Shared Task: Multilingual Parsing from Raw Text to Universal Dependencies. In *Proceedings of the CoNLL 2018 Shared Task: Multilingual Parsing from Raw Text to Universal Dependencies*, Brussels, Belgium.

Yuhao Zhang, Peng Qi, and Christopher D. Manning. 2018. Graph convolution over pruned dependency trees improves relation extraction. In *Proceedings of the 2018 Conference on Empirical Methods in Natural Language Processing*, pages 2205–2215, Brussels, Belgium, October-November. Association for Computational Linguistics.

An Industry Evaluation of Embedding-based Entity Alignment

Ziheng Zhang[1]*, **Jiaoyan Chen**[2]*, **Xi Chen**[1]*†,
Hualuo Liu[1], **Yuejia Xiang**[1], **Bo Liu**[1], **Yefeng Zheng**[1]
[1]Tencent Jarvis Lab, Shenzhen, China
[2]Department of Computer Science, University of Oxford, UK
{zihengzhang, jasonxchen}@tencent.com, jiaoyan.chen@cs.ox.ac.uk
lhl18@mails.jlu.edu.cn, {yuejiaxiang, raymanliu, yefengzheng}@tencent.com

Abstract

Embedding-based entity alignment has been widely investigated in recent years, but most proposed methods still rely on an ideal supervised learning setting with a large number of unbiased seed mappings for training and validation, which significantly limits their usage. In this study, we evaluate those state-of-the-art methods in an industrial context, where the impact of seed mappings with different sizes and different biases is explored. Besides the popular benchmarks from DBpedia and Wikidata, we contribute and evaluate a new industrial benchmark that is extracted from two heterogeneous knowledge graphs (KGs) under deployment for medical applications. The experimental results enable the analysis of the advantages and disadvantages of these alignment methods and the further discussion of suitable strategies for their industrial deployment.

1 Introduction

Knowledge graphs (KGs), such as DBpedia (Auer et al., 2007), Wikidata (Vrandečić and Krötzsch, 2014) and YAGO (Suchanek et al., 2007) are playing an increasingly important role in various applications such as question answering and search engines. The construction of KGs usually includes several components, such as Named Entity Recognition (NER) (Li et al., 2018), Relation Extraction (RE) (Zhang et al., 2019a), and Knowledge Correction (Chen et al., 2020). However, the content of an individual KG is often incomplete, leading to a limited knowledge coverage especially in supporting applications of a specific domain (Färber et al., 2018; Demartini, 2019). One widely adopted solution is to merge multiple KGs (e.g., an enterprise KG with fine-grained knowledge of a specific domain and a general-purpose KG with an extensive coverage) with the assistance of an alignment system which discovers cross-KG mappings of entities, relations, and classes (Otero-Cerdeira et al., 2015; Yan et al., 2016).

Embedding-based *entity alignment* has recently attracted more attention due to the popularity of KGs with big data (i.e. a large number of facts) such as Wikidata. Traditional alignment systems such as PARIS (Suchanek et al., 2011) and LogMap (Jiménez-Ruiz and Grau, 2011), which usually reply on lexical matching and semantic reasoning (e.g., for checking the violation of relation domain and range), are believed to be weak in utilizing the contextual semantics especially the graph structure of such large KGs. To address this problem, some novel embedding-based methods have been proposed with the employment of different KG embedding methods such as TransE (Bordes et al., 2013) and Graph Neural Networks (GNNs) (Scarselli et al., 2008) as well as some algorithms from active learning (Berrendorf et al., 2020), multi-view learning (Zhang et al., 2019b) and so forth.

We find all these embedding-based entity alignment methods rely upon *seed mappings* for supervision or semi-supervision in training. They are usually evaluated by benchmarks extracted from DBpedia, Wikidata and YAGO, all of which are constructed from the same source, namely Wikipedia. These methods typically build their models with 30% (or even higher) of all the ground-truth mappings, and the training and validation sets are randomly extracted, sharing the same distribution as the test set.

---

*The first three authors contributed equally.
†Xi Chen is the corresponding author.

Proceedings of the 28th International Conference on Computational Linguistics: Industry Track, pages 179–189
Barcelona, Spain (Online), December 12, 2020

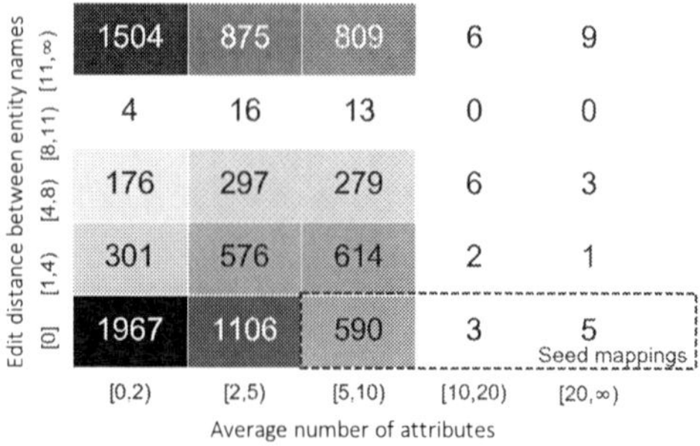

Figure 1: Distribution of mappings of two sampled medical KGs. The horizontal axis denotes the average number of attributes and the vertical axis denotes the edit distance between entity names.

In industrial applications, however, such seed mappings require not only expertise but also much human labour for annotation, especially when the two large KGs come from totally different sources. Even though a small number of seed mappings can be annotated, they are usually biased in comparison with the remaining for prediction with respect to entity name, attribute, graph structure and so on. Figure 1 shows the distribution of all the mappings of two sampled medical KGs from Tencent Technology (cf. Section 3.1 for more details), with two dimensions – the similarity between names of mapping entities and the average attribute number of mapping entities. When we directly invited experts or utilized downstream applications to annotate mappings, the annotated mappings, which could act as the seed mappings for training, usually lie in the bottom right area (seen in the red block in Figure 1) with high name similarity and large attribute number. Thus, we believe that the seed mappings should have the following characteristics to make the evaluation of these supervised methods more practical. Firstly, the seed mappings should take a small proportion of all the mappings, such as 3% that is far smaller than previous experimental settings. Secondly, the seed mappings should be biased towards the remaining mappings with respect to the entity name similarity, the average attribute number, or both. Such biases are ignored in the current evaluation.

In this work, we systematically evaluate four state-of-the-art embedding-based KG alignment methods in an industrial context. The experiment is conducted with one open benchmark from DBpedia and Wikidata, one industry benchmark from two enterprise medical KGs with heterogeneous contents, and a series of seed mappings with different sizes, name biases and attribute biases. The performance analysis considers all the testing mappings as well as different splits of them for fine-grained observations. These methods are also compared with the traditional system PARIS. To the best of our knowledge, this is the first work to evaluate and analyse the embedding-based entity alignment methods from an industry perspective. We find that these methods heavily rely on an ideal supervised learning setting and suffer from a dramatic performance drop when being tested in an industrial context. Based on these results, we can further discuss the possibility to deploy them for real-world applications as well as suitable sampling strategies. The new benchmark and seed mappings can also benefit the research community for future studies, which are publicly available at `https://github.com/ZihengZZH/industry-eval-EA`.

2　Preliminaries and Related Work

2.1　Embedding-based Entity Alignment

Most of the existing embedding based entity alignment methods conform to the following three-step paradigm: *(i)* embedding the entities into a vector space by either a translation based method such as TransE (Bordes et al., 2013) or Graph Neural Networks (GNNs) (Scarselli et al., 2008) which recursively aggregate the embeddings of the neighbouring entities and relations; *(ii)* mapping the entity embeddings in the space of one KG to the space of another KG by learning a transformation matrix, sharing embeddings of the aligned entities, or swapping the aligned entities in the associated triples; *(iii)* searching an entity's counterpart in another KG by calculating the distance in the embedding space using metrics such as the cosine similarity. It is worth noting that the role of the seed mappings mainly lies in the second step, aligning the embeddings of two KGs.

Specifically, we evaluate four methods, namely **BootEA** (Sun et al., 2018), **MultiKE** (Zhang et al., 2019b), **RDGCN** (Wu et al., 2019) and **RSN4EA** (Guo et al., 2018). On the one hand, they have achieved the state-of-the-art performance in the ideal supervised learning setting, according to their own evaluation and the benchmarking study (Sun et al., 2020); on the other hand, they are representative to different techniques that are widely used in the literature. The four methods are introduced as follows.

BootEA is a semi-supervised approach, which adopts translation-based models for embedding and iteratively trains a classifier by bootstrapping. In each iteration, new likely mappings are labelled by the classifier and those causing no conflict are added for training in the following iteration.

MultiKE utilizes multi-view learning to encode different semantics into the prediction model. Specifically, three views are developed for entity names, entity attributes, and the graph structure respectively.

RDGCN applies a GCN variant, Dual-Primal GCN (Monti et al., 2018) to utilize the relation information in KG embedding. It can better utilize the graph structure than those translation-based embedding methods, especially in dealing with the triangular structures.

RSN4EA firstly generates biased random walks (long paths) of both KGs as sequences and then learns the embeddings by a sequential model named Recurrent Skipping Network. The seed mappings here are used to generate cross-KG walks, thus exploring correlations between cross-KG entities.

2.2 Seed Mappings

As far as we know, the current embedding-based entity alignment methods mostly rely on the seed mappings, whose roles are introduces in Section 2.1, for supervised or semi-supervised learning. Specially, we can consider some heuristic rules with, for example, string and attribute matching to generate the seed mappings, as done by the method IMUSE (He et al., 2019), but the impact of the seed mappings is similar and the study of such impact also benefit the distant supervision methods.

In addition, although some semi-supervised approaches such as BootEA (Sun et al., 2018) and SEA (Pei et al., 2019) are less dependent on the seed mappings, their performance, when trained on a small set of seed mappings, may vary from data to data and be impacted by the bias of the seed mappings.

In the own evaluation of these methods and the recent benchmark study (Sun et al., 2020), 20% and 10% of all the ground truth mappings are used for training and validation respectively, and more importantly, they are randomly selected, thus maintaining the same distribution as the testing mappings. This violates the real-world scenarios in the industry, where annotating seed mappings is costly and the annotated ones are usually biased, as discussed in Section 1. Actually, there are relatively few studies that investigate the seed mappings and those investigated only consider the proportion of the seeding mappings. In Sun et al. (2018) and Wu et al. (2019), the proposed methods are evaluated with the proportion of the seed mapping for training varying from 10% to 40%. However, the minimum proportion still leads to a very large number (e.g., 1.5K) of seed mappings in aligning two big KGs.

2.3 Benchmarks

The current benchmarks used to evaluate the embedding-based methods are typically extracted from DBpedia, Wikidata, and YAGO. They can be divided into two categories. The first includes those for cross-lingual entity alignment such as DBP15K (Sun et al., 2017) and WK3l60k (Chen et al., 2018), both of which support the alignment between DBpedia entities in English and DBpedia entities in other languages, such as Chinese or French. These benchmarks usually only support within KG alignment. The second includes those for cross-KG entity alignment such as DWY15K (Guo et al., 2018) and DWY100K (Sun et al., 2018), both of which are for the alignment between DBpedia and Wikidata/YAGO.

As discussed in Sun et al. (2020), entities in these aforementioned benchmarks have a significant bias in comparison with normal entities in the original KGs; for example, those DBpedia entities in WK3l60k have an average connection degrees of 22.77 while that of all DBpedia entities is 6.93. Thus, these benchmarks are not representative to DBpedia, Wikidata, and YAGO. To address this issue, Sun et al. (2020) proposed a new iterative degree-based sampling algorithm to extract new benchmarks for both cross-lingual entity alignment within DBpedia and cross-KG entity alignment between DBpedia and Wikidata/YAGO. Although the new benchmarks are more representative w.r.t. the graph structure, the entity labels defined by *rdfs:label* are removed, which include important name information, which makes them less representative to real-world alignment contexts. More importantly, since DBpedia, Wikidata, and YAGO are constructed from the same source Wikipedia, the entities for alignment often have similar names, attributes, or graph structures. These benchmarks are therefore not applicable in the real-world alignment which in contrast, aims at KGs from different sources to complement each other. To make an industry evaluation, we constructed a new benchmark from two industrial KGs (cf. Section 3.1).

It is worth noting that Ontology Alignment Evaluation Initiatives[1] has been organizing a KG track since 2018 (Hertling and Paulheim, 2020). The benchmarks used are those KGs extracted from several different Wikis from Fandom;[2] for example, starwars-swg is a benchmark with mappings between two KGs from Star Wars Wiki and Star Wars Galaxies Wiki. Multiple benchmarks are adopted, but their scales are limited; for example, 4 out of 5 used in 2019 have less than 2K entity mappings. As the two KGs of a benchmark are about two hubs of one concrete topic (such as the movie and the game of Star Wars), the entity name has little ambiguity and becomes a superior indicator for alignment. Thus they are not suitable industrial benchmarks for evaluating the embedding-based entity alignment methods.

3 Data Generation

3.1 Industrial Benchmark

To evaluate the embedding-based entity alignment methods in an industrial context as discussed above, we first extract a benchmark from two real-world medical KGs for alignment. One KG is built upon multiple authoritative medical resources, covering fine-grained knowledge about illness, symptoms, medicine, etc. It is deployed to support applications such as question answering and medical assistants in our company. However, some of its entities have incomplete information with many important attributes missing, which limits its usability. We extract around 10K such entities according to the feedback from downstream applications. They are then aligned with another KG to improve the information completeness. That KG is extracted from the information boxes of Baidu Baike[3], the largest Chinese encyclopedia, via NLP techniques (such as NER and RE) as well as some handcrafted engineering work. We refer to crowdsourcing for annotating the mappings, where heuristic rules, based on labels and synonyms, and a friendly interface for supporting information check are used for assistance. Finally, we obtain $9,162$ one-to-one entity mappings, based on which one sub-KG is extracted from one original KG. Specifically, the sub-KG includes triples that are composed of entities associated with these mappings. The two sub-KGs are named as MED and BBK, and the new benchmark is named as MED-BBK-9K.

Table 1: Statistics of MED-BBK-9K and D-W-15K.

Benchmark	KGs	#Entities	Relation			Attribute		
			#Relations	#Triples	Degree	#Attributes	#Triples	Degree
MED-BBK-9K	MED	9,162	32	158,357	34.04	19	11,467	1.24
	BBK	9,162	20	50,307	10.96	21	44,987	4.91
D-W-15K	DBpedia	15,000	167	73,983	8.55	175	66,813	4.40
	Wikidata	15,000	121	83,365	10.31	457	175,686	11.59

More details of MED-BBK-9K and another benchmark D-W-15K, which is extracted by the iterative degree-based sampling method under the setting of V2 (Sun et al., 2020), are shown in Table 1, where # denotes the number and degree is the rate between the triple number and the entity number. Statistics of relation triples and attribute triples are separately presented in Table 1. Note that a relation is equivalent to an object property connecting two entities, while an attribute is equivalent to a data property associating an entity with a value of some data type. Two entity mapping examples of MED-BBK-9K are depicted in Figure 2, where the green ellipses indicate the aligned entities across KGs, the white ellipses and the solid arrows indicate their relation triples[4], and the red rectangles and the dash arrows indicate the attributes

---

182

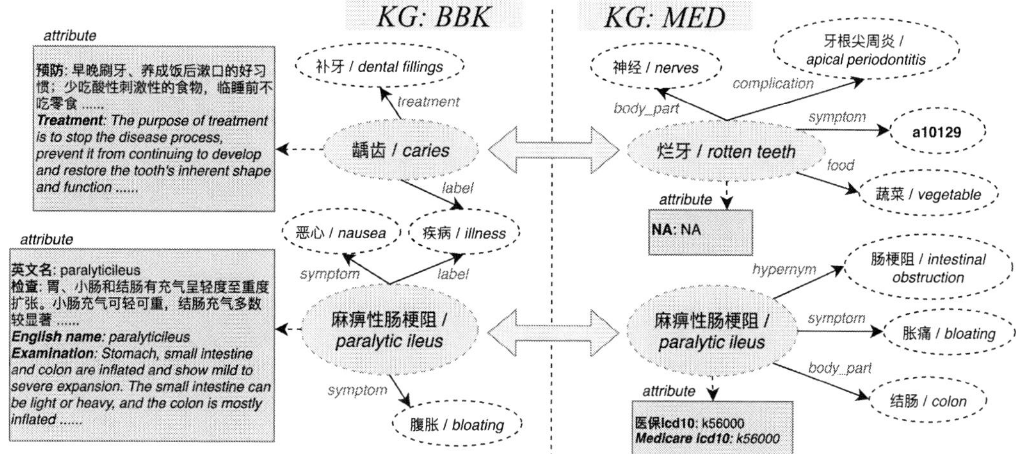

Figure 2: Two mapping examples from MED-BBK-9K with *English translations*.

which include normal values, sentence descriptions, and noisy values. Through the statistics and the examples, we can conclude that KGs in MED-BBK-9K are quite different from KGs in D-W-15K, with a higher relation degree, less attributes, higher heterogeneity, etc.

3.2 Biased Seed Mappings

Besides the industrial benchmark, we also develop a new approach to extract biased seed mappings for the industrial context. We first introduce two variables, s_{name} and n_{attr}, in which s_{name} is the normalized Levenshtein Distance – an edit distance metric (Navarro, 2001) in $[0, 1]$ for the name strings of entities of each mapping, and n_{attr} is the average number of attributes of entities of each mapping. For Wikidata entities in D-W-15K, we use the attribute values of *P373* and *P1476* as the entity names, while for DBpedia entities we use the entity name in the URI. Note when one or both entities in one mapping has multiple names, we adopt the two names leading to the highest similarity i.e., the lowest s_{name}. Meanwhile, all the names are pre-processed before calculating s_{name}: dash, underline and backslash are replaced by the white space, punctuation marks are removed, letters are transformed into lowercase.

With s_{name} and n_{attr} calculated, we divide all the mappings into three different splits according to either the name similarity or the attribute number. For the name similarity, the mappings are divided into "same" (s_{name}=1.0), "close" ($s_{name} < 1.0$) and "different" (s_{name} is NA, i.e., no valid entity name) for both MED-BBK-9K and D-W-15K. From the attribute number, the mappings are divided into "large" ($n_{attr} \geq k_1$), "medium" ($k_2 \leq n_{attr} < k_1$) and "small" ($n_{attr} < k_2$), where (k_1, k_2) are set to $(5, 2)$ for MED-BBK-9K and set to $(10, 4)$ for D-W-15K.

We further develop an iterative algorithm to extract the seed mappings with name bias and attribute bias. Its steps are shown below, with two inputs, namely the set of all the mappings $\mathcal{M}_{all}$ and the size of seed mappings N_{seed}, and one output, namely the set of biased seed mappings $\mathcal{M}_{seed}$.

(1) Initialize the biased seed mapping set $\mathcal{M}_{seed}$.

(2) Assign each mapping in $\mathcal{M}_{all}$ a score: $z = z_{name} + z_{attr}$, where z_{name} is set to 4, 3 and 1 if the mapping belongs to "same", "close" and "different" respectively, and z_{attr} is set to 4, 3 and 1 if the mapping belongs to "large", "medium" and "small" respectively. Note all the mappings in $\mathcal{M}_{all}$ are assigned a score of 8, 7, 6, 5, 4, or 2.

(3) Move the mapping with the highest score in $\mathcal{M}_{all}$ to $\mathcal{M}_{seed}$. Randomly select one if multiple mappings in $\mathcal{M}_{all}$ have the highest score.

(4) Check whether the size of $\mathcal{M}_{seed}$ has been equal to or larger than N_{seed}. If yes, return $\mathcal{M}_{seed}$; otherwise, go to Step (3).

With the above procedure, we can also obtain seed mappings that are name biased alone by setting $z = z_{name}$, and seed mappings that are attribute biased alone by setting $z = z_{attr}$. Note the seed mappings $\mathcal{M}_{seed}$ include both training mappings and validation mappings. In our experiment, the former occupies two thirds of the seed mappings while the latter occupies one third.

4 Evaluation

4.1 Experimental Setting

We first conduct the overall evaluation (cf. Section 4.2). Specifically, the methods BootEA, MultiKE, RDGCN, and RSN4EA are tested under *(i)* an **industrial context** where the seed mappings are both name biased and attribute biased, and the rate of training (resp. validation) mappings is 2% (resp. 1%), and *(ii)* an **ideal context** where the seed mappings are randomly selected without bias, and the rate of training (resp. validating) mappings is 20% (resp. 10%). We then conduct ablation studies where three impacts of seed mappings are independently analysed, including size, name bias, and attribute bias.

In both overall evaluation and ablation studies, we calculate metrics Hits@1, Hits@5, and mean reciprocal rank (MRR) with all the testing mappings. For each testing mapping, the candidate entities (i.e., all the entities in the target KG) are ranked according to their predicted scores; Hits@1 (resp. Hits@5) is the ratio of testing mappings whose ground truths are ranked in the top 1 (resp. 5) entities; MRR is the Mean Reciprocal Rank of the ground truth entity. Meanwhile, to further analyse the impact of the seed mappings on different kinds of testing mappings, we divide the testing mappings into two three-fold splits – "same", "close" and "different" from the name biased aspect, and "small", "medium" and "large" from the attribute biased aspect.

We adopt the implementation of BootEA, MultiKE, RDGCN, and RSN4EA in OpenEA, while their hyperparameters are adjusted with the validation set. Specifically, the batch size is set to 5000, the early stopping criterion is set to when Hits@1 begins to drop on the validation set (checked for every 10 epochs), the maximum epoch number is set to 2000. As MultiKE and RDGCN utilize literals, the word embeddings are produced using a fastText model pre-trained on Wikipedia 2017, UMBC webbase corpus and statmt.org news dataset[5]. To run them on MED-BBK-9K, the Chinese word embeddings are obtained via a medical-specific BERT model pre-trained on big medical corpora from Tencent Technology[6].

We finally compare these embedding-based methods with a state-of-the-art conventional system named PARIS (v0.3)[7], which is based on lexical matching and iterative calculation of relation mappings, class mappings and entity mappings with their correlations (logic consistency) considered (Suchanek et al., 2011). We adopt the default hyperparameters to PARIS. Note that PARIS requires no seed mappings for supervision. As PARIS does not rank all the candidate entities, we use Precision, Recall, and F1-score as the evaluation metrics. For the embedding-based methods, Hits@1 in our one-to-one mapping evaluation is equivalent to Precision, Recall, and F1-score.

4.2 Overall Results

Table 2 presents the results of those embedding-based methods on both D-W-15K and MED-BBK-9K under the ideal context and the industrial context. On one hand, we find that *the performance of all four methods dramatically decreases when the testing context is moved from the ideal to the industrial*, the latter of which is much more challenging with less and biased seed mappings. For instance, considering the average MRR of all four methods on all testing mappings, it drops from 0.661 to 0.262 on D-W-15K, and from 0.327 to 0.118 on MED-BBK-9K.

We also find that the performance decreasement, when moved to the industrial context, varies from one testing mapping split to another. Considering the name-based splitting, the decreasement is the most significant on the "different" split, and the least significant on the "same" split. Take MultiKE on MED-BBK-9K as an example, its Hits@1 decreases by 11.4%, 13.9% and 43.1% on the "same", "close" and "different" splits respectively. As a result, the methods including MultiKE and RDGCN perform better on the "same" split than on the "close" and the "different" splits. It meets our expectations because the seed mappings in the industrial context, which are sampled with a bias toward those with high name

---

[5]The word embeddings are publicly available at `https://fasttext.cc/docs/en/english-vectors.html`.
[6]Other Chinese word embedding models would suffice to reproduce comparable experimental results.
[7]`http://webdam.inria.fr/paris/`

Table 2: Overall results under the ideal context and the industrial context.

		Models	Name-based Splits (Hits@1)			Attr-based Splits (Hits@1)			All Test Mappings		
			Same	Close	Diff.	Small	Medium	Large	Hits@1	Hits@5	MRR
D-W-15K	Ideal	BootEA	.868	.902	.753	.721	.821	.912	.818	.922	.864
		MultiKE	.977	.254	.216	.306	.488	.661	.484	.622	.554
		RDGCN	.942	.934	.305	.330	.734	.827	.629	.756	.687
		RSN4EA	.718	.718	.579	.536	.663	.753	.650	.797	.717
	Industrial	BootEA	.050	.051	.023	.015	.040	.053	.037	.092	.065
		MultiKE	.968	.211	.036	.086	.392	.605	.368	.426	.402
		RDGCN	.945	.872	.062	.110	.559	.759	.489	.539	.514
		RSN4EA	.055	.060	.029	.016	.046	.065	.043	.092	.068
MED-BBK-9K	Ideal	BootEA	.334	.259	.328	.388	.201	.265	.307	.495	.399
		MultiKE	.342	.173	.072	.269	.149	.195	.213	.367	.289
		RDGCN	.550	.217	.056	.348	.270	.242	.306	.425	.365
		RSN4EA	.238	.121	.226	.277	.114	.095	.195	.311	.253
	Industrial	BootEA	.006	.003	.003	.006	.002	.004	.004	.011	.010
		MultiKE	.303	.149	.041	.218	.137	.155	.179	.322	.252
		RDGCN	.329	.083	.013	.201	.120	.086	.158	.239	.199
		RSN4EA	.008	.002	.007	.009	.001	.000	.005	.013	.011

similarity, are close to the "same" split and far away from the "different" split. However, such a regular is violated when we consider the attribute based seed mapping splits. As to MultiKE tested by the "large" testing split, its performance decreasement when moved to the industrial context is the least significant on D-W-15K, which is as expected, but is the most significant on MED-BBK-9K. Thus MultiKE performs worse on the "large" testing split than on the "small" testing split (with 28.9% lower Hits@1), although the former is more close to the seed mappings. One potential explanation is that mappings with more than 5 attributes (mappings in the "large" testing split) in MED-BBK-9K tend to have duplicate attributes and some attribute values are sentences that cannot be fully utilized by these methods.

On the other hand, we find that *MultiKE and RDGCN are much more robust than BootEA and RSN4EA in the industrial context on both D-W-15K and MED-BBK-9K.* Although MultiKE and RDGCN do not perform as well as in the ideal context, their performance is still promising. Specifically, when measured by all testing mappings, RDGCN performs better than MultiKE on D-W-15K with 27.9% higher MRR and 32.9% higher Hits@1 but performs worse than MultiKE on MED-BBK-9K with 21.3% lower MRR and 11.7% lower Hits@1. The performance of BootEA and RSN4EA is poor in the industrial context; their Hits@1, Hits@5, and MRR on all testing mappings or on different testing splits are all lower than 0.1 for both benchmarks. This means that they are very sensitive to the size or/and the bias of the seed mappings (cf. Section 4.3 for the ablation studies).

4.3 Ablation Studies

4.3.1 Size Impact

According to the results in the "With No Bias" setting in Table 3, we can first find that *MultiKE and RDGCN are relatively robust w.r.t. a small training mapping size.* Considering their Hits@1 measured on all the test mappings, it drops slightly from 0.484 to 0.394 and from 0.629 to 0.513 respectively when the training mapping size is significantly reduced from 20% to 2%. On the "same" testing split and the "large" testing split, both of which are close to the training mappings, the performance of MultiKE and RDGCN keeps relatively good when trained by 2% of the mappings. On the other two splits, which are more biased compared with training mappings, the performance of MultiKE and RDGCN, however, decreases more significantly.

Furthermore, we find that *BootEA and RSN4EA are very sensitive to the training mapping size.* For example, the MRR of BootEA (resp. RSN4EA) measured by all the test mappings decreases from 0.864 to 0.153 to 0.051 (resp. from 0.717 to 0.132 to 0.044) when the training ratio decreases from 20% to 4% to 2%. The performance of BootEA is beyond our expectation as it is a semi-supervised algorithm designed for a limited number of training samples. Besides all the testing mappings, their performance decreasement is also quite significant on different testing splits including the "same" and the "large".

Table 3: Results on D-W-15K under different settings (biases and ratios) of the training mappings.

Settings		Models	Name-based Splits (Hits@1)			Attr-based Splits (Hits@1)			All Test Mappings		
			Same	Close	Diff.	Small	Medium	Large	Hits@1	Hits@5	MRR
With No Bias	20%	BootEA	.868	.902	.753	.721	.821	.912	.818	.922	.864
		MultiKE	.977	.254	.216	.306	.488	.661	.484	.622	.554
		RDGCN	.942	.934	.305	.330	.734	.827	.629	.756	.687
		RSN4EA	.718	.718	.579	.536	.663	.753	.650	.797	.717
	4%	BootEA	.104	.087	.092	.078	.085	.125	.096	.206	.153
		MultiKE	.975	.217	.088	.159	.440	.647	.413	.513	.467
		RDGCN	.898	.901	.123	.163	.650	.754	.521	.605	.562
		RSN4EA	.105	.079	.090	.071	.078	.133	.093	.168	.132
	2%	BootEA	.024	.022	.030	.028	.025	.026	.026	.073	.051
		MultiKE	.969	.224	.048	.121	.428	.639	.394	.463	.433
		RDGCN	.900	.895	.107	.147	.636	.761	.513	.582	.547
		RSN4EA	.026	.015	.031	.025	.021	.034	.027	.056	.044
With Name Bias	20%	BootEA	.871	.903	.535	.433	.737	.931	.645	.766	.702
		MultiKE	.978	.285	.080	.085	.230	.318	.185	.335	.261
		RDGCN	.966	.924	.111	.102	.521	.641	.362	.441	.402
		RSN4EA	.786	.800	.391	.271	.631	.827	.514	.656	.580
	4%	BootEA	.733	.817	.358	.260	.633	.802	.554	.642	.596
		MultiKE	.971	.209	.053	.106	.391	.609	.358	.427	.398
		RDGCN	.956	.905	.076	.128	.616	.766	.491	.544	.518
		RSN4EA	.198	.185	.087	.051	.147	.228	.138	.228	.182
	2%	BootEA	.031	.031	.017	.013	.026	.034	.024	.069	.049
		MultiKE	.968	.195	.027	.093	.389	.617	.360	.404	.388
		RDGCN	.956	.871	.056	.118	.606	.766	.490	.541	.516
		RSN4EA	.054	.040	.027	.018	.036	.062	.038	.084	.062
With Attribute Bias	20%	BootEA	.789	.870	.397	.365	.734	.936	.565	.682	.621
		MultiKE	.975	.358	.078	.145	.488	.767	.334	.459	.398
		RDGCN	.946	.919	.109	.168	.667	.885	.437	.522	.479
		RSN4EA	.725	.816	.309	.277	.670	.834	.489	.611	.546
	4%	BootEA	.704	.819	.337	.245	.622	.800	.538	.611	.574
		MultiKE	.972	.211	.057	.115	.430	.662	.383	.450	.421
		RDGCN	.922	.908	.091	.133	.630	.798	.501	.557	.529
		RSN4EA	.192	.213	.083	.056	.156	.228	.141	.232	.185
	2%	BootEA	.052	.051	.023	.017	.039	.059	.037	.094	.066
		MultiKE	.968	.229	.041	.104	.426	.651	.384	.449	.421
		RDGCN	.915	.895	.078	.122	.615	.785	.497	.552	.524
		RSN4EA	.068	.073	.027	.018	.050	.083	.049	.096	.073

4.3.2 Name Bias Impact

The name bias impact from the seed mappings can be evaluated by comparing the settings of "With Name Bias" and "With No Bias" in Table 3. With 20% of the mappings for training, MultiKE and RDGCN are more negatively impacted by the name bias than BootEA and RSN4EA; for example, the MRR measured by all the test mappings drops by 52.9% and 41.5% respectively, while that of BootEA and RSN4EA drops only by 18.8% and 19.1% respectively.

Specifically, considering different testing mapping splits, the negative impact on MultiKE and RDGCN mainly lies in the "different" split (e.g., Hits@1 of RDGCN drops from 0.305 to 0.111), while the impact on the "same" and the "close" is relatively limited and sometimes even positive. Mappings in the "different" testing split, which have very biased distributions as the training mappings, are sometimes known as long-tail prediction cases, and the above phenomena indicate their universality and difficulty in an industrial context. On the other hand, the negative impact of name bias on MultiKE and RDGCN is still much less than the negative impact of the small size on BootEA and RSN4EA. Thus when impacted by both small size (using 2% of the mappings for training) and name bias, BootEA and RSN4EA perform poorly. It is also worth noting that RDGCN outperforms other methods by a large margin in the "close" split under all the experimental settings; for example, its Hits@1 reaches 0.905 and 0.871 with 4% and 2% training mappings while that for MultiKE is only 0.209 and 0.195 respectively.

4.3.3 Attribute Bias Impact

The attribute bias impact from the seed mappings can be analysed by comparing the settings of "With Attribute Bias" and "With No Bias" in Table 3. When 20% mappings are used for training, its negative impact on all four methods are similar; for example, the MRR of BootEA, MultiKE, RDGCN, and RSN4EA on all testing mappings drops by 28.1%, 28.2%, 30.3%, and 23.8% respectively. The negative impact is especially significant on the "small" testing split as its average attribute number is very different from that of the training mappings. In contrast, the impact on the "large" testing split is even positive for all four methods; for example, when trained by 4% of the mappings, Hits@1 of RSN4EA increases from 0.133 to 0.228. Especially, under the attribute bias, reducing the training mappings size has limited impact on MultiKE and RDGCN, and sometimes the impact is even positive that for example, the MRR of MultiKE and RDGCN on all testing mappings increases by 5.8% and 10.4% respectively when the training mapping ratio drops from 20% to 4%.

4.4 Comparison with Conventional System

This subsection presents the comparison between the embedding-based methods and the conventional system PARIS (Suchanek et al., 2011), using results in both Table 2 and Table 4. Note that Hits@1 in Table 2 is equivalent to Precision, Recall, and F1-Score in our evaluation with all one-to-one mappings. Although PARIS is an automatic system needing no supervision, it still significantly outperforms all four embedding based methods on both D-W-15K and MED-BBK-9K. On MED-BBK-9K whose two KGs for alignment are more heterogeneous, the outperformance of PARIS is even more significant; for example, the F1-score of PARIS is 0.493, while the best of the four embedding based methods is 0.307 (resp. 0.179) when trained in the ideal (resp. industrial) context. One important reason we believe is that these embedding based methods ignore the overall reasoning and the correlation of different mappings, while PARIS utilizes them by an iterative workflow and makes holistic decisions. Luckily, such reasoning capability and inter-mapping correlations can also be considered in the embedding-based methods, and this indicates an important direction for the future industrial application.

Table 4: Results of conventional system PARIS on D-W-15K and MED-BBK-9K.

Benchmark	Metric	Name-based Splits			Attr-based Splits			All Test Mappings
		Same	Close	Diff.	Small	Medium	Large	
	Precision	.998	.998	.900	.868	.980	.999	.956
D-W-15K	Recall	.980	.975	.707	.640	.914	.987	.846
	F1-score	.989	.986	.792	.736	.946	.993	.898
	Precision	.910	.669	.778	.879	.748	.757	.814
MED-BBK-9K	Recall	.505	.248	.258	.417	.293	.314	.354
	F1-score	.649	.362	.388	.565	.422	.444	.493

5 Conclusion and Discussion

In this study, we evaluate four state-of-the-art embedding-based entity alignment methods in an ideal context and an industrial context. To build the industrial context, a new benchmark is constructed with two real-world KGs, and the seed mappings are extracted with different sizes, different name and attribute biases. The performance of all four investigated methods dramatically drops when being evaluated in the industrial context, worse than the traditional system PARIS. Specifically, MultiKE and RDGCN are sensitive to name and attribute bias but robust to seed mapping size; BootEA and RSN4EA are extremely sensitive to seed mappings size, leading to poor performance in the industrial context.

Based on these empirical findings, we recommend to specifically design strategies in crowdsourcing (with tool assistance) to ensure the annotated samples in different name and attribute distributions. In our industrial context where the seed mappings are limited, adopting MultiKE or RDGCN is demonstrated to be a better choice for cross-KG alignments. Meanwhile, as mentioned in the evaluation, an ensemble of such embedding based methods with PARIS or LogMap, which considers the correlation between mappings, is also a promising solution for better performance. Finally, we also plan to develop a robust model that can utilize a complete set of attributes, especially those with values of textual descriptions.

References

Sören Auer, Christian Bizer, Georgi Kobilarov, Jens Lehmann, Richard Cyganiak, and Zachary Ives. 2007. DBpedia: A nucleus for a web of open data. In *The Semantic Web*, pages 722–735. Springer.

Max Berrendorf, Evgeniy Faerman, and Volker Tresp. 2020. Active learning for entity alignment. *arXiv Preprint*, January. arXiv: 2001.08943.

Antoine Bordes, Nicolas Usunier, Alberto Garcia-Duran, Jason Weston, and Oksana Yakhnenko. 2013. Translating embeddings for modeling multi-relational data. In *Advances in Neural Information Processing Systems*, pages 2787–2795.

Muhao Chen, Yingtao Tian, Kai-Wei Chang, Steven Skiena, and Carlo Zaniolo. 2018. Co-training embeddings of knowledge graphs and entity descriptions for cross-lingual entity alignment. In *Proceedings of the 27th International Joint Conference on Artificial Intelligence*, pages 3998–4004.

Jiaoyan Chen, Xi Chen, Ian Horrocks, Erik B. Myklebust, and Ernesto Jimenez-Ruiz. 2020. Correcting knowledge base assertions. In *Proceedings of The Web Conference 2020*, WWW '20, page 1537–1547, New York, NY, USA. Association for Computing Machinery.

Gianluca Demartini. 2019. Implicit bias in crowdsourced knowledge graphs. In *Companion Proceedings of The 2019 World Wide Web Conference*, pages 624–630.

Michael Färber, Frederic Bartscherer, Carsten Menne, and Achim Rettinger. 2018. Linked data quality of DBpedia, Freebase, OpenCyc, Wikidata, and YAGO. *Semantic Web*, 9(1):77–129.

Lingbing Guo, Zequn Sun, Ermei Cao, and Wei Hu. 2018. Recurrent skipping networks for entity alignment. *arXiv Preprint arXiv:1811.02318*.

Fuzhen He, Zhixu Li, Yang Qiang, An Liu, Guanfeng Liu, Pengpeng Zhao, Lei Zhao, Min Zhang, and Zhigang Chen. 2019. Unsupervised entity alignment using attribute triples and relation triples. In *International Conference on Database Systems for Advanced Applications*, pages 367–382. Springer.

Sven Hertling and Heiko Paulheim. 2020. The knowledge graph track at OAEI. In *European Semantic Web Conference*, pages 343–359. Springer.

Ernesto Jiménez-Ruiz and Bernardo Cuenca Grau. 2011. LogMap: Logic-based and scalable ontology matching. In *International Semantic Web Conference*, pages 273–288. Springer.

Jing Li, Aixin Sun, Jianglei Han, and Chenliang Li. 2018. A Survey on Deep Learning for Named Entity Recognition. *CoRR*, abs/1812.09449.

Federico Monti, Oleksandr Shchur, Aleksandar Bojchevski, Or Litany, Stephan Günnemann, and Michael M Bronstein. 2018. Dual-primal graph convolutional networks. *arXiv preprint arXiv:1806.00770*.

Gonzalo Navarro. 2001. A guided tour to approximate string matching. *ACM Computing Surveys*, 33(1):31–88.

Lorena Otero-Cerdeira, Francisco J. Rodríguez-Martínez, and Alma Gómez-Rodríguez. 2015. Ontology matching: A literature review. *Expert Systems with Applications*, 42(2):949–971.

Shichao Pei, Lu Yu, Robert Hoehndorf, and Xiangliang Zhang. 2019. Semi-supervised entity alignment via knowledge graph embedding with awareness of degree difference. In *The World Wide Web Conference*, pages 3130–3136.

Franco Scarselli, Marco Gori, Ah Chung Tsoi, Markus Hagenbuchner, and Gabriele Monfardini. 2008. The graph neural network model. *IEEE Transactions on Neural Networks*, 20(1):61–80.

Fabian M. Suchanek, Gjergji Kasneci, and Gerhard Weikum. 2007. YAGO: A core of semantic knowledge. In *Proceedings of the 16th international conference on World Wide Web*, pages 697–706.

Fabian M. Suchanek, Serge Abiteboul, and Pierre Senellart. 2011. PARIS: Probabilistic alignment of relations, instances, and schema. *Proceedings of the VLDB Endowment*, 5(3).

Zequn Sun, Wei Hu, and Chengkai Li. 2017. Cross-lingual entity alignment via joint attribute-preserving embedding. In *International Semantic Web Conference*, pages 628–644. Springer.

Zequn Sun, Wei Hu, Qingheng Zhang, and Yuzhong Qu. 2018. Bootstrapping entity alignment with knowledge graph embedding. In *Proceedings of the 27th International Joint Conference on Artificial Intelligence*, pages 4396–4402.

Zequn Sun, Qingheng Zhang, Wei Hu, Chengming Wang, Muhao Chen, Farahnaz Akrami, and Chengkai Li. 2020. A Benchmarking Study of Embedding-Based Entity Alignment for Knowledge Graphs. *Proc. VLDB Endow.*, 13(12):2326–2340, July.

Denny Vrandečić and Markus Krötzsch. 2014. Wikidata: A Free Collaborative Knowledge Base. *Communications of the ACM*, 57(10):78–85.

Yuting Wu, Xiao Liu, Yansong Feng, Zheng Wang, Rui Yan, and Dongyan Zhao. 2019. Relation-aware entity alignment for heterogeneous knowledge graphs. In *Proceedings of the 28th International Joint Conference on Artificial Intelligence*, pages 5278–5284.

Zhuang Yan, Li Guoliang, and Feng Jianhua. 2016. A survey on entity alignment of knowledge base. *Journal of Computer Research and Development*, 1:165–192.

Ningyu Zhang, Shumin Deng, Zhanlin Sun, Guanying Wang, Xi Chen, Wei Zhang, and Huajun Chen. 2019a. Long-tail relation extraction via knowledge graph embeddings and graph convolution networks. In *Proceedings of the 2019 Conference of the North American Chapter of the Association for Computational Linguistics: Human Language Technologies, Volume 1 (Long and Short Papers)*, pages 3016–3025, Minneapolis, Minnesota, June. Association for Computational Linguistics.

Qingheng Zhang, Zequn Sun, Wei Hu, Muhao Chen, Lingbing Guo, and Yuzhong Qu. 2019b. Multi-view knowledge graph embedding for entity alignment. In *Proceedings of the 28th International Joint Conference on Artificial Intelligence*, pages 5429–5435.

Learning Domain Terms - Empirical Methods to Enhance Enterprise Text Analytics Performance

Gargi Roy, Lipika Dey, Mohammad Shakir, Tirthankar Dasgupta

TCS Research and Innovation, India

{roy.gargi,lipika.dey,m.shakir,dasgupta.tirthankar}@tcs.com

Abstract

Performance of standard text analytics algorithms are known to be substantially degraded on consumer generated data, which are often very noisy. These algorithms also do not work well on enterprise data which has a very different nature from News repositories, storybooks or Wikipedia data. Text cleaning is a mandatory step which aims at noise removal and correction to improve performance. However, enterprise data need special cleaning methods since it contains many domain terms which appear to be noise against a standard dictionary, but in reality are not so. In this work we present detailed analysis of characteristics of enterprise data and suggest unsupervised methods for cleaning these repositories after domain terms have been automatically segregated from true noise terms. Noise terms are thereafter corrected in a contextual fashion. The effectiveness of the method is established through careful manual evaluation of error corrections over several standard data sets, including those available for hate speech detection, where there is deliberate distortion to avoid detection. We also share results to show enhancement in classification accuracy after noise correction.

1 Introduction

A large part of enterprise data such as customer complaints, project management documents, client communications, risk reports, emails etc. can yield rich insights and actionable intelligence for improving enterprise processes. Text analytics solutions built with machine learning methods are employed for the purpose. There is also an increasing emphasis on robotic process automation (RPA) where the focus is on automating enterprise tasks. Tasks that do not involve active or deep cognitive abilities can be easily automated. However, if the task involves reading and interpretation of natural language content, there is a need to ensure that the machine interpretation of the content is correct before it is sent for automated downstream processing. Given the volumes of such communication that is generated for any organization in the digital world, automated processing of these content is beneficial to ensure timely response to customers, timely resolution and also generate predictive insights.

It is well known that the quality of analytical results are largely dependent on the quality of input text. Thus, all text analytics solutions are preceded by pre-processing and cleaning steps to help yield better results. Though there exists standard dictionaries to aid the cleaning process, these dictionaries are not enough to deal with enterprise text, due to their inherent nature. Internal enterprise communication like emails, messages etc. contains words, abbreviations and terms that are very domain specific and not available in general purpose thesaurus. This includes terms representing names of services, products or groups etc. They also contain lots of acronyms that are not always standardized but get created along the way and are well understood within a community. Consumer generated content like customer complaints, call logs etc. additionally contain spelling distortions of products and services. The real problem posed by enterprise text is that there is no demarcation between domain words that "appear to be noisy" since they are not part of a dictionary and words that are "true noise" because it is wrongly spelt or misused. For any cleaning to be done for enterprise text, it has to be first resolved whether the unrecognizable term

Proceedings of the 28th International Conference on Computational Linguistics: Industry Track, pages 190–201
Barcelona, Spain (Online), December 12, 2020

is an enterprise term or a true noise term and then correct it appropriately. Without this, even word or phrase frequencies cannot be generated properly.

Interestingly we found a resonance of the problem while dealing with social media text. There are not only spelling mistakes and typos - but deliberate distortion of traditional words and phrases while writing them down. Some of these are conventional short-hands and some are done to avoid online detection. This is one of the problems faced by online hate speech detectors. Hence detecting and replacing these words with the correct word is an important problem in that scenario also.

Let us illustrate the different types of errors and their significance through the following examples.

- Let us assume a certain repository refers often to the name "Flipkart." This is a non-dictionary term, but may be recognized as a Named Entity if written correctly in a text. However, the more crucial issue is detecting distortions of it in consumer generated text. While analyzing a set of customer communications involving the organization, we found the following mentions - "fipkart", "flipcart", "flipcardt" etc. which are easily recognizable as erroneous mentions of the name by a human, but not by a computer. The performance of many downstream text analytics solutions are affected by this since the frequency computation of the term is affected by these errors.

- The second example will show that not all errors are with respect to named entities only. Analysis of a text repository for a bank yields the following different references to the term "account" - accont, acnt, act etc. While the last two are abbreviated references, the first one is a typo. A standard spell-correction algorithm employing shortest edit-distance based correction corrects "accont" as "accost", which is obviously wrong. Such situations need context-based correction.

- In a third example, we take the case of a specific issue where there is no error, but only "apparent error" introduced by enterprise terms. In a particular repository, a term called "gess" appears very often. This is a company internal term for the organization, referring to a particular service. There are multiple references to this term in the company's internal text repository. A standard spell checker would tend to correct this term to "guess" - which would once again be incorrect.

- Social media abounds in such examples. The terms such as "ebloa", "snapchatt" which are mis-spellings of non-dictionary yet important, non-noise terms - "ebola" and "snapchat" respectively, where the first one is a virus name that caused epidemic and the second one is a multimedia messaging application. Where as, "presidrnt" is a misspelling of the dictionary term "president". In hate speech data, we found lots of spelling distortions of an Internet slang - "lmao", such as "lmfao", "lmaoooooo", "lmmfao", "lmfaooo", and our method was able to capture them.

The above examples illustrate that text cleaning, especially while dealing with enterprise text, involves segregation of non-dictionary domain terms from true noise words. Since terminologies differ within groups in an enterprise, and also evolve over time, one time dictionary creation is not a solution. As products, processes and tasks evolve over time, the terminologies also change. Hence, there is a need for designing methods that can ingest a given enterprise or social media repository and clean it correctly in an efficient fashion before embarking on a text analytics journey.

In this work, we propose novel unsupervised method that can analyze any enterprise document repository and clean it effectively. Initially, all words in the repository are segregated into two categories - dictionary and non-dictionary words. Any standard linguistic dictionary can be used for the purpose. The key idea is to segregate the domain words from true noise words and then correct the noise words accordingly. The domain words, when recognized, get included in the dictionary. The remaining noise words are corrected incrementally. The whole act is achieved via an iterative method using the following two steps of Analyze and Infer.

Analyze - This step analyzes the word distributions of the dictionary and non-dictionary words and classifies them into different frequency groups.

Infer - This step facilitates the movement of non-dictionary words to the dictionary and finally correct the noise words, based on word structures, their frequency groups and contextual similarities. Similarities between words are established using multiple distance functions that combine traditional edit-distance based measures, phoneme based similarity as well as contextual similarities computed using word embeddings that are created for each repository. The word2vec skip-gram model (Mikolov et al., 2013) is used for creating the word embeddings. The vector dimensions are adjusted to take care of small repositories.

The above steps are applied in an iterative fashion till no movement of word is possible. The validity and effectiveness of the method are established through multiple experiments. We also provide performance analysis of the proposed algorithms to show that the proposed method is highly efficient. Thus it can be used to clean any new repository before applying text analytics algorithms to achieve the best results.

2   Related Work

Most of the noise detection and correction work for text center around spellchecking and spelling correction (Subramaniam et al., 2009). A standard way to do so is to use edit distance based methods (Ristad and Yianilos, 1998) with respect to a standard dictionary. Other methods include noisy channel model for detecting misspellings (Brill and Moore, 2000; Lai et al., 2015), linguistic and statistical approach (Schierle et al., 2008) and graph based approach to correct spelling errors in domain-centric search for emails (Bao et al., 2011). Neural word embeddings for context sensitive spelling correction have also been considered in (Gong et al., 2019; Fivez et al., 2017; Flor, 2012). The work by (Flor et al., 2019) also uses orthographic and phonetic similarity and contextual information for automatic spelling correction. However, none of the above works consider segregation of non-dictionary domain words from noise. Hence, most of these methods are not applicable for enterprise text which deserves special attention. In (Li et al., 2018), methods have been specified for acronym disambiguation in enterprise text. However other errors are not addressed in this. In (Lu et al., 2019), methods are presented for correcting errors contextually, based on neighboring words and edit distance measures. However, these also do not take care of enterprise domain words and consider them as errors. Although, (Shakir et al., 2019) has attempted to identify domain terms over true error terms based on the assumption that domain and correct terms are more uniformly distributed across documents, this assumption does not work always. It is often found that some spelling mistakes also occur uniformly and with high frequency. Thus there is a need to work on unsupervised, robust and repeatable methods for detecting true noise terms in enterprise text and correct them. This work addresses that need.

3   Enterprise text cleaning - a prelude to analytics

Consumer generated text is inherently noisy. Hence all text analytics tasks start with mandatory pre-processing and cleaning steps as follows. These texts are found to be fraught with random use of upper cases, spaces and punctuation marks. Social media has also given rise to a set of new terms that represent phrases, and may be expressed by a non-traditional combination of characters. For example, the term 4u represents "for you". Certain errors are also introduced due to the underlying digital platforms. Incorrect conversion of characters to symbols or icons fall under this category. Rule based pre-processors are implemented to remove the above noises. After the removal of unwanted elements, the text is tokenized using the modified twitter tokenizer (Dey and Roy, 2015). The modification is done in such a manner that it suits the semi-formal enterprise text tokenization. Afterwards, stop words are removed and words are normalised to lower case letters. The next step is to perform noise correction, which involves recognition of noisy terms and restoring them to their correct forms. The next section explains the proposed steps to do this for enterprise text.

4   Correcting Noisy terms in Enterprise Text

In this section we present the details of the proposed noise correction algorithm. To begin with, all tokens in the text repository are segregated into two groups, dictionary and non-dictionary, depending on whether they belong to a standard language dictionary or not. Each token is tagged with their category. Further, the frequency of each token is computed and ranked.

For a token w, its frequency is given by the number of occurrence of w in the corpus and is denoted by w_f. The rank of w, denoted by w_r, is determined by ordering the words in descending order of frequency. The word with highest frequency gets rank one, second highest will have rank two and so on.

Let the set of tokens that are detected as dictionary words be indicated by $\mathbf{V}$, and the set of non-dictionary tokens be denoted by $\mathbf{N}$. The task now is to reduce the cardinality of $\mathbf{N}$ by identifying tokens that can be moved from it to $\mathbf{V}$. This happens iteratively through the following actions.

Analyze - This step analyzes the relative frequencies and ranks of tokens and classifies them into different frequency groups.

Infer - This step checks the similarities among tokens in terms of their structures, frequency groups and contextual presence in text. The final movement is inferred based on a weighted similarity computed using multiple distance functions that combine traditional edit-distance based measures, phoneme based similarity as well as contextual similarities computed using word embeddings that are created for each repository.

The next two subsections describe the above steps in detail.

4.1 Analyzing word frequencies in Repository

Zipf's law (Zipf, 1932; Manning et al., 1999) states that the log-log plot of the rank versus frequency of words in a corpus usually follows a linear pattern. This distribution is computed from all words in the corpus. Usually, the noise words occur less frequently, hence their individual frequencies are very low. Consequently, it is assumed that their ranks are very high and are concentrated at the tail of the distribution. Though the Zipf's law has been found to represent word distributions from different kinds of repositories like News, story books etc. quite well, we observed that it fails to represent enterprise text correctly. The distributions shown in top row of Figure 1 shows this. The distortion is noticeable towards the side of high-frequency or top ranked words. Delving deeper, we found that the dictionary and non-dictionary words show two different trends. While the relative occurrence of high-frequency dictionary words in the repository is less than expected, the relative occurrence of high-frequency non-dictionary words is much higher than expected. The log-log plot of Zipf's distribution for dictionary and non-dictionary words plotted separately in middle and lower bands of Figure 1 illustrate this. The reason obviously lies in the fact that enterprise content, especially parts of it, are far more repetitive in nature and hence the pattern breaks. Intuition therefore suggests that, analyzing the repository to find the tokens that cause the deviation from linearity should be a good idea to spot domain words.

Given that the repository is already segregated into two sets of tokens $\mathbf{V}$ and $\mathbf{N}$, this is accomplished as follows:

(a). For each set $\mathbf{V}$ and $\mathbf{N}$, the zipf's distribution is plotted using log-log scale of rank w_r versus frequency w_f of the tokens belonging to the set. A linear regression minimizing the standard error, is then applied, to determine the best fitting line to both the distributions independently. The standard error is defined by the absolute value of the difference between predicted and actual values.

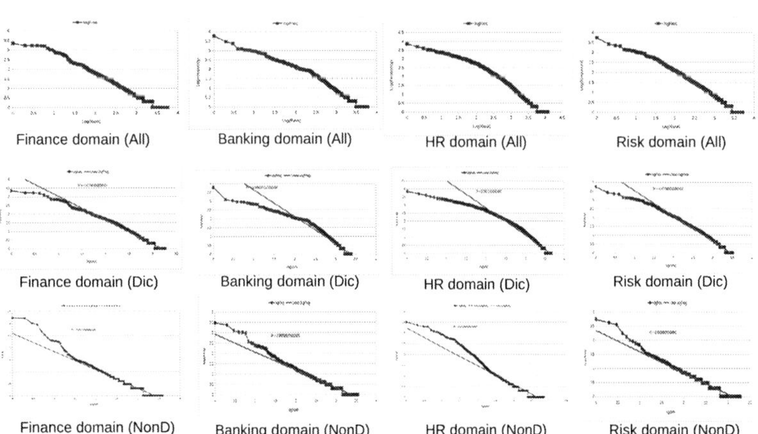

Figure 1: Log-log plot of rank versus frequency of all, dictionary (Dic) and non-dictionary (NonD) terms in four different enterprise content.

The next task was to find natural groups of words in each set, such that all words in a group are likely to belong to the same error category, indicating that these words would have similar kind of distribution and hence similar roles to play in the repository. The natural breaks are determined using Jenks optimization method (Jenks, 1977) on the standard error between the regression line and the original frequency curve. The optimal number of natural breaks are determined by applying Jenks optimization method. Jenks optimization method, which is also called goodness of variance fit (GVF), divides a set of values into groups or classes such that intra-class variance is minimized while maximizing inter-class variance. The value of GVF ranges from 0 to 1 where 0 signifies "No Fit" and 1 signifies "Perfect Fit". The value of GVF, denoted by η, is a parameter fed to the process which helps the process terminate with an optimal number of classes within an acceptable error limit. The method starts with class number equal to 2, and then iteratively increases the number of classes till the error limit crosses η. In our implementations, we have used 0.85 as the value of η. Function 2 depicts this.

Jenks natural breaks, also called classes play a very useful role in determining the role of words within a repository. Each class in each set is assigned a unique identity. In this work, the class associated to the highest-frequency side of the regression line is assigned the identity 1 in both the cases. Thus, for both the sets $\mathbf{V}$ and $\mathbf{N}$, it can be stated that a word belonging to Jenk's class i in that set appears with higher frequency in the repository than a word belonging to class $i + 1$ in the same set. Each token w in each set can now be associated to a class identity, based on the class it belongs to. For token w, its class is denoted by w_i^S, where the superscript S takes value $\mathbf{V}$ or $\mathbf{N}$, depending on the parent set of w and i denotes the class number.

The class identity of a token w is utilized by the inference process to decide whether the token should be retained as a domain term or be declared a noise and hence corrected.

4.2 Inferring nature of words - segregating true noise terms from domain terms

As stated in the earlier section, the objective of the inference mechanism is to determine whether a non-dictionary token is a wrongly spelt dictionary word or a domain word, that should be retained as it is. The decision is taken based on the Jenk's class of the noise word and also it's similarity to other words in the repository.

Traditional noise detection and correction methods have assumed all wrongly spelt words in a text to be errors and attempt to correct them using similarity measures with known words. Some commonly used similarity measures used in literature are Jaro-Winkler distance (Jaro, 1989; Winkler, 1990), Fuzzy distance, Levenshtein distance (Levenshtein, 1966), orthographic similarity (Weber, 1970; Van Orden, 1987) etc. Table 1 shows comparative results for these measures. It is seen that Jaro-Winkler distance is the most effective measure.

A second type of similarity that can be used to determine the likelihood of two tokens being same is based on phonetic similarity. Phonetic similarity plays a very important role in enterprise text which contains many non-familiar words. These words are often spelt wrong, but have a spelling which "sounds similar" to the original word. This is the reason why we see many occurrences of "Flipcart" for the term is "Flipkart". There are standard ways of deriving the phonetic representation of any word and thereafter compute pair-wise phonetic similarity of words. For phonetic representation (denoted by $ph(w)$), we have used Double Metaphone algorithm (Philips, 2000) that has a large code length and we used up to 25, which we have found to be sufficient for encoding the words.

However none of the above measures can capture contextual similarity or dissimilarity of words. So we propose to use word vectors to capture context of words. Since enterprise text has non-standard vocabulary, no existing model serves the purpose and word vectors have to be built for every repository. Unlike, other embedding generation models, our focus is on building word vectors from small repositories rather than large ones.

To obtain the word vectors for all words in a repository, we start with a pre-processed tokenized corpus from which stop words are removed. The word2vec (Mikolov et al., 2013) algorithm which uses the skip-gram model is utilized to generate the word vectors. The word vector for token w is denoted by w^v. The skip-gram model is specifically chosen since it has shown to work well for small data and can represent rare terms also. We have used window size of five and vector dimension of 20, as the vocabulary sizes for each repository is not very large. The dimension can be varied.

While word embeddings can encapsulate context, character embeddings for words have been found to help in recognizing new words in a vocabulary that have partial overlaps with known words. They play an important role in recognizing different lemmatizations of the same form, different entities of the same type by recognizing a particular suffix or prefix and so on. To generate the character embedding vectors (denoted by w^c), we have used a standard Chars2vec library (Engineering, 2019) that comes with a pre-trained model with different vector dimensions. We have used 50 as the dimension since the vocabularies are small.

For a word w_i, its vector embedding is denoted by w_i^v and it's character vector is denoted by w_i^c. We have used cosine similarity as a measure to compute similarity between two vectors.

4.3 Recognizing domain terms and correcting Noise terms

We now present an approach that can detect domain terms in a completely unsupervised way and further assist in cleaning the repository text by correcting noise. It may be noted that, domain terms need not be only non-dictionary, terms like "account" or "banks" are domain terms for financial content.

In order to achieve this, the first step is to characterize the words as belonging to one of the following four categories, which are maintained as different sets - *i*) Dictionary domain term - denoted by $\mathbf{D}'$, *ii*) Non–dictionary domain term denoted by $\mathbf{D}''$, *iii*) A noise word which is a distortion of a dictionary term $\mathbf{E}'$ and *iv*) A noise term which is a distortion of a non-dictionary term $\mathbf{E}''$.

The movement of words from one set to another set occurs throughout the process until no more movement

Noise	Correction	JW	FD	LD	OS
acccessible	accessible	0.98	26	1	0.97
calculte	calculate	0.98	16	1	0.88
accont	account	0.97	10	1	0.87
acconut	account	0.97	11	2	0.83
accout	account	0.97	13	1	0.87
balnce	balance	0.97	7	1	0.85
adjustmentrs	adjustment	0.97	28	2	0.77
hoildays	holidays	0.97	5	2	0.85
cahnged	changed	0.96	2	2	0.57
ccorrect	correct	0.96	17	1	0.7
deatils	details	0.96	5	2	0.83
calim	claim	0.94	2	2	0.49
ddeduction	deduction	0.94	23	1	0.72
excempeted	exempted	0.91	18	2	0.82
apalgamation	amalgamation	0.9	5	1	0.72
kundly	kindly	0.9	1	1	0.55
aalowance	allowance	0.86	2	1	0.66

Table 1: Different spelling similarities between a pair of words. JW: Jaro-Winkler distance, FD: Fuzzy distance, LD: Levenshtein Distance, OS: Orthographic Similarity

is possible. As edit distance based spelling similarity is computationally expensive, we have designed our algorithm in a way that it reduces time and computational complexity and does not compute similarity measures for all possible pair of words which takes $O(n^2)$, instead efficiently we choose to compute through hierarchically relaxing constraints.

Step 1 - All terms in Jenk's class 1 of $\mathbf{V}$ are declared as dictionary domain terms and are added to $\mathbf{D}'$. Terms like *account, bank, appraisal, mobile, customer* etc. come under this category, depending on which dataset is being analyzed.

Step 2 - Target now is to detect domain words from the set of non-dictionary terms $\mathbf{N}$. For each $w_i \in \mathbf{N}$, it's phonetic representation $ph(w_i)$ is compared with phonetic representation of the dictionary words belonging to the set $\mathbf{V}$. Let $\mathbf{V_m} \subseteq \mathbf{V}$ such that each word $w_j \in \mathbf{V_m}$ satisfy all the following properties (a) w_j and w_i have exactly similar phonetic representation (b) $JW(w_i, w_j) > \alpha_1$ and $Sim(w_i^c, w_j^c) > \alpha_2$, where α_1 and α_2 are user controlled parameters, that are kept high.

Now we pick up the word w_j in $\mathbf{V_m}$ which has highest frequency as the candidate correction term. If the frequency of w_j is higher than frequency of w_i, then w_i is assumed to be a wrongly spelt occurrence of w_j. Hence w_i is added to $\mathbf{E}'$ with w_j marked as a correction for w_i.

However, if w_j has lower frequency than w_i, then there is a chance that w_i may be a domain word and not a wrongly spelt occurrence of w_j. However this has to be verified. The frequencies and Jenk's class numbers of w_i and w_j are considered for the purpose. Contextual similarities of the words are also checked.

Since frequencies and class numbers have different orders of magnitude, so an analysis is done (given in Function 3) on the relative difference (Törnqvist et al., 1985) of class numbers and frequencies as given in Equation 1 and Equation 2 The corresponding functions are given in Function 5 and Function 4 respectively. These equations have been designed using the sigmoid function, so that both the values remain within 0 to 1. Where, w_i^S and w_i^f denote the class number and the frequency of word w_i. $max\{x, y\}$ and $min\{x, y\}$ return the maximum and minimum of $\{x, y\}$ respectively. In Equation 2, logarithm to the base 10 is used to represent the large range of values in a compact way and also to capture the multiplicity of the large number i.e. "how large the number is in multiple", with respect to the small number.

$$d_s = \sigma(ln(\frac{max\{w_i^S, w_j^S\} - min\{w_i^S, w_j^S\}}{min\{w_i^S, w_j^S\}})), \ where \ \sigma(x) = \frac{e^x}{e^x + 1} \tag{1}$$

$$d_l = \sigma(log_{10}(max\{w_i^f, w_j^f\}) - log_{10}(min\{w_i^f, w_j^f\})), \ where \ \sigma(x) = \frac{e^x}{e^x + 1} \tag{2}$$

The higher the values of d_l and d_s, lower the possibility of them to be the same word. If d_l is higher than a user defined threshold, say θ_1, then we don't go for any further analysis and declare w_i to be a domain word which needs no correction. Hence, w_i is moved from $\mathbf{N}$ to $\mathbf{D}''$.

An example of this is a term *GESS* which is very close phonetically to *guess* but is actually a domain term. Hence it has a much higher frequency and rank than the dictionary word guess. Hence a correction would not be appropriate in this case. Rather the word should be retained as it is.

If the difference in relative frequencies between w_j and w_i are low, then we further check the value of d_s along with the cosine similarity between their word vector representations, $Sim(w_i^v, w_j^v)$. If $d_s > \theta_2$ and $Sim(w_i^v, w_j^v) \leq \theta_3$, then we infer that w_i is a domain term. The class number of a word captures its relative significance in a repository, independent of the actual frequency values. This value is used to control the identification of unknown words in a cautious fashion by imposing the following restriction - an unknown or error word which has a higher class in $\mathbf{N}$ is not allowed to be identified as a misspelling of a word belonging to a lower class in $\mathbf{V}$ indiscriminately. This is the key feature of the proposed work that enables detection of domain words correctly. The cosine similarity of word vectors further establish the contextual similarity, since the neighbours of a word are taken into consideration while constructing the embeddings. Occurrences of terms like *STURCTURE* which is a very common typos for the intended term STRUCTURE are corrected at this stage since both the terms have same phonetic representation and also a substantial overlap in their context.

Step 3 - Now, we concentrate on the words in $\mathbf{N}$ which do not have an exact but approximately phonetically similar counterpart in $\mathbf{V}$. Some of these words may also be domain words while others may be errors. $\mathbf{N}$ is alphabetically sorted based on the phonetic representation strings by representing it as a Red-Black tree which is self-balancing binary search tree and sorted based on the natural ordering of the keys (here, phonetic representation string of the words are the key). All words that have matching phonemes in first two positions are grouped together through obtaining the sub tree (in-order traversal) whose key ranges are specified by the above condition i.e. matching of first two characters. Function 6 depicts this where ξ is the approximation constraint and set to two in this work (as we are matching first two characters of the phonetic representations).

Thus $\mathbf{N}$ gets divided into several smaller subsets. Figure 2 shows a portion of the above mentioned tree and the smaller subsets obtained are shown in curly brackets along with their matched phonemes in first two positions. For each subset $\mathbf{N_j} \in \mathbf{N}$, we now compute pair-wise Jaro-wrinkler

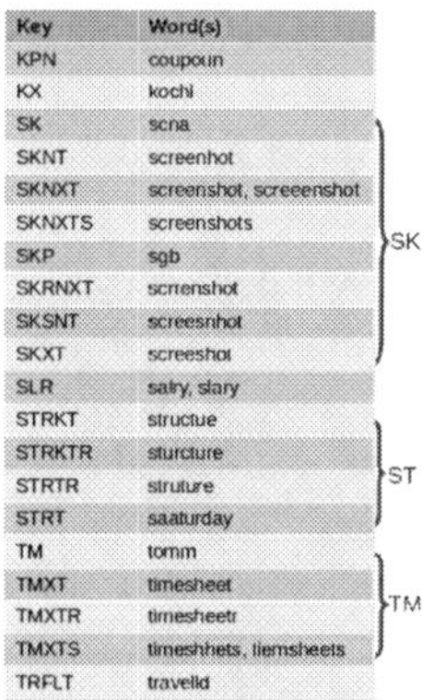

Key	Word(s)	
KPN	coupoun	
KX	kochi	
SK	scna	
SKNT	screenhot	
SKNXT	screenshot, screeenshot	
SKNXTS	screenshots	
SKP	sgb	SK
SKRNXT	scrrenshot	
SKSNT	screesnhot	
SKXT	screeshot	
SLR	salry, slary	
STRKT	structue	
STRKTR	sturcture	
STRTR	struture	ST
STRT	saaturday	
TM	tomm	
TMXT	timesheet	
TMXTR	timesheetr	TM
TMXTS	timeshhets, tiemsheets	
TRFLT	travelld	

Figure 2: A part of $\mathbf{N}$ as phoneme wise sorted, balanced binary search tree

distance between the words as well as between their phonetic representations, the cosine-similarities of their character and word vector representations. These measures are then used to construct tightly connected graphical components over the text representation space, such that each node in this graph may be considered as altered representations of each other. Thus, from the three subsets in Figure 2, the following three updated subsets are obtained. {*screenhot, screenshot, screeenshot, screenshots, scrrenshot, screesnhot, screeshot*}, {*structue, sturcture, struture*}, {*timesheet, timesheetr, timeshhets, tiemsheets*}. If any of these nodes now represent a word which has already been identified as a noisy representation of a dictionary word, i.e. $\in \mathbf{E}'$, then all words in this component are also moved to $\mathbf{E}'$. This is repeated for all subsets containing phonetically similar words. These words are removed from their corresponding subsets in $\mathbf{N}$. For example, from the above mentioned subsets consider the second subset, *sturcture* has been identified earlier and *structure* is suggested as correction. So, now both *struture, structue* are identified as errors with *structure* as suggested correction. Thus, the terms whose phonetic representations are not exactly same as that of any dictionary word but are typos, are corrected appropriately now.

For the remaining non-empty subsets that have cardinality greater than two, the frequency distribution of the words within the subset is generated and tested for anomaly detection using Grubbs' test (Grubbs and others, 1950). If Grubb's test detects the highest frequency word as an anomaly, then the word is considered as a domain term and is moved to $\mathbf{D}''$ while the others are considered as erroneous representations of it and moved to $\mathbf{E}''$. For subsets with two elements we apply Equation 2 which computes relative difference between the frequencies with threshold γ which is set to be 0.75 in this work, and apply the same logic as earlier to decide whether a term is a domain term and move it accordingly to $\mathbf{D}''$. Otherwise we keep it as it is in $\mathbf{N}$ since no correction can be suggested for it. Continuing from the earlier example, thus, *screenshot* and *timesheet* are now recognised as non-dictionary domain term (which are very common in many enterprise repositories) respectively from the first and third sub set and the other words are identified as misspelling of the recognised domain term and suggested correction accordingly.

Step 4 - Finally, the identified erroneous terms in $\mathbf{E}'$ and $\mathbf{E}''$ are replaced by their candidate corrections in the corpus. The entire corpus is again segregated into dictionary and non-dictionary terms (say $\mathbf{V}'$, $\mathbf{N}'$ respectively) and Jenk's classes are once again generated as earlier. Finally, the words belonging to the two highest ranked classes of $\mathbf{V}'$ are considered as domain dictionary terms and maintained as $\mathbf{D}'$ while the corresponding terms from $\mathbf{N}'$ are inferred as non-dictionary domain terms and moved to $\mathbf{D}''$. The execution of the algorithm is presented in Algorithm 1.

Algorithm 1: IdentifyCorrect

Input : Corpus tokens, $\mathbf{C}$
Output: $\mathbf{D}'$, $\mathbf{D}''$, $\mathbf{E}'$, $\mathbf{E}''$

1 $\{\mathbf{N}, \mathbf{V}\} \leftarrow$ segregate words in $\mathbf{C}$
2 **for** $w \in \mathbf{C}$ **do**
3   $\quad \{w_f, w_r, w^v, w^c, ph(w)\} \leftarrow compute\ features(w)$
4 $\mathbf{W}^{\mathbf{N}} \leftarrow$ PlotFitBreak($\mathbf{N}$)
5 $\mathbf{W}^{\mathbf{V}} \leftarrow$ PlotFitBreak($\mathbf{V}$)
6 **for** $w \in \mathbf{N}\ and\ w' \in \mathbf{V}$ **do**
7   $\quad$ Efficient phonetic match s.t. $ph(w) = ph(w')$
8   $\quad$ **if** $JW(w, w') > \alpha_1\ and\ Sim(w^c, w'^c) > \alpha_2$ **then**
9    $\quad\quad$ **if** $(w_f > w'_f)$ **then**
10    $\quad\quad\quad w_i^N \leftarrow$ get class number of w from $\mathbf{W}^{\mathbf{N}}$
11    $\quad\quad\quad w_i'^V \leftarrow$ get class number of w' from $\mathbf{W}^{\mathbf{V}}$
12    $\quad\quad\quad w_{type} \leftarrow$ AnalyseRelativeDifference($w, w', w_i^N, w_i'^V$,
13    $\quad\quad\quad w_f, w'_f, Sim(w^v, w'^v)$)
14    $\quad\quad\quad$ **if** $w_{type}\ is\ domain$ **then**
15     $\quad\quad\quad\quad \mathbf{D}'' \leftarrow w$
16    $\quad\quad\quad$ **else**
17     $\quad\quad\quad\quad \mathbf{E}' \leftarrow w$ and w' is correction for w
18 Represent $\mathbf{N}$ as phonetic representation-wise sorted balanced binary search tree
19 **for** $w \in \mathbf{N}$ **do**
20   $\quad \mathbf{A} \leftarrow$ GetApproxPhonemeMatch($w, \mathbf{N}, \xi$)
21   $\quad$ **for** $w' \in \mathbf{A}$ **do**
22    $\quad\quad$ **if** $JW(w, w') > \beta_1\ and\ Sim(w^c, w'^c) > \beta_2\ and$
23    $\quad\quad Sim(w^v, w'^v) > \beta_3\ and\ JW(ph(w), ph(w')) > \beta_4$ **then**
24     $\quad\quad\quad \mathbf{Y} \leftarrow \{w, w'\}$
25 Compute set $\mathbf{X}$ containing all such set $\mathbf{Y}$ which contains spelling wise, phonetically and contextually consistent non-dictionary terms
26 **for** $\mathbf{Z} \in \mathbf{X}$ **do**
27   $\quad$ **if** $\exists w \in \mathbf{Z}$ *s.t.* $w \in \mathbf{E}'$ **then**
28    $\quad\quad$ Move all other words of $\mathbf{Z}$ to $\mathbf{E}'$ with correction equal to correction of w and remove $\mathbf{Z}$ from $\mathbf{X}$
29 **for** $\mathbf{Z} \in \mathbf{X}$ **do**
30   $\quad w$ is the word with maximum frequency w_f in $\mathbf{Z}$
31   $\quad$ **if** $|\mathbf{Z}| \geq 3$ **then**
32    $\quad\quad$ **if** w_f *is sufficiently large than frequencies of other words in* $\mathbf{Z}$ *using Grubbs' test* **then**
33     $\quad\quad\quad \mathbf{D}'' \leftarrow w$ and $\mathbf{E}'' \leftarrow (\mathbf{Z} - \{w\})$
34   $\quad$ **if** $|\mathbf{z}| = 2$ **then**
35    $\quad\quad$ **if** $RelDiffLargeRange(w_f, w'_f)) > \gamma\ where\ w, w' \in \mathbf{z}$ **then**
36     $\quad\quad\quad \mathbf{D}'' \leftarrow w$ and $\mathbf{E}'' \leftarrow w'$
37 **for** $w \in \mathbf{E}' \cup \mathbf{E}''$ **do**
38   $\quad$ Replace w with its correction w' and update frequency of w'
39 $\mathbf{N}' \leftarrow$ update $\mathbf{N}$
40 $\mathbf{V}' \leftarrow$ update $\mathbf{V}$
41 $\mathbf{W}^{\mathbf{N}'} \leftarrow$ PlotFitBreak($\mathbf{N}'$)
42 $\mathbf{W}^{\mathbf{V}'} \leftarrow$ PlotFitBreak($\mathbf{V}'$)
43 $\mathbf{D}' \leftarrow$ get words from first two classes from $\mathbf{W}^{\mathbf{V}'}$
44 $\mathbf{D}'' \leftarrow \mathbf{D}'' \cup$ get words from first two classes from $\mathbf{W}^{\mathbf{N}'}$

4.4 Time complexity analysis:

The algorithm is designed and implemented efficiently. At every step, we have reduced comparisons by applying the different similarity checking functions in a hierarchical fashion as discussed in Steps $1 - 4$ earlier. By grouping the dictionary words according to their phonetic representation and keeping them in an hash table with the phonetic representation code as key, the search for phonetically similar words is accomplished in $O(1)$ time. The hash sets are typically small. Application of the conditions based on high Jaro-wrinkler and character vector similarities, reduces the set of possible terms for candidate matches for an error term even further. The cosine similarity computation to check for contextual similarity is therefore conducted between very few pairs of words only. For efficient computation of line 19, the non-dictionary words and their phonetic code are stored in a sorted tree map, where the sub map is retrieved based on the approximation constraint for each non-dictionary word, which takes $O(log(m''))$ time assuming that the sub map contains m'' number of non-dictionary terms where $m'' \ll m$, assuming m to be the cardinality of $\mathbf{N}$, hence the total time is $(m * log(m''))$.

Algorithm 2: PlotFitBreak

Input : Set of words: $\mathbf{W}$
Output: Set containing every word from $\mathbf{W}$ with its class number
1 Plot rank versus frequency in log-log scale within $\mathbf{W}$
2 Apply linear regression on the plot
3 Compute standard error of the regression
4 Compute Jenks natural breaks on the standard error iteratively (starting from 2) until the goodness of variance fit reaches to η
5 Mark the class number of the words in $\mathbf{W}$ according to the natural breaks

---

Algorithm 3: AnalyseRelativeDifference

Input : Non-dictionary word: w, dictionary word: w', class number of the words: w_i^N, $w_i'^V$, frequency of the words: w_f, w_f', cosine similarity between the word vectors of w, w': $Sim(w^w, w'^w)$
Output: Type of a word - domain or not
1 **if** $RelDiffLargeRange(w_f, w_f') \geq \theta_1$ **then**
2 $\quad$ w is a domain word
3 **else if** $RelDiffSmallRange(w_i^N, w_i'^V) \geq \theta_2$ and $Sim(w^w, w'^w) \leq \theta_3$ **then**
4 $\quad$ w is a domain word

Algorithm 4: RelDiffLargeRange

Input : Frequencies of words: w_f, w_f'
Output: Relative difference between w_f, w_f': d
1 $max \leftarrow$ getMaximum(w_f, w_f')
2 $min \leftarrow$ getMinimum(w_f, w_f')
3 d $\leftarrow \sigma(log_{10}(max) - log_{10}(min))$, $\sigma(x) = \frac{e^x}{e^x + 1}$

Algorithm 5: RelDiffSmallRange

Input : Class number of words: $w_i^N, w_i'^V$
Output: Relative difference between $w_i^N, w_i'^V$: d
1 $max \leftarrow$ getMaximum$(w_i^N, w_i'^V)$
2 $min \leftarrow$ getMinimum$(w_i^N, w_i'^V)$
3 d $\leftarrow \sigma(ln(\frac{max - min}{min}))$, $\sigma(x) = \frac{e^x}{e^x + 1}$

Algorithm 6: GetApproxPhonemeMatch

Input : A word: w, sorted, balanced binary search tree: $\mathbf{W}$, approximation constraint: ξ
Output: Set of words: $\mathbf{W}'$
1 $\mathbf{W}' \leftarrow$ Return the sub tree from $\mathbf{W}$ whose key ranges from first letter of ph(w) to the number of letters specified in ξ
2 $\mathbf{W}' \leftarrow \mathbf{W}' \cup w$

---

5 Results

This section presents the results and evaluation of our techniques. We have done manual evaluation for error correction as well as performed experiments to show that noise cleaning indeed enhances the performance of classification. We have done all of these for 7 sets of enterprise data. We also applied our method on 3 hate speech data sets to detect distortions of slang words. For these sets also we report enhancement in classification performance after correction of errors.

Data set description: Dataset 1 to dataset 7 are internal enterprise data sets pertaining to different domain such as, risk, contigency, finance, banking and HR. These data sets contain internal organizational mails, communications, customer complaints, customer requests. The other five data sets are as follows. *i*) Dataset 8: This data set (Weissenbacher et al., 2018) contains tweets mentioning different drug names, their side effects. *ii*) Dataset 9: This data set contains customer complaints with multi-label annotation in telecom domain (Dasgupta et al., 2016). The complaints has been generated within India. Dataset 10: This Offensive Language Identification Dataset (OLID) (Zampieri et al., 2019) contains annotated offensive social media content. *iii*) Dataset 11: This data set (Davidson et al., 2017) contains tweets with racist, sexist, homophobic and offensive content. Although this dataset contains annotations, we did not consider the annotations. *iv*) Dataset 12: This dataset (de Gibert et al., 2018) contains posts extracted from Stormfront, a white supremacist forum. This data set is annotated, however, we have used those texts which are annotated as hate speech. One of the evaluation criteria was downstream task of classification to show that the noise cleaning actually enhances the classification performance. Of the above, data sets 5, 6, 7, 9 and 10 are labeled. For these we present results for classification before and after cleaning. Classification has been done using Gradient Boosting classifier. Dataset 9 is multi-labeled, hence has been classified using Multilabel k Nearest Neighbours classifier. Classification results are presented using accuracy, precision, recall and F1-Scores.

Performance evaluation: All these experiments were run on a standard machine with Intel® Core™ i7-4600U CPU @ 2.10GHz 4 with 15.6 GiB memory having 64-bit ubuntu 18.04 LTS operating system. Error correction results were manually evaluated for subsets of words for all the 12 data sets and the performance is presented in Table 2. The evaluation was done against annotated set with given ground truths. The table shows that the precision of correction is very high at around 90%. Analysis shows that most of the unresolved error words are names of people and places, land marks and house/building names etc. sometimes as a part of main text or signature in case of emails. These usually have very low

Data Set	Domain	# of documents	Corpus Tokens	Unique Non-Dictionary Terms	Domain Dictionary Terms		Error Terms						
							Resolved	Domain Terms		Misspelling of Dictionary Terms		Misspelling of NonDictionary Terms	
					Detected	Correct(%)		Detected	Correct(%)	Detected	Correct(%)	Detected	Correct(%)
1	Risk	9942	7211	3022	27	27(100%)	1457	565	546(97%)	760	636(84%)	132	124(94%)
2	Contigency	9942	6640	2525	142	139(98%)	1067	505	495(98%)	481	438(91%)	81	74(91%)
3	Risk	9387	5251	1934	100	100(100%)	746	317	303(96%)	387	367(95%)	42	32(76%)
4	Contigency	9387	5448	1965	165	165(100%)	626	240	233(97%)	353	325(92%)	33	29(88%)
5	Finance	2147	5865	3967	29	29(100%)	1092	447	430(96%)	427	316(74%)	218	158(73%)
6	Banking	2360	6843	4122	41	41(100%)	766	137	131(96%)	431	356(83%)	198	135(68%)
7	HR	16357	12201	7309	67	67(100%)	3272	381	369(97%)	2261	1884(84%)	630	339(62%)
8	Twitter	5383	10766	5192	1157	1130(98%)	370	150	143(95%)	220	170(77%)	-	-
9	Telecom	5394	17263	10009	130	129(99%)	4102	255	236(93%)	3105	2403(77%)	772	567(73%)
10	Offensive	13241	17784	5973	225	225(100%)	619	287	266(93%)	243	217(89%)	89	75(84%)
11	Hate tweet	24783	32552	21228	505	498(99%)	5701	2208	1933(88%)	2718	236(91%)	775	719(93%)
12	Hate post	958	3382	588	598	597(100%)	179	144	135(94%)	35	29(83%)	-	-

Table 2: Manual evaluation of domain and error term detection and correction for the error terms

Performance	Multi Class								Multi-label	
	Dataset5 (Finance)		Dataset6 (Banking)		Dataset7 (HR)		Dataset10 (Offensive)		Dataset9 (Telecom)	
	raw	clean	raw	clean	raw	clean	raw	clean	raw	clean
Precision	0.924	0.96	0.425	0.5	0.878	0.89	0.79	0.8	0.54	0.58
Recall	0.922	0.96	0.418	0.47	0.849	0.87	0.63	0.66	0.32	0.38
F1-Score	0.923	0.96	0.421	0.48	0.863	0.88	0.7	0.72	0.409	0.46
Accuracy	0.927	0.96	0.444	0.48	0.855	0.89	0.75	0.77	0.44	0.46

Table 3: Classification performance of the data sets with and without cleaning

frequencies and high variance. Table 3 present the classification performance (before and after cleaning) showing that performance is enhanced (around 3-13%) after cleaning.

Table 4 presents a slang term in row 1 and it's distortions encountered very often in hate speech data (dataset 11). It is purposefully distorted to avoid automatic detection by word-based filters. Columns 2 - 5 in this table show that no single distance measure would be able to capture these, since they vary a lot from the original term. Our multi-pronged approach are able to detect these types of distortions also very well. Hence this approach can be more effective in detecting such terms from social media.

Non-dictionary term	Phonetic code	$JW(t,t')$	$Sim\,(t^v, t'^v)$	$Sim(t^c, t'^c)$
motherfuckin	M0RFKN	**1**	**1**	**1**
motherfuckas	M0RFKS	**0.93**	0.75	0.88
mufuckin	MFKN	0.84	**0.97**	0.74
muthafucka	M0FK	0.78	**0.96**	0.83
mothafucka	M0FK	0.89	**0.94**	0.9
muthafuckin	M0FKN	0.87	**0.97**	0.89
mothafuckin	M0FKN	0.95	0.92	**0.97**
muthafukin	M0FKN	0.84	**0.94**	0.9
muhfuckin	MFKN	**0.87**	0.86	0.85
muthaufckin	M0FKN	0.84	0.76	**0.89**
muhhfuckin	MFKN	0.84	**0.96**	0.88

Table 4: Non-dictionary slang (in bold and denoted as t') along with its different distorted versions (denoted as t) are detected from a hate speech data set (Dataset11)

6 Conclusion

This work presents an efficient method for identifying domain terms over true noise terms from enterprise text and thereafter clean the text appropriately to enhance performance of text analytics programs. The methods, though empirical, have been derived after careful analysis of many large enterprise repositories. Experimental evaluation shows that the method proposed is highly accurate in determining domain terms and also correct errors. The effectiveness of the approach is also established through improvement in classification accuracy after correction. Though designed for enterprise text, it was found that the method can be very fruitfully engaged in detecting errors in hate speech data originating in social media. Since these words are deliberately distorted, the errors in this case do not follow any specific pattern and are more difficult to determine. We have shown that our combined approach performs very well in such scenarios also. We are now working on formalizing the error detection and correction in enterprise text as an optimization problem. We are also working on an interactive system such that the method can receive rewards for a correct action and penalized for a wrong one. This can be effectively used for designing better systems which can utilize reinforcement learning for cleaning enterprise text. Detecting and removing names and other low frequency errors is also on the agenda.

References

Zhuowei Bao, Benny Kimelfeld, and Yunyao Li. 2011. A graph approach to spelling correction in domain-centric search. In *Proceedings of the 49th Annual Meeting of the Association for Computational Linguistics: Human Language Technologies*, pages 905–914.

Eric Brill and Robert C Moore. 2000. An improved error model for noisy channel spelling correction. In *Proceedings of the 38th annual meeting of the association for computational linguistics*, pages 286–293.

Tirthankar Dasgupta, Lipika Dey, and Ishan Verma. 2016. Fuzzy multi-label classification of customer complaint logs under noisy environment. In *International Joint Conference on Rough Sets*, pages 376–385. Springer.

Thomas Davidson, Dana Warmsley, Michael Macy, and Ingmar Weber. 2017. Automated hate speech detection and the problem of offensive language. In *Proceedings of the 11th International AAAI Conference on Web and Social Media*, ICWSM '17, pages 512–515.

Ona de Gibert, Naiara Perez, Aitor García-Pablos, and Montse Cuadros. 2018. Hate Speech Dataset from a White Supremacy Forum. In *Proceedings of the 2nd Workshop on Abusive Language Online (ALW2)*, pages 11–20, Brussels, Belgium, October. Association for Computational Linguistics.

Lipika Dey and Gargi Roy. 2015. Auto-correction of consumer generated text in semi-formal environment. In *7th Language and Technology Conference: Human Language Technologies as a Challenge for Computer Science and Linguistics. Fundacja Uniwersytetu im. Adama Mickiewicza w Poznaniu*, pages 203–207.

Intuition Engineering. 2019. Chars2vec: Character-based language model for handling real world texts with spelling errors and human slang.

Pieter Fivez, Simon Suster, and Walter Daelemans. 2017. Unsupervised context-sensitive spelling correction of clinical free-text with word and character n-gram embeddings. In *BioNLP 2017*, pages 143–148.

Michael Flor, Michael Fried, and Alla Rozovskaya. 2019. A benchmark corpus of English misspellings and a minimally-supervised model for spelling correction. In *Proceedings of the Fourteenth Workshop on Innovative Use of NLP for Building Educational Applications*, pages 76–86, Florence, Italy, August. Association for Computational Linguistics.

Michael Flor. 2012. Four types of context for automatic spelling correction. *TAL*, 53(3):61–99.

Hongyu Gong, Yuchen Li, Suma Bhat, and Pramod Viswanath. 2019. Context-sensitive malicious spelling error correction. In *The World Wide Web Conference*, pages 2771–2777.

Frank E Grubbs et al. 1950. Sample criteria for testing outlying observations. *The Annals of Mathematical Statistics*, 21(1):27–58.

Matthew A Jaro. 1989. Advances in record-linkage methodology as applied to matching the 1985 census of tampa, florida. *Journal of the American Statistical Association*, 84(406):414–420.

G.F. Jenks. 1977. *Optimal data classification for choropleth maps: George F. Jenks*. Occasional paper. University of Kansas. Department of Geography.

Kenneth H Lai, Maxim Topaz, Foster R Goss, and Li Zhou. 2015. Automated misspelling detection and correction in clinical free-text records. *Journal of biomedical informatics*, 55:188–195.

Vladimir I Levenshtein. 1966. Binary codes capable of correcting deletions, insertions, and reversals. In *Soviet physics doklady*, volume 10, pages 707–710.

Yang Li, Bo Zhao, Ariel Fuxman, and Fangbo Tao. 2018. Guess me if you can: Acronym disambiguation for enterprises. In *Proceedings of the 56th Annual Meeting of the Association for Computational Linguistics (Volume 1: Long Papers)*, pages 1308–1317.

Chris J Lu, Alan R Aronson, Sonya E Shooshan, and Dina Demner-Fushman. 2019. Spell checker for consumer language (cspell). *Journal of the American Medical Informatics Association*, 26(3):211–218.

Christopher D Manning, Christopher D Manning, and Hinrich Schütze. 1999. *Foundations of statistical natural language processing*. MIT press.

Tomas Mikolov, Kai Chen, Greg Corrado, and Jeffrey Dean. 2013. Efficient estimation of word representations in vector space. *arXiv preprint arXiv:1301.3781*.

Lawrence Philips. 2000. The double metaphone search algorithm. *C/C++ users journal*, 18(6):38–43.

Eric Sven Ristad and Peter N Yianilos. 1998. Learning string-edit distance. *IEEE Transactions on Pattern Analysis and Machine Intelligence*, 20(5):522–532.

Martin Schierle, Sascha Schulz, and Markus Ackermann, 2008. *From Spelling Correction to Text Cleaning – Using Context Information*, pages 397–404. 01.

Mohammad Shakir, Gargi Roy, Aninda Sukla, Tirthankar Dasgupta, Geetika Sharma, and Lipika Dey. 2019. Framework for analyzing and improving quality of available data for enterprise automation tasks. In *DCCL workshop at ACM SIGKDD Conference on Knowledge Discovery and Data Mining*.

L Venkata Subramaniam, Shourya Roy, Tanveer A Faruquie, and Sumit Negi. 2009. A survey of types of text noise and techniques to handle noisy text. In *Proceedings of The Third Workshop on Analytics for Noisy Unstructured Text Data*, pages 115–122.

Leo Törnqvist, Pentti Vartia, and Yrjö O Vartia. 1985. How should relative changes be measured? *The American Statistician*, 39(1):43–46.

Guy C Van Orden. 1987. A rows is a rose: Spelling, sound, and reading. *Memory & cognition*, 15(3):181–198.

Rose-Marie Weber. 1970. A linguistic analysis of first-grade reading errors. *Reading Research Quarterly*, pages 427–451.

Davy Weissenbacher, Abeed Sarker, Michael Paul, and Graciela Gonzalez. 2018. Overview of the third social media mining for health (smm4h) shared tasks at emnlp 2018. In *Proceedings of the 2018 EMNLP Workshop SMM4H: The 3rd Social Media Mining for Health Applications Workshop & Shared Task*, pages 13–16.

William E Winkler. 1990. String comparator metrics and enhanced decision rules in the fellegi-sunter model of record linkage.

Marcos Zampieri, Shervin Malmasi, Preslav Nakov, Sara Rosenthal, Noura Farra, and Ritesh Kumar. 2019. Predicting the Type and Target of Offensive Posts in Social Media. In *Proceedings of NAACL*.

George Kingsley Zipf. 1932. Selected studies of the principle of relative frequency in language.

Model-agnostic Methods for Text Classification with Inherent Noise

Kshitij Tayal *
University of Minnesota
Twin Cities
`tayal@umn.edu`

Rahul Ghosh *
University of Minnesota
Twin Cities
`ghosh128@umn.edu`

Vipin Kumar
University of Minnesota
Twin Cities
`kumar001@umn.edu`

Abstract

Text classification is a fundamental problem, and recently, deep neural networks (DNN) have shown promising results in many natural language tasks. However, their human-level performance relies on high-quality annotations, which are time-consuming and expensive to collect. As we move towards large inexpensive datasets, the inherent label noise degrades the generalization of DNN. While most machine learning literature focuses on building complex networks to handle noise, in this work, we evaluate model-agnostic methods to handle inherent noise in large scale text classification that can be easily incorporated into existing machine learning workflows with minimal interruption. Specifically, we conduct a point-by-point comparative study between several noise-robust methods on three datasets encompassing three popular classification models. To our knowledge, this is the first time such a comprehensive study in text classification encircling popular models and model-agnostic loss methods has been conducted. In this study, we describe our learning and demonstrate the application of our approach, which outperformed baselines by up to 10 % in classification accuracy while requiring no network modifications. Code for this paper is hosted at www.kshitijtayal.com/code/model-agnostic-methods.

1 Introduction

Text classification is a fundamental problem in natural language processing, where the objective is to categorize text into a set of predefined classes. It has been shown to be valuable in many domains, such as social media (Kateb and Kalita, 2015), cognitive-biometric recognition (Pokhriyal et al., 2016) and e-commerce (Yu et al., 2012). Modern-day enterprises are heavily dependent on the performance of text classification models, where even a marginal improvement in the performance can accrue billions of dollars (Singh, 2019) and substantially improve the customer experience.

Currently, DNN (Zhou et al., 2016; Devlin et al., 2018) are the state of the art machine learning models widely deployed for text classification tasks in major enterprises (Bernardi et al., 2019; Haldar et al., 2019; Liu et al., 2019). Like any other supervised classifiers, the performance of these DNN trained using standard cross-entropy loss is strongly dependent on the quality and quantity of the data. However, collecting high-quality manual labels is time-consuming and expensive. At the same time, there are less expensive sources to collect labeled data, such as Mechanical Turk (Kittur et al., 2008), search engine meta data, and social media tags. These inexpensive large datasets have a high level of noise, as multiple annotators generate the labels under different skill-set and biases. In e-commerce, an example of one such confusing case is when the same product title is labeled differently by agents into separate but related categories, as shown in Fig. 1. Blindly trusting these large inexpensive datasets as gold-standard can decrease the performance of models.

Learning from noisy labels is an active area of research in computer vision, and several model cognizant approaches (Wu et al., 2018; Lefkimmiatis, 2018) have been proposed. However, these approaches work on building complex network architecture to handle noise and require substantial back-

---

equal contribution

Proceedings of the 28th International Conference on Computational Linguistics: Industry Track, pages 202–213
Barcelona, Spain (Online), December 12, 2020

ground knowledge and training to operate. For many enterprises, the performance of text classification models plays a crucial role in their revenue earnings, and the difficulty of implementing complex architecture becomes a bottleneck. Conversely, there is minimal research studying the performance of the model-agnostic methods to handle inherent label noise, that can be easily incorporated into existing machine learning workflows with no network modifications for large scale text classification tasks.

Under model agnostic schemes, there are several different lines of work which include modeling noise-transition matrix (Patrini et al., 2017; Goldberger and Ben-Reuven, 2016; Sukhbaatar et al., 2014), training auxiliary network (Jiang et al., 2017; Guo et al., 2018), training with clean labels (Malach and Shalev-Shwartz, 2017), label regularization (Szegedy et al., 2016), data augmentation (Zhang et al., 2017), and noise-robust loss functions. In this work, we focus our attention on techniques that do not add any overhead computation. Specifically, we evaluate label smoothing regularization, data augmentation technique, and state

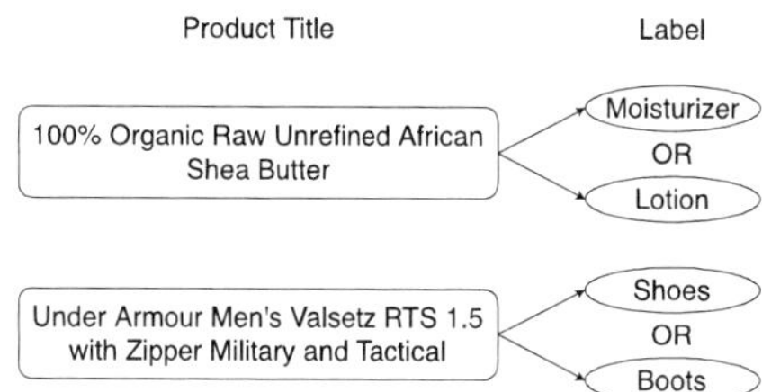

Figure 1: Noisy labels arising due to labels assigned by multiple annotators.

of the art noise-robust loss functions (Reed et al., 2014; Wang et al., 2019; Ma et al., 2018; Zhang and Sabuncu, 2018) to examine its effect in mitigating inherent label noise for large scale text datasets. These methods are simpler and easy to implement than other lines-of-work in tackling noisy labels, which either gets very complex (Jiang et al., 2017) or has strong assumptions on the type of noise present (Sukhbaatar et al., 2014). We conduct our study on large web-scale text data scraped from popular e-commerce platforms, which contains a significant number of classes leading to a higher inherent noise due to annotator confusion. In contrast with previous work (Li et al., 2019; Jindal et al., 2019), we do not introduce any external noise into our dataset. To the best of our knowledge, no previous study has been done to study model-agnostic methods in mitigating inherent label noise for large scale text classification. To summarize, the main contributions of our work are as follows:

- We propose the use of model-agnostic methods to handle inherent noise in the context of text classification on large scale datasets. To our knowledge, this is the first attempt to use model-agnostic methods for text classification.

- We perform extensive experiments on three real-world datasets scraped from popular e-commerce platform. We show that our approach outperforms baselines with a margin of 10% in classification accuracy using three popular classification models.

2   Related Work

In this section, we provide a brief literature review for model agnostic methods popularly used in machine learning to handle noise. These include modeling label noise, training auxiliary network, data augmentation, noise-robust loss functions, and regularization schemes.

Existing literature in modeling label noise can be further subdivided into two groups: class-conditional and instance-conditional label noise. The first group assumes that the noise is independent of the instance and models the transition probability from true class to noisy class. (Mnih and Hinton, 2012) assumed the class-conditional label noise for binary classification task and consequently use an EM-based algorithm to learn the model parameters and the noise transition matrix. (Sukhbaatar et al., 2014) extended the multi-class counterpart of class-conditional noise and proposed a constrained linear layer at the top of the softmax layer, which under some strong assumptions can be interpreted as the noise transition matrix. A similar work by (Patrini et al., 2017) uses forward and backward methods to explicitly model the noise transition matrix and also provide a way to estimate the noise transition matrix. The second group assumes that the label noise is conditioned for each instance. (Xiao et al., 2015) developed a noise model, where noise is modeled on the instance and its class. Similarly, (Vahdat, 2017) model the noise through Conditional Random Fields (CRF), where the clean labels are modeled as latent variables during training.

Under training auxiliary network, (Malach and Shalev-Shwartz, 2017) proposed training two different networks which back-propagate the loss when the predictions of the two network disagree. Mentor network (Jiang et al., 2017), another popular method, learns a sample weighting scheme to supervise the training of a base network, termed StudentNet, that learns under label noise contingencies. Similarly, (Guo et al., 2018) present an unsupervised approach to learn the curriculum based on the complexity of the instance in the feature space. Supporting the loss function category, (Natarajan et al., 2013) presented robust surrogate loss functions for handling noisy labels in a binary classification task. Mean absolute error (MAE) (Ghosh et al., 2017) was shown to be inherently robust to label noise for the classification task. Similarly bootstrapping loss function (Reed et al., 2014) was proposed, which introduced a weighted combination of target labels and network predictions to compensate for noisy samples. While (Reed et al., 2014) uses a fixed hyper-parameter as weights, D2L (Ma et al., 2018) proposes to use the subspace complexity score of the model as weights which gets updated at every iteration. To overcome the limitation of MAE, Generalized Cross Entropy (Zhang and Sabuncu, 2018) was proposed, which is a combination of MAE and categorical cross entropy (CCE) loss. Symmetric cross-entropy (Wang et al., 2019) augments the standard CCE, similar to symmetric KL-divergence, with the noise robust reverse cross-entropy.

Data augmentation and regularization schemes are some other ways introduced to make the learning procedure robust to noisy labels. These include, mixup (Zhang et al., 2017), that uses convex combinations of training data points and its corresponding labels, and Label Smoothing Regularization (LSR) (Szegedy et al., 2016), where a smoothing parameter is used to modify the hard one-hot labels into soft labels to mitigate over-fitting to noisy labels.

3 Method

3.1 Problem Setting

In this paper we consider the text classification problem where each data instance is described as features $x \in \mathbb{R}^d$ and label $y \in \{0,1\}^K$ (one hot encoded vector). x is the vector representation of a text, where d is the dimensionality of the embedding vector and K are the number of classes.

Table 1: Summary statistics of datasets

Dataset	#Samples	#Unique Words	#Class
Beauty	207574	118215	342
Electronics	362142	424368	823
Automotive	243296	228234	1818

Data: We conduct our study on large web-scale product title data scraped from Amazon (He and McAuley, 2016)[1]. The datasets are broken down by categories, and we make use of three such categories i.e. **Electronics**, **Beauty** and **Automotive**. Table 1 shows the characteristics of these datasets. Each dataset contains product titles, metadata for each product (also bought, also viewed, bought together, buy after viewing), and their categories. For each product, its category is a path from a coarse-grained label to a fine-grained label. We use the product titles as inputs and the fine grained label from the above metadata as the product label. E.g., a product in category `Electronics` $\Rightarrow$ `Computers & Accessories` $\Rightarrow$ `Cables & Accessories`, will have `Cables & Accessories` as its label. We do a 70:30 split of our dataset $\mathcal{D} = \{x_i, y_i\}_{i=1}^N$ into training set $\mathcal{D}^{Train}$ and test set $\mathcal{D}^{Test}$ such that $\{\mathcal{D}^{Train} \cap \mathcal{D}^{Test} = \emptyset\}$ and $\{\mathcal{D}^{Train} \cup \mathcal{D}^{Test} = \mathcal{D}\}$.

Goal: Our objective is to learn a classification model $f(x, \theta)$ on the training set $\mathcal{D}^{Train}$ which learns an accurate mapping function f such that it makes correct prediction on test sample $x_i \in \mathcal{D}^{Test}$. Here θ are the parameters of the DNN.

3.2 Model-agnostic Methods

The underlying principle of training classification models is to minimize a loss function and accordingly update the network parameters. In the classification task, categorical cross entropy (CCE) loss is one such loss function which measures the performance of a classification model whose output is a likelihood

---

[1] http://jmcauley.ucsd.edu/data/amazon/links.html

estimation $f(\boldsymbol{x};\theta)$ between 0 to 1 scale. The CCE loss is given by

$$\mathcal{L}_{CCE} = -\frac{1}{N}\sum_{i=1}^{N}\sum_{j=1}^{K} y_{ij} log(f_j(\boldsymbol{x}_i;\theta)) \tag{3.1}$$

where, y_{ij} is the j'th element of $\boldsymbol{y}_i$. The features, label and network prediction of the i'th instance are denoted by $\boldsymbol{x}_i$, $\boldsymbol{y}_i$ and $f(\boldsymbol{x}_i;\theta)$ respectively. K is the number of classes and N is the number of training examples. The number of parameters in most deep architectures are very large and often exceeds the size of the data used for training. There is significant theoretical and empirical evidence that in such over-parametrized DNN, the output of the trained model matches the training labels exactly (Zhang et al., 2016). Consequently, if the training labels contain noise, the learned weights can be sub-optimal leading to high test error in-spite of low training losses. In the following segment, we briefly describe noise-robust learning methods we used in our evaluation to overcome inherent noise in large datasets.

3.2.1   Label Smoothing Regularization (LSR)

CCE loss encourages the model to be more confident on its predictions by minimizing the probabilities of the given class which can be particularly harmful in case of noisy labels, as the model overfits on the noisy examples resulting in poor generalization performance. To regularize the model and make it more adaptable, (Szegedy et al., 2016) proposed to use a mixture of the original ground truth distribution with another fixed distribution u in place of the original labels. The target label is modified as $y'_{ij} = (1-\epsilon)y_{ij} + \epsilon u(j)$, where, $u(j)$ is used as a fixed prior distribution over labels weighted by ϵ. Thus, using this weighted target label, the loss function takes the following form

$$\mathcal{L}_{LSR} = -\frac{1}{N}\sum_{i=1}^{N}\sum_{j=1}^{K} [(1-\epsilon)y_{ij}log(f_j(\boldsymbol{x}_i;\theta)) + \epsilon u(j)log(f_j(\boldsymbol{x}_i;\theta))] \tag{3.2}$$

3.2.2   Bootstrapping

Proposed by (Reed et al., 2014), Bootstrapping loss function expands the prediction objective with a notion of consistency. A prediction is consistent if an identical prediction is made given similar percepts, where the idea of similarity is between model features estimated from the input data. Bootstrapping loss function dynamically updates the target labels by using a convex combination of the current model's prediction and the (possibly noisy) training label. The weight of the convex combination is administered by hyperparameter β. This process provides the model justification to "disagree" with inconsistent training label, and efficiently re-label the data while training. This approach is referred to as soft bootstrapping when the predicted probabilities are directly used to generate target labels as follows

$$\mathcal{L}_{boot\text{-}soft} = -\frac{1}{N}\sum_{i=1}^{N}\sum_{j=1}^{K} [\beta y_{ij} + (1-\beta)f_j(\boldsymbol{x}_i;\theta)]log(f_j(\boldsymbol{x}_i;\theta)) \tag{3.3}$$

Similarly, the approach is referred to as hard bootstrapping when the predicted class probabilities are replaced by their one-hot encoded vector based on the maximum apriori probability (MAP) estimate as follows

$$\mathcal{L}_{boot\text{-}hard} = -\frac{1}{N}\sum_{i=1}^{N}\sum_{j=1}^{K} [\beta y_{ij} + (1-\beta)z_{ij}]log(z_{ij}) \tag{3.4}$$

where, $z_i = \mathbb{1}[k= \text{argmax } f_j(\boldsymbol{x}_i;\theta), j = i \ldots K]$

3.2.3   Mixup

(Zhang et al., 2017) proposed a simple data augmentation technique that works on the vicinal risk minimization principle (Chapelle et al., 2001), where virtual data instances created in the vicinity of training data instances are used for risk minimization. Mixup constructs virtual training examples under the assumption that linear interpolation of feature vectors should lead to linear interpolation of associated targets and thus takes the form

$$\tilde{x} = \lambda \boldsymbol{x}_i + (1 - \lambda)\boldsymbol{x}_j \qquad \tilde{y} = \lambda \boldsymbol{y}_i + (1 - \lambda)\boldsymbol{y}_j \tag{3.5}$$

where, $\boldsymbol{x}_i, \boldsymbol{x}_j$ are raw feature vectors and $\boldsymbol{y}_i, \boldsymbol{y}_j$ are the corresponding one-hot labels. λ is sampled from a beta distribution Beta(α, α), for $\alpha \in (0, \infty)$. Increasing α results in virtual examples further from the training examples. The authors hypothesize that learning linear interpolations of real instances is easier than memorizing random noisy labels and thus this strategy should avoid the model to overfit to the corrupted labels.

3.2.4 Dimensionality Driven Learning (D2L)

(Ma et al., 2018) introduced a new prospect for understanding DNN generalization by examining the dimensionality of the representation subspace of training samples. They explain that DNN exhibits a two-stage learning style when training with noisy labels, i.e., 1) an early stage of dimensionality compression that models low dimensional subspace that approximately resembles the underlying distribution and 2) a later stage of dimensionality expansion that expands subspace dimensionality to overfit noisy labels. Thus, to avoid noisy labels, a label smoothing strategy is proposed, which finds an optimal trade-off between the model prediction and the training labels. Specifically, the model is trained with the training labels until a turning point is found, at which point the model starts to overfit. This turning point is determined based on Local Intrinsic Dimensionality (LID) (Houle, 2017), which is a measure of the subspace dimensionality at each epoch. Specifically, at any epoch for a training instance $\boldsymbol{x}$, LID is calculated as:

$$LID(\boldsymbol{x}, X_B) = - \left(\frac{1}{k} \sum_{i=1}^{k} \log \frac{r_i(g(\boldsymbol{x}), g(X_B))}{r_{max}(g(\boldsymbol{x}), g(X_B))} \right)^{-1} \tag{3.6}$$

where, X_B is a random batch selected from the training set, g is the second-to-last DNN layer, $r_i(g(\boldsymbol{x}), g(X_B))$ is the distance between $\boldsymbol{x}$ and its i-th nearest neighbor in the transformed space and r_{max} is the largest value among the k nearest neighbors thus denoting the radius of the neighborhood. After the turning point is established, the training labels are smoothed by adding the network prediction to them, and these smoothed labels are used for training the models. Smoothed labels are calculated as follow:

$$\overset{*}{y} = \alpha_t y + (1 - \alpha_t)\hat{y}, \text{ where } \quad \alpha_t = exp\left(-\lambda \frac{LID_t}{\min_{j=0}^{t-1} LID_j} \right) \tag{3.7}$$

is a LID-based factor that updates at the t-th training epoch. y is the raw label, $\hat{y}$ is the predicted label, and $\lambda = j/T$, (T: total epochs) is a weighting that indicates diminishing confidence in the raw labels when the training proceeds to the dimensionality expansion stage. Dimensional expansion is evaluated in terms of the ratio of two average LID scores: the current epoch's score, and the lowest score encountered at earlier epochs. The ratio exceeds one as the learning enters the dimensional expansion stage, and after that, the exponential decay factor starts to support the current model prediction. The training loss can then be refined as:

$$\mathcal{L}_{D2L} = -\frac{1}{N} \sum_{i=1}^{N} \sum_{j=1}^{K} \overset{*}{y}_{ij} log(f_j(\boldsymbol{x}_i; \theta)) \tag{3.8}$$

where, N is the total number of training samples.

3.2.5 Generalized Cross Entropy (GCE)

Proposed by (Zhang and Sabuncu, 2018), GCE is a generalization of CCE and mean absolute error (MAE) with hyperparameter q, where $q \in [0, 1]$. When $q \to 0$, the loss becomes CCE, and likewise becomes MAE/unhinged loss when $q = 1$. During training with CCE, the loss function implicitly puts more stress on samples where the model disagrees with the target labels, which is useful when training data is clean but can cause overfitting to noisy labels. Conversely, MAE weighs all predictions equally, which makes it more robust to noisy labels (Ghosh et al., 2017). However, in our experiments with product title classification tasks, we see that the neural network was not able to converge and gave an abysmal result on the test dataset. This finding is coherent with other authors' works (Fonseca et al., 2019; Zhang and Sabuncu, 2018). GCE addressed the challenge by taking advantage of both the noise-robustness provided by MAE and the implicit weighting scheme of CCE. The GCE loss is given by

$$\mathcal{L}_{GCE} = -\frac{1}{N}\sum_{i=1}^{N}\sum_{j=1}^{K}\frac{1 - (y_{ij}f_j(\boldsymbol{x}_i;\theta))^q}{q}, q \in [0,1] \tag{3.9}$$

3.2.6 Symmetric Cross Entropy (SL)

Cross-entropy by itself is not sufficient for learning generalizable models in presence of noisy labels. The training labels don't represent the true class, whereas after a few iterations of training the model output can start to get closer to the true class distribution. Therefore, in addition to the standard CCE, (Wang et al., 2019) propose to use the reverse cross entropy (RCE) in the loss function and the final loss is a weighted combination of both as given below

$$\mathcal{L}_{SL} = \alpha\mathcal{L}_{CCE} + \beta\mathcal{L}_{RCE} = -\frac{1}{N}\sum_{i=1}^{N}\sum_{j=1}^{K}\alpha y_{ij}log(f_j(\boldsymbol{x}_i;\theta)) + \beta f_j(\boldsymbol{x}_i;\theta)log(y_{ij}) \tag{3.10}$$

where, α and β are two hyperparameters. Here, the CCE loss helps in convergence whereas the RCE loss is noise tolerant and penalizes the model predictions that has been optimized for the noisy training labels.

4 Experiments and Results

In this section, we evaluate several model-agnostic approaches discussed above on three large scale datasets shown in Table 1 and attempt to answer the following questions:

- Do model-agnostic methods give a substantial gain in performance for large web-scale data having inherent noise over baseline?

- How does the performance vary for model-agnostic methods under different types of models?

- How the behavior of model-agnostic methods change as we introduce external noise? Is there any correlation between performance gain and the number of class label?

4.1 Learning Models

In this section, we provide a brief discussion of the models used in our comparative study. **FFNN:** In this work, we use FFNN (Rumelhart et al., 1985) with average pooling operation (Shen et al., 2018) on input feature with two hidden layers having 1024 and 512 units respectively. We employ a ReLU activation function for non linearity with 0.2 dropout followed by a output layer of K output values, where K is the number of classes. **CNN:** 1D CNN (Kim, 2014) and fixed the maximum length of sentence to 10 and embedding dimension 128. In our network architecture, we use one convolutional layer having 128 filters with a convolution window/kernel size of 5 followed by max-pooling and finally a fully connected layer with 512 neurons. **LSTM:** For LSTM (Hochreiter and Schmidhuber, 1997), we use the same sentence length and embedding size as CNN. In our network architecture, the first layer of LSTM is the embedding layer

Table 2: Hyperparameters for model-agnostic methods

Method	Hyper-parameters
LSR	$\epsilon = 0.3$
$Boot\text{-}hard$	$\beta = 0.3$
$Boot\text{-}soft$	$\beta = 0.3$
$mixup$	$\alpha = 0.2$
GCE	$q = 0.3$
SL	$\alpha = 2, \beta = 1$

Table 3: Relative performance of different model-agnostic methods against cross-entropy loss with no external noise

MODEL	DATASET	$CCE(\%)$	LSR	$BootHard$	$BootSoft$	$mixup$	$D2L$	GCE	SL
FFNN	Beauty	68.16	0.79	0.1	1.19	**2.63**	2.45	2.43	1.13
	Electronics	70.36	0.91	0.2	1.09	2.57	**3.49**	3.18	1.62
	Automotive	73.19	1.82	0.42	1.08	**3.02**	1.83	1.42	1.31
LSTM	Beauty	68.76	1.31	1.05	1.69	1.59	1.81	**1.98**	1.28
	Electronics	66.16	2.03	0.53	1.59	**2.86**	2.55	1.63	1.81
	Automotive	73.50	1.24	0.34	0.79	2.34	**3.73**	1.09	1.32
CNN	Beauty	60.33	3.93	4.19	3.93	3.91	**6.41**	5.37	3.08
	Electronics	56.79	5.35	1.95	4.75	4.67	**9.8**	5.6	4.37
	Automotive	64.36	4.3	2.41	2.95	3.59	**10.74**	9.4	3.56

followed by variational dropout. The next layer is the LSTM layer, with 256 memory units, followed by the output layer of K output values. More recently, researchers have started to apply graph convolutional networks (Tayal et al., 2019; Yao et al., 2019) for text classification. Preliminary results are encouraging; however, they bring in the additional complexity of the graph. In this work, we restrict ourselves to more popular techniques, i.e., FFNN, CNN, LSTM.

4.2 Experimental setup

We trained all models for a maximum of 75 epochs using Adam optimizer (Kingma and Ba, 2014) with 0.001 learning rate and terminate training if the validation loss does not reduce for 10 continuous epochs. To remove bias between different model runs, the train, validation, and test set are kept consistent for all models. We refer the model trained on cross-entropy loss as baseline. Individual words are encoded using glove embeddings (Pennington et al., 2014). For electronics dataset, we fixed hyperparameter for each of the methods using grid search based on their average performance on 5 fold cross-validation. Due to constraints in the use of computational hardware, we fixed the same hyperparameters (Table 2) for other datasets too.

4.3 Results

Table 3 reports the relative performance of the different model-agnostic methods. The column for CCE shows the absolute baseline accuracy, and other columns represent the percentage improvement achieved by model-agnostic methods over their cross-entropy trained counterpart. We highlight best performing methods for each row and make the following high-level observations from our results: a) All values in result table 3 are positive, which strengthens our statement that there is inherent noise in large text datasets, which can result in overfitting of DNNs trained on standard CCE loss, and b) $D2L$ is the top-performing method that gave the best result consistently over CCE, followed by GCE and $mixup$. Likewise, *boot-hard* and *boot-soft* worked well over CCE but not as high as other methods.

Continuing to expand on the above observations, $D2L$ is the best performing model, which suggests that dimensionality driven learning strategy is highly tolerant to noisy labels and works best for large scale text classification. The performance improvement is much more visible when CNN is used in conjunction with $D2L$.

GCE, which is a generalization of cross-entropy and MAE has comparable performance with $D2L$ and consistently outperforms CCE. This shows the benefit of using the noise-robustness feature of MAE in conjunction with CCE.

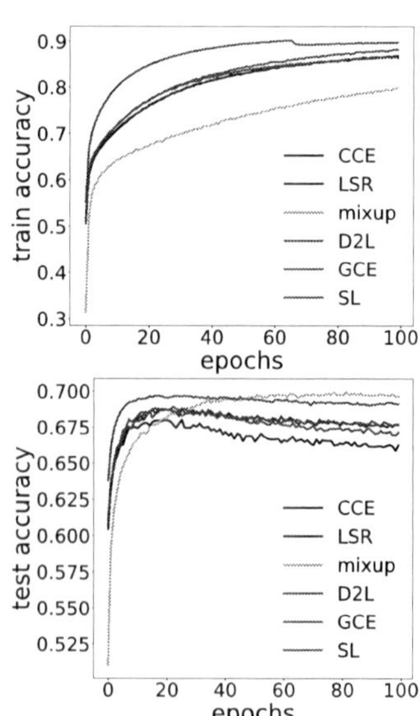

Figure 2: Train and Test accuracy against number of epochs for FFNN on Beauty dataset

Table 4: Relative performance of different model-agnostic methods against cross-entropy loss with 20% noise

MODEL	DATASET	$CCE(\%)$	LSR	$Boot\text{-}hard$	$Boot\text{-}soft$	$mixup$	$D2L$	GCE	SL
FFNN	Beauty	66.42	0.53	1.2	1.84	2.12	**2.78**	2.78	1.25
	Electronics	68.80	0.83	0.58	1.09	2.81	**3.62**	3.38	1.9
	Automotive	70.90	1.76	1.71	2.75	3.03	**4.49**	2.91	2.74
LSTM	Beauty	67.11	1.49	**3.01**	1.22	0.86	1.80	2.94	1.71
	Electronics	63.73	2.73	-1.6	0.41	3.69	**5.60**	4.06	3.0
	Automotive	70.90	2.0	0.71	2.28	2.38	**4.59**	3.07	2.02
CNN	Beauty	54.71	7.27	10.38	11.99	5.1	**13.03**	12.5	6.62
	Electronics	53.33	5.57	-4.56	1.5	9.52	**15.15**	9.1	5.18
	Automotive	59.06	6.3	4.25	6.86	10.04	**16.44**	10.68	5.81

Likewise, SL uses a combination of reverse cross-entropy, which adds value when used in conjunction with CCE. $mixup$, a simple data augmentation technique gave impressive gain for FFNN and LSTM. However, it didn't perform well on CNN as compared to other methods, which showcase the gap in learning when hundreds of unique class labels are present. Likewise, LSR has average performance gains due to the huge number of classes present in our dataset. The huge number of classes reduces the label smoothing effect of the approach, which relies on the addition of a fixed uniform label distribution to the one-hot labels.

$Boot\text{-}hard$ and $Boot\text{-}soft$ performed fine, but not as high as other methods. We attribute this to hyperparameter β, which is fixed for each epoch and controls the convex combination of the model prediction and the training label. $D2L$, on the other hand, overcame this and set its parameter for each epoch in an automated fashion using model complexity.

Although our goal is not to compare the performance between different models, we cannot help but notice that for the Automotive dataset, $D2L$ and GCE were able to bring the performance of CNN closer to that of FFNN. We thereby conclude that in some cases model-agnostic methods can further help to make existing models more powerful.

4.4 Accuracy Curves

Figure 2 denotes training and test accuracies at every epoch attained by FFNN on the beauty dataset. We observe that the classifier trained using CCE first learns discriminative patterns, which is evident from high test accuracy in the initial epochs. Later the test accuracy decreases as the model starts overfitting on the noisy labels, which explains the increase in train accuracy (CCE training curve overlapped by LSR). This validates report from other works (Zhang et al., 2016; Arpit et al., 2017) that DNNs first learn predictive patterns from easily separable instances and later overfits to the noisy labels. On the contrary, training with model-agnostic methods limits overfitting to noisy labels and achieved higher test accuracies.

Specifically, $D2L$ and $mixup$ are the most effective methods in limiting the overfitting effect. We note that low training accuracy of $mixup$ is on linear interpolated data, while test accuracy is on original test samples. These observations serve as an empirical justification for the use of model-agnostic approaches.

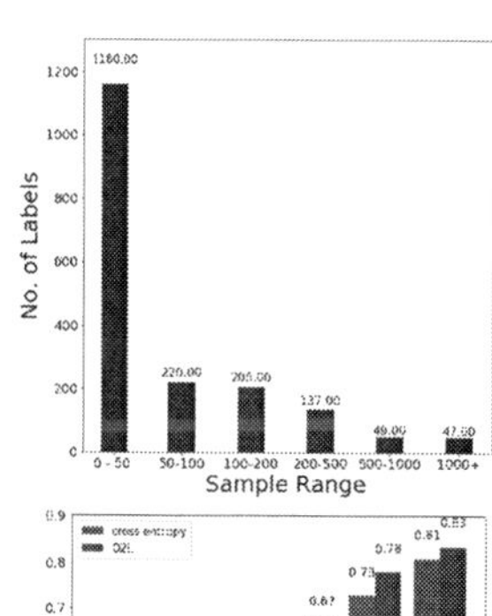

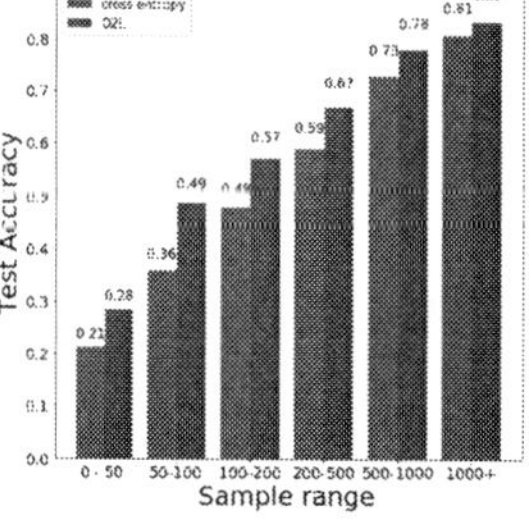

Figure 3: Top: distribution of labels with respect to the sample range for the automotive dataset. Bottom: Test accuracy comparison b/w CCE loss and D2L across different sample range.

4.5 Noise Robustness

To further evaluate the performance of model-agnostic methods, we randomly flipped 20% training labels and compared the model performance on the test set where the labels are not touched. Table 4 reports the performance when external noise is added. All the settings are the same as in Section 4.3. As with no noise, we note that $D2L$ is consistently the top performer, and the margin becomes more distinct. Specifically, if we look at CNN, it gave 13.03%, 15.15%, and 16.44% gain for beauty, electronics, and automotive dataset, respectively, which translates to absolute performance of 61.82 %, 61.32 %, 68.51%. These numbers are close to the result given by $D2L$ when no noise was present, concluding that $D2L$ is more stable in the presence of noise. We also observe that $Boot\text{-}hard$ loss function breaks down when we increase the noise, particularly when used with LSTM and CNN in the Electronics dataset.

We further experimented by flipping 40% training labels and find that most of the approaches gave an inferior performance as compared to CCE, thereby concluding that model-agnostic methods do not perform well with very large noise.

4.6 Data Imbalance

As with any large dataset with hundreds of classes, our data set is imbalanced (Figure 3 -top), purporting that we have more classes with fewer samples and fewer classes with more samples. In this section, we study whether the performance gain is uniform throughout the class space, or it changes with the number of samples/class. To evaluate, we select automotive dataset having 1818 labels and compare the performance of the CNN model trained using $D2L$ and CCE loss. Notably, we divide the classes into 6 categories according to the number of samples in the dataset i.e., 0-50, 50-100, 100-200, 200-500, 500-1000, 1000+. Figure 3 (bottom) displays the test accuracy for both the models across six categories. We observe that the highest gain in performance is achieved for the classes with 50-100 samples, followed by 100-200 samples, 200-500 samples. 1000+ samples make the lowest gain in performance. Thus from these observations, we reason that the model agnostic methods is more advantageous for classes having samples in the range 50-500, while classes having more samples gets a limited advantage.

4.7 Impact of number of class label

In this section, we investigate the relationship between class label size and performance gain. As the number of classes increases, it presents an additional complexity on model learning to learn the accurate boundary. We observe that some model-agnostic methods performance gain have positive correlation with the number of class label. Specifically, in Table 3, when $D2L$ is used with CNN, we observe performance gain of 6.41 %, 9.8 %, 10.74 %, which directly relates to class label size of 342, 823 and 1818 for beauty, electronics, and automotive dataset respectively. The same trend continues in table 4 when we flip 20% of the labels. We observe this trend owing to the fact that as the number of class labels increases, the annotator becomes more confused in labeling, which results in more inherent noise in the datasets. Thus the use of model-agnostic methods becomes more necessary when training machine learning models on large datasets with hundreds and thousands of categories.

4.8 Comparison with large expressive models

In this section, we compare model-agnostic method performance with a large expressive model like pre-trained BERT (Devlin et al., 2018). We consider three pre-trained BERT models (trained on Wikipedia and the Book Corpus dataset) having 2, 4, and 6 layers respectively and fine-tune them on our inputs using standard CCE loss. The models were fine-tuned for 600 epochs using a batch size of 500 and a learning rate of $1e-5$. Table 5 provides test error for all BERT model. From the results, we conclude that FFNN with $D2L$ can easily outperform the fine-tune BERT models (2-4-6 layers) consistently over all the three datasets, which reiterates the use of noise-robust loss functions. We can additionally increase the complexity of BERT models by adding more layers, but then the model will be highly com-

Table 5: BERT model performance

DATASET	L-2	L-4	L-6
Beauty	64.7	67.3	70.6
Electronics	56.2	62.7	65.2
Automotive	57.9	65.8	67.3

plex and cannot be used for inference in production. Due to computational hardware constraints, we leave for future work to explore such a model's performance and how these model-agnostic approaches will work for BERT when trained from scratch.

5 Conclusion

In this study, we demonstrate the effectiveness of model-agnostic methods in advancing the performance of machine learning models for large scale text classifications. While most of the machine learning literature focused on building complex networks to handle noise, very few works have studied the performance of simpler methods that can give a significant impact. To the best of our knowledge, this is the first attempt to apply model agnostic methods requiring no network modifications to handle inherent noise for text classification datasets. We fill the gap in existing literature, where applying these methods to large scale text classification tasks is not the norm. Although we have shown improvements for data scraped from e-commerce platforms, the methods mentioned above can be applied to any large text classification task. The methods mentioned are easy to implement and can be easily integrated into any machine learning workflows without breaking the existing code-base. In contrast to previous works, we did not add noise and hypothesize that large dataset having thousands of samples and hundreds of unique classes can inadvertently introduce noise. Moreover, this paper serves as a brief literature review of model-agnostic methods that can be applied to text classification and other related domains, requiring no network modifications and minimal computation overhead.

Acknowledgement

This research was supported by National Science Foundation under the grant 1838159 and 1739191. Access to computing facilities was provided by the University of Minnesota Supercomputing Institute.

References

Devansh Arpit, Stanislaw Jastrzkbski, Nicolas Ballas, David Krueger, Emmanuel Bengio, Maxinder S Kanwal, Tegan Maharaj, Asja Fischer, Aaron Courville, Yoshua Bengio, et al. 2017. A closer look at memorization in deep networks. In *Proceedings of the 34th International Conference on Machine Learning-Volume 70*, pages 233–242. JMLR. org.

Lucas Bernardi, Themistoklis Mavridis, and Pablo Estevez. 2019. 150 successful machine learning models: 6 lessons learned at booking. com. In *Proceedings of the 25th ACM SIGKDD International Conference on Knowledge Discovery & Data Mining*, pages 1743–1751.

Olivier Chapelle, Jason Weston, Léon Bottou, and Vladimir Vapnik. 2001. Vicinal risk minimization. In *Advances in neural information processing systems*, pages 416–422.

Jacob Devlin, Ming-Wei Chang, Kenton Lee, and Kristina Toutanova. 2018. Bert: Pre-training of deep bidirectional transformers for language understanding. *arXiv preprint arXiv:1810.04805*.

Eduardo Fonseca, Manoj Plakal, Daniel PW Ellis, Frederic Font, Xavier Favory, and Xavier Serra. 2019. Learning sound event classifiers from web audio with noisy labels. In *ICASSP 2019-2019 IEEE International Conference on Acoustics, Speech and Signal Processing (ICASSP)*, pages 21–25. IEEE.

Aritra Ghosh, Himanshu Kumar, and PS Sastry. 2017. Robust loss functions under label noise for deep neural networks. In *Thirty-First AAAI Conference on Artificial Intelligence*.

Jacob Goldberger and Ehud Ben-Reuven. 2016. Training deep neural-networks using a noise adaptation layer.

Sheng Guo, Weilin Huang, Haozhi Zhang, Chenfan Zhuang, Dengke Dong, Matthew R Scott, and Dinglong Huang. 2018. Curriculumnet: Weakly supervised learning from large-scale web images. In *Proceedings of the European Conference on Computer Vision (ECCV)*, pages 135–150.

Malay Haldar, Mustafa Abdool, Prashant Ramanathan, Tao Xu, Shulin Yang, Huizhong Duan, Qing Zhang, Nick Barrow-Williams, Bradley C Turnbull, Brendan M Collins, et al. 2019. Applying deep learning to airbnb search. In *Proceedings of the 25th ACM SIGKDD International Conference on Knowledge Discovery & Data Mining*, pages 1927–1935.

Ruining He and Julian McAuley. 2016. Ups and downs: Modeling the visual evolution of fashion trends with one-class collaborative filtering. In *proceedings of the 25th international conference on world wide web*, pages 507–517. International World Wide Web Conferences Steering Committee.

Sepp Hochreiter and Jürgen Schmidhuber. 1997. Long short-term memory. *Neural computation*, 9(8):1735–1780.

Michael E Houle. 2017. Local intrinsic dimensionality ii: multivariate analysis and distributional support. In *International Conference on Similarity Search and Applications*, pages 80–95. Springer.

Lu Jiang, Zhengyuan Zhou, Thomas Leung, Li-Jia Li, and Li Fei-Fei. 2017. Mentornet: Learning data-driven curriculum for very deep neural networks on corrupted labels. *arXiv preprint arXiv:1712.05055*.

Ishan Jindal, Daniel Pressel, Brian Lester, and Matthew Nokleby. 2019. An effective label noise model for dnn text classification. *arXiv preprint arXiv:1903.07507*.

Faris Kateb and Jugal Kalita. 2015. Classifying short text in social media: Twitter as case study. *International Journal of Computer Applications*, 111(9).

Yoon Kim. 2014. Convolutional neural networks for sentence classification. *arXiv preprint arXiv:1408.5882*.

Diederik P Kingma and Jimmy Ba. 2014. Adam: A method for stochastic optimization. *arXiv preprint arXiv:1412.6980*.

Aniket Kittur, Ed H Chi, and Bongwon Suh. 2008. Crowdsourcing user studies with mechanical turk. In *Proceedings of the SIGCHI conference on human factors in computing systems*, pages 453–456.

Stamatios Lefkimmiatis. 2018. Universal denoising networks: a novel cnn architecture for image denoising. In *Proceedings of the IEEE conference on computer vision and pattern recognition*, pages 3204–3213.

Junnan Li, Yongkang Wong, Qi Zhao, and Mohan S Kankanhalli. 2019. Learning to learn from noisy labeled data. In *Proceedings of the IEEE Conference on Computer Vision and Pattern Recognition*, pages 5051–5059.

Bang Liu, Weidong Guo, Di Niu, Chaoyue Wang, Shunnan Xu, Jinghong Lin, Kunfeng Lai, and Yu Xu. 2019. A user-centered concept mining system for query and document understanding at tencent. In *Proceedings of the 25th ACM SIGKDD International Conference on Knowledge Discovery & Data Mining*, pages 1831–1841.

Xingjun Ma, Yisen Wang, Michael E Houle, Shuo Zhou, Sarah M Erfani, Shu-Tao Xia, Sudanthi Wijewickrema, and James Bailey. 2018. Dimensionality-driven learning with noisy labels. *arXiv preprint arXiv:1806.02612*.

Eran Malach and Shai Shalev-Shwartz. 2017. Decoupling" when to update" from" how to update". In *Advances in Neural Information Processing Systems*, pages 960–970.

Volodymyr Mnih and Geoffrey E Hinton. 2012. Learning to label aerial images from noisy data. In *Proceedings of the 29th International conference on machine learning (ICML-12)*, pages 567–574.

Nagarajan Natarajan, Inderjit S Dhillon, Pradeep K Ravikumar, and Ambuj Tewari. 2013. Learning with noisy labels. In *Advances in neural information processing systems*, pages 1196–1204.

Giorgio Patrini, Alessandro Rozza, Aditya Krishna Menon, Richard Nock, and Lizhen Qu. 2017. Making deep neural networks robust to label noise: A loss correction approach. In *Proceedings of the IEEE Conference on Computer Vision and Pattern Recognition*, pages 1944–1952.

Jeffrey Pennington, Richard Socher, and Christopher Manning. 2014. Glove: Global vectors for word representation. In *Proceedings of the 2014 conference on empirical methods in natural language processing (EMNLP)*, pages 1532–1543.

Neeti Pokhriyal, Kshitij Tayal, Ifeoma Nwogu, and Venu Govindaraju. 2016. Cognitive-biometric recognition from language usage: A feasibility study. *IEEE Transactions on Information Forensics and Security*, 12(1):134–143.

Scott Reed, Honglak Lee, Dragomir Anguelov, Christian Szegedy, Dumitru Erhan, and Andrew Rabinovich. 2014. Training deep neural networks on noisy labels with bootstrapping. *arXiv preprint arXiv:1412.6596*.

David E Rumelhart, Geoffrey E Hinton, and Ronald J Williams. 1985. Learning internal representations by error propagation. Technical report, California Univ San Diego La Jolla Inst for Cognitive Science.

Dinghan Shen, Guoyin Wang, Wenlin Wang, Martin Renqiang Min, Qinliang Su, Yizhe Zhang, Chunyuan Li, Ricardo Henao, and Lawrence Carin. 2018. Baseline needs more love: On simple word-embedding-based models and associated pooling mechanisms. *arXiv preprint arXiv:1805.09843*.

Shelly Singh. 2019. Natural language processing market worth $26.4 billion by 2024. *https://www.bloomberg.com/press-releases/2019-12-10/natural-language-processing-market-worth-26-4-billion-by-2024-exclusive-report-by-marketsandmarkets.*

Sainbayar Sukhbaatar, Joan Bruna, Manohar Paluri, Lubomir Bourdev, and Rob Fergus. 2014. Training convolutional networks with noisy labels. *arXiv preprint arXiv:1406.2080.*

Christian Szegedy, Vincent Vanhoucke, Sergey Ioffe, Jon Shlens, and Zbigniew Wojna. 2016. Rethinking the inception architecture for computer vision. In *Proceedings of the IEEE conference on computer vision and pattern recognition*, pages 2818–2826.

Kshitij Tayal, Rao Nikhil, Saurabh Agarwal, and Karthik Subbian. 2019. Short text classification using graph convolutional network. *NIPS workshop on Graph Representation Learning.*

Arash Vahdat. 2017. Toward robustness against label noise in training deep discriminative neural networks. In *Advances in Neural Information Processing Systems*, pages 5596–5605.

Yisen Wang, Xingjun Ma, Zaiyi Chen, Yuan Luo, Jinfeng Yi, and James Bailey. 2019. Symmetric cross entropy for robust learning with noisy labels. In *Proceedings of the IEEE International Conference on Computer Vision*, pages 322–330.

Xiang Wu, Ran He, Zhenan Sun, and Tieniu Tan. 2018. A light cnn for deep face representation with noisy labels. *IEEE Transactions on Information Forensics and Security*, 13(11):2884–2896.

Tong Xiao, Tian Xia, Yi Yang, Chang Huang, and Xiaogang Wang. 2015. Learning from massive noisy labeled data for image classification. In *Proceedings of the IEEE conference on computer vision and pattern recognition*, pages 2691–2699.

Liang Yao, Chengsheng Mao, and Yuan Luo. 2019. Graph convolutional networks for text classification. In *Proceedings of the AAAI Conference on Artificial Intelligence*, volume 33, pages 7370–7377.

Hsiang-Fu Yu, Chia-Hua Ho, Prakash Arunachalam, Manas Somaiya, and Chih-Jen Lin. 2012. Product title classification versus text classification. *Csie. Ntu. Edu. Tw*, pages 1–25.

Zhilu Zhang and Mert Sabuncu. 2018. Generalized cross entropy loss for training deep neural networks with noisy labels. In *Advances in neural information processing systems*, pages 8778–8788.

Chiyuan Zhang, Samy Bengio, Moritz Hardt, Benjamin Recht, and Oriol Vinyals. 2016. Understanding deep learning requires rethinking generalization. *arXiv preprint arXiv:1611.03530.*

Hongyi Zhang, Moustapha Cisse, Yann N Dauphin, and David Lopez-Paz. 2017. mixup: Beyond empirical risk minimization. *arXiv preprint arXiv:1710.09412.*

Peng Zhou, Zhenyu Qi, Suncong Zheng, Jiaming Xu, Hongyun Bao, and Bo Xu. 2016. Text classification improved by integrating bidirectional lstm with two-dimensional max pooling. *arXiv preprint arXiv:1611.06639.*

ScopeIt: Scoping Task Relevant Sentences in Documents

Vishwas Suryanarayanan[*]   **Barun Patra**[*]   **Pamela Bhattacharya**

Chala Fufa   **Charles Lee**

Microsoft
{visuryan, bapatra, pamelabh, chfufa, charlle}@microsoft.com

Abstract

A prominent problem faced by conversational agents working with large documents (Eg: email-based assistants) is the frequent presence of information in the document that is irrelevant to the assistant. This in turn makes it harder for the agent to accurately detect intents, extract entities relevant to those intents and perform the desired action. To address this issue we present a neural model for scoping relevant information for the agent from a large document. We show that when used as the first step in a popularly used email-based assistant for helping users schedule meetings[1], our proposed model helps improve the performance of the intent detection and entity extraction tasks required by the agent for correctly scheduling meetings: across a suite of 6 downstream tasks, by using our proposed method, we observe an average gain of 35% in precision without any drop in recall. Additionally, we demonstrate that the same approach can be used for component level analysis in large documents, such as signature block identification.

1   Introduction

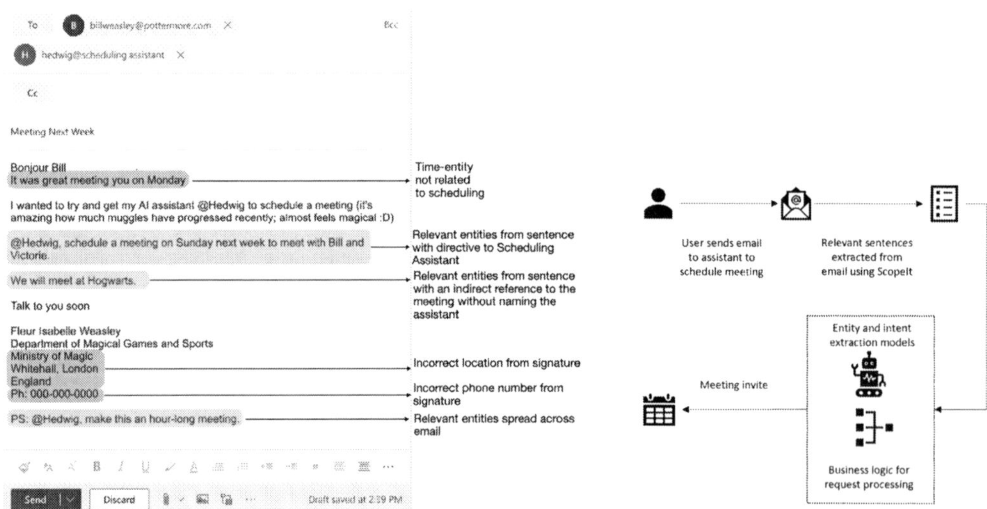

(a) A typical email encountered by the Scheduling Assistant   (b) The Email processing workflow

Intelligent personal digital assistants (IPDA) such as Microsoft Cortana, Amazon Alexa, Apple Siri, and Google Assistant, are becoming increasingly popular. These assistants make use of natural language to communicate, which leads to faster task completion, improving the user's productivity. A typical interaction with such a digital assistant requires a trigger (such as saying the assistant's name), followed

---

[*]Equal Contribution

[1]We use Hedwig in lieu of the actual persona of the agent throughout this paper

Proceedings of the 28th International Conference on Computational Linguistics: Industry Track, pages 214–227
Barcelona, Spain (Online), December 12, 2020

by a short phrase or sentence describing the user's ask of the digital assistant. Some examples of these conversations are: *"Cortana, what is the weather now?"*, *"Alexa, play next"*, *"Siri, turn off Bluetooth"*, *"Hey Google, take me home"*.

While most such assistants are voice based and communicate synchronously with the user, working mostly with short, targeted directives; there also exist email-based assistants that communicate and provide assistance asynchronously and thus have to work with much larger textual queries. Notable examples from the scheduling space are assistants like Cortana from Microsoft Scheduler, Amy and Andrew from x.ai, and Clara from Clara labs. These assistants require that the meeting organizer add them in the email with the attendees, and delegate the scheduling task to the assistant. Fig 1a shows an example of an email that an organizer can send to their virtual assistant. After receiving the email, the assistant needs to identify intents and entities of interest for scheduling the meeting correctly. For example, the duration of the meeting, where the meeting is (location), required and optional attendees, the type of meeting being requested (e.g. lunch, coffee), etc. This intent detection and entity extraction from large documents (eg: emails) can be challenging for two reasons:

- Information for scheduling the meeting could be spread across the document where most of the content is irrelevant

- Most generic open source entity extraction models are recall-heavy as they often are context independent, and consequently detect entities that are not relevant for scheduling.

Both the issues can be mitigated by building models (feature-based and/or neural) trained on the task at hand. However as we show in §6, these models can still get confused by the irrelevant information in the document and their performance can be improved by identifying relevant sentences of the document.

We model this problem of finding relevant sentences in a large document as a sentence-level binary classification problem, where every sentence in the email is either considered to be relevant or irrelevant to the context of scheduling meetings. While we focus on scheduling as an example throughout this paper, we believe our approach would be useful for domains outside of scheduling. We show that when used as a preprocessing step (Fig 1b), a good performance of our proposed model (ScopeIt) on the task of identifying relevant sentences in an email boosts the performance of the downstream intent classifiers and entity extractors. Additionally, we show the utility of the same model for signature block detection in component level analyses of emails. We demonstrate that our method can identify signature blocks for signature removal tasks, often required for pre-processing emails for text to speech systems, or for anonymizing email corpora.

The main contributions of this work are:

- We propose a novel model (ScopeIt) for scoping out task relevant sentences from a large document that outperforms strong baseline methods

- We illustrate the benefits of using ScopeIt as a preprocessing step and show that it improves the performance of a suite of downstream intent classifiers and entity detectors for the meeting scheduling task; improving precision by 35% (average) without any drop in recall. To the best of our knowledge, this is the first work to explore the utility of scoping task relevant sentences as a preprocessing step for tackling problems involving large text corpora.

- We show that our proposed architecture also performs better than publicly available baselines on the component level tasks like signature detection and generalizes better to real world data.

We present our approach to the problem of scoping out relevant sentences in §2. In §3, we describe our experimental setup and introduce the baselines we compare our approach against. We discuss ScopeIt's performance in §4. We analyze the embedding space induced by ScopeIt in §5 to understand why it performs well. In §6 we show the effectiveness of using ScopeIt as a preprocessing step on downstream intent classification and entity extraction tasks. We then show the performance of ScopeIt on the signature detection task (§7). In §8 we discuss the related work. Finally, we conclude in §9.

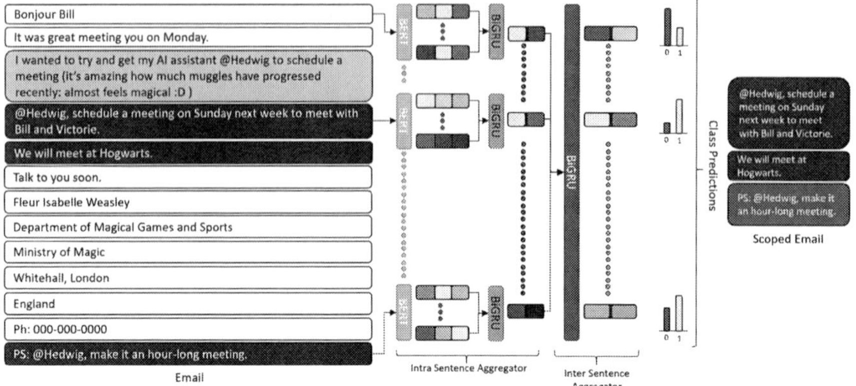

Figure 1: The model architecture: Contextual embeddings for each token in a sentence are first generated using BERT, following which, a BiGRU is used to generate the sentence embeddings. A BiGRU then aggregates information across the document. Finally, we predict the probability of selecting a sentence.

2 Proposed Method

In this section, we outline our approach to the problem of scoping out relevant sentences for a NLP-based scheduling assistant. Our approach consists of 2 parts: a preprocessing module and a neural model. An incoming email is first passed through the preprocessing module. The preprocessed email is then tokenized, indexed and passed through the neural model to generate a confidence score for each sentence. The model is trained end-to-end with human-labeled gold scores denoting the relevant sentences of the email. We also adopt some data augmentation methods to improve model generalization.

2.1 Preprocessing Module

The preprocessing step fixes any issues due to improperly decoded text (mojibake characters). Furthermore, since we use the wordpiece tokenizer[2] to tokenize each word into its constituent wordpieces, having raw urls or emails often generates a large number of uninformative wordpieces[3]. In order to circumvent this issue, we replace all urls and emails with special tokens (eg: URLTOKEN, EMAILTO-KEN). We keep track of the original urls/emails, and invert the token replacement after obtaining the confidence scores from the neural model.

2.2 Neural Model

Our neural model consists of 3 different modules: an intra-sentence aggregator to aggregate information within a sentence, an inter-sentence aggregator to share information across different sentences, and a classifier to predict the final relevance score of each sentence (Fig 1). Given a document, we first tokenize it into sentences using NLTK's sentence tokenizer. We then use the wordpiece tokenizer to tokenize each sentence. Let $\mathcal{X} = \{w_{1,1} \cdots w_{m,l_m}\}$ be the tokenized document, where $w_{i,j}$ denotes the jth wordpiece of the ith sentence and l_m denotes the length of the mth sentence. We predict the relevance of each sentence using the following approach:

$$(e_{i,1}, \cdots e_{i,l_i}) = BERT(w_{i,1} \cdots w_{i,l_i})$$

$$(h_{f_{i,1}} \cdots h_{f_{i,l_i}}) = \overrightarrow{Seq2SeqEncoder}(e_{i,1}, \cdots e_{i,l_i}) \quad (f_{s_1}, \cdots f_{s_m}) = \overrightarrow{Seq2SeqEncoder}(e_{s_1}, \cdots e_{s_m})$$

$$(h_{bi,1} \cdots h_{bi,l_i}) = \overleftarrow{Seq2SeqEncoder}(e_{i,1}, \cdots e_{i,l_i}) \quad (p_{s_1}, \cdots p_{s_m}) = (\sigma(f_{s_1}), \sigma(f_{s_2}) \cdots \sigma(f_{s_m}))$$

$$e_{s_i} = [h_{f_{i,l_i}}; h_{bi,1}]$$

---

[2] https://github.com/google/sentencepiece
[3] E.g "https://coling2020.org/pages/call_for_papers.html" generates 20 wordpieces

Intra Sentence Aggregator: Let $s_i = \{w_{i,1} \cdots w_{i,l_i}\}$ be the ith sentence. We generate contextual embeddings for each token $w_{i,j}(1 \leq j \leq l_i)$. We use BERT (Devlin et al., 2018) for generating the embeddings. Note that generating embeddings for each sentence independently, along with replacing urls with special tokens, allows us to circumvent the issue of BERT having a maximum of 512 positional embeddings (i.e we can now encode 512 * $num\_sentences$ wordpieces). Since we want to avoid back-propagating through BERT for compute constraints, using the [CLS] token (as is commonly done to generate sentence representations) doesn't work. Consequently, we use a Seq2Seq encoder to better adapt the contextual embeddings to the task. We then concatenate the final forward and backward hidden dimensions to get the sentence embedding $e_{s_i}, 1 \leq i \leq m$ for each sentence:

Inter Sentence Aggregator: Given sentence embeddings $\{e_{s_1} \cdots e_{s_m}\}$, we use a Seq2Seq encoder to aggregate information across different sentences. This allows the model to capture context based on other sentences around it, enabling us to capture document level features. A final Sigmoid output layer generates the probability of each sentence being relevant:

The model is trained with a binary cross entropy loss using gold annotated relevance scores, i.e. given annotations for the sentences $\mathcal{Y} = \{y_1, y_2, \cdots y_m\}$:

$$\mathcal{L} = -\sum_{i=1}^{m} y_i \log(p_{s_i}) + (1 - y_i) \log(1 - p_{s_i}) \tag{1}$$

2.3 Data Augmentation

Given that most emails received by the scheduling assistant have some information pertinent to scheduling, we augment the training data with irrelevant emails (i.e emails not relevant to scheduling). These emails are sampled from the Enron dataset (Cohen, 2015; Klimt and Yang, 2004). Further, we observed that the model was confused when given texts that did not resemble general email writing styles. To avoid this bias, we augment the dataset with negative samples from the IMDb and Yelp datasets (Kotzias et al., 2015). Furthermore, we observed that the original dataset had a bias of having relevant information being present at the beginning of the email. In order to account for that bias, we also shuffled passages of text within each email except the salutation and signature, and augment our dataset with the shuffled emails. We do so to ensure that the resulting shuffled emails are not nonsensical. We also augment the dataset by first creating templates for emails that are representative of the emails the system would receive, and then randomly replacing proper nouns in the email templates. Additional details can be found in Appendix A.

3 Experiments on Scoping Relevant Sentences

3.1 Dataset and Experimental Setup

We show the performance of ScopeIt on an internal dataset for identifying relevant sentences from emails for the context of scheduling. The details of pertaining to the dataset creation can be found in Appendix A. Table 1 shows the instances present in the train, validation and test splits. During evaluation, any sentence with score > 0.5 is classified as relevant and others are classified as irrelevant. We use the F1 score of the sentence relevance prediction task as the metric of evaluation. We report the hyperparameters and training details in Appendix B.

3.2 Baselines

Seq2Seq Encoder: This model does not use BERT for generating contextual embeddings. Instead, a standard word-level BiGRU model is used as the sentence encoder to generate sentence embeddings, with the vocabulary set to the top 10,000 most frequently occurring words encountered in the training data. The sentence embeddings are then projected using a feed-forward layer to generate the relevance probabilities.

No Inter-Sentence Aggregator: This model uses BERT for generating the contextual embeddings, and then a BiGRU encoder to generate the sentence embeddings. It however does not make use of any inter-sentence aggregator; instead a feed-forward layer directly generates the relevance probabilities.

BERT with [CLS] only: This model just uses the [CLS] token of BERT for generating the sentence embedding vector. Note that we don't fine-tune the BERT model.

ScopeIt Without Data Augmentation: Our proposed model without any data augmentation (§2.3)

BertSum: A state of the art extractive summarization model leveraging BERT (Liu and Lapata, 2019). We use the implementation provided by the authors.

Split	n_docs	n_internal	n_sent	n_pos	n_neg
train	21875	10546	233307	24428	208879
validate	2436	1176	25866	2699	23167
test[4]	1215	1015	12055	1716	10339

Table 1: Relevance Scoping Dataset Details

Model	F1 Score
BERT [CLS]	0.81
Seq2Seq Encoder	0.83
No Inter-Sentence Aggregator	0.89
BertSum (Liu and Lapata, 2019)	0.90
ScopeIt Without Data Augmentation	0.93
ScopeIt	**0.94**

Table 2: Performance for Relevance Scoping

4 Main Results

Table 2 shows the performance of ScopeIt compared to the baseline models. Since the BERT [CLS] model is not fine-tuned, it does not perform as well as any of the models where the Seq2Seq encoders are trained. Unsurprisingly, the models with BERT augmented embeddings outperform the standard Seq2Seq encoder model substantially. We observe that the inter-sentence aggregator also improves performance. Finally, the model with data-augmentation outperforms all of the baselines. We believe this is because of two reasons. First, most emails have a prior of being relevant, simply because the user cc'd the scheduling assistant. Consequently, the model predicted some sentences as relevant, even for emails which did not have any. Augmenting the data with completely irrelevant emails helps overcome that bias. Further, for most emails, the relevant scope occurs in the beginning of the email. Hence, baseline models bias towards scoring the beginning of the email higher than the end, even if the beginning was not particularly relevant. Training with the shuffling data augmentation mitigates the issue.

Our proposed model also performs better than BertSum. We hypothesize this is because our dataset is orders of magnitude smaller than the CNN/Daily Mail dataset (Hermann et al., 2015) used by Liu and Lapata (2019). And while finetuning BERT models for general tasks does not require as much data, BertSum uses a formulation very different from the original BERT model (Devlin et al., 2018)[5]. Consequently, finetuning BERT to adapt to these modification potentially requires more data. Moreover, BertSum still suffers from the 512 wordpiece restriction (§2.1), while ScopeIt does not.

5 Clustering in the Embedding Space

We next investigate if sentence embeddings generated by ScopeIt exhibit any clusters that make semantic sense. On preliminary analysis, some clusters that we observed in the data were salutations, signature blocks and sentences containing entities associated with scheduling meetings. We hypothesize that similar clusters should be observed in the sentence embedding space. To test this hypothesis, we propose the following experiment: given the embedding of a sentence belonging to a certain cluster (the query sentence), retrieve the top k nearest neighbor sentence embeddings from a set of sentence embeddings generated by ScopeIt. If similar clusters exist in the embedding space, then sentences associated with the retrieved embeddings should belong in the same cluster as the query sentence.

Due to space constraints, we describe the methodology of the embedding experiment in Appendix C, and report our main findings here. We observe that salutations and signatures are clustered together. We also observe sub-clusters wherein sentences containing similar entities or intents are clustered with sentences containing similar information. Moreover, we find that these sentence embeddings also capture

---

[4]We augment the test set with 200 completely irrelevant emails to gauge the model performance for that scenario.

[5]Specifically, they use alternating type tokens for each sentence, with each sentence separated with a [SEP] token and a [CLS] token, and use the [CLS] token of the sentence to generate the sentence embedding.

the context in which the sentences occur: syntactically similar query sentences get mapped to different clusters based on the context in which they occur.

6 Improvements to Downstream Tasks

Our main motivation for developing ScopeIt was the hypothesis that using relevant sentences in place of the entire document would improve the performance of downstream NLP tasks. In this section we highlight the impact ScopeIt has on 6 downstream tasks, 5 of which are either associated with detecting an intent related with scheduling a meeting or extracting the necessary entities. The models for tackling these tasks use the scoped message generated by ScopeIt as the input. We also consider the "Non-actionable Emails" task which helps the scheduling assistant identify emails that it should ignore. The models used for each task vary: they can either be context independent regex models, or context aware neural models. For each of these tasks, we first describe what the task is, and then describe the model(s) used for solving it. Finally, to show the impact of ScopeIt, for each task, we give the model(s) the original unaltered email and the scoped version as input, and compare the performance difference. We summarize the results of these experiments in §6.1. Note that there is no overlap between the data used for the analysis presented in this section and the data used for training ScopeIt.

1. Meeting Type When the scheduling assistant receives an email and has determined that the email has an intent to schedule a meeting, the Meeting Type task tries to classify the meeting request into one of the broad classes of meeting types as defined by the system. Each of the categories have special meeting properties that help the assistant populate the meeting details. Some examples of these meeting types defined are Lunch (which constrain the times to schedule), Conference Call (require a Remote Bridge), Phone call etc. The assistant uses an ensemble of different models to classify the meeting requests into these classes. For this case study, we focus on the model responsible for detecting a call or a conference call intent, which maps to the Phone Call and Conference Call meeting type classes, respectively.

  Example Input: *"Let us get together on a Team's call."*
  Expected Output: Conference Call Intent

  This task is modeled as a multi-label classification task, and we use a context aware deep network to tackle it. We use a model similar to the one proposed in (Mullenbach et al., 2018). Specifically, we generate a contextual embedding using BERT for each token in the email. Then, an attention method (Bahdanau et al., 2014), one for each label, is used to aggregate the embeddings into a document embedding, which is then passed through a sigmoid layer to generate the probability for each label. The entire model is trained end to end by minimizing the negative log likelihood of the gold labels. While using ScopeIt, we only select sentences that occur above a particular threshold (0.01), and feed the concatenation of those sentences as inputs to the model.

2. Meeting Duration The scheduling assistant needs to extract the duration for the meeting from the meeting organizer's email. If there wasn't a duration entity detected, the system uses the default duration set by the organizer in their meeting preferences.

  Example Input: *"Hedwig, schedule a meeting for 30 minutes."*
  Expected Output: 30 minutes.

  We use LUIS[6] for extracting the duration of a meeting from the meeting requests. LUIS is the Language Understanding Service in Microsoft Azure Cognitive Services that provides natural language intelligence for conversational AI applications (Williams et al., 2015). In order to utilize LUIS' high recall duration extraction model in the context of scheduling meetings, we select sentences scored above 0.01 by ScopeIt, and feed the concatenation of the sentences as the input to LUIS' duration extraction model.

3. Meeting Phone Number When users schedule a phone call, the system needs to extract phone numbers from the organizer or attendee to add to the meeting invite.

  Example Input: *"Hedwig, please schedule a call with Albus. My phone number is +1 000-000-0000. Regards, Gellert Grindelwald"*

---

[6]`https://www.luis.ai/home`

Expected Output: +1 000-000-0000.

We use LUIS for extracting the phone numbers from an email. We extract sentences scored above a threshold of 0.01 by ScopeIt, concatenate the sentences, and feed that as an input to the high recall phone number extraction model.

4. Meeting Location   In order to schedule the meeting at the right location, the system needs to extract the intended location expressed by the organizer.

    Example Input: *"Hedwig, schedule a meeting. Hagrid, let's meet at the 3 Broomsticks."*

    Expected Output: the 3 Broomsticks

This is modeled as an entity extraction problem and consequently we fine-tune BERT for tagging (similar to the BERT for NER, as done in Devlin et al. (2018)). We concatenate sentences scored above a certain threshold by ScopeIt and pass it as an input to the model.

5. Meeting Timezone   Users typically express multi timezones in two ways: express time zones by explicitly mentioning timezone abbreviations like "EST", or implicitly by indicating the city and sometimes the country where the meeting is going to be held.

    Example Input: *"Hedwig, schedule an online meeting with Ron Weasley next week. Ron is in EST, and I am going to be working from Dublin for that week."*

    Expected Output: EST, Dublin

By using ScopeIt to filter out sentences irrelevant to scheduling the meeting, the system is able to leverage recall-heavy time zone entity extractors, and city and country extractors to find the right time zones. It utilizes LUIS for time zone entity extraction and LU (Location Understanding) from Bing to extract cities and countries from the input text. These utterances are subsequently resolved for their time zone offsets.

6. Non-actionable Emails   When the scheduling assistant processes a request, the system might receive emails from meeting participants which are irrelevant to scheduling. For example, after the meeting organizer has sent a request to the scheduling assistant (Hedwig, in the prior examples), one of the invitees might reply to the email thread with all meeting participants including the assistant saying, *"Thanks for setting this up. Look forward to meeting you."* In these cases, there is no action required from the system's point of view and the email can be safely ignored. Similar to the approach stated in the previous tasks, sentences in the email that are scored above a threshold are extracted and concatenated. If there are no sentences in the email above the relevance threshold, the email is considered irrelevant and is ignored by the system.

6.1   Results

Task	Task Type	Model Type	Metric	Before ScopeIt	After ScopeIt	Δ
Meeting Type	Classification	Context Aware	Accuracy	0.72	0.96	+0.24
Non-actionable Emails	Classification	Context Aware	Accuracy	N/A	0.96	+ 0.96
Duration	Extraction	Context Independent	Accuracy	0.88	0.92	+0.04
Phone Number	Extraction	Context Independent	Precision	0.46	0.98	+0.52
			Recall	1	1	0
Location	Extraction	Context Aware	Precision	0.73	0.96	+0.23
			Recall	0.92	0.96	+0.04
Timezone	Extraction	Context Independent	Precision	0.37	0.67	+0.30
			Recall	0.92	0.96	+0.04
	Average		Accuracy			+0.14
			Precision			+0.35
			Recall			+0.02

Table 3: A summary of all improvements resulting from the ScopeIt's preprocessing

Table 3 summarizes the utility of using ScopeIt. For the intent classification and duration extraction tasks, we see an average increment of 0.14 in the accuracy. An interesting observation is that even the context aware neural model benefits strongly (+0.24 accuracy improvement).

For the entity extraction models, we observe a strong increase in precision, with an average increase of 0.35. The context independent models benefit strongly when we strip out the irrelevant parts of the document: as shown in the example in Figure 1a, phone numbers extracted by the context independent regex based model are often found in the signature block of the email. A similar behavior is also observed in the timezone extraction task, where locations in the signature often get picked up as timezones. As hypothesized, once the email is scoped to only the relevant parts, these models get a substantial boost in precision. A similar gain is also observed for the BERT Location extractor.

An interesting observation is that the recall for these extraction models also improves. On further investigation, we found that this can be attributed to an increase in the true positives. For the BERT Location extraction, this makes sense, since a simplified input allows the model to reason better about the location. For the timezone task, we hypothesize that the LU model has additional heuristics and that the heuristics perform better on the simplified inputs.

Using ScopeIt also offers the benefit of making regex models feasible to use. This is especially advantageous since regex-based models have faster inference times and require much less data to build than their neural counterparts.

Finally, ScopeIt also helps the scheduling assistant decide between which emails to process and which ones to ignore, which plays a crucial role for an email-based agent. People often use reply-all while interacting with each other on an email thread. This leads to the agent receiving emails whose contents are not relevant to the task of scheduling the meeting. Using ScopeIt ensures that those emails are ignored by the agent.

7   Signature Block Detection

As described in §5, we observed that sentences with similar semantics were clustered close to each other in the sentence embedding space. We use this observation to apply our model to component detection in email, specifically for signature block identification. We show the model's performance on a publicly available dataset, and show that it outperforms the baseline model. We also hypothesize that the publicly available systems for extracting signatures are not suitable for real-world use-cases, as they are often trained on well structured emails using hand crafted features, and hence are not robust to the variety of writing styles that people employ in the real world. In order to validate this hypothesis, we test the effectiveness of the baseline on our use-case.

7.1   Dataset and Experimental Setup

We use the 20-Newsgroup dataset consisting of emails annotated with signature blocks (Carvalho and Cohen, 2004). This dataset is publicly available [7]. We use a standard split of 80%, 10% and 10% as the training, validation, and testing splits. In order to validate our hypothesis about the efficacy of the publicly available baseline on our use-case, we annotate 625 emails with signature blocks and then test the performance of the baseline as well as our model (trained on the 20-Newsgroup dataset) on this annotated dataset. The number of instances in the dataset can be found in Table 4.

7.2   Baseline

We compare against a publicly available signature detection tool Jangada(Carvalho and Cohen, 2004). Jangada uses a CRF model with handcrafted features, and is trained on the 20-Newsgroup dataset.

7.3   Results on Signature Block Detection

As seen in Table 5, our proposed neural model outperforms Jangada on the 20 Newsgroup dataset. We also validate our hypothesis: when we use Jangada for our real world use-case to remove signatures, we observe that while it has a high precision, the recall drops drastically (0.224); making it impractical to

---

[7]https://www.cs.cmu.edu/~vitor/codeAndData.html

Dataset	Split	n_docs	n_sent	n_pos	n_neg
20 Newsgroup	train	465	20629	18076	2553
	val	52	1797	1522	275
	test	100	4547	4054	493
Manually Annotated	train	501	6055	2043	4012
	val	62	670	227	443
	test	62	663	260	403

Table 4: Signature Detection: Dataset Details

Dataset	Model	Precision	Recall	Fscore
20 Newsgroup	Jangada	0.98	0.971	0.975
	ScopeIt	0.992	0.999	**0.996**
Manually Annotated	Jangada	0.908	0.224	0.359
	ScopeIt	0.995	0.884	**0.936**

Table 5: Performance: Jangada Vs ScopeIt

use in production. On the other hand, ScopeIt, even when trained on 20 Newsgroup, generalizes much better (recall 0.885, fscore: 0.936).

8 Related Work

Our problem of relevance scoping in documents is similar to extractive summarization. Extractive summarization deals with selecting subsets (usually sentences) of a document that succinctly summarizes it. For the case of this scheduling assistant, scoping out the relevant part in an email document is in essence selecting the subset of sentences from the email that accurately summarizes the scheduling intent and specifies the parameters necessary to schedule a meeting correctly. Both traditional feature based methods using word probability, TF-IDF weights, sentence position and sentence length features (Luhn, 1958; Eduard and Lin, 1998; Cao et al., 2015; Ren et al., 2016) and recent neural methods (Nallapati et al., 2017; Zhou et al., 2018; Narayan et al., 2018; Liu et al., 2019; Liu and Lapata, 2019) have been used for the task of extractive summarization. Liu and Lapata (2019) show the benefit of using pretrained language models (Peters et al., 2018; Radford et al., 2018; Devlin et al., 2018; Dong et al., 2019; Zhang et al., 2019) for the same task. Their proposed model BertSum leverages interval segment embeddings to distinguish multiple sentences within a document. BertSum further also finetunes the BERT embeddings to learn the segment embeddings during training, which potentially requires more data; and can also only encode upto 512 wordpiece long documents. In contrast, we used hierarchical RNNs (similar to (Nallapati et al., 2017; Zhou et al., 2018)), with the pretrained embeddings forming the embedding layer (Fig. 1); thereby allowing us to encode emails much larger than 512 tokens long.

Intent classification and entity extraction tasks in the context of conversational understanding have been studied both in academia and corporate research laboratories (de Mori et al., 2008). There exists a rich body of research in user intent identification from targeted queries (Wang et al., 2014). However, these methods don't work as well when applied to large documents. We showed that scoping out the relevant parts in a document improves performance of classification and extraction tasks on large queries. To the best of our knowledge, this is the first work to explore the utility of extractive summarization as a preprocessing step for tackling problems involving large text corpora.

There has been extensive research on the topic of identifying signature blocks and reply lines from an email (Carvalho and Cohen, 2004; Minkov et al., 2005; Balog and de Rijke, 2006; Xiaoqin, 2015). (Balog and de Rijke, 2006; Xiaoqin, 2015) present heuristic driven methods for unsupervised identification of the signature body, while (Carvalho and Cohen, 2004) present a CRF based approach for identifying and extracting signature and reply lines from Email. We showed in §7 that our proposed method also works well for removing signatures and also generalizes better.

9 Conclusion

In this paper, we proposed a simple method for scoping relevant information within emails and the impact the model had on a suite of tasks that are vital for the scheduling assistant. We also showed our models applicability on the task of Signature Detection. We show that it performs better than existing publicly available baselines and generalizes better on real world use-cases.

In this work we showed that our model works well with emails. For future work, we plan on investigating the impact of our proposed method for other tasks that process large textual inputs (Eg: document classification, sentiment analysis on large reviews). Furthermore, using BERT for inference poses latency challenges in a production system. A promising direction of future work that we plan on investigating is leveraging distilled versions of BERT (Sun et al., 2019; Wang et al., 2020) for the task.

References

Dzmitry Bahdanau, Kyunghyun Cho, and Yoshua Bengio. 2014. Neural machine translation by jointly learning to align and translate. *arXiv preprint arXiv:1409.0473*.

Krisztian Balog and Maarten de Rijke. 2006. Finding experts and their eetails in e-mail corpora. In *Proceedings of the 15th international conference on World Wide Web*, pages 1035–1036.

Ziqiang Cao, Furu Wei, Sujian Li, Wenjie Li, Ming Zhou, and Houfeng Wang. 2015. Learning summary prior representation for extractive summarization. In *Proceedings of the 53rd Annual Meeting of the Association for Computational Linguistics and the 7th International Joint Conference on Natural Language Processing (Volume 2: Short Papers)*, pages 829–833.

Vitor R. Carvalho and William W. Cohen. 2004. Learning to extract signature and reply lines from email. In *CEAS 2004 - First Conference on Email and Anti-Spam*, Mountain View, CA.

Kyunghyun Cho, Bart Van Merriënboer, Caglar Gulcehre, Dzmitry Bahdanau, Fethi Bougares, Holger Schwenk, and Yoshua Bengio. 2014. Learning phrase representations using rnn encoder-decoder for statistical machine translation. *arXiv preprint arXiv:1406.1078*.

William W. Cohen. 2015. Enron email dataset.

R de Mori, F Bechet, D Hakkani-Tur, M McTear, G Riccardi, and G Tur. 2008. Spoken language understanding. *IEEE Signal Processing Magazine*, 25(3):50–58, 9.

Jacob Devlin, Ming-Wei Chang, Kenton Lee, and Kristina Toutanova. 2018. Bert: Pre-training of deep bidirectional transformers for language understanding. *arXiv preprint arXiv:1810.04805*.

Li Dong, Nan Yang, Wenhui Wang, Furu Wei, Xiaodong Liu, Yu Wang, Jianfeng Gao, Ming Zhou, and Hsiao-Wuen Hon. 2019. Unified language model pre-training for natural language understanding and generation. In *Advances in Neural Information Processing Systems*, pages 13042–13054.

Hovy Eduard and Chin-Yew Lin. 1998. Automated text summarization and the summarist system. In *Proceedings of a workshop on held at Baltimore*.

Matt Gardner, Joel Grus, Mark Neumann, Oyvind Tafjord, Pradeep Dasigi, Nelson F. Liu, Matthew Peters, Michael Schmitz, and Luke S. Zettlemoyer. 2017. Allennlp: A deep semantic natural language processing platform.

Karl Moritz Hermann, Tomas Kocisky, Edward Grefenstette, Lasse Espeholt, Will Kay, Mustafa Suleyman, and Phil Blunsom. 2015. Teaching machines to read and comprehend. In *Advances in neural information processing systems*, pages 1693–1701.

Diederik P Kingma and Jimmy Ba. 2014. Adam: A method for stochastic optimization. *arXiv preprint arXiv:1412.6980*.

Bryan Klimt and Yiming Yang. 2004. Introducing the enron corpus. In *CEAS*.

Dimitrios Kotzias, Misha Denil, Nando de Freitas, and Padhraic Smyth. 2015. From group to individual labels using deep features. In *Proceedings of the 21th ACM SIGKDD International Conference on Knowledge Discovery and Data Mining*, KDD '15, page 597–606, New York, NY, USA. Association for Computing Machinery.

Yang Liu and Mirella Lapata. 2019. Text summarization with pretrained encoders.

Yang Liu, Ivan Titov, and Mirella Lapata. 2019. Single document summarization as tree induction. In *Proceedings of the 2019 Conference of the North American Chapter of the Association for Computational Linguistics: Human Language Technologies, Volume 1 (Long and Short Papers)*, pages 1745–1755, Minneapolis, Minnesota, June. Association for Computational Linguistics.

Hans Peter Luhn. 1958. The automatic creation of literature abstracts. *IBM Journal of research and development*, 2(2):159–165.

Einat Minkov, Richard C. Wang, and William W. Cohen. 2005. Extracting personal names from email: Applying named entity recognition to informal text. In *Proceedings of Human Language Technology Conference and Conference on Empirical Methods in Natural Language Processing*, pages 443–450, Vancouver, British Columbia, Canada, October. Association for Computational Linguistics.

James Mullenbach, Sarah Wiegreffe, Jon Duke, Jimeng Sun, and Jacob Eisenstein. 2018. Explainable prediction of medical codes from clinical text. In *Proceedings of the 2018 Conference of the North American Chapter of the Association for Computational Linguistics: Human Language Technologies, Volume 1 (Long Papers)*, pages 1101–1111, New Orleans, Louisiana, June. Association for Computational Linguistics.

Ramesh Nallapati, Feifei Zhai, and Bowen Zhou. 2017. Summarunner: A recurrent neural network based sequence model for extractive summarization of documents. In *Thirty-First AAAI Conference on Artificial Intelligence*.

Shashi Narayan, Shay B. Cohen, and Mirella Lapata. 2018. Ranking sentences for extractive summarization with reinforcement learning. In *Proceedings of the 2018 Conference of the North American Chapter of the Association for Computational Linguistics: Human Language Technologies, Volume 1 (Long Papers)*, pages 1747–1759, New Orleans, Louisiana, June. Association for Computational Linguistics.

F. Pedregosa, G. Varoquaux, A. Gramfort, V. Michel, B. Thirion, O. Grisel, M. Blondel, P. Prettenhofer, R. Weiss, V. Dubourg, J. Vanderplas, A. Passos, D. Cournapeau, M. Brucher, M. Perrot, and E. Duchesnay. 2011. Scikit-learn: Machine learning in Python. *Journal of Machine Learning Research*, 12:2825–2830.

Matthew Peters, Mark Neumann, Mohit Iyyer, Matt Gardner, Christopher Clark, Kenton Lee, and Luke Zettlemoyer. 2018. Deep contextualized word representations. In *Proceedings of the 2018 Conference of the North American Chapter of the Association for Computational Linguistics: Human Language Technologies, Volume 1 (Long Papers)*, pages 2227–2237, New Orleans, Louisiana, June. Association for Computational Linguistics.

Alec Radford, Karthik Narasimhan, Tim Salimans, and Ilya Sutskever. 2018. Improving language understanding by generative pre-training. *URL https://s3-us-west-2. amazonaws. com/openai-assets/researchcovers/languageunsupervised/language understanding paper. pdf*.

Pengjie Ren, Furu Wei, Zhumin Chen, Jun Ma, and Ming Zhou. 2016. A redundancy-aware sentence regression framework for extractive summarization. In *Proceedings of COLING 2016, the 26th International Conference on Computational Linguistics: Technical Papers*, pages 33–43.

Siqi Sun, Yu Cheng, Zhe Gan, and Jingjing Liu. 2019. Patient knowledge distillation for BERT model compression. In *Proceedings of the 2019 Conference on Empirical Methods in Natural Language Processing and the 9th International Joint Conference on Natural Language Processing (EMNLP-IJCNLP)*, pages 4323–4332, Hong Kong, China, November. Association for Computational Linguistics.

Zhuoran Wang, Hongliang Chen, Guanchun Wang, Hao Tian, Hua Wu, and Haifeng Wang. 2014. Policy learning for domain selection in an extensible multi-domain spoken dialogue system. In *Proceedings of EMNLP 2014*. Association for Computational Linguistics.

Wenhui Wang, Furu Wei, Li Dong, Hangbo Bao, Nan Yang, and Ming Zhou. 2020. Minilm: Deep self-attention distillation for task-agnostic compression of pre-trained transformers. *arXiv preprint arXiv:2002.10957*.

Jason D Williams, Eslam Kamal, Mokhtar Ashour, Hani Amr, Jessica Miller, and Geoff Zweig. 2015. Fast and easy language understanding for dialog systems with microsoft language understanding intelligent service (luis). In *Proceedings of the 16th Annual Meeting of the Special Interest Group on Discourse and Dialogue*, pages 159–161.

Yuan Xiaoqin. 2015. Unsupervised extraction of signatures and roles from large-scale mail archives. *International Journal of Security and Its Applications*, 9(4):229–238.

Xingxing Zhang, Furu Wei, and Ming Zhou. 2019. HIBERT: Document level pre-training of hierarchical bidirectional transformers for document summarization. In *Proceedings of the 57th Annual Meeting of the Association for Computational Linguistics*, pages 5059–5069, Florence, Italy, July. Association for Computational Linguistics.

Qingyu Zhou, Nan Yang, Furu Wei, Shaohan Huang, Ming Zhou, and Tiejun Zhao. 2018. Neural document summarization by jointly learning to score and select sentences. *arXiv preprint arXiv:1807.02305*.

A   Dataset Creation Details

The dataset is built by sampling 12737 emails from an internal dataset. These emails were split into a train and test set first at a 90%-10% split, and then the train set was split again at a 90%-10% split to form the training and validation datasets. In order to measure the inter-annotator agreement for the dataset, we randomly sample 200 emails, which were then annotated by another annotator. The Cohen's kappa (κ) measured was 0.89.

This dataset is augmented with negative samples from the Enron dataset, which are used to account for emails from a professional settings, which are not related to scheduling. This is done by using a list of disqualification words that remove emails that could potentially be referring to meetings. The disqualification words for Enron are as follows: "book a room", "let's meet", "meeting", "conference room", "meet", "invitation", "location", "half an hour", "30 mins", "30 minutes", "45 mins", "schedule" and "reserve". If any of these phrases are found in the email, the same disqualifies them as a negative. A total of 5429 emails were added from the Enron dataset.

To account for emails that do not conform to regular language used in a professional setting, text data was sampled and added from the Yelp and IMDB subsets from the UCI Sentiment Labelled Sentences dataset. Specifically, 1000 documents and 748 documents were sampled from the Yelp and IMDB subsets respectively, after similar disqualification rules. These were added to the train and validation dataset in the same proportions as before. The data augmentation was necessary to ensure the model is not biased to believe that all documents contain something relevant. We also add 200 examples to the test set to check if the trained models learn discard completely irrelevant documents.

Other data augmentation methods included random replacement and random swapping. For random replacement, proper nouns in templatized emails were replaced. Finally, the dataset was further augmented by random swapping of passages for longer emails (with > 3 passages). The last and first passages were not swapped, as these generally tended to be salutation or signature blocks. These account for the remainder of the data points in the dataset.

B   Hyperparameters and Training Details

We use the BERT-Base, Multilingual Cased[8] model for generating the contextual embeddings. We do not fine-tune the BERT model for any of the models due to compute constraints. We use a 2 layer BiGRU encoder (Cho et al., 2014) (hidden dimension of 128) as the Seq2SeqEncoder for the intra-sentence aggregator, and a 2 layer BiGRU (hidden dimension of 128) as the Seq2Seq Encoder for the inter-sentence aggregator. The model was trained with gradient descent for 50 epochs. We used Adam (Kingma and Ba, 2014) as the optimizer with a learning rate of 0.0001. The learning rate was annealed by a factor of 0.5 if the validation loss failed to improve over 5 epochs, and also use early stopping with a patience of 8. All our models were developed using the AllenNLP framework (Gardner et al., 2017). For tuning the models, a grid search over the following learning rates was done: $\{1e-2, 5e-3, 1e-3\}$, as well as a batch size of $\{4, 8, 16, 32\}$ (beyond that caused out of memory issues). All models were trained on a single K80 instance.

C   Clustering in Embedding Space

To generate the set of sentence embeddings, we use the aforementioned publicly available Enron dataset. We randomly sample 10000 of the 500000 emails present in the dataset, and generate sentence embeddings for all the emails, obtaining ≈ 100000 sentence embeddings. We then generate a typical email that a user might send to their scheduling assistant and use sentences from those emails as query sentences to probe the sentence embedding space. We use Scikit-learn's (Pedregosa et al., 2011) NearestNeighbors method [9] for the NN computation, and retrieve 3 NN sentences.[10] We redact personal information like names, phone numbers in order to preserve the privacy of the users in the Enron dataset.

---

[8] https://github.com/google-research/bert/blob/master/multilingual.md

[9] https://scikit-learn.org/stable/modules/neighbors.html

[10] Specifically, we retrieve the sentence generating the embedding as well as the email containing the sentence. This is done to provide context, since these sentence embeddings also take context into consideration.

Original Email	Query	Cluster Type	NN With Surrounding Context
Hey Harry **I'm using Hedwig to schedule a** **meeting! @Hedwig, schedule a meeting for next week, in Hogsmade.** Thanks, Ronald Weasley The Burrow Ottery St. Catchpole England	Hey Harry	Salutation	*Hi Richard,* Per my voicemail, are you available for w/Greg *Jim,* Is there going to be a conference call or some other type of weekly meeting ⋯ *Hi Shirley,* Is this meeting still set for tomorrow? ⋯
	@Hedwig, schedule a meeting for next week, in Hogsmade.	Date-time availab-ility intent	⋯ call memo that we will forward on early next week. *Chris Long will be in touch on Tuesday to help coordinate the recommended call.* ⋯ ⋯ Any possibility of rescheduling to another day? *Sally is available Thursday, June 1.* ⋯ Susan, *please organize a meeting with Steve, Kim, and Tracey early next week, say Monday or Tuesday* ⋯
	Ronald Weasley	Signature	⋯ Thank you *Mona ******** ⋯ Thanks, Larry ******** ⋯ Thanks, Patti*
Hey Ron, Sounds's good. **Let's meet at the Three Broomsticks. @Hedwig, Ron will call me. My phone number is 000-000-0000.** Thanks, Harry Potter Ph: 000-000-0000	My phone number is 000-000-0000.	Phone availability intent	⋯ I should contact your assistant to schedule a meeting. *If you need to contact me immediately, please call my cell phone at 000-000-0000.* ⋯ ⋯ *he is available for a meeting (or conference call) to discuss the GE facility agreement sometime tomorrow - either am or after 300.* ⋯ Hey Suz *Is Sheila still planning on having the GE call tomorrow?*
	Ph: 000-000-0000	Signature	⋯ Thanks. *Rahul* ⋯ Larry ******** *(000) 000-0000* ⋯ Director *Government Affairs - The Americas*

Table 6: Nearest Neighbor Analysis on the Enron Dataset. **Red** denotes the scoped email as predicted by ScopeIt. *Blue* denotes the actual nearest neighbor in the context. Best viewed in color

Table 6 shows the results of the NN analysis. We use **Red** to denote the final scoped out email as predicted by ScopeIt, and we use *Blue* to denote the actual NN of the query sentence. As shown in the table, the queried NNs belong to the same cluster as the query. We see that salutations and signatures get clustered together. We also observe sub-clusters wherein sentences containing date-time availability or phone call intents get mapped to sentences containing similar information. We also observe that contextual information is captured by these contextual embeddings. As shown by the second generated email, syntactically similar query sentences can get mapped to different clusters, based on the context in which they occur.

Uncertainty Modeling for Machine Comprehension Systems using Efficient Bayesian Neural Networks

Zhengyuan Liu, Pavitra Krishnaswamy, Ai Ti Aw, Nancy F. Chen
Institute for Infocomm Research, A*STAR, Singapore
{liu_zhengyuan,nfychen}@i2r.a-star.edu.sg

Abstract

While neural approaches have achieved significant improvement in machine comprehension tasks, models often work as a black-box, resulting in lower interpretability, which requires special attention in domains such as healthcare or education. Quantifying uncertainty helps pave the way towards more interpretable neural networks. In classification and regression tasks, Bayesian neural networks have been effective in estimating model uncertainty. However, inference time increases linearly due to the required sampling process in Bayesian neural networks. Thus speed becomes a bottleneck in tasks with high system complexity such as question-answering or dialogue generation. In this work, we propose a hybrid neural architecture to quantify model uncertainty using Bayesian weight approximation but boosts up the inference speed by 80% relative at test time, and apply it for a clinical dialogue comprehension task. The proposed approach is also used to enable active learning so that an updated model can be trained more optimally with new incoming data by selecting samples that are not well-represented in the current training scheme.

1   Introduction

Neural approaches demonstrate strong learning capability, achieve significant improvement in various natural language processing tasks (Devlin et al., 2019), and are increasingly applied in real-world applications (Du et al., 2019; J Kurisinkel and Chen, 2019). However, neural models typically operate as black-box functions and thus lack interpretability. Interpreting (or even if only partially) the output from neural models is important in domains such as healthcare, when a model is prone to make incorrect diagnosis (Settles, 2012). To tackle this issue, one approach is to evaluate the confidence of an output generated by a model regarding an input, which is through quantifying *model uncertainty* or *epistemic uncertainty*. When the uncertainty measure of the model is high, one could be prompted to intervene in the automated decision process by either overriding the system's decision or escalating the situation to a domain expert. This approach would also favor model training with new incoming streams of data that may be ill-represented in the current setting.

Different from the label probability produced by models, epistemic uncertainty is derived from the weight variance under the observation on a certain distribution. Bayesian neural networks (BNNs) (Denker and LeCun, 1990; Buntine and Weigend, 1991), in which prior distributions are applied as additional constraints to weights, have been shown to be effective for quantifying epistemic uncertainty. Instead of obtaining deterministic weights, Bayesian methods update weights via distribution-based estimation (Kendall and Gal, 2017). Therefore, one can sample different possible weights and forward inputs through the network multiple times, then obtain epistemic uncertainty according to the variance of a set of predictions. Moreover, drawing experience from past work, modeling within a Bayesian framework can lead to potentially better representations and predictions in various tasks (Kendall and Gal, 2017; Xiao and Wang, 2019).

Most previous studies applied Bayesian neural approaches on classification or regression tasks. In this paper, we focus on modeling and utilizing epistemic uncertainty for question-answering (QA) systems

Proceedings of the 28th International Conference on Computational Linguistics: Industry Track, pages 228–235
Barcelona, Spain (Online), December 12, 2020

in natural language processing, and tackling the aforementioned issues in the healthcare domain. Since the neural network architectures for QA tasks are relatively more complex, there is a need to balance the learning quality and inference speed. To this end, we propose a hybrid neural architecture by integrating Bayesian approximation to a base neural model and optimize its training strategy. We conduct experiments on a clinical conversational scenario in Section 4.1 and a question-answering benchmark dataset (see Appendix B). The result shows that our approach can achieve better performance and is capable of modeling epistemic uncertainty. Furthermore, we analyze the characteristics of the quantified uncertainties and conduct an active learning experiment on the clinical corpus.

2　In Relation to Other Work

Neural question-answering approaches, often applied to machine comprehension tasks, have achieved rapid progress lately, benefiting from large-scale corpora (Rajpurkar et al., 2016), semantic vector representations (Pennington et al., 2014), sophisticated neural architectures (Seo et al., 2017), and deep contextual language models (Devlin et al., 2019), pushing the state-of-the-art performance on various benchmarks. However, the extent to which these systems truly understand language remains unclear, and models are vulnerable to adversarial samples (Jia and Liang, 2017).

As an effective approach to model weight variance and generate predictions, Bayesian neural networks and their variants have been applied in computer vision for image classification (Kendall and Gal, 2017) and autonomous vehicles to better model safety (McAllister et al., 2017). In natural language processing, uncertainty modeling has been adopted in sentiment analysis, named entity recognition and language modeling (Xiao and Wang, 2019). Such approaches have also proved effective in domain-specific active learning such as named entity recognition (Shen et al., 2017). To the best of our knowledge, we take the first stab to introduce neural epistemic uncertainty modeling in question-answering tasks.

Making Bayesian neural networks tractable on large-scale practical problems has been a focus in the research field since the 1990's (Denker and LeCun, 1990; Hinton and Van Camp, 1993; Barber and Bishop, 1998). More recently, several approximation methods have been proposed, including Bayes-by-Backprop (Blundell et al., 2015), which places a prior distribution over model parameters and calculates the Kullback-Leibler (KL) divergence between approximated and expected posterior distribution; and Monte-Carlo Dropout (Gal and Ghahramani, 2016), which applies dropout in both training and inference stages to approximate Bayesian variational inference. Sampling from approximated posterior distribution using gradient uncertainty can also be used to represent uncertainty in predictions (Park et al., 2018).

3　Methodology

3.1　Modeling Epistemic Uncertainty with Bayesian Neural Networks

A traditional neural model $f^{\mathcal{W}}(.)$ with a specific network architecture $f(.)$ learns and optimizes weights $\mathcal{W}$ by point estimation, therefore the inference process is deterministic. However, in practice, there is a degree of uncertainty associated with the weights (epistemic uncertainty), which can be modeled by representing the weights $\mathcal{W}$ as a distribution. To this end, Bayesian neural networks aim to estimate the posterior distribution of $\mathcal{W}$, based on the observation of data $\mathcal{D}$. Here, the posterior is denoted as $p(\mathcal{W}|\mathcal{D})$ and once it is estimated, the prediction of an input x is generated by marginalizing over the posterior:

$$p(y|x, \mathcal{D}) = \int_{\mathcal{W}} p(y|f^{\mathcal{W}}(x))p(\mathcal{W}|\mathcal{D})d\mathcal{W} \tag{1}$$

However, the exact solution is intractable, thus variational inference (Graves, 2011) is used to estimate the true posterior $p(\mathcal{W}|\mathcal{D})$ with an approximation $q(\mathcal{W})$ parametrized by θ. This approximation is typically obtained by minimizing the KL divergence between the two distributions, and can be performed by Bayes-by-Backprop (Blundell et al., 2015) or Monte-Carlo Dropout (Gal and Ghahramani, 2016). At the inference stage, we can draw weights from the approximated posterior $\widehat{\mathcal{W}} \sim q(\mathcal{W})$.

With the approximated weight distribution, we can employ a weight sampling scheme to represent

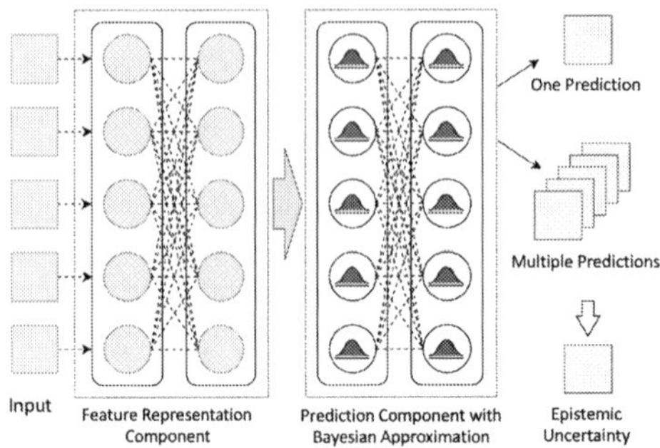

Figure 1: Overview of the hybrid framework extended from a traditional neural network. The epistemic uncertainty is calculated upon multiple predictions.

epistemic uncertainty. For the sample x_i, the neural model outputs o_i as prediction via softmax operation:

$$o_i = \text{Softmax}(\text{f}^{\widehat{\mathcal{W}}}(\text{x}_\text{i})). \tag{2}$$

In our question-answering setting, since the final output is generated as an answer span (Wang and Jiang, 2016) and the prediction is a classification task pointing on the input sequence (Vinyals et al., 2015), we quantify the uncertainty at the start and end positions respectively. More specifically, we conduct the Monte-Carlo (MC) integration by repeating the inference process m times, then the answer span is selected based on the mean of all sampled predictions. For any input text x_i, we denote the probability of the answer span starting at token t as p_{i_t}. Then, the epistemic uncertainty of answer span starting token is quantified as:

$$U(p_{i\_t}|x_i) = \frac{1}{m} \sum_{j}^{m} (p_{i\_t}^{j})^2 - \text{E}(p_{i\_t})^2 \tag{3}$$

where x_i is the text sequence input, m is the weight sampling time, $p_{i\_t}^{j}$ is the probability produced by the jth sampling, and E denotes the expectation of all predictions. The final uncertainty output is the sum of both ends of the predicted answer span.

3.2 Hybrid Neural Architecture

Since uncertainty quantification in Bayes-by-Backprop and Monte-Carlo Dropout needs multiple sampling and forward iterations, inference time is linearly increased. In practical scenarios, machine comprehension and dialogue tasks often require deeper and larger neural architectures than classification or regression tasks, thus the inference process becomes more time-consuming. On the other side, in neural language approaches, the implicit linguistic features are modeled hierarchically from token and sentence to document level in a deep contextualized architecture (Clark et al., 2019), and semantic-related features at top neural layers play an important role in the machine comprehension task. Therefore, to speed up the inference process without sacrificing the uncertainty modeling capability, we propose a hybrid neural architecture (see Figure 1). More specifically, we split a neural network for question-answering into two sub-functions: (1) feature representation component, which is a traditional neural network, and (2) prediction component with Bayesian approximation, in which we adopt the Bayesian weight estimation. As the feature representation component produces deterministic outputs, the hybrid model will only conduct weight sampling on the prediction component, thus significantly reducing the inference time. Moreover, by integrating Bayesian weight approximation in Section 3.1 to a base neural network, the hybrid model can still be trained in an end-to-end way,[1] and we can obtain epistemic uncertainty via Equation 3.

---

[1]There are two training strategies of the hybrid model: joint training from scratch and warm-up training with deterministic weights, and the latter performed slightly better in our experiment.

Model	Exact Match	F1 Score	Train Time (Iter.)	Test Time (Iter.)
Base Model (Bi-DAF)	77.45	79.55	0.236	0.053
Pure Bayes-by-Backprop	78.86	80.90	0.597	4.371
FAB Bayes-by-Backprop	78.57	80.41	0.318	0.828
Pure MCDO	**79.33**	**81.71**	0.435	3.250
FAB MCDO (Our final model)	79.04	81.35	0.238	0.652

Table 1: Left: evaluation scores of various Bayesian models in the clinical scenario. Right: training and inference speed (seconds per iteration) comparison (batch size=128, sampling times=100).

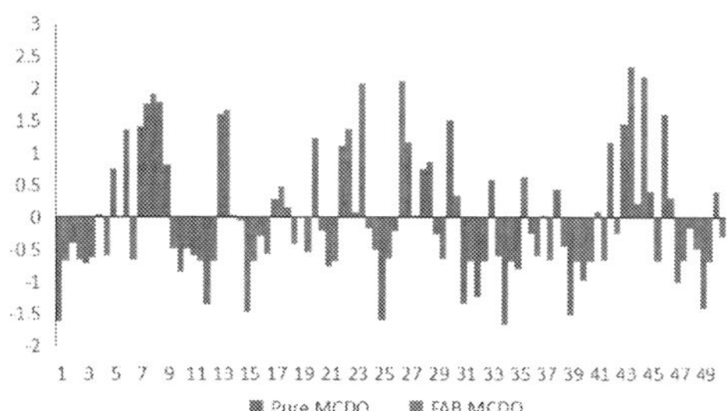

Figure 2: Epistemic uncertainty values of 50 examples. Scores from both models (Pure MCDO and FAB MCDO) have been z-score normalized.

4 Experiments and Results

4.1 Question-Answering on Clinical Conversations

We evaluated the proposed approach on a spoken dialogue comprehension corpus, consisting of nurse-to-patient symptom monitoring conversations (Liu et al., 2019). This corpus was inspired by real dialogues in the clinical setting where nurses enquire about symptoms of patients. Linguistic structures at the semantic, syntactic, discourse and pragmatic levels were abstracted from these conversations to construct templates for simulating multi-turn dialogues. These conversations cover 9 topics/symptoms (e.g., headache, cough). For each conversation, the average word number[2] is 255 and the average interactive turn number is 15.5. For the comprehension task, questions were raised to query different attributes of a specified symptom; e.g., *How frequently did you experience chest pain?* Answer spans were labeled with start and end indices. The training, validation and test set[3] are 30k, 3k and 1k respectively.

We choose Bi-Directional Attention Flow network (Seo et al., 2017) as the base architecture,[4] which fuses question-aware and context-aware attention and performs competitively in various question-answering corpora. Pre-trained word embeddings from Glove (Pennington et al., 2014) were utilized and fixed during training. Out-of-vocabulary words were replaced with the *[unk]* token. The hidden size and embedding dimension were set to 300, and batch size was set to 128. During training, the validation-based early stop strategy was applied. During prediction, we selected answer spans using the maximum product of the start and end position. In our Bayes-by-Backprop (BBB) implementations, weights in the prediction component were sampled from a mixture of two Gaussian distributions with small variances (Blundell et al., 2015) during inference for uncertainty modeling. In our Monte-Carlo Dropout (MCDO) implementations, dropout in the Bayesian approximation component was permanently enabled during training and inference for uncertainty modeling. L2 weight regularization was added to the feature representation component. All models were implemented in Pytorch (Paszke et al., 2019). More details of hyper-parameter configuration are described in Appendix A.

---

[2]The input sequence length is set of 300, and all text samples are tokenized and padded before feeding to the encoder.

[3]The data used for training and validation are simulated dialogue samples as described in (Liu et al., 2019), and the test set is derived from anonymized samples that acquired as part of a research study approved by the SingHealth Centralised Institutional Review Board (Protocol 1556561515).

[4]We also implemented RNet(Wang et al., 2017) for the question-answering task, in our settings, it performed similar to Bi-DAF. Moreover, we adopted and fine-tuned BERT (Devlin et al., 2019) as a contextual representation backbone; however, the performance did not benefit from it, since the spoken dialogue content is quite different from the pre-trained content.

Model	Train Size	Exact Match	F1 Score
Training on Set A	15k	52.50	56.87
Random Selection (+5K from Set B)	20k	60.69	65.38
FAB MCDO Selection (+5k from Set B)	20k	66.80	70.64
Training on Full Dataset (Set A + Set B)	30k	79.04	81.35

Table 2: Evaluation results on Bayesian uncertainty based active selection and random collection.

As shown in Table 1, models with uncertainty estimation components achieve higher performance than the base model, and MCDO models perform better. Compared with applied Bayesian estimation on all weights (Pure MCDO), our Feature-and-Bayesian (FAB) model still obtains comparable results. Meanwhile, in the inference stage, the FAB MCDO model is significantly faster than the Pure MCDO model. Then, we quantify the epistemic uncertainty with MCDO models as described in Section 3.1. We set the Monte-Carlo sampling instances to 100, and collect all the predictions. Then we calculated the variance of the softmax probability at the start and end positions respectively. As shown in Figure 2, the epistemic uncertainties of the two models were similar. Moreover, there was a certain overlap (69%) when we ranked the 1k test samples with their uncertainty scores and selected the top-k ones (k=300). This indicates that we can refer to the FAB model's uncertainty output with shorter inference time.

4.2 Active Learning on Clinical Conversation QA

Based on the previous result, we explore to apply the proposed hybrid model to active learning. Since it is time-consuming to annotate a large number of clinical data samples from the electronic health records (EHR), we expect to utilize epistemic uncertainty to identify samples that are potentially the most helpful for training (Siddhant and Lipton, 2018). To this end, we split the training set in Section 4.1 to two subsets (set A and set B), and conducted active learning in two steps: (1) We trained the FAB MCDO model on set A (15k samples); (2) We evaluated the epistemic uncertainty on all samples of set B (15k samples); (3) We selected 5k samples in set B with the highest uncertainty scores, added them to the training set, and re-trained the model from scratch. We also randomly selected 5k samples from set B as control. As shown in Table 2, FAB MCDO selection obtains larger performance improvement than the random scheme, achieving 87% performance of full set training with 66.7% samples. Moreover, although adopting various Bayesian active learning methods is beyond the scope of this paper, the proposed model can also be used with other acquisition functions such as BatchBALD (Kirsch et al., 2019).

5   Conclusion

In this work, we defined how to quantify epistemic uncertainty in question-answering tasks. We further proposed a hybrid neural architecture that achieves performance comparable to regular Bayesian neural networks but offers greater efficiency, speeding up the inference processing time by 80% relative. The proposed approach also enabled active learning for dialogue comprehension tasks so that an updated model was trained more optimally with new incoming data by selecting training samples that may not have been well-represented in the current training dataset.

Acknowledgements

Research efforts were supported by funding and infrastructure for Digital Health from the Institute for Infocomm Research (I2R), Science and Engineering Research Council, A*STAR, Singapore (Grant Nos SSF A1818g0044, IAF H19/01/a0/023). The clinical data acquisition was funded by the Economic Development Board (EDB), Singapore Living Lab Fund, and Philips Electronics Hospital to Home Pilot Project (EDB grant reference number: S14-1035-RF-LLF H and W). We gratefully acknowledge valuable inputs on the clinical data from the Department of Cardiology and Health Management Unit, Changi General Hospital, Singapore. We thank Weiwen Xu, Yang Guo, and Savitha Ramasamy for insightful discussions and the anonymous reviewers for their precious feedback to help improve and extend this piece of work.

References

David Barber and Christopher M Bishop. 1998. Ensemble learning in bayesian neural networks. *Nato ASI Series F Computer and Systems Sciences*, 168:215–238.

Charles Blundell, Julien Cornebise, Koray Kavukcuoglu, and Daan Wierstra. 2015. Weight uncertainty in neural network. In Francis Bach and David Blei, editors, *Proceedings of the 32nd International Conference on Machine Learning*, volume 37 of *Proceedings of Machine Learning Research*, pages 1613–1622, Lille, France, 07–09 Jul. PMLR.

Wray L. Buntine and A. Weigend. 1991. Bayesian back-propagation. In *Complex systems*, volume 5(6), pages 603–643.

Kevin Clark, Urvashi Khandelwal, Omer Levy, and Christopher D. Manning. 2019. What does BERT look at? an analysis of BERT's attention. In *Proceedings of the 2019 ACL Workshop BlackboxNLP: Analyzing and Interpreting Neural Networks for NLP*, pages 276–286, Florence, Italy, August. Association for Computational Linguistics.

John S. Denker and Yann LeCun. 1990. Transforming neural-net output levels to probability distributions. In *Proceedings of the 1990 Conference on Advances in Neural Information Processing Systems 3*, NIPS-3, pages 853–859, San Francisco, CA, USA. Morgan Kaufmann Publishers Inc.

Jacob Devlin, Ming-Wei Chang, Kenton Lee, and Kristina Toutanova. 2019. BERT: Pre-training of deep bidirectional transformers for language understanding. In *Proceedings of the 2019 Conference of the North American Chapter of the Association for Computational Linguistics: Human Language Technologies, Volume 1 (Long and Short Papers)*, pages 4171–4186, Minneapolis, Minnesota, June. Association for Computational Linguistics.

Nan Du, Kai Chen, Anjuli Kannan, Linh Tran, Yuhui Chen, and Izhak Shafran. 2019. Extracting symptoms and their status from clinical conversations. In *Proceedings of the 57th Annual Meeting of the Association for Computational Linguistics*, pages 915–925, Florence, Italy, July. Association for Computational Linguistics.

Yarin Gal and Zoubin Ghahramani. 2016. Dropout as a bayesian approximation: Representing model uncertainty in deep learning. In *international conference on machine learning*, pages 1050–1059.

Alex Graves. 2011. Practical variational inference for neural networks. In J. Shawe-Taylor, R. S. Zemel, P. L. Bartlett, F. Pereira, and K. Q. Weinberger, editors, *Advances in Neural Information Processing Systems 24*, pages 2348–2356. Curran Associates, Inc.

Geoffrey Hinton and Drew Van Camp. 1993. Keeping neural networks simple by minimizing the description length of the weights. In *in Proc. of the 6th Ann. ACM Conf. on Computational Learning Theory*. Citeseer.

Litton J Kurisinkel and Nancy Chen. 2019. Set to ordered text: Generating discharge instructions from medical billing codes. In *Proceedings of the 2019 Conference on Empirical Methods in Natural Language Processing and the 9th International Joint Conference on Natural Language Processing (EMNLP-IJCNLP)*, pages 6165–6175, Hong Kong, China, November. Association for Computational Linguistics.

Robin Jia and Percy Liang. 2017. Adversarial examples for evaluating reading comprehension systems. In *Proceedings of the 2017 Conference on Empirical Methods in Natural Language Processing*, pages 2021–2031, Copenhagen, Denmark, September. Association for Computational Linguistics.

Alex Kendall and Yarin Gal. 2017. What uncertainties do we need in bayesian deep learning for computer vision? In *Advances in neural information processing systems*, pages 5574–5584.

Andreas Kirsch, Joost van Amersfoort, and Yarin Gal. 2019. Batchbald: Efficient and diverse batch acquisition for deep bayesian active learning. In *Advances in Neural Information Processing Systems*, pages 7026–7037.

Zhengyuan Liu, Hazel Lim, Nur Farah Ain Suhaimi, Shao Chuen Tong, Sharon Ong, Angela Ng, Sheldon Lee, Michael R. Macdonald, Savitha Ramasamy, Pavitra Krishnaswamy, Wai Leng Chow, and Nancy F. Chen. 2019. Fast prototyping a dialogue comprehension system for nurse-patient conversations on symptom monitoring. In *Proceedings of the 2019 Conference of the North American Chapter of the Association for Computational Linguistics: Human Language Technologies*, pages 24–31, Minneapolis, Minnesota, June. Association for Computational Linguistics.

Rowan McAllister, Yarin Gal, Alex Kendall, Mark Van Der Wilk, Amar Shah, Roberto Cipolla, and Adrian Vivian Weller. 2017. Concrete problems for autonomous vehicle safety: Advantages of bayesian deep learning. In *International Joint Conferences on Artificial Intelligence, Inc.*

Chanwoo Park, Jae Myung Kim, Seok Hyeon Ha, and Jungwoo Lee. 2018. Sampling-based bayesian inference with gradient uncertainty. *arXiv preprint arXiv:1812.03285*.

Adam Paszke, Sam Gross, Francisco Massa, Adam Lerer, James Bradbury, Gregory Chanan, Trevor Killeen, Zeming Lin, Natalia Gimelshein, Luca Antiga, et al. 2019. Pytorch: An imperative style, high-performance deep learning library. In *Advances in Neural Information Processing Systems*, pages 8024–8035.

Jeffrey Pennington, Richard Socher, and Christopher Manning. 2014. Glove: Global vectors for word representation. In *Proceedings of the 2014 Conference on Empirical Methods in Natural Language Processing*, pages 1532–1543. Association for Computational Linguistics.

Pranav Rajpurkar, Jian Zhang, Konstantin Lopyrev, and Percy Liang. 2016. Squad: 100,000+ questions for machine comprehension of text. In *Proceedings of the 2016 Conference on Empirical Methods in Natural Language Processing*, pages 2383–2392. Association for Computational Linguistics.

Minjoon Seo, Aniruddha Kembhavi, Ali Farhadi, and Hannaneh Hajishirzi. 2017. Bidirectional attention flow for machine comprehension. In *Proceedings of the 5th International Conference for Learning Representations*.

Burr. Settles. 2012. Active learning. In *Synthesis Lectures on Artificial Intelligence and Machine Learning*, volume 6.1, pages 1–114.

Yanyao Shen, Hyokun Yun, Zachary Lipton, Yakov Kronrod, and Animashree Anandkumar. 2017. Deep active learning for named entity recognition. In *Proceedings of the 2nd Workshop on Representation Learning for NLP*, pages 252–256, Vancouver, Canada, August. Association for Computational Linguistics.

Aditya Siddhant and Zachary C. Lipton. 2018. Deep Bayesian active learning for natural language processing: Results of a large-scale empirical study. In *Proceedings of the 2018 Conference on Empirical Methods in Natural Language Processing*, pages 2904–2909, Brussels, Belgium, October-November. Association for Computational Linguistics.

Oriol Vinyals, Meire Fortunato, and Navdeep Jaitly. 2015. Pointer networks. In C. Cortes, N. D. Lawrence, D. D. Lee, M. Sugiyama, and R. Garnett, editors, *Advances in Neural Information Processing Systems 28*, pages 2692–2700. Curran Associates, Inc.

Shuohang Wang and Jing Jiang. 2016. Machine comprehension using match-lstm and answer pointer. *CoRR*, abs/1608.07905.

Wenhui Wang, Nan Yang, Furu Wei, Baobao Chang, and Ming Zhou. 2017. Gated self-matching networks for reading comprehension and question answering. In *Proceedings of the 55th Annual Meeting of the Association for Computational Linguistics (Volume 1: Long Papers)*, pages 189–198. Association for Computational Linguistics.

Yijun Xiao and William Yang Wang. 2019. Quantifying uncertainties in natural language processing tasks. In *Proceedings of the AAAI Conference on Artificial Intelligence*, volume 33, pages 7322–7329.

A   Training Configuration for Clinical QA Scenario

The hyper-parameters of the model adopted on the clinical dialogue comprehension task is shown in Table 3. Moreover, In our hybrid neural architecture, we adopt several strategies which empirically benefit the performance in the training process: (1) In the warm-up training epochs, all weights of the hybrid architecture were updated jointly, with a warm-up learning rate of $2e-5$. (2) After warm-up training, the prediction component was trained with Bayesian weight estimation by sampling from a mixture of two prior Gaussian distributions, where $\sigma_1 = 0.05$ and $\sigma_2 = 0.1$ (Blundell et al., 2015) or applying Monte Carlo Dropout (Gal and Ghahramani, 2016), and we assigned a learning rate of $1e-3$ to the prediction component while that of the feature representation component was set to $1e-4$; (3) Layer normalization was added in the last layer of the feature representation component, providing feature outputs with lower variance.

Parameter	Value	Parameter	Value
Feature Layer Dropout Rate	0.3	Bayesian Layer Dropout Rate	0.5
Optimize Algorithm	Adam	Learning Rate	0.0001
Warm-up Learning Rate	0.00002	Warm-up Training Epoch	2
Hidden Size	300	Batch Size	128
Gradient Norm Clipping	3.0	Max Input Length	300

Table 3: Hyper-parameters for the clinical dialogue comprehension task.

B   Evaluation on a Reading Comprehension Benchmark Corpus

In this section, we adapt our approach in a common question-answering benchmark corpus: SQuAD (Rajpurkar et al., 2016). Different from the domain-specific dialogue dataset, models for this benchmark can significantly benefit from utilizing large-scale pre-trained contextual representation. Therefore, following our design in Section 3, here we use a pre-trained language model BERT (Devlin et al., 2019) as the feature representation component, and add two linear layers with Bayesian approximation for the prediction component. We trained the *"bert-base-uncased"* version of BERT along with the prediction component, with a separate optimizer and different learning rate and weight decay configurations. As shown in Table 4, the model can achieve higher performance than the baseline. The uncertainty calculated on all samples of the evaluation set is shown in Figure 3.

Model	EM Score	F1 Score
BERT for QA (Traditional)	81.22	88.52
BERT for QA (FAB Bayes-by-Backprop)	81.30	89.81
BERT for QA (FAB MCDO)	81.75	90.05

Table 4: Evaluation results on the SQuAD development set.

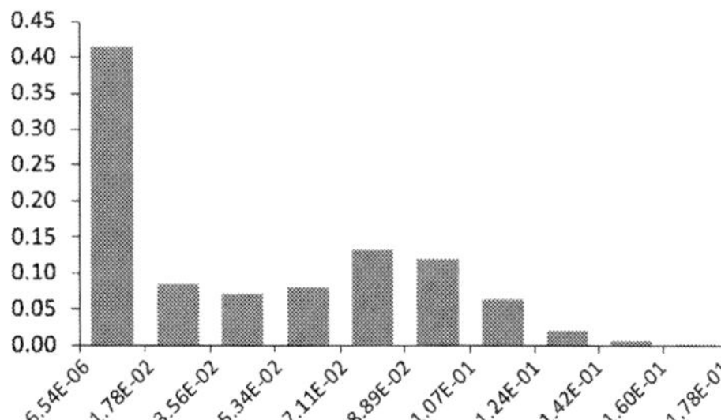

Figure 3: Histogram of epistemic uncertainty values on the SQuaAD evaluation set. X axis is the epistemic uncertainty value. Y axis is the proportion of sample.

Regularized Graph Convolutional Networks for Short Text Classification

Kshitij Tayal
University of Minnesota
Twin Cities
tayal@umn.edu

Saurabh Agrawal
Amazon
Palo Alto, CA 94301
airan@amazon.com

Nikhil Rao
Amazon
Palo Alto, CA 94301
nikhilsr@amazon.com

Xiaowei Jia
University of Pittsburgh
Pennsylvania
xiaowei@pitt.edu

Karthik Subbian
Amazon
Palo Alto, CA 94301
ksubbian@amazon.com

Vipin Kumar
University of Minnesota
Twin Cities
kumar001@umn.edu

Abstract

Short text classification is a fundamental problem in natural language processing, social network analysis, and e-commerce. The lack of structure in short text sequences limits the success of popular NLP methods based on deep learning. Simpler methods that rely on bag-of-words representations tend to perform on par with complex deep learning methods. To tackle the limitations of textual features in short text, we propose a Graph-regularized Graph Convolution Network (GR-GCN), which augments graph convolution networks by incorporating label dependencies in the output space. Our model achieves state-of-the-art results on both proprietary and external datasets, outperforming several baseline methods by up to 6% . Furthermore, we show that compared to baseline methods, GR-GCN is more robust to noise in textual features.

1 Introduction

Short-text classification is a common problem in information retrieval (Ji et al., 2014) and has applications in several domains including e-commerce (Yu et al., 2012; Shen et al., 2009), social media (Kateb and Kalita, 2015), healthcare (Pestian et al., 2007) and cognitive-biometric recognition (Pokhriyal et al., 2016). In this paper, we develop a short text classification technique for solving two problems relevant to product search on e-commerce platform: 1) **Product Query Classification (PQC)** - When the customer enters a free form query, it is important to understand their product type intent to recommend and advertise the relevant products. We classify customer search queries to one or more product types (e.g., shoe, televisions, skis), and 2) **Product Title Classification (PTC)** - We classify billions of product titles to one or more product categories. This is important for sellers to place their items in the correct product category and retrieve it when a customer queries it.

Unlike traditional text classification, classifying short-texts poses additional challenges. First, short texts in e-commerce typically involve sentences with an average length of 3 (for queries) to 15 words (for product titles). Second, unlike longer texts such as blogs or news articles, these customer queries or product titles lack "natural" language structure and are often plagued with spelling errors. For example, in PQC, queries like `Nike running`, `shoes size 9`, `nike shos` (misspelling variants) all belong to the `shoes` category. In addition, queries contain non-target language text and non-language text (like model/part numbers), which introduces noise in the embedding. A similar challenge could also be faced in PTC problem, where products from the same class have high diversity in their title texts. For example, titles `PhotoFast microSD to MS Pro Duo CR-5300`, `Kingston microSD Card` and `8GB card for Blackberry Storm 9530` all belong to the same genre of `microSD` card products and hence need to be listed under the same category. All these factors make it difficult to separate product-type classes by purely relying on text which is heterogeneous and contains noise.

In this work, we propose to enhance the textual information by leveraging additional knowledge about relationships between input short-texts as well as among class labels. For PQC, we can derive similarities

Proceedings of the 28th International Conference on Computational Linguistics: Industry Track, pages 236–242
Barcelona, Spain (Online), December 12, 2020

between input user queries from (anonymized) user logs, by looking at commonly purchased items in response to different queries. The intuition is that two queries that consistently lead to the purchase of a same set of items might have similar product-type intents. Likewise, in PTC, we can estimate similarity between two input product titles from historical information such as co-views. Similarly, in output space, relationships between product-type classes can be modeled using product-category taxonomies, which are typically hand-curated and readily available in e-commerce applications.

Such auxiliary information can be naturally represented in graphical form, where each node represents a short-text (input graph) or a class label (output graph), while an edge indicates magnitude of similarity between two nodes. We thus propose a Graph-regularized Graph Convolution Network (GR-GCN) approach, which augments the graph convolutional network (Tayal et al., 2019) to incorporate such graphical information in an end to end learning framework. The two key aspects of GR-GCN are: i) a GCN that leverages dependencies in the input space to learn more informative representations of nodes(input short texts), and ii) a graph-regularization (GR) term in the objective function that exploits label similarities to penalize contrasting predictions for similar class labels on each input sample, thereby restricting the solution space and making our approach more robust to noise in the data.

We perform extensive experiments on one proprietary, and two public datasets and demonstrate the improvement in classification accuracy for GR-GCN upto 6% compared to text-based baselines. Further, we add noise in the input data and show that the graph's presence makes our method more robust to noise as compared to baseline methods based on just textual features.

2 Proposed Approach

Let $\mathbf{X} \in \mathbb{R}^{n \times d}$ be a matrix with each row being the embedding vector of an input sample and $\mathbf{Y} \in \mathbb{R}^{n \times L}$ be the label indicator matrix. Here d is the dimension of embedding and L number of class labels. Let $\mathcal{G}_\mathcal{I} = (\mathcal{V}_\mathcal{I}, \mathcal{E}_\mathcal{I})$ be the graph on input samples, with a corresponding adjacency matrix $A_\mathcal{I} \in \mathbb{R}^{n \times n}$, $\bar{A}_\mathcal{I} = A_\mathcal{I} + I$. Let $\mathcal{G}_o = (\mathcal{V}_o, \mathcal{E}_o)$ be the graph in output space, with $A_o \in \mathbb{R}^{L \times L}$ being the adjacency matrix on the output labels.

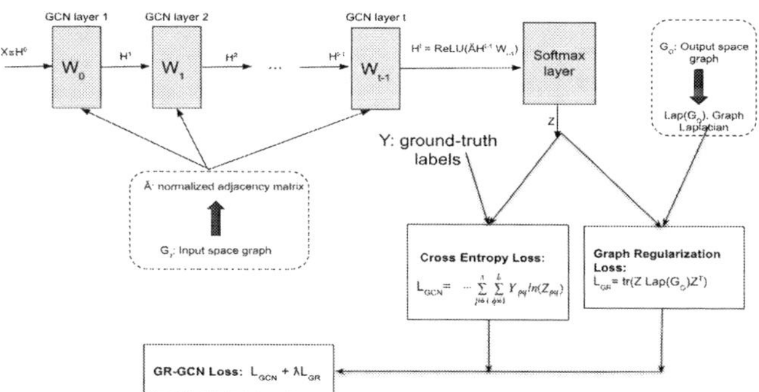

Figure 1: Schematic Illustration of GR-GCN. The GCN is used to learn node representations that respect the input graph structure, while the graph regularization is used to learn representations that respect the output graph structure.

Figure 1 illustrates our approach: GR-GCN. In this work, we use a 2-layer GCN (Kipf and Welling, 2016) on $G_\mathcal{I}$. The parameters are learnt by miniminizing the GR-GCN loss function: $L_{GCN} + \lambda L_{GR}$, where $L_{GCN} := \mathcal{L}(f_\theta(x), y)$ is the cross-entropy loss between the GCN predictions $f_\theta(x)$ for node x, parameterized by θ and the ground truth y. $L_{GR} := \sum_{i,j \in \mathcal{E}_o} \|f_\theta(x_i) - f_\theta(x_j)\|^2$ is the graph Laplacian based regularization that acts on the output node representations, and forces the predictions of adjacent nodes in the output graph to be similar. As we demonstrate in the experiments, this additional regularization makes our model especially robust to noise. Regularizers of the form L_{GR} have shown to be successful in factorization models (Johnson and Zhang, 2007; Rao et al., 2015; Zhou et al., 2012), and to the best of our knowledge, we are the first to apply it to regularize the output space for GCNs.

3   Graph Construction

Table 1: Summary statistics of datasets

Dataset	#Docs	#Training	#Test	#Unique Words	#Edges	#Class	Average Length
Internal	200000	160000	40000	41880	3642910	2290	3.38
Electronics	188626	150,900	37,726	291,804	962,444	796	14.23
Home	279788	223,830	55,958	176,754	6549,740	1100	9.63

In this section, we discuss the construction of graphs in input space and output space in the context of the two application problems that we focus on in this paper.

3.1   Product Query Classification (PQC):

The goal of PQC is to predict the product-type intent of user-typed search queries on an e-commerce website. To create the input graph, we use anonymous user logs that hold knowledge about query association. Intuitively, any two queries leading to the purchase of same items are more likely to have similar product-type intent. Following the intuition, we construct the graph such that for any two queries i and j, the adjacency matrix $A_\mathcal{I}$ is constructed as A_{ij} = number of common purchases between query i and query j. To construct the output graph between product labels , we first represent each label (product category) with the mean of embeddings of the titles of products that belong to this category. We then apply cosine similarity between embedding vectors of labels to construct the output graph, and discard edges that do not meet the threshold.

3.2   Product Title Classification (PTC):

The goal of PTC is to classify products into product categories. Specifically, each input sample is the title of a product, while the output label is a product category. To construct graph $G_\mathcal{I}$, we use the co-viewed metadata of each product. Specifically, for two product titles i and j, the input matrix $A_\mathcal{I}$ is constructed as A_{ij} = number of co-view between title i and title j. As with PQC problem, we used the same procedure to obtain the output space graph between labels. Co-views, is an intuitive means to construct the input graph, since items that are co-views are typically substitutes of each other. Thus, neighbors on the co-view graph tend to have similar categorization.

4   Experiments and Results

We evaluate GR-GCN approach on three datasets described in Table 1. For PQC, we used a proprietary e-commerce dataset (referred to as *Internal* dataset henceforth), whereas for PTC problem, we used a publicly available dataset consisting of Amazon product titles and other metadata including co-views for two departments: *Electronics* and *Home & Kitchen* (referred to as Home in this paper). (He and McAuley, 2016) [1].

Table 2: Classification accuracy of GR-GCN compared to multiple baselines

Model	Internal	Electronics	Home
TF-IDF + LR (Salton and Buckley, 1988)	80.9	59.70	61.2
CNN-rand (Kim, 2014)	79.45	55.87	61.42
CNN-non-static (Kim, 2014)	82.75	58.75	64.19
CharCNN (Zhang et al., 2015)	80.36	61.72	63.18
LSTM (Gers et al., 1999)	80.35	60.09	61.3
Bi-LSTM (Graves and Schmidhuber, 2005)	81.38	60.19	61.00
fastText (Joulin et al., 2016)	83.67	61.4	64.03
Graph-CNN-C (Defferrard et al., 2016)	80.08	58.60	59.25
Text GCN (Yao et al., 2019)	80.25	61.77	65.31
SWEM (Shen et al., 2018)	86.86	62.85	64.81
GR-GCN	**92.10**	**64.63**	**67.85**

---

[1] http://jmcauley.ucsd.edu/data/amazon/links.html

All pre-trained word embeddings are $128\text{-}d$ learned by training FastText (Bojanowski et al., 2017; Joulin et al., 2016). For GR-GCN, we used a 2-layer GCN with learning rate 0.1, dropout set to 0.1 and L2 regularization factor λ of $1e^{-7}$. All the datasets are split into 70 % training, 10% validation, and 20 % testing.

4.1 Baselines :

The following are brief descriptions of the baselines in the comparative study. We have grouped our baselines into three categories i.e., Text Models (text features only), Graph Models (graph relation information only), and Text + Graph Models (uses both textual and graph information).

Text Models: **TF-IDF+LR**: Bag-of-words model with TF-IDF as feature and Logistic Regression as a classifier. Low-frequency words appearing less than 5 times were removed. **CNN**: Two variants of CNN proposed in (Kim, 2014) are used: i) **CNN-rand** uses randomly initialized word embeddings and, ii) **CNN-non-static** uses pre-trained word embeddings. **CharCNN**: Character-level CNNs as proposed in (Zhang et al., 2015) **LSTM**: A simple LSTM block with 256 hidden states. We input pre-trained word embeddings. **Bi-LSTM**: Bidirectional LSTM block with 256 hidden states. We input pre-trained word embeddings. **fastText**: text classification tool from facebook (Joulin et al., 2016). It averages words embedding, then feeds into a linear classifier. **SWEM**: employing average pooling operation (Shen et al., 2018) of feature and afterwards using feed forward network with architecture 256-512-1024-C as classifier, where C is the number of classes.

Graph Models: **Graph-CNN-C**: CNN model that performs convolutions across word embeddings relation graph using Chebyshev filter (Defferrard et al., 2016)

Text+Graph Models: **Text GCN**: GCN model where we construct corpus graph using documents and word as nodes (Yao et al., 2019).

4.2 Quantitative Results

For all baselines, we used default parameters as in their original paper/implementation. The results are summarized in Table 2. GR-GCN can be seen to outperform all baseline models in classification accuracy by a margin of 6% for the Internal dataset, 2.8% on Electronics and 3.8% on Home dataset. Further, we make the following observations from our results: **1)** A simple model, TF-IDF + LR performs well on short text datasets beating CNN random on internal and electronics datasets and performing comparably on home dataset. This reinforces our observation that short text documents often lack the structure that complex models such as neural networks can capture, and in some cases, using the latter might over parameterized the problem. **2)** LSTM based methods that use pre-trained embeddings also do not perform better than TFIDF based methods, for a similar reason: the word order is seldom important in user typed queries and product titles, and there's no "natural language" structure to exploit. **3)** TextGCN shows competitive performance on Electronics and Home dataset but performs poorly on the internal dataset. This is because the texts in the internal dataset are super short, with an average length below 4, contain many spelling errors, and the label space is vast. On further examination, we noticed that due to spelling errors, TextGCN is creating a lot of spurious nodes in the graph, which is a limitation of the learning graph from the corpus.

4.3 Impact of Incorporating Auxiliary Graphs

To evaluate the effect of each graph (input and output) individually on model performance, we perform two more experiments. In first experiment we incorporate output graph to the best "Text" performance model in our baselines (SWEM) and measure the performance. We refer to this model as SWEM-GR-*out*. In the second experiment, we only use the input graph,

Model	Internal	Electronics	Home
SWEM	86.86	62.85	64.81
GR-GCN	92.10	64.63	67.85
SWEM-GR-*out*	86.90	63.26	65.20
GR-GCN-*inp*	91.95	63.99	66.9

Table 3: Performance Comparison

thus eliminating the graph regularization. We
refer to this model as GR-GCN-*inp*. Results are summarized in Table 3. We observe that both input
and output graphs in their individual capacity are adding meaning to the classification accuracy.

4.4 Robustness comparison

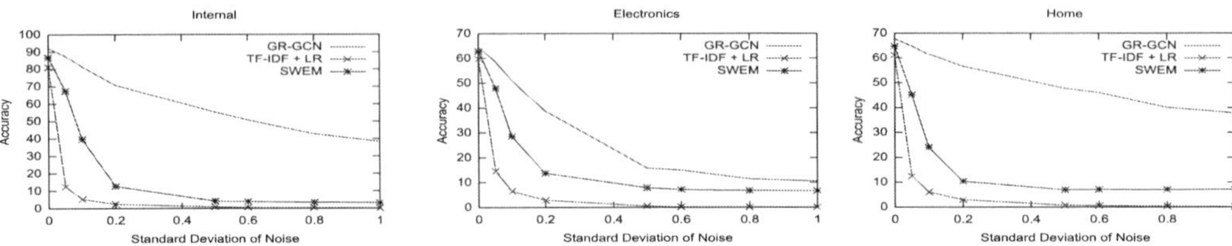

Figure 2: Test accuracy by varying standard deviation of added noise (best seen in color). GR-GCN
consistently outperforms the baselines.

Search queries on e-commerce platforms contain a lot of misspelled keywords that introduce noise
in the embedding. To simulate this behavior in our model, we evaluate the robustness of GR-GCN
by introducing Additive White Gaussian Noise with zero mean and varying standard deviations in our
embedding(Zhang and Yang, 2018). Figure 2 reports test accuracy with varying standard deviation (σ)
of the noise. We compare GR-GCN with two text-base baselines: **TF-IDF+LR**, a simple bag of words
model and **SWEM** (Shen et al., 2018), a state of the art deep learning model. We see test performance of
TF-IDF + LR, and SWEM drops immediately with minimal noise, while GR-GCN is robust to noise. On
Internal dataset with $\sigma = 0.05$, TF-IDF performance drops to 12%, SWEM performance drops to 67%,
while GR-GCN performance dropped to 87%. We attribute this noise-tolerant feature to the presence of
input and output graph, which other methods lack.

4.4.1 Effect of the size of the Labelled Data

To assess the impact of the size of the labeled data, we tested the top-performing models with varying
proportions of the training data. Figure 3 reports test accuracy with various sized subsamples of the
training datasets. We observe that GR-GCN can achieve higher test accuracy with limited labeled documents. For example, with just 20% training data, GR-GCN achieves 87 % accuracy on the Internal
dataset, surpassing all other baselines that are trained on 100 % training data.

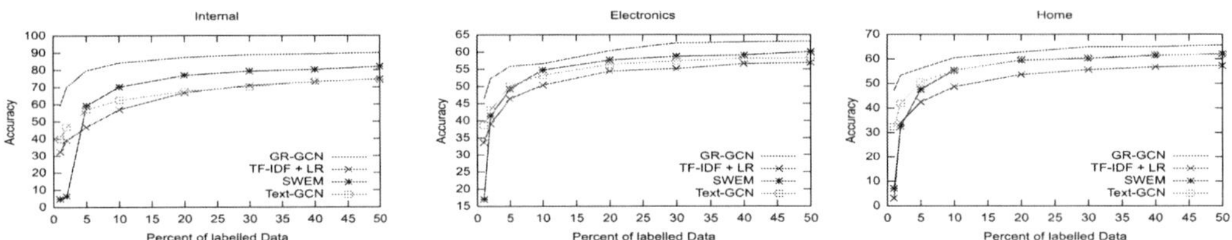

Figure 3: Test accuracy by varying training data (best seen in color).

5 Conclusion

In this paper, we propose GR-GCN to classify short texts that capture dependency on two levels, i.e.,
within the text samples (input space graph) and amongst the output label (output space graph). We
demonstrated its efficacy on two commercial e-commerce applications and its robustness to noise.

We note that the proposed method can add value to other domains like medical science, where the
input graph can capture drug similarity, and the output graph can capture the relationship among various
types of illness; remote sensing, where the input graph can capture the distance, depth etc. between
different ground points and output graph can capture similarity between similar labels such as pasture
and vegetation as well as distinguish between entirely different labels such as river and residence.

References

Piotr Bojanowski, Edouard Grave, Armand Joulin, and Tomas Mikolov. 2017. Enriching word vectors with subword information. *Transactions of the Association for Computational Linguistics*, 5:135–146.

Michaël Defferrard, Xavier Bresson, and Pierre Vandergheynst. 2016. Convolutional neural networks on graphs with fast localized spectral filtering. In *Advances in neural information processing systems*, pages 3844–3852.

Felix A Gers, Jürgen Schmidhuber, and Fred Cummins. 1999. Learning to forget: Continual prediction with lstm.

Alex Graves and Jürgen Schmidhuber. 2005. Framewise phoneme classification with bidirectional lstm and other neural network architectures. *Neural networks*, 18(5-6):602–610.

Ruining He and Julian McAuley. 2016. Ups and downs: Modeling the visual evolution of fashion trends with one-class collaborative filtering. In *proceedings of the 25th international conference on world wide web*, pages 507–517. International World Wide Web Conferences Steering Committee.

Zongcheng Ji, Zhengdong Lu, and Hang Li. 2014. An information retrieval approach to short text conversation. *arXiv preprint arXiv:1408.6988*.

Rie Johnson and Tong Zhang. 2007. On the effectiveness of laplacian normalization for graph semi-supervised learning. *Journal of Machine Learning Research*, 8(Jul):1489–1517.

Armand Joulin, Edouard Grave, Piotr Bojanowski, and Tomas Mikolov. 2016. Bag of tricks for efficient text classification. *arXiv preprint arXiv:1607.01759*.

Faris Kateb and Jugal Kalita. 2015. Classifying short text in social media: Twitter as case study. *International Journal of Computer Applications*, 111(9).

Yoon Kim. 2014. Convolutional neural networks for sentence classification. *arXiv preprint arXiv:1408.5882*.

Thomas N Kipf and Max Welling. 2016. Semi-supervised classification with graph convolutional networks. *arXiv preprint arXiv:1609.02907*.

John P Pestian, Christopher Brew, Paweł Matykiewicz, Dj J Hovermale, Neil Johnson, K Bretonnel Cohen, and Włodzisław Duch. 2007. A shared task involving multi-label classification of clinical free text. In *Proceedings of the Workshop on BioNLP 2007: Biological, Translational, and Clinical Language Processing*, pages 97–104. Association for Computational Linguistics.

Neeti Pokhriyal, Kshitij Tayal, Ifeoma Nwogu, and Venu Govindaraju. 2016. Cognitive-biometric recognition from language usage: A feasibility study. *IEEE Transactions on Information Forensics and Security*, 12(1):134–143.

Nikhil Rao, Hsiang-Fu Yu, Pradeep K Ravikumar, and Inderjit S Dhillon. 2015. Collaborative filtering with graph information: Consistency and scalable methods. In *Advances in neural information processing systems*, pages 2107–2115.

Gerard Salton and Christopher Buckley. 1988. Term-weighting approaches in automatic text retrieval. *Information processing & management*, 24(5):513–523.

Dou Shen, Ying Li, Xiao Li, and Dengyong Zhou. 2009. Product query classification. In *Proceedings of the 18th ACM conference on Information and knowledge management*, pages 741–750. ACM.

Dinghan Shen, Guoyin Wang, Wenlin Wang, Martin Renqiang Min, Qinliang Su, Yizhe Zhang, Chunyuan Li, Ricardo Henao, and Lawrence Carin. 2018. Baseline needs more love: On simple word-embedding-based models and associated pooling mechanisms. *arXiv preprint arXiv:1805.09843*.

Kshitij Tayal, Rao Nikhil, Saurabh Agarwal, and Karthik Subbian. 2019. Short text classification using graph convolutional network. *NIPS workshop on Graph Representation Learning*.

Liang Yao, Chengsheng Mao, and Yuan Luo. 2019. Graph convolutional networks for text classification. In *Proceedings of the AAAI Conference on Artificial Intelligence*, volume 33, pages 7370–7377.

Hsiang-Fu Yu, Chia-Hua Ho, Prakash Arunachalam, Manas Somaiya, and Chih-Jen Lin. 2012. Product title classification versus text classification. *Csie. Ntu. Edu. Tw*, pages 1–25.

Dongxu Zhang and Zhichao Yang. 2018. Word embedding perturbation for sentence classification. *arXiv preprint arXiv:1804.08166*.

Xiang Zhang, Junbo Zhao, and Yann LeCun. 2015. Character-level convolutional networks for text classification. In *Advances in neural information processing systems*, pages 649–657.

Tinghui Zhou, Hanhuai Shan, Arindam Banerjee, and Guillermo Sapiro. 2012. Kernelized probabilistic matrix factorization: Exploiting graphs and side information. In *Proceedings of the 2012 SIAM international Conference on Data mining*, pages 403–414. SIAM.

Association for Computational Linguistics
209 N. Eighth Street
Stroudsburg, Pennsylvania 18360

ISBN 978-1-7138-2522-7